People at Work

People at Work

Life, Power, and Social Inclusion in the New Economy

EDITED BY

Marjorie L. DeVault

New York University Press
New York and London

NEW YORK UNIVERSITY PRESS
New York and London
www.nyupress.org

© 2008 by New York University
All rights reserved

Library of Congress Cataloging-in-Publication Data
People at work : life, power, and social inclusion in the new economy /
edited by Marjorie L. DeVault.
p. cm.   Includes bibliographical references and index.
ISBN 978–0–8147–2003–5 (cloth : alk. paper)
ISBN 978–0–8147–2004–2 (pbk. : alk. paper)
1. Work—Social aspects.   2. Industrial sociology.
I. DeVault, Marjorie L., 1950–
HD6955.P464   2008
306.3'6—dc22   2007038650

New York University Press books are printed on acid-free paper,
and their binding materials are chosen for strength and durability.

Manufactured in the United States of America

c 10 9 8 7 6 5 4 3 2 1
p 10 9 8 7 6 5 4 3 2 1

Contents

Acknowledgments

This book grew from a conference at Syracuse University, in February 2004, that was made possible by a grant from the American Sociological Association's Fund for the Advancement of the Discipline, which is supported in part by the National Science Foundation and skillfully administered at ASA by Roberta Spalter-Roth. We received additional funding for the conference from Syracuse University's Department of Sociology, Maxwell School of Citizenship and Public Affairs, Social Science Program, Moynihan Institute of Global Affairs, and Senate Committee on LGBT Concerns. The conference gave us time for sustained collaborative discussion directed toward developing insights about the broad sweep and common technologies of economic restructuring in the diverse locations we were investigating.

I'm sure that our intellectual indebtedness to Dorothy E. Smith is evident throughout the text, but I am pleased to thank her again here for her generosity and for the intellectual engagement that has inspired me to pursue these issues. She told me years ago that she didn't have "all the answers" (as I seemed to believe) and that I should work out my own adaptations of her approach. I have enjoyed that project and tried to work in ways that are faithful to her vision, but of course I am responsible for the ways in which my implementation of the approach falls short. Dorothy and Joan Acker were inspiring plenary speakers at our conference, and I thank both of them for giving us leadership there; I'm also grateful to other conference attendees who contributed to our thinking, and to James Biddle for videotaping the proceedings.

I've learned a great deal from each contributor to this book and I thank them all for their participation in the project. Marie Campbell deserves particular mention for the enormously helpful comments she provided as

I prepared the editorial material for the book. My partner, Robert Chibka, has been, as always, an insightful critic and loyal supporter. And, finally, I wish to thank our editor, Ilene Kalish, who is smart, efficient, and fun to work with, as well as the other staff at New York University Press who have made the production of this book a smooth and enjoyable endeavor.

Introduction

As I travel from my teaching job in Syracuse, New York, to my home in Boston, Massachusetts, I rub shoulders with other professionals and business travelers moving through the airport—often connected to work via cell phone and laptop. As I pass through airport security, I encounter teams of workers doing x-ray screening—usually middle-aged white workers in Syracuse, but not in Boston, where the team turned predominantly white after September 11, 2001, but since then has gradually become more ethnically mixed again. I buy food in the Syracuse airport from white women and in Boston from Asian and Caribbean immigrants, marked by their appearance and speech. Like other North Americans, I am increasingly aware that my everyday life is shaped by events and activities far removed from my workplace and home. I think of the jobs lost in factory closings since I came to Syracuse in the 1980s and of the low-wage service jobs in shopping malls that have replaced them; of the high-tech workers who lost jobs as their bubble burst; of immigrant health-care workers in long-term-care facilities; and of those in other parts of the world who make so many of my clothes or speak to me on the phone when I need help with my computer. Sitting in the airport—grading papers, waiting to get home—I hear the news on the TV monitor hanging overhead: the commentators assure us that the economy looks good. That's one account of things, but I know that there are many stories to tell about work and life in a world undergoing fundamental transformation.

In the accounting categories of employers and states, the people I encounter in my travels may be categorized as full- or part-time employees and their salaries or wages tallied as part of the cost of labor. They may be U.S. citizens, with all the associated rights, or part of the growing pool of immigrant labor, with or without legal permission to work. And some of their activities may be understood and accounted for as part of the nation's productivity, while other work they do falls out of that picture. Such descriptive labels point to the categories through which work and social policy are administered in the U.S. and other Western nations. Like any representation (including my earlier narrative description), each of these accounting categories captures some elements of the lives they refer to and leaves out many more.

The people behind these textual sketches live varied, embodied lives, with different capacities that change over time; their activities braid together paid work and relations with others, of mutual responsibility, care, and dependence. Our goal in this book is to examine the ways that these and other people's lives are represented in the textual machinery of a changing world and to explore the consequences of those representations. We offer a mode of analysis—institutional ethnography (Smith 1987, 2005)—designed for exploring a regime of social policy from the standpoint of those subject to it. We strive to keep both lives and texts in view.

People at work are always embodied, of course; we all live physical lives, located in particular material settings, with limitations imposed by our human bodies and all their frailties. People use their bodies in work, and work always takes a physical toll, though quite differently in different kinds of work. Furthermore, if workers are to continue in their jobs, their bodies must be sustained, in households and through services of various kinds that may be provided collectively or purchased within or outside homes. The somewhat redundant notion of the "embodied worker" calls attention to this fundamental fact. The phrase also provides us with points of entry to the investigation of workplace organization and social policy, both of which often assume what Joan Acker (1990) has labeled an "unencumbered" or disembodied worker. It may seem obvious that workers live in bodies, but employers and policymakers have often acted as if they didn't.

Early second-wave feminist sociologists recognized a fundamental clash between the embodied, everyday experiences of women workers—especially experiences of bearing and raising children and the insistent tugs of caregiving responsibilities—and the inflexible "clockwork" and demands of most paid jobs (Hochschild 1975). Dorothy Smith (1987) argued that mothers lived with a sharp disjuncture between the everyday world of caregiving and the world of work, where one is meant to act as if those grounded demands did not exist. A bit later, Acker began to write about "Hierarchies, Jobs, and Bodies" (1990), suggesting that organizations are designed as if workers were unencumbered by any extraneous needs or limitations; those assumptions produce problems for all workers, but especially for women who are mothers and caregivers. The contradiction that Hochschild, Smith, and Acker pointed to thirty years ago has only deepened as the economy has come to be characterized by heightened inequality and uncertainty. And, although these authors wrote specifically about women and family carework, the contradictions of sustaining paid employment under contemporary conditions have sharpened for virtually all workers, though of course in different forms.

These feminist scholars, and others who argue for fuller inclusion in economic life, were aimed at a moving target—an increasingly global economy undergoing a period of radical change. Their critique was directed toward the "family wage" system characteristic of the Western industrial economies of the nineteenth and twentieth centuries—a work arrangement that produced and was sustained by breadwinner-housewife heterosexual families. Now, these national economies are undergoing substantial changes: both jobs and workers flow across national borders; "good jobs"—often associated with new technologies and requiring new technical skills—are increasingly scarce and contingent; workers are asked to take on increasing risks; and states are withdrawing resources from the provision of social services, borrowing their logics of accountability from those of business enterprises (V. Smith 2001). Together, these changes are profoundly altering lives (and the fortunes of nations) around the world.

Analysts sometimes refer to these changes as consequences of deindustrialization and globalization and point to the emergence of what is often labeled a New Economy. The terms themselves reveal the importance of language, since these words carry the impression of an impersonal process to which people must inevitably adapt. A language of economic restructuring is perhaps more useful, since its verb form at least suggests that people are at work behind these changes. Jobs and workers do not simply float across borders in the currents of an economic sea; they are pushed and pulled by the global strategies of multinational corporate leaders. Political leaders devise strategies designed to enhance or sustain national economies (and, often, the interests of class strata within nations), and the members of international economic organizations such as the International Monetary Fund and the World Bank increasingly set the terms within which they do that—insisting on reductions in the public welfare programs that so many people rely on to sustain families. Workers and their advocates also strategize around these changes, seeking not only stability of employment but also a basis for sustaining home and family lives (Mohanty 1997).

The organizing idea of this book is that the diverse lives of people at work, varied as they might seem on the ground, are lived out in their different ways in a common landscape, located in and shaped by an ongoing global process of economic restructuring. The analytic method we use—institutional ethnography—brings the inquiry back to people and their activities.

Institutional Ethnography

The Canadian sociologist Dorothy Smith developed the institutional ethnography approach out of feminist insights and first presented it as a sociology for (rather than about) women (1987, 1990a); she thinks of it now more broadly as a sociology for people (2005, 2006), and it has attracted increasing interest as a method of use to many groups (Campbell and Gregor 2002; Smith 2006). Combining theory and method, institutional ethnography emphasizes connections among the sites and situations of everyday life, management/professional practice, and policymaking, considered from people's locations in everyday life (Smith 1987). The notion of a standpoint or location anchoring the research is fundamental to institutional ethnography, but the research is not confined to the everyday lives of the anchor group at this point of entry. Rather, the institutional ethnographer traces how those lives are organized through the social relations of their contexts. The goal is not simply to assert a macrosociological (or structural) argument to frame microsociological findings: institutional ethnographers reject that distinction, and, as the analysis moves from one setting to another, the researcher strives always to attend to the activities of the people constituting and operating institutional machinery. In most settings, texts of various kinds are key to these activities and especially to linkages among sites; texts and their uses are often the sources of translocal coordination. Thus, institutional ethnographers attend closely to the production and uses of texts and to the ways that texts (and the concepts and discourses they contain and reproduce) travel—both literally and figuratively—from one setting to another.

The institutional ethnography approach is especially well suited for analyses of economic restructuring as it unfolds. The dominant mode of contemporary governance (in most arenas, and increasingly) is now discursive, and institutional ethnographers pay particular attention to textually mediated social organization. In addition, we investigate both local experiences and regimes of governance. We conduct inquiries into what people do and how they fare, but always in light of the organizational practices and schemes of accountability that define a particular terrain on which they act. The focus on regimes can highlight aspects of restructuring that are less easily visible in research that focuses primarily on individuals or on outcomes.

Our analytic goals are to locate the discursive pivot points of social organization, within "maps" of the institutional processes that shape people's organizational and extra-organizational lives. Such analytic maps can pinpoint areas of trouble for people subject to these regimes, as well as indicate directions for potential reforms that address their troubles (Mykhalovskiy and McCoy 2002; Pence 2001; G. Smith 1990). To the extent that our analyses can do this work, the institutional ethnography approach can be seen as a radically democratic policy tool. I return to this possibility in the concluding chapter.

Elements and Methods of Institutional Ethnography

An institutional ethnography begins with a point of entry and a problematic, or puzzle, in some site of embodied experience—an actual place where one can find people at work, doing things together. The researcher's goal is to investigate how activities in that site are connected to and shaped by activities conducted elsewhere. Typically, there is an anchor group whose experience provides a standpoint for the research. This standpoint has no specific or static content—it does not imply that all immigrant workers or all students with disabilities, for example, share a particular experience (that's clearly not the case). Instead, the standpoint taken up in the research provides the problematic and also serves as a touchstone: as the researcher explores coordinative processes in the wider institutional context, she always considers the consequences of institutional action for that immigrant worker or that disabled student. This conceptualization of experience and standpoint are based in a "generous concept of work" (Smith 1987) at the heart of institutional ethnographic analysis.

Attention to work processes. Institutional ethnographers understand work processes as the fundamental grounding of social life. They do not privilege paid work but keep in mind the broader requirements of embodied existence—people's need to sustain themselves, their connections of mutual care and dependence, and the activities that nurture and educate a next generation. This generous concept of work is meant to keep such caring labors in view. It directs us to other kinds of work, as well—work undertaken by paid employees that is outside their job descriptions, the extra work taken up by those marked as "different" to facilitate their inclusion in workplace and community, the work that clients do to access social services, and so on. The intent is to move beyond ideological definitions of work and workers in order to explore how work lives are actually put together.

Historically, women's work has been especially unacknowledged and undervalued, and feminist scholars have long argued for an expansion in our understandings of women's efforts. From the early feminist economist Charlotte Perkins Gilman (see Lengermann and Niebrugge-Brantley 1998), to the European Wages for Housework movement, which began in the 1970s (Dalla Costa and James 1972, and see Karides 2002), to the international development workers who organized for gender justice (Desai 2002), feminist scholars and activists have pressed for recognition of the unpaid work done by women. Dorothy Smith's early writing on institutional ethnography (1987) drew from this rich strand of thought: she saw that the control and appropriation of work happened, in part, through organizational strategies that highlight and support some kinds of work while leaving other tasks unacknowledged, to be done without recognition, support, or any collective responsibility.

Texts and textualization. Texts and "textually mediated social organization" (Smith 1990b) are central to institutional ethnographic analysis. The focus on texts emerges from empirical observation as well as from theory; it comes from the insight that technologies of social control are increasingly and pervasively textual and discursive. Texts such as medical charts, enrollment reports, strategic plans, and so on are mechanisms for coordinating activity across many different sites. Attention to these types of textual coordination can make visible just how the links among settings are put in place.

Many organizational texts are produced by working up the complex actualities of everyday life through a process of textualization that results in a typified representation. There are myriad examples: when a woman visits her primary-care doctor, for example, she is discussed (and speaks) as a patient. She gives information that might (or might not) be understood as symptoms, and her stories are translated into medical language and charted; the doctor's accounting staff translate all these activities into a few numbers on a page, which stand as an account of their work (but not hers) for the insurance company. When the same woman travels across borders, she presents a passport. She may stand in line fidgeting, with a sore back, wondering if she'll get home in time for dinner, but for official purposes she is simply a U.S. citizen who will sit in Row 19, seat A. Similarly, if you visit my office, you'll usually find me wearing casual clothing, but for the photo on my university's Web page I put on a suit jacket and a scarf, aiming to look appropriately professional. And that page lists my publications but provides no account of the hours I spend talking with students.

In each of these examples, some aspects of experience are highlighted in the textual representation, while others are treated as irrelevant. Representations are crafted in more or less standardized formats—shaped by the forms used for recording medical information, the software that tracks airline passengers, and so on. In each example, textualization is collective activity, and those who are typified usually participate in these processes. Finally, it is important to note that the moment of textualization, for each actor, is one moment in an extended course of action; people anticipate textualization, and, when it is completed, they expect to use its product elsewhere. The medical office staff, for example, sends a record of the visit to the insurance company in order to obtain payment; the patient takes an order for lab work to the clinic for further evaluation or a prescription to the pharmacy in order to begin a course of treatment at home. These routine exchanges of textual material link the places where things get done; they are significant because they organize those doings, making some but not other things possible, shaping opportunities for action. Institutional ethnographers follow texts in order to explore and analyze the social relations that connect people across the myriad sites of action in contemporary societies.

Mapping social relations. The analytic phase of an institutional ethnography proceeds by tracing the social relations people are drawn into through their work activities. The term "social relations" is used here in its Marxist sense—to refer to connections among people and work processes; it orients the researcher to sequences of action that extend beyond local sites. Dorothy Smith explains: "It is useful analytically to think of social relations as temporal sequences in which the foregoing intends the subsequent and in which the subsequent 'realizes' or accomplishes the social character of the preceding" (2005: 228). The patient presents herself to the physician with an account of symptoms; the doctor responds with an examination and diagnosis and proposes a course of treatment. These coordinated actions (and the actions that follow) produce, or accomplish, a medical encounter. The point of following social relations is to see how people in one place are aligning their activities with relevances produced elsewhere (McCoy 2006).

Institutional ethnographers use a related and more specific concept, that of "ruling relations" (Smith 1999, 2005: 277), to refer to a distinctive formation of textually based power that arose and became dominant with the development of corporate capitalism in developed nations. This complex web of discourse and practice encompasses not only state and economy but also academic, professional, and bureaucratic knowledge and associated practices. The categories and concepts of these institutional complexes routinely textualize lived experience so that people's circumstances can be "worked up" to fit administrative and managerial schemata; they objectify experience in order to make it amenable to management. The patient's symptoms are recorded on the chart, the doctor's actions summarized in the codes of health insurers.

In organizational studies, this kind of textual coordination may be quite focused and relatively easy to see, as in professional-client relations in health-care, social-work, and educational settings. Similarly, such coordination in organizations is often accomplished through specific moments of textualized accountability: hourly workers punch time cards, supervisors complete performance evaluations, academics prepare lists of their grants and publications—and such texts are consequential, taken up in specific sites of organizational decision making as representations of work accomplished. Life and work outside formal organizational sites—in households and family groupings, for example—is typically more diffusely and unevenly coordinated through texts. But Alison Griffith and Dorothy Smith (2005), in an institutional ethnographic study of mothering discourse, show how organizations such as schools depend on the expected performance of mothering work; teachers cannot teach unless mothers get children to school on time, and the kind of teaching they can do is shaped by what children have already learned, a product at least in part of parental efforts that may vary considerably from one neighborhood to another. These observations suggest that the alignment of some households (but not others) with the coordinative logics of other institutions may be a primary mechanism for the reproduction of inequalities. The products of mothering work are recognized in the institution—discussed through notions of children's "readiness" for schooling, for example—but the work itself is left largely unacknowledged.

By contrast, the generous concept of work used by institutional ethnographers directs the researcher to recover the work that is actually being done and to provide a more complete accounting of social organization—or, in colloquial terms, to show how things are "put together." The generous concept of work directs the researcher to set aside institutional definitions and ask more straightforwardly, "What's getting done?" and then "Who's doing it?" Simply accounting for all of the work of the setting often provides a much clearer picture of "how it works." But one can also use the generous concept of work to link actors with one another, going on to ask, "Who do these people hand off to?" or "Where does the product of this work go next?" In tracing those connections, one begins to see the coordination of work and the relations of power that make things happen one way and not another.

The institutional ethnographic approach can provide distinctive contributions to analyses of economic restructuring and neoliberal governance. For those on the ground, it may often seem that "these things just happen" (Jackson 1995). Institutional ethnography provides an analysis that is "something like a map" (Smith 2006) to show who is at work, where, making things happen as they do. In the next section, I provide an overview of economic transformation in the past half-century, pointing not only to what has changed but also to some of the discursive frames and associated institutional technologies through which change has been discussed and managed.

What's New in the New Economy?

The ensemble of activities and processes we call the economy is always in flux, and capitalist economies continually change as institutional actors seek new forms of profit making. Yet we can identify periods of relative stability, achieved through state management of the economy, and significant moments of change, when the interlocking arrangements of an entire regime of accumulation shift. Regulation theory provides a way of locating and specifying these shifts (Brodie 1994); our approach is related but focuses on how such restructuring is accomplished on the ground. Contemporary discourses of a New Economy mark such a period of restructuring; we argue that, in addition to naming changes, these discourses also demand and constitute change.

Since the 1980s, neoliberal political and economic theorizing has gained ascendancy in Western and other nations (Harvey 2005); its ideas provide the overarching discourses that now most forcefully explain past and present changes and also orchestrate state and individual responses. Neoliberal thinkers tout market processes, typically conceived abstractly, as natural and efficient ways to organize human life. Opponents of neoliberalism argue for limits to market strategies, attention to workers' interests (Clawson 2003), and a stronger welfare state (Folbre 2001), Their voices are relatively muted in contemporary debates—but never absent.

1. *Who works? A discourse of work and dependency.* Labor struggles through the nineteenth century brought a twentieth-century industrial compromise in work arrangements that scholars have labeled Fordism (Gottfried 1995), emphasizing long-term employment and a family household that would sustain and reproduce workers: the male worker would receive a family wage, set high enough for him to support a homemaker wife. Though the realities never matched this model, state policies evolved around such a regime, providing public services to support these business enterprises and a modest safety net to patch up the caretaking arrangements based in family households. This Fordist regime began to crumble in the aftermath of the Second World War as capitalists began to organize their enterprises globally rather than nationally, seeking new efficiencies by using cheaper labor. The resulting changes, labeled deindustrialization in North America, have chipped away at the traditional jobs of the male breadwinner and brought many more former housewives into paid labor.

As many feminist analysts have noted, women's increasing participation in paid labor has far exceeded any increase in male participation in carework. For women workers, the new regime simply added a "second shift" (Hochschild 1989), and the double shift has come to be seen as typical, even for mothers of young children. This new construction entered the "genealogy of dependency" so cogently analyzed by Nancy Fraser and Linda Gordon (1994), and the discourse of dependency that emerged became part of the rationale for the welfare restructuring that took place in the 1990s in the United States—a set of changes that envisioned mothers' needs for support as temporary and made paid work a condition for receiving assistance. As Nancy Naples (1997) has shown in an analysis of the congressional hearings that led up to these changes, this discourse identified the good mother as one who works to support her children and the welfare-reliant mother at home as dependent, with a strongly negative moral judgment attached. Paid work, in these accounts, is presented as the basis for an ideal of self-sufficiency and thus for full inclusion in social life—a worthy, empowering activity that makes a good parent. Ironically, many of the affluent women workers who are taken as self-sufficient have achieved that status by hiring and relying on low-paid immigrant domestic and careworkers (see Ehrenreich and Hochschild 2002; Hondagneu-Sotelo 2001).

Reproductive labor lurks in the background of these discourses, but, despite a great deal of useful scholarship, it is rarely acknowledged fully and usefully in social policy making (Folbre 2001). The architects of U.S. welfare-to-work programs, for instance, recognize that single working mothers need assistance not only with child care but with tasks of daily self-maintenance and the expenses of travel to the job, and most states have built minimal levels of such (temporary) assistance into their programs. Similarly, large employers seeking to attract and retain highly skilled workers recognize that workers who lack a stay-at-home spouse often need such assistance, and they have begun to invent a varied array of new benefits and services to address those needs. Yet, such needs are construed in policy frameworks as temporary and exceptional, rather than ordinary. And, despite the common needs of these different groups of workers, policies for welfare recipients and higher-wage workers have developed along quite separate tracks and, as Randy Albelda (2001) observes, are rarely considered side by side.

Discourses of dependency resonate even more profoundly for people with disabilities. Marta Russell (1998) points out that the transition from feudal to industrial economies freed people from one form of political domination but also required those without wealth to find work, beg, or perish. She suggests that the then-new industrial economy brought into consciousness the idea of disability and points out that, since that time, disability has been defined at least in part (as in U.S. social security law) in terms of a person's ability to perform paid work. But if paid work becomes the key to social inclusion, the value of human life seems to be defined by the ability to meet the procrustean demands of paid jobs (Wendell 1996). The experiences of people with disabilities alert us to important questions about embodied work, yet they are rarely included in discussions of work in the New Economy, an omission that follows the history of employment policy for these groups, who have generally been treated in distinct and separate tracks (O'Brien 2001).

2. *Constructions of competition and skill.* Economic ideologies typically feature the economy as an organismic entity, developing according to its own logic; in these discourses, people are viewed as living at the mercy of its demands. The very phrase New Economy has served to call on individuals to change themselves, and the notion of skill—always a political matter (Jackson and Jordan 2000)—has been central to these processes. One of the rhetorical frames of New Economy discourse asserts that the work people do now, and especially work in new technology-based fields, demands

new and higher-level skills than were required in the past. Competition is naturalized in most economic discourse: political leaders talk as if it's obvious that individuals will compete within local labor markets, cities within a national economy, and nations within a global market for jobs. The level and type of skill associated with a national population is seen as key to attracting employers who will offer particular kinds of jobs, and there is a hierarchy of jobs—labeled good and bad ones (V. Smith 2001)—to match a constructed hierarchy of skills.

These paradoxical discourses involve both an individualizing rhetoric and one that erases and homogenizes individuals. At the individual level of the job search—a term associated with downsized professionals and the welfare or employment insurance recipients pushed into job seeking—individuals are encouraged to see themselves as bundles of skill, to market themselves (constructing what some resumé consultants refer to as "a brand called you"), and to engage in continual self-reconstruction (V. Smith 2001). These discourses promote education and training, giving rise to a great array of trainings that offer impressive certificates but that may or may not lead to sustainable employment (Lafer 2002), and they shape the kinds of training on offer, as programs are increasingly designed in consultation with those identified as business-community stakeholders (Folbre 2001; Grahame 1998; Jackson 1987, 1995). And discourses of skill and competition are increasingly reaching into public schooling and university education, where new emphases on assessment can be seen as efforts to ensure a fit between students' preparation and the demands of the New Economy.

On the other hand, employers seeking a workforce rely on constructions that associate skills with particular groups—not a new strategy but one that organizes and justifies new developments. For example, garment-industry outsourcers now explain that certain sewing skills can no longer be found in North America but exist only in countries where wage levels are conveniently low (Collins 2003). Employers both see and cultivate particular inclinations and capacities in local workforces (Salzinger 2003), and states develop economic strategies responsive to those constructions (Alexander 1997; Banerjee this volume). These strategies produce global labor markets with consequences for all workers, even as they mark and rely on racialized differences.

3. *Fiscal discipline: Privatization and accountability.* Another strand of neoliberal economic ideology emphasizes the efficiency of the market. This idea underpins global policies of structural adjustment, privatization, and

a "new managerialism" in the public sector (Rankin and Campbell 2006). These policies are introducing profound changes in the national infrastructures of collective responsibility that previously helped—however unevenly—to support and sustain a workforce.

Work lives, whether in public- or private-sector workplaces, are inextricably bound to public-sector services and supports. In the Fordist industrial regime, the public welfare state—including not only public assistance and social security but also housing subsidies and access to public utilities, universal education, and a public health system—has been critical for the reproduction of labor. As restructuring has proceeded, nations in the global South have been pressed toward market-oriented reforms as a condition for entering a global economy; at the same time, the industrialized nations of the North have faced the competitive pressures of that economy and rising expenditures on health and social welfare programs. A number of feminist analysts are tracking these changes, arguing that retrenchment in the welfare state increases the burden of unpaid work shouldered by women throughout the world (Bakker 1994; Neysmith 2000) and shifts the boundaries of public and private spheres (Brodie 1994). But in both South and North, arguments for the privatization of public-sector activities have gained increasing traction. On the basis of appealing rhetorics and technologies of efficiency and accountability—who wouldn't want "more bang for the buck"?—principles of the market are coming to organize (and shrink) collective provisions for social welfare.

Overview of Chapters

The authors represented here are exploring the circumstances of diverse groups of workers, all of whom are navigating the terrain of the New Economy sketched in this essay. Some contributors are longtime practitioners of institutional ethnography, while others, engaged in more conventional ethnographic research, joined our project in order to explore the approach; thus, some chapters present research explicitly designed as institutional ethnography, while others offer studies that contribute useful pieces to the picture without the focused look at textual technologies of an institutional ethnographic analysis.[1] Our studies fit together because they are focused on people's activities and because those activities are understood as always interconnected. We have stories to tell about people in specific places. But the object of our analysis, collectively, is the regime—the "connective tissue" located in text—that is realigning practice in the myriad sites of everyday work and life.

The first section of the book introduces key elements in the ideologies that have developed as underpinnings of the so-called New Economy: ideologies that emphasize competitiveness, accountability, personal responsibility and work as empowerment, and a new managerialism that spreads business logic to the public sector and even the family. The first chapter, by Nancy Jackson and Bonnie Slade, begins in one high-tech Canadian workplace—the kind of enterprise often touted as promising the jobs of the future that demand new and higher skills. Jackson and Slade explore demands for literacy in this kind of work and introduce us to a national (and international) discourse that points to a purported "crisis" of literacy skills. They explain that competing on the basis of quality brings textualized forms of accountability; the new demand is not only that the product be right but also that the texts asserting its quality be in order. However, the company's labor strategies introduce a racialized hierarchy of jobs that actually produces the shop floor practices that come to be understood as literacy problems. The analysis raises questions about the textual constructions of literacy that drive national and local agendas for job training; we also begin to see the reach of such practices into other arenas, such as public education and human services.

Chapter 2, by Alison Griffith and Lois André-Bechely, explores new relations of accountability in the public sector (here, in schooling) and the ways that parents as well as teachers are drawn into the work that produces student outcomes on standardized assessment measures. These authors explore technologies of measurement that are changing the landscape of public education, as new testing and publishing enterprises emerge to serve an international market (and one can think of related trends within higher education, in efforts to standardize liberal arts curricula and assess their outcomes and in efforts to align the curricula of community and vocational colleges with the training needs of local business interests [Jackson 1995; McCoy 1998]). In both private- and public-sector workplaces, such ideologies of accountability resonate with common-sense ideas about effectiveness; in practice, however, the experience-based judgments and authority of those on the ground may be eroded in favor of abstracted representations of quality or learning.

This chapter also demonstrates how work is shifted back into the household, onto the shoulders of parents and consumers. The push for accountability—constructed through the test scores of a group of children—

requires remedial work with those children who need help to reach the grade-level standard at the appropriate point in time. Parents are recruited by teachers to assist with that work and guided in doing it by the commercial test-preparation enterprises that not only sustain but also profit from these regimes of accountability. Thus, an erosion of public education for children is hidden within a rhetoric of responsibility and accountability.

Logics of personal responsibility and accountability are also shaping the work of local community groups, such as the one discussed by Nancy Jurik in chapter 3, which examines the establishment of a microlending program in the southwestern United States. Local activists seeking strategies for poverty alleviation found in microenterprise development (a strategy for providing support to individuals building very small businesses) a theory of empowerment through work that resonated in multiple ways with dominant New Economy discourses, and that resonance made their program fundable. They promised not only to serve the low-income clients who were also the target of welfare-to-work efforts of the era but also to do so in ways that were consistent with a bottom-line entrepreneurial logic. Once the activists began their work, however, they found that this structure of accountability pushed them toward traditional business models, rather than toward the more expansive social assistance they had envisioned.

The entrepreneurship featured in the microlending model fits neatly with the New Economy emphasis on self-sufficiency and individual empowerment through work. In that respect, it parallels the trend toward reductions in public assistance—exemplified in the 1990s restructuring of the U.S. social welfare program, designed to move clients from welfare to work. The neoliberal theorizing behind welfare restructuring aims to push workers toward self-sufficiency, conceptualized as personal responsibility for seeking and sustaining paid employment. It relies on a logic of individualism, envisioning for the most part an unencumbered client who simply chooses to accept work that is offered or not (see also Solomon, chapter 7; Scott and London, chapter 8; and Ridzi, chapter 11 this volume). In much the same way, the microlending approach envisions an entrepreneur who need only apply wise business practices to succeed, focusing only minimal attention on structural obstacles or the competing pressures of caring for others.

Self-sufficiency is a key term in the new policy discourses, but it is also a malleable notion, applied unevenly in ways that hide some dependencies and highlight others. Rannveig Traustadóttir's discussion in chapter 4 explores the issue of work and self-sufficiency for disabled youth in Iceland and how the European Union (EU) is addressing such issues in its relatively progressive disability policy. Several decades of disability-rights activism have established principles of access and inclusion, and the right of access to work has been seen as a key dimension of social inclusion. But movement activists have envisioned participation with appropriate supports and the understanding that everyone needs assistance from others. By contrast, the neoliberal thinking behind welfare retrenchment aims to push workers into the labor force with little regard for their desires or the kinds of support that facilitate genuine inclusion. Traustadóttir's sketch of this policy terrain suggests that advocates for inclusion have significant footholds in EU policymaking and have made considerable progress, but she also warns that policies seem increasingly to be shaped within an economic framework that pulls away the social infrastructure meant to support young disabled workers as they move into the labor force.

The chapters in Part I make visible a logic of market-based competition and personal accountability. Workers and companies, students and teachers, clients and the organizations that serve them—all are seen as necessarily in competition with others. Given such an account, employers can argue that they simply cannot afford to take responsibility for workers, and states can insist on belt-tightening fiscal reforms. They are not only making that argument but also developing increasingly sophisticated managerial tools for measuring and monitoring outcomes and bringing expenditures under closer scrutiny. Such institutional technologies are changing the bases for organizational decision making and often justify organizational shedding of responsibility for employees (Acker 2006). Thus, discourses that emphasize a global market-based competitiveness and accountability set the stage for insisting that workers survive on their own, making do as best they can.

The two sections that follow trace out, in various ways, how the key terms of these ideologies are crafted into text-based state and managerial strategies that organize particular sites of work and mobilize labor within and across national borders. Two chapters examine the incorporation of immigrant labor in the United States. Payal Banerjee's study of skilled Indian information technology (IT) workers (chapter 5) illustrates a flexible labor strategy akin to that used by Bonnie Slade's high-tech employer, while Nancy Naples's analysis (chapter 6) explores the longer-term incorporation of Mexican immigrant labor in midwestern U.S. food-processing plants. Both analyses focus on texts as mechanisms of incorporation; Banerjee examines the use of the H1-B visa by employers and labor vendors and its consequences for workers, while Naples considers the various texts of citizenship—such as the driver's license—that allow immigrants access to the communities in which they work. And both analyses illustrate that texts are activated, in complex and sometimes contradictory ways, not only by those in positions of power but also by those subject to regimes of rule.

Banerjee's analysis highlights the H1-B visa program as a political arrangement, crafted in both India and the United States. She also demonstrates that, while the visa is a particularly determinative text—one has it or not, enters or is barred—its power to shape the daily lives of workers comes in the way it is activated in a sequence of mediating organizations. And IT workers themselves learn the terms of H1-B life and take up its challenges, seeking their own work in the United States, taking on more and more of the burdens of the flexibility that benefits their multiple employers. Ironically, their skill and agency are knitted into a web of exploitation.

The Mexican and Mexican American workers that Naples studied stay in their midwestern U.S. communities long enough to establish settled family lives. But a close analysis illustrates the uneven ways that employers, state agencies, and other community residents include and exclude them. Legal permission to work and even U.S. citizenship do not lead to full inclusion, which must be negotiated in the range of community spaces and organizations of daily life. From the schools and parks where young people gather to grocery stores and churches, it is daily activity that includes and excludes these new residents. And while some of those processes are interpersonal ones, many interactions between longer-term residents and newcomers are shaped by the policies and texts of state and community governance—by the provision of English-language instruction and interpreter services, by access to housing and recreational facilities, by practices of local law enforcement, and so on.

These chapters track immigrant workers who are expected to bear on their own the burdens of their own daily maintenance and their families' needs for care and connection. Racialized differences related to descent and citizenship are woven into labor and state strategies to construct groups that can be positioned as outside the scope of employer or public-sector responsibility. But one can also see an emphasis on personal responsibility within the domestic labor markets of the United States and other postindustrial economies. Paid work has come to be seen as desirable for nearly everyone, with little regard for other responsibilities they may shoulder (Fraser and Gordon 1994). The imperative to shape oneself into an unencumbered worker (Acker 1990), endlessly available to an employer, takes varied forms in different realms of work; those varied modes of control and workers' responses to them are addressed in the third section of the book.

The current promotion of paid employment over caregiving appears in starkest form in the United States in the 1996 restructuring of public assistance for low-income mothers, who are increasingly expected to move into the labor force. The restructuring that established the TANF program—making assistance time limited and linking it to job seeking for all those deemed employable—has evolved in somewhat different local forms within a basic legislative framework and no doubt will continue to change over time. Indeed, the policymakers who designed the program have been especially concerned to avoid subversion of program goals by front-line workers, and new technologies of accountability and performance monitoring are being brought into this realm in order to track and control implementation (Ridzi 2004). Two chapters in this section examine the experiences of this group of workers as new programs have been implemented, while Frank Ridzi's discussion in the next section (chapter 11) analyzes some of the consequences of the accounting procedures designed to shrink expenditures in this area.

In chapter 7, Brenda Solomon discusses her study of job training for nursing assistants early in the development of the welfare-to-work programs. The program she analyzes was presented to young, low-income mothers as one that offered skill development that would move them toward economic independence; it was also closely tied to labor needs in the local small-town economy, preparing them for difficult, low-wage jobs at the local nursing home. Solomon relies on the generous concept of work to show the full range of the women's efforts even to sustain their attendance in the program and also to show how the trainer goes beyond her job description in her efforts to bring the women's practices into line with expectations for "employability."

The chapter by Ellen Scott and Andrew London (chapter 8) focuses on a period further along the trajectory of welfare reform and explores the consequences of time limits to assistance—the ultimate implementation of an ideology of personal responsibility. Limiting benefits seems a simple idea—likely understood by many policymakers as a kind of tough-love spur to self-sufficiency. In the county that London and Scott studied, welfare staff dubbed "self-sufficiency coaches" conducted telephone conferences to help prepare those being cut off and conducted child-safety reviews in advance of time limits. But the detailed ethnographic accounts provided in this chapter reveal that these text-based versions of safety-net support are insufficient in at least some cases—sometimes with devastating results. The picture these authors present is mixed, but, even in the best cases, they introduce us to women who (like those in Brenda Solomon's study) have taken whatever low-wage jobs they can find in local labor markets. Some who reach the time limit find that they must rely on parents or partners with whom they have violent histories. And, in some cases, women find themselves simply alone and without help—"like an animal trying to survive in the woods," as one poignantly puts it. The stark demand for self-sufficiency may seem reasonable in the textual world of policy; in the lived world of clients, it looks like an abandonment of any collective responsibility to assist vulnerable citizens.

Those in jobs that are more secure are insulated from some of the pressures of economic restructuring, but they may feel its effects in subtler ways. In the professions, work has been controlled historically through the training and ethical injunctions of the field; personal responsibility for managing and monitoring work effort has been built into the professional role. As in other jobs, however, professionals are expected to devote themselves to work, performing as if they have no other, mundane responsibilities (and, historically, many professional men have relied on wives to attend to other obligations of sustenance and care for others). In chapter 9, Catherine Solomon discusses the experiences of young faculty members in contemporary research universities, focusing on a rhetoric of "stardom" in their talk about work and their decisions about balancing work and family responsibilities. Her analysis suggests that faculty members (and perhaps other professional workers) may increasingly be forced to choose between a total devotion to work that brings the job security that goes with being a "star" and a lower-tier position that does not carry equivalent benefits and security.

The last chapter in this section (chapter 10) provides a tentative look at some of the issues of support for workers with disabilities. Katrina Arndt draws from her study of the college experiences of students who are deaf-blind to consider one participant's foray into the world of work via a college internship. The students she studied were enrolled in one of only a few U.S. colleges for the deaf, one that provides excellent supportive services. But the students' relatively unusual visual impairments meant that they often needed additional help, tailored to their distinctive needs. The students knew their own capacities and the kinds of assistance they could use most effectively, and they worked hard to explain and negotiate such assistance. That kind of work is one of the requirements for inclusion in any social setting, including a future workplace; Arndt's analysis suggests that too often it may be work that those with disabilities are expected to shoulder themselves.

These chapters introduce us to people navigating new demands and opportunities. They also explore representations of these people's work that provide only partial accounts—the employment plan or training-program curriculum, the college internship that shows up on a transcript, the diffuse notion of the academic star. These analyses display the two-sided character of such bits of text (Rankin and Campbell 2006): they operate both to organize individual activity and to provide official accounts that travel elsewhere, in forms worked up for management and decision making. The woman who manages to complete the training program is deemed employable, regardless of her other responsibilities; the student who sits through an unsatisfactory internship is thought to have gained work experience; and so on.

The final section focuses on these managerially oriented modes of knowing work and workers, in particular the frameworks of accountability that have developed in the public sector in an era of budgetary scrutiny. It takes us further into the sites of institutional activity that operate the machinery of accountability, considering front-line sites of program delivery and the managerial oversight of these kinds of state support. Thus, these chapters explore simultaneously the effects of economic restructuring on work within the public sector and also restructuring's effects on programs of state support for those who cannot so easily meet the demands of paid work on their own.

In chapter 11, Frank Ridzi uses a county appeals process as a point of entry to understanding new approaches in two U.S. welfare programs: TANF welfare-to-work support for mothers deemed employable and Medicaid funding for people with disabilities who need home health support. In both programs, clients and caseworkers develop formal plans for support, and those texts are extremely consequential. Ridzi's account of two appeal hearings suggests that once such texts are in place, they carry a version of reality that is quite difficult to amend—and increasingly a version of reality that places heavy new burdens on clients. In these programs, for instance, clients are expected to hire and manage their own "providers" of carework—that is, child-care workers and home health aides. Such programs do seem to give clients more autonomy than they may have had in the past. In practice, however, this system often puts them at odds with caregivers they depend on and gives them all the difficult choices that typically face managers of low-income workers. It effectively caps funding and leaves clients (supposedly "empowered") to manage as best they can; it may also give welfare staff reduced autonomy to exercise discretion in decision making.

Of course, institutional technologies do not always work as their designers intend and, in chapter 12, Yvette Daniel examines a Canadian educational funding policy that went wrong. Instituted as a "resource-led" strategy for curbing expenditures on support for students with special needs, this provincial funding exercise required that teachers and administrators assess and document needs in their schools and districts so that scarce funding could be focused effectively. But that straightforward notion produced a complex and ultimately wasteful web of activities, as administrators and school personnel hurried to establish the most favorable baseline budget levels they could in a competitive funding environment. One might, of course, read this account simply as the kind of local subversion program managers have worried about as school staff try to game the system. I suggest, however, that the story also points to the kinds of problems that often arise when objectified modes of knowing students are substituted for the more grounded and particular knowing of the teachers, parents, and professionals who spend time with children.

Daniel's analysis also points to some of the ironies built into these types of accountability. The rush to transform children into cases with "special needs" illustrates one problem with such modes of categorization: a label—though perhaps undesirable in other ways, and often unsheddable— may be the only route to services that can be tailored to the individual. These are the kinds of dilemmas that produce front-line subversion and that often leave front-line workers feeling puzzled and demoralized as they observe their well-intentioned efforts leading in directions they did not intend. Daniel's analysis, based on her own professional participation (and dismay) in this implementation work, stands as an example of how institutional ethnography might be used within various practice settings to illuminate how local procedures are organized and where they lead.

Finally, Marie Campbell's analysis in chapter 13 focuses on practices of accountability and fiscal restraint as they organize the work of home health aides, their supervisors and schedulers, and the disabled clients who depend on them. She traces one of many ways that provincial government in British Columbia has relied on the principles of new public management to reduce welfare expenditures. As in the United States (Ridzi, chapter 11), payments for social services such as home support are increasingly bundled into block-grant funding to states and provinces, which then contract out for services. This kind of decoupling is supported by the textual measurement of services and quality; the provincial health authority requires that home health agencies provide "continuity of care," for example, and they collect continuity statistics. Campbell's analysis illustrates, however, that knowing about continuity in this textual form does not usually tell much about the consistency and adequacy of care and assistance that are so consequential for clients.

Like many preceding analyses, Campbell's study reveals a managerial discourse and technologies that respond to competing imperatives, with rhetorical threads drawn from discourses of empowerment and inclusion, efficiency and accountability, fairness and necessity—all skillfully woven into an account that assumes (and glosses over) cutbacks in services. In the textualized version of restructuring, those with mandated responsibility to provide services can meet a textual standard of accountability, while not knowing what actually happens when a particular provider meets an individual client—in this case, when Teresa needs to lift Fred from bed to toilet. As Campbell shows, such concrete moments of need and assistance are organized in multiple sites of ruling and justified through the conceptual currencies of the time.

It is possible to know and think in other ways, and institutional ethnography is meant to support those kinds of knowing grounded in people's embodied activity. These studies take up aspects of the fundamental transformations under way in the organization of work and workers' lives and follow these changes into the sites of ruling where relations among people and states are being reshaped. The consequences of change unfold in the spaces we all occupy daily—they are visible around us—but the motors and mechanisms of change are more distant. Institutional ethnography can bring those technologies of change more clearly into view—a first step toward considering how work and life might be differently organized. In the concluding chapter, I say more about how the method might be used to those ends.

NOTE

1. Though I don't want to make too much of these boundaries, for readers interested in clarification I would group the chapters into those designed as IE studies (Jackson/Slade, Jurik, Griffith/André-Bechely, Ridzi, Daniel, and Campbell); those influenced by the approach (Naples, Solomon, Richards Solomon, Arndt); and those using related political-economic or other qualitative approaches in ways that contribute to our collective project (Traustadóttir, Banerjee, Scott/London).

PART I

Ideologies of the Neoliberal Economy

This section introduces key ideological building blocks in a dominant view of economic change that circulates within and from sites of administration and management—the conceptual currencies of policymakers. Each chapter begins in a specific place—in a high-tech, "high-performance" Canadian workplace; at kitchen tables in Ontario and in California; among members of a community organization and its low-income clients in the southwestern United States; and in the lives of disabled youth in Iceland—with the activities of people at work in those places. Each analysis then traces out and explores threads of the ruling relations that have been crafted to align local activity with the (sometimes contradictory) institutional discourses emerging elsewhere; these include discourses of competitiveness; accountability and efficiency; and individual empowerment and inclusion achieved through participation in economic activity.

The conceptual currencies introduced in these analyses appear throughout the book, though in different forms that adapt them to particular institutional realms. They work, in part, through their double character (Rankin and Campbell 2006), which can recruit local actors to a reorganization of consciousness and thereby align their activity with ruling agendas. Empowerment through paid work, for example, may be understood in the context of an individual's life as a route to economic security, pride in accomplishment, and recognition as a full member of society. Within the managerial logic of the new economy, however, the same concept can refer to a stark version of independence in which individuals increasingly shoulder all the responsibilities and risks of their own and others' sustenance. Our analyses call attention to these conceptual currencies and examine, in some detail, how they aim at such alignments with managerial goals in particular cases and sites.

"Hell on My Face"
The Production of Workplace Il-literacy

NANCY JACKSON AND BONNIE SLADE

Editor's Introduction

In this chapter, Nancy Jackson and Bonnie Slade examine the notion of work-place literacy, considering both policy and practice. Bonnie's work as a team leader in a Canadian electronics plant grounds their analysis in the ways that permanent employees and skilled immigrant contract workers operate on a daily basis. Her on-the-ground frustrations provide the kind of puzzle that opens up an extended analysis in an institutional ethnography; in this case, that analysis links workers' activities with the company's flexible labor re-gime and the demands for elaborated textual forms of accountability arising outside the company. Quality is increasingly defined textually, producing an additional layer of work. And the production regime is racialized, since it is the primarily North American–born permanent workers who are positioned through the company's managerial strategies to contribute textually to qual-ity control. The analysis links the discussions of policymakers addressing an ostensible crisis of literacy and the ways that workers manage—and are man-aged by—these new demands for text-based accountability. The juxtaposition of the policy discourse with the view of texts-in-use on the shop floor suggests that supposed problems of literacy may often be not problems of individual skill so much as perverse effects of textually mediated production and a flex-ible labor regime.

* * *

The New Economy is bringing new stresses to working life. Many jobs are changing, and mostly not for the better; they are often part-time, more precarious, with lower wages and fewer benefits. At the same time, even such arguably bad jobs are said to involve higher skills and thus new requirements for employees. In this context, poor literacy skills are increasingly cited by employers and policymakers as a problem of crisis proportion, posing a threat to the global competitiveness and the prosperity of industrialized nations.

This chapter challenges the dominant discourse about a "literacy crisis" at work, with its emphasis on skill deficits of individuals. We argue that framing the issues this way conceals critical processes of organizational restructuring that are changing the nature and meaning of literacy at work. These changes focus on a growing labyrinth of workplace texts used to govern both work and workers, as part of documenting and standardizing work in the name of "quality" and productivity. The centrality of these texts to systems of work intensification and performance monitoring can foster fear, avoidance, or resistance among employees. Thus, paperwork is often a site of struggle; when it does not get done, complaints about literacy are usually not far behind.

But closer examination of these troubles shows that they are often not about the functional skill levels of individuals but rather about changes in the social relations of work. The concept of literacy has come to stand for this complex textual relation between the demands of powerful institutions and the lives of individuals. Here we will explore these dynamics in a manufacturing environment, but similar issues will be familiar to workers in service, health, retail, and many other workplaces in both the private and the public sectors.

This essay speaks in two voices, based on the experiences of the two authors. In the first half of the paper, Nancy draws on accounts of workplace change found in social studies of work, particularly analyses of lean production and quality assurance, to situate an understanding of workplace literacy within a broader picture of widespread changes in the organization of work. She argues that everyday demands of reading and writing are increasingly embedded in a web of textual relations that are complex and highly contested. While this way of framing the problem of "literacy" will be familiar to readers of other studies in the social organization of knowledge, it stands in some contrast to the dominant discourse around workplace literacy (see Belfiore et al. 2004).

The second part of the chapter is a first-person narrative account of Bonnie's reflection on her experience as a team leader on a high-tech manufacturing line. She takes us onto the shop floor to examine the organization and implications of everyday literacy practices in this environment. She argues that "literacy" in this workplace was much less about individuals' ability to read and write than about forms of textual communication, either paper or electronic, that subordinated front-line workers and excluded them from the exercise of power in their workplace.

Literacy: Discourse of Crisis, Danger, and Blame

A critical perspective on the meaning and uses of the concept of literacy is far from new in academic life. There is a long tradition of critical studies showing how the concept of literacy has been used in various ways across the centuries to manage populations for the benefit of powerful interests: the church of the Middle Ages, or the industrialists of the early twentieth century (Graff 1987; Hautecoeur 1997; Larson 2001). There is also a critical literature on the social construction of skill, written from feminist, labor, and other critical perspectives, that shows how skill labels have been used historically to organize categories of privilege and exclusion that reproduce hierarchies of gender, race, and other dimensions of difference (Cockburn 1983; Connell 1987; deWolff 2000; Galabuzi 2005; Green 2001; Jackson 1991; Slade and Mirchandani 2005). Curiously, these critical analyses of skill categories have rarely been connected to the notion of literacy.

Indeed, over the past decade or so, the principal analyses of adult literacy have come not from academics at all, or even from community advocates as in past, but rather from employer groups, business councils, and other labor-market and economic think tanks. Their interest in literacy is reflected in mainstream newspapers and magazines in North America, featuring articles with rhetorical headlines such as "Literacy Problems Cost U.S. Companies $60 Billion Annually in Lost Productivity . . . What's Your Company Doing About It?" (Baynton 2001).

Under pressure from the business community, national governments of many political stripes have begun to pay more attention to literacy. Some, including the United States, the United Kingdom, Australia, New Zealand, and South Africa, have moved to develop more comprehensive national policy frameworks (Jackson 2005b). Even more significant may be the actions of supranational policy bodies like the Organization for Economic Cooperation and Development (OECD) and UNESCO, which have supported the Canadian government in developing the International Adult Literacy Survey (IALS) and the U.S. government in creating the National Adult Literacy Survey (NALS). The objective of this survey process is to measure and profile literacy levels among the working-age population in more than thirty countries across the world. The first round of these surveys began in 1994, with the most recent version, called the Adult Life Skills Survey (ALSS), starting to report in 2003 with data from seven countries, including the United States and Canada (see National Center for Education Statistics 2003; Statistics Canada 2003; OECD and Statistics Canada 1997, 2000).

Results from these surveys have caught the attention of governments across the industrialized world, particularly the claim that large portions of the working-age populations do not have adequate literacy levels to support everyday life and work. Depending on the country and which iteration of the surveys is cited, between one-third and more than two-thirds of adult populations in countries surveyed[1] are said to lack the minimum skill level (Level 3) considered by experts to be suitable for coping with the increasing demands of the emerging knowledge society and the information economy (OECD and Statistics Canada 1995). American newspapers reported sensationally that "half of America's adults are functionally illiterate!" (Sticht 2001a).

There have been many controversies among experts about the methodology, reliability, and meanings of the findings of these surveys (Sticht 2001a, 2001b). Perhaps the point that gained the most attention was the large disparity reported between measured performance on a set of task-based test items and the views about performance ability expressed in the self-assessment portion of the survey. Respondents were asked how well their reading, writing, and numeracy skills met the demands of their daily lives and work. Quite consistently, adults believed their own skills to be much higher than their measured performance. For example, in the United States, among adults rated by the first NALS test results as being in the bottom two categories (Levels 1 and 2) of literacy functioning, most reported that "they could read and write English 'well' or 'very well'" (Sticht 2001a). Similarly, in Canada, among adults assessed as being at Level 1 on the task performance scale, almost half (48 percent) rated themselves as having "excellent" or "good" reading skills, and only 22 percent said their skills were "poor" (Sticht 2001b: 21). Other contrasting reports have long been reported elsewhere in the academic literature (Prinsloo and Breier 1996; Darville 1999) and are familiar to literacy practitioners. According to Darville (1999), "Whatever IALS measures, it is neither people's general abilities to function, nor their abilities to use reading in situations where they have occasion to" (p. 281).

These anomalies in survey results have produced quite different reactions among some government officials. As one senior official in the Canadian government, speaking on a panel at a government sponsored conference on literacy in 2002, observed, "People are illiterate, and they don't even know it! This is very dangerous!"[2] For this official, the problem is self-evident: the test scores are simply right, and individuals are simply wrong about their own abilities. But, for our purposes in this essay, this talk of danger and blame offers not an explanation but more puzzling data. What might be going on behind these heated controversies and official alarm about a "literacy crisis" in Canada and elsewhere?

In the following pages, we aim to shed light on this puzzle by looking first at what the literature can tell us about changing uses of text at work and then by exploring a concrete example of an electronics manufacturing workplace. In both parts, we will show how the concept of literacy can function as an ideological construct that obscures powerful interests at play in even routine job tasks of a "high-performance" workplace.

High-Performance Work

Volumes have been written in the past two decades about workplace restructuring, revealing a sea change in the philosophy of management for workplaces of all kinds, both private- and public-sector. The manufacturing sector has been central to these developments, with the decline of mass production and the emergence of new approaches to the theory and (sometimes) practice of manufacturing, known variously as post-Fordism, flexible or lean production, agile manufacturing, high performance, or just "the new workplace." All of these terms refer in various ways to evolving approaches to increasing productivity through more intensive management of both material and human resources, largely influenced since the 1980s by the so-called Japanese manufacturing revolution.[3]

In this chapter we use the term "high performance" to refer broadly to this climate of pressure to do "more with less." High-performance workplaces are said to operate in a highly competitive market by changing quickly in response to customer needs and by competing on the basis of quality assurance (QA) as well as cost (Womack et al. 1990). In this context, "quality" has a technical meaning defined by ISO certification (International Organization for Standards), operationalized as adherence to standard operating procedures (SOP), and demonstrated through systematic recording of production data on the shop floor. Achieving this standard depends heavily on prescribed use of text, either paper or electronic, by front-line workers. Maintaining ISO certification requires regular on-site audits to ensure conformity with ISO standards, and failure to pass an audit can mean a serious threat to staying in business.

A second and closely related aspect of high-performance production is continuous improvement (CI). Like quality assurance, CI is a highly technical practice involving the systematic use of an ongoing cycle of planning, executing, checking, and refining operations to improve efficiencies and to eliminate waste in all aspects of the production process. All this depends on intensive recordkeeping and is referred to in the Japanese management literature as "speaking with data" (Imai 1997: 197). Data come from many sources, including the most routine use of charts, checklists, and logbooks, sometimes computerized, as part of the daily work tasks of employees in all kinds of workplaces. Thus, whether by hand or by computer, "speaking with data" also depends centrally on literacy practices of front-line workers.

These connections among ISO, CI, and the use of text are at the center of the widespread concern about a "literacy crisis" at work (Belfiore et al. 2004; Jackson 2000/2001). Until the 1990s, production environments often involved very little paperwork. Production control was exercised through an oral culture of supervision. But today, all that has changed. Supervisors, team leaders, and even some middle managers in the high-performance workplace are caught between the competing demands of "getting the product out the door" and doing the paperwork. Shop-floor workers commonly see the paperwork as an add-on and a second priority, while for senior managers and quality assurance experts, the *data*—in the form of paper or electronic text—are increasingly the form of work that counts. The texts increasingly stand in for the product and mediate business relationships through real-time and just-in-time communications between suppliers and customers. Thus, the use of text, electronic or paper, in this setting is inseparable from the exercise of managerial power.

To show how all this works in real life, we turn to Bonnie's experience in an electronics manufacturing firm. She shows us how the demands of reading and writing in this setting are embedded in a textual organization of work that is complex and highly contested. From this vantage point, we see that the charge of "literacy problems" arises less as a description of the actual education and performance abilities of individuals than as an ideological construct that blames certain workers for the tensions and competing interests in workplace life.

The "Hell on My Face"

When I was asked by Nancy and Tim[4] if I had enjoyed my job as a team leader on an electronic manufacturing assembly line, I scowled and said, "Can't you tell by the hell on my face?" Tim leaned forward in his chair and said, "Hmm, could you tell us about that?" As I described my former workplace and the frustrations I had experienced, Nancy and Tim asked me questions about *how* my workplace functioned. When they first asked me about the role of texts, I told them that there weren't many texts; I remembered instructional manuals and logbooks, but they seemed relatively unimportant to me in terms of my daily activities and responsibilities. However, as we continued our dialogue about my work in the plant, we discovered that texts were profoundly important, both to understanding the nature of the work and to identifying my frustrations with my job. Here I will try to make those tensions visible.

For seven years, I worked in a large, global, ISO9001-registered electronics contract manufacturing company. I was one of approximately fifty surface mount technology (SMT) team leaders in the plant whose job was to lead a small team of workers through the first manufacturing step in the production of electronic circuit boards, such as memory cards and motherboards. The physical work of making circuit boards was relatively straightforward, since the processes for each machine and each product were documented in manufacturing instructions (MIs); although there were wide variations in the types of products that we built, the process itself was highly prescribed.

Adherence to standardized operating procedures (SOP) is a cornerstone of the ISO9001 approach. Texts, or, more specifically, "controlled documents," were the vehicle for achieving standardization of work processes within one plant, as well as among geographically distant plants. All approved procedures for each stage of the production needed to be explicitly documented. The MIs, for example, contained product-specific process steps, including details on which parts should be on the board, how much solder paste should be applied, and how to handle the boards.

At the beginning of each shift, my first responsibility was to check the production board to find out which product we were building. My second task was to print all the relevant MIs to ensure that the team had the most current set of instructions. Not only did all processes have to be documented, but each document had an "owner" (rather than an author), a number, and a revision number. An owner of a document was the person, usually a process engineer, who was responsible for the correct maintenance of the document in compliance with ISO. As team leader, it was my responsibility to ensure that the team was using the correct revision number of the document; this requirement meant that most team leaders printed a new set of documents each shift just to be safe. In theory, we were allowed to do only what was detailed in the MI; in practice, there were often more effective ways to get the work done. Yet, if we were audited by a quality specialist or internal ISO auditor and asked why we were doing something in particular, we would need to be able to show the relevant section of the appropriate document to justify our actions. These documentary requirements were essential in order for the plant to maintain the ISO9001 certification. Thus, documents governed our work both by defining the acceptable range of our actions and by curbing our discretion.[5]

At the same time, workers were also active producers of texts in the workplace. The SMT line process involved the mechanical application of solder paste on a circuit board, the mechanical placement of electronic components on top of the solder paste, and the thermal cycling of the board in a fifty-foot oven to melt and solidify the solder paste. As the components were tiny (some measured 0.008 inch by 0.006 inch) and intricate (some parts were 0.5 inch by 0.5 inch, with 240 leads), workers had to be able to pay attention to small detail. A long conveyer belt transported the circuit board from operation to operation. All of the machines were controlled by software that, in theory, reduced the role of the worker to activating the process using "Go" buttons; in practice, a great deal of human intervention was required to make the production line run smoothly and to document and monitor the process. Part of that work was to record machine data from each step of the process in logbooks; as I reflect on my experience, this activity turned out to be central to my experience of frustration in the job.

On the assembly line, there were four paper logbooks for solder paste measurements, to document when new parts were added to the placement machines and to record the results of the weekly oven profile test. There were also three points in the production process where the employee's number was electronically linked to the bar code identification on every circuit board he or she processed. These data were used to track manufacturing problems back to the specific employee. The required paperwork for the team leader included the "End of Shift Report," which involved recording the actual number of circuit boards manufactured during each shift.

One of my biggest problems was ensuring that these logbooks were filled in properly. Production demands conflicted with these requirements for recording the process, but, as team leader, I was held accountable for both tasks. I was usually able to keep on top of the required paperwork for the team leader; however, checking that the logbooks had been properly filled in by the contract workers at the end of each shift was something that I never had time for. I saw this task as a pesky distraction from the "real" work of getting the product out the door. My attitude toward what counted as real work was shaped by middle-management actions that clearly sent the message that meeting production targets was our main priority. If the team failed to meet the production targets on a shift, I, as team leader, would be questioned by my manager about what had gone wrong. I would also have to complete a form detailing the problems we had encountered on the shift (more paperwork!).

It was only at the time of the ISO audits that the gaps in logbooks would be noticed. When an audit was approaching, there would be a big panic about whether the documents were thorough enough to pass the audit. Each department had a quality specialist who had to ensure that the logbooks, employee training records, and all instructional documents were up to date and complete. At audit time, these specialists had a big job on their hands. This "catch-up" documentary work fell heavily on team leaders, as we were expected to "fix" the logbooks to show a consistent, coherent set of data. Not surprisingly, we would often have to fabricate data after the fact in order to appear to be in compliance with audit specifications. The workers who had worked on the shifts with missing data were most often long gone (and even if they still were employed by the company, they wouldn't have remembered the measurements). Team leaders like me learned to play the game to keep our jobs.

The expectation that team leaders would "smooth out" the gaps and omissions in the logbooks created a climate of resentment toward the contract workers whose job it was to make regular entries in the books. The failure to complete logbooks was often seen by team leaders as evidence of deficiencies in the literacy abilities of individual contract workers. It was not uncommon to hear a team leader grumble, "Why can't they even fill in the logbooks? Don't they know how to read and write?"

But a closer look at the organization of paperwork in this workplace provides an alternative explanation to this common-sense way of understanding the problem. For contract workers, just like team leaders, the logbooks were the part of the work that could be ignored in that moment when there was a push to produce product. Thus, to keep up with the other demands, contract workers would neglect the logbooks. As I wouldn't have time to check at the end of each shift, the gaps in data collection, then, would be discovered only at audit time. The omissions in the logbooks mattered to me because my performance was evaluated on the basis not only of whether I had met production targets but also whether I had satisfied the documentary requirements; my personal evaluation directly impacted my annual salary and "team incentive bonus."[6] For the contract workers, however, there was no compelling reason to make regular logbook entries, as their work performance was never reviewed, their time in the plant was short-lived, and management actions, they could see, clearly indicated that building the product was the priority.

Eventually, I realized there were several more layers to this story, revealing profound contradictions in the hiring practices in the plant. For example, each SMT line was operated by four workers, three of whom had expertise on only one part of the process; only I, as team leader, was trained on all of the machines. Yet I was also the only permanent employee on my team. The other team members were employed on six-month contracts renewable three times to a maximum of eighteen months. This practice meant that skilled and experienced workers left the company on a weekly basis, resulting in constant disruption to the team. Yet, when "lean manufacturing" was the buzzword of the plant, management articulated a goal of having all team members cross-trained on more than one machine. As a team leader, I wholeheartedly agreed with this goal. However, I was frustrated by the barriers to achieving it when company hiring policies and practices favored short-term contract workers. But that's not all. Strangely, the company's hiring process for these short-term contract positions was both rigorous and time consuming. The minimum requirement for contract positions was a postsecondary degree from any country, an acceptable score on the Test of English as a Foreign Language (TOEFL), and the successful completion of a thirty-to-forty-five-minute scenario-based interview. These hiring practices ensured that the contract workers on the manufacturing floor were highly educated people with a high degree of fluency in English. Most workers were recent male immigrants to Canada, usually with more than one university degree; these hiring criteria ensured a highly literate workforce, yet the way these highly educated workers were utilized by the company suggested otherwise.

The contract workers not only had to deal with relentless and conflicting production demands and resulting tensions but also experienced a more generalized exclusion from key communication practices in the plant. Permanent employees were equipped with individual email accounts so that they could communicate with other workers in other departments or on other shifts. We were also given training on how to create and work with documents so that we would be able to own documents and take the lead in technical problem solving at regular quality meetings. Permanent employees were expected to be involved in cross-shift and cross-department communication and were given the tools to accomplish this. In sharp contrast, contract workers did not have personal email accounts; they had access only to a general department email account. As a result, they lost both their individual identities as employees and any sense of privacy in communication. They were not permitted to create new documents, lead process-improvement projects, or meet with employees on other shifts or in other departments. At the Learning Centre, they were restricted to functional training on how to fill in logbooks. In other words, the contract workers were actively excluded from the main electronic textual practices that tied together much work of the plant. In a very real sense, the value of workers to the company could be gauged by their access to such literacy practices as the ability to communicate through email, access texts, and create new work processes via text. Exclusion from this textual realm also meant exclusion from real power in the workplace. Ironically, it was actually highly educated workers who were being "made illiterate" by the workplace practices that subordinated and excluded them from the literacy practices of the organization.

Finally, I also came to understand the significance of the fact that the majority of these workers were people of color. In my two years as a team leader, I worked with people from all areas of the world. It was an uncomfortable experience for me, as a Canadian-born white woman with a B.A. in women's studies and an electronics engineering technician diploma, to be supervising contract workers with graduate degrees and years of professional work experience.[7] Although many contract workers had more experience and knowledge of the SMT line than I did, especially during my first three months as team leader, as the permanent employee, I was in a position of power. Because the majority of permanent employees in manufacturing were also white and the majority of the contract workers were people of color, there was a strange neocolonial feel to the workplace that made me uneasy. Eventually, I saw how this process of exclusion and subsequent labeling of contract workers as "deficient" was itself a process of racialization—that is, differences in people's "race" were readily treated as an indication of their skill levels and as a determinant of their work performance.

Conclusions: "Il-literacy" as Organizational Course of Action

When Bonnie began to discuss her experience in this plant with Tim and Nancy, she was frustrated that the skills and knowledge of contract workers were systematically undervalued and unrewarded by the company. This was not incidental, accidental, or an oversight; it was an organizational course of action central to the labor-market strategy of this large corporation. She was keenly aware that it was a form of racialized discrimination. But what did it have to do with literacy?

Together we unraveled these connections. In this setting, as in many others, the concept of literacy was at the center of a complex textual relation between the changing demands of powerful institutions and the increasingly precarious lives of individuals. Here was a group of highly literate workers who were accused of having poor literacy on the basis of how they functioned in the plant. How they functioned, however, turned out to have little to do with individual skills or skill deficits. Instead, it was part of an organizational course of action in which some workers (and not others) were hired into temporary and subordinate positions and then excluded from key literacy practices in the plant. These arrangements were designed to monitor and control the work process and were justified in terms of the imperative to turn a profit on every shift. The literate work of filling in "logbooks" in this scenario became a key mechanism in this process of control and thus a site of struggle and contestation. The "hell" on Bonnie's face was a point of entry to uncovering these arrangements.

This particular story focuses on a relation between permanent, North American–born employees and highly skilled immigrant workers of color. Indeed, as the number of highly skilled immigrants grows in many industrialized countries, creating a workforce of newcomers who are technically skilled but socially and culturally vulnerable to exclusion, the type of situation explored in this chapter may well occur more frequently. But the dynamics described here can apply not only to the situation of immigrant workers. The label of "illiteracy" in this scenario is an ideological construct that can be used to blame anyone whose interests or performance conflict with the imperative of increased productivity.

Indeed, we recognize that there are many people in workplaces who are not highly educated and who do actually lack skills and/or experience in the use of texts, both electronic and print. Such individuals may indeed encounter challenges at work and sometimes in other areas of their lives. But many years of research in adult literacy show that such people often find innovative (and usually collaborative) ways to live and work well in the face of these challenges (Darrah 1997; Darville 1998; Prinsloo and Breire 1996). So when headlines claim that such individuals are the cause of a "$60 billion problem" and a threat to the prosperity of nations, it is important to ask what is actually happening here, and where is this trouble coming from.[8] When we look more broadly, we see that literacy levels are being touted as a growing problem for transnational corporations in their search for a labor force unencumbered by national borders (as well as by national taxation and labor laws). In response, the concept of literacy has been redesigned or reinvented—through new technologies such as the IALS/ALSS surveys—as a tool that assesses, labels, ranks, and organizes whole populations according to their value as a resource for production, and thus for capital accumulation on a transnational scale. Having IALS data to certify the "employability" of the population is increasingly like having ISO certification; it means that the nation is "open for business" in the global economy.

In this competitive environment, poor scores on international literacy tests may indeed cause "trouble" or pose "dangers," but ones that are quite different from those implied in alarmist speeches and headlines. For example, governments are particularly sensitive about where they rank in international literacy reports, particularly if published test scores suggest that their workforce is "illiterate" and thus a bad risk for corporate investment. This could be seen as a threat to the economic status of any nation in the global marketplace. Relatedly, there may be political dangers for public officials if they are seen to be failing in their responsibility for labor force development. So the Canadian official who spoke with such alarm may have been accurately reflecting (and projecting) her own fears. But her way—and the dominant way—of framing the issues collapses these economic relations into a property—and a responsibility—of individuals.

Constructing illiteracy as a problem of crisis proportions is key to making it into a site of administrative action (Smith 1990a; Darville 1999, 2002). Yet, it is revealing to note that the kind of action that is being taken most frequently in response to this issue is not to provide more literacy instruction to increase the functional levels of adults. On the contrary, funds available for adult literacy programming are reported to be shrinking internationally, though there is widespread new investment in literacy for children (Jackson 2005a; Khan 2000; Sivasubramaniam 2005; World Bank 1995).

Instead, the most pervasive response of governments and employers has been to insert literacy testing as a requirement for entry to a growing range of opportunities and services. Testing is now commonplace not only for new job applicants but also as part of compulsory certification for people who want to keep jobs they already have. Tests are being required variously as a condition of registering with an employment agency, getting into a training program, applying for social assistance, and receiving (un)employment insurance, or whatever else remains of a "social safety net" in industrialized countries (Shragge 1997). In theory, a failed test in most of these settings is said to trigger compulsory literacy instruction; in practice, since resources for instruction are scarce, the immediate impact is often exclusion from services and opportunities.

Thus, while literacy may not be experienced by individuals as a problem in the routine conduct of their lives, it is being made to matter by powerful interests that have harnessed it to their own purposes. In the process, corporate interests have overtaken human interests as the centerpiece of the literacy movement.

NOTES

The authors wish to acknowledge funding for this research from the Canadian Networks of Centres of Excellence: The Automobile in the 21st Century.

1. Countries for which survey results have been reported now include Australia, Belgium (Flanders), Bermuda, Canada, Italy, Germany, Ireland, the Mexican State of Nuevo Leon, the Netherlands, New Zealand, Norway, Poland, Sweden, Switzerland (French- and German-speaking), the United Kingdom, and the United States.

2. Statement recorded in field notes by Nancy Jackson, who attended the conference.

3. For discussion of these issues, see Ackers, Smith, and Smith 1996; Delbridge 2000; Handy 1988; James, Veit, and Wright 1997; Kidd 1994; Piore and Sabel 1984; Pollert 1991; Story 1994; Womack et al. 1990.

4. I was working as a research assistant with Nancy Jackson and Tim Diamond on a project called "Texts as a Tool of Restructuring." We recorded our meetings and had them transcribed. These texts have been important in tracing how my awareness developed over the year that we worked together.

5. The documents were more of a shield than a source of information; I found out about production changes verbally, at shift crossover, from the other team leader. However, it was unacceptable in the ISO9001 environment to say that I was doing something because the other shift leader had verbally communicated it to

me. I needed that piece of paper (which was often fifteen pages long) to validate my actions should I be audited. The mantra of ISO at that time was something like "Say [i.e., document] what you do, do what you say, prove that you have done it." Because of these expectations, each team leader would print the documents at the beginning of every shift and, most likely, never look at them.

6. The "team incentive bonus" initially applied only to permanent employees. Twice it was extended to contract workers, but both of those years the bonus was not paid to contract workers as the company reported that it had failed to meet "threshold" profit levels.

7. My experiences in this workplace have been the impetus for my graduate research. For more detailed analysis of the deprofessionalization of immigrant women engineers in Canada, see Slade 2003a.

8. Experienced workplace educators know the importance of starting with an "organizational needs analysis" rather than individual skills testing to understand the complexity of workplace challenges that frequently get labeled as "literacy" problems.

[2]

Institutional Technologies
Coordinating Families and Schools, Bodies and Texts

ALISON I. GRIFFITH AND LOIS ANDRÉ-BECHELY

Editor's Introduction

The conceptual currencies related to skill and competitiveness introduced in the preceding chapter have been carried not only through arenas of literacy and job training but also to the various layers of state-supported education, where they connect the efforts of teachers (and, as we'll see, parents, as well) with employers' concerns for educating workers. This chapter examines the push for accountability in primary education and extends the idea of interinstitutional discourses that carry ruling ideas across institutional realms and national borders.

Alison Griffith and Lois André-Bechely begin with work that mothers do to meet accountability standards in the public schools, and sketch out a map of the extended relations of that accountability. They show us mothers attempting to fill in with extra tutoring where underfunded schools and overworked teachers may not be able to meet accountability demands—in much the same way that family caregivers may fill in with unpaid child-care work as low-income mothers are pressed into the labor force (Scott and London chapter 8 and Ridzi chapter 11 this volume), or with informal nursing as hospital stays are shortened (Rankin and Campbell 2006).

The institutional technologies that coordinate these activities in schools and homes are rationalized procedures for producing knowledge of what's happening locally—forms of measurement and reporting that make local activity governable from sites of administration. For example, the standardized tests that have assumed increasing importance in primary schools incorporate particular, objective ways of accounting for children's learning, and these objective and processable representations of school learning are replacing more grounded judgments of educators and parents. These standardized modes of

performance reporting are also tied to internationally developed curricula
and, increasingly, to the products of an international educational industry.

Griffith and André-Bechely find the products of that growing enter-
prise in the kitchens where they met mothers and children at work; they in-
troduce us to the commercially produced texts that guide and support unpaid
work outside the public educational system and that also provide new sources
of profit for large educational publishers. Thus, their analysis draws attention
to linkages not only across institutional areas and national borders but also
across the increasingly permeable boundaries of public and private provision
for education, health, and social welfare

* * *

In Los Angeles, a second grader sits at a working-class African American
family's kitchen table. She is doing an assignment from the *Open Court*
Reading textbook, part of the series adopted by her urban elementary
school. Also on the table is a test-preparation workbook for the second-
grade level of the CAT-6, the standardized test required by California. The
young girl's mother bought the test preparation workbook at a local teacher
supply store for ten dollars, following the recommendation of a teacher at
her daughter's school. Each night, while she cooks dinner and after her
daughter finishes her regular homework, the mother helps her daughter go
through the workbook so that the young girl will be better prepared to do
well on the standardized tests she will soon take.

In Toronto, another child is doing a reading assignment, which is
aligned to provincial curriculum standards for which a new version of a
Canadian standardized test, the CAT-3,[1] has been developed. He, too, is using the *Open Court Reading* text and a test-preparation workbook bought
from a local bookshop on the recommendation of the community center
tutor. His English is coming along well, and his parents, who speak only
Farsi, wish they could better help their son prepare for the upcoming tests.

These two stories are drawn from research done in Canada and the
United States that explores the educational work of mothers with children
in elementary school. The similarities in these stories are striking, yet they
are occurring in different countries with different educational systems,
different educational policies, and different school demographics. Across
national boundaries, students undertake educational work in local classrooms that has been developed by international educational publishing
corporations and prepare for standardized tests required by educational
policies that, across provincial and state boundaries, have strong similarities in terms of content and process. As educational systems in the United

States and Canada are being transformed by a global educational enterprise, by educational policy-borrowing across national boundaries, and by a local educational focus on standards and accountability, parents' educational work in the family also becomes coordinated with those economic and policy changes.

Over the past ten years, school systems in the United States and Canada have undergone extensive restructuring, particularly in the areas of finance, accountability, standardization and testing. Regardless of, or perhaps in concert with, the standardizing practices of current educational reforms, parents and educators struggle to meet new educational goals that have been established locally in boards of education and school districts and translocally through a global educational discourse. Yet, the intersection between these globalizing discourses, educational change, and families' local experience with schooling is unexplored.

In our research and writing, we have been exploring how local changes in schooling are being shaped by a global discourse on educational restructuring. In particular, we are interested in the ways that educational policies frame up the issues embedded within them in such a way that the issues can be made administratively actionable. The educational actions that flow from a policy, then, bring with them an administrative process that manages our interaction with the identified issues. Recursively, the language of the policy can be tracked back to the globalized discourse that shaped the issue in the first place. For example, many of the current changes in education in Ontario are embedded in a conception of the need to change schooling to provide for Canada's participation in a global economy—that is, to produce a labor force whose skills "fit" with the needs of global capital. From this conception of social change flow the policy solutions of accountability and standardization, mandated in educational policies such as the No Child Left Behind Act of 2001 (NCLB) in the United States and the Government of Ontario's Bill 160: The Education Quality Act (1995). What we see in classrooms as a result of these policy mandates is a new standardized curriculum, accompanied by standardized testing and standardized reporting—the new institutional technologies of standardization and accountability.

In the different national educational contexts of Canada and the United States, internationally developed reading series, like *Open Court Reading* mentioned earlier, are shaping local school and family practices in similar ways (Jenkins 2004). These curricula are linked to the accountability reforms in public education, particularly to standardized testing processes.

Educational restructuring in K-12 education in the diverse educational settings of Toronto and Los Angeles directs the work of students and teachers in classrooms, *as well as* the educational work of families. The introductory stories tell of one way that a global educational discourse embedded in the institutional technologies of standardization and accountability can appear at the kitchen tables of families with children in public school.

Exploring the Terrain

The institutional technologies that we are seeing in our research are not specific to educational contexts. New institutional technologies can be linked to the social and economic transformation taking place across public service institutions. The Canadian and U.S. economies are increasingly global and racially diverse (Brodie 1994; Spivak 1999). Typically, the emphasis in discussions of the changing economy has been on the transformation of the private sector. Yet, substantial changes are occurring in public institutions under various descriptors as "restructuring," "privatizing," "marketizing," and "outsourcing." As capital shifts from a regional to a global context, uneven and contested changes are manifested in the work of public-sector professionals and their clients within and across organizations. We can see this trend particularly in the human-service domains of education, health care, and social work. We suggest that current and ongoing changes to the traditionally defined public sector are important to explore in that they affect all segments of Canadian, U.S., and other Western societies. Of particular interest to us are the new institutional technologies that are central to the process of transforming human-service organizations within a globalizing economy.

The term "institutional technologies" refers to the formalized, technically developed, and rationalized procedures that regulate the everyday operations of institutions. As the public sector is changing, these ordinary work routines are becoming ever more digitized and more similar across institutional and national boundaries. The new institutional technologies include standardized, often computer-mediated, always textually mediated work processes that link professionals and nonprofessionals in social institutions. They provide the administrative ground on which various levels of management in a social institution can assess and coordinate action.

Although institutions differ widely in their organization, contemporary social change is interinstitutional. Developing and developed institutional technologies are reorganizing the everyday work of nurses and other health workers in communities and hospitals, social workers in municipal agencies, and educators in K-12 and postsecondary schools. The new institutional technologies are changing the relationship between professionals and nonprofessionals and directly affecting the lives of those people who fall within their institutional mandate. Changes in social institutions are intensifying the educational work of parents in the home (André-Bechely 2005; Griffith and Smith 2005), are relying on standardized assessments to move children out of risky family situations (Swift 1995), and are, increasingly, depending on families and communities for health-care services (Campbell 1999; Rankin and Campbell 2006). Institutional technologies are reshaping the work and relationships of people who participate in the public sector—those who provide services and those who receive services.

The economy's shift toward competition as the basis for successful participation in the global marketplace has penetrated policy and practice in both the Canadian and U.S. public sectors. Public-service institutions are actively addressing themselves to businesslike management strategies to help accommodate reductions in social spending. These changes are consistent with new human-service program goals of supporting individual effort, self-reliance, and competitiveness in those who, in an earlier time, would have been seen as "needing services."

The availability of sophisticated information-based technologies enables human-service organizations to become sensitive to market influences in institutional planning, decision making, and action. Indeed, it might be said that the early-twenty-first-century revolution in information and communication makes such a transformation in human services possible. Knowledge, in processable forms, has become a resource of the greatest importance for determining the most efficient course of action in health care, social services, and educational services. Institutional technologies that harness knowledge for the purposes of planning, resource utilization, program management, and evaluation are transforming the public sector—ranging from the processes of service-delivery systems to the required expertise of practitioners.

The new institutional technologies "work" for the purposes of organizing and managing effectively the new forms of public service. They also create distinctive new problems. Just as the innovations of rational management and bureaucracy advanced organizational action in an earlier historical period, the new institutional technologies have their own Achilles' heel(s). Human-service undertakings now operate on information that displaces people as knowing subjects. Working from informational data bases instead of from the more traditional hands-on interaction, decision making, and professional judgment means that the manifold functions of the service sector must be reconceptualized in specific ways. Whether organizational texts are for processing people for eligibility, assessing results of programs, determining the most cost-efficient interventions, or determining whose need is greatest for placement on waiting lists, they are constructed for the purpose of decision making about the efficient deployment of human services.

Thus, knowing, in other than objective ways, has been called into question. Yet, systems that are automated and objective must continue to rely on knowledgeable people and on the experiential input of individuals themselves to keep them operating successfully. Our research is focused at this juncture—the intersection of the new institutional technologies and the actual activities of people who work in or use human-service organizations in the transforming public sector.

The transformation of social institutions in the public sector reaches into the lives of most Americans and Canadians, and particularly into the traditional sphere of women's work. The majority of the participants in the public institutional sector, sometimes called the "sphere of reproduction," are women. The professionals employed in social work, nursing, community health, and education, as well as the support workers (e.g., practical nurses, intake assistants, and educational assistants), are primarily female. So, too, their institutional work is oriented to that part of society in which women have primary care-taking responsibility—the disabled, the family, the child. Thus, the transformation of the public sector is also a transformation in women's professional, nonprofessional, and family-based work, values, and identities.

The new institutional technologies are one instance of the textually mediated conversations that permeate social institutions. As Smith (1987, 2005) notes, texts are ubiquitous in our social world. Texts coordinate the apparently individual but socially organized points of connection between people working in different parts of institutional complexes of activity. In the research on education and on globalization, we are struck by the unexamined, textually mediated communications that coordinate the work and understandings of people in different social sites, nations, and, indeed, globally oriented agencies. The two stories we told earlier are thoroughly saturated by textual relations that extend from the kitchen table to the school to the Ministry or Department of Education, to policies, to neoliberal educational restructuring. So, too, the phenomenon often called globalization is thoroughly textualized. For example, converging educational policies are informed by theories of the market that are being taught through textbooks in M.B.A. programs around the world. In the international education market, universities are changing regulations and policies to admit students from other countries on the basis of educational equivalencies portrayed in school transcripts sent within educational packages. Bilateral and multilateral trade agreements—written agreements—shape the work of government ministries that credential public and private universities. And so on.

Digitally oriented institutional texts are an empirically interesting feature of institutional restructuring. Our interaction with texts is a moment of activity, taking time and energy—in other words, work—and thus can be described and analyzed. As the human-service professional (teacher, social worker, nurse) activates the textual relations through her ongoing work practices—doing report cards, estimating risk assessments, doing welfare intake, entering patient classification forms—she enters into the extended textual relations of the institution. Of interest to us are the processes through which institutional technologies, with their embedded globalized policy discourses, orient the everyday activities of those who work within the social institution *and* those whose lives intersect with it.

As we engage with texts, we coordinate the local and the translocal, managing and smoothing over the disjunctures between our experience and the relations of power and knowledge that shape and are shaped by education policies. Changes in K-12, and increasingly in higher education, focus the work of students and teachers in classrooms, as well as the educational work of families that support or enhance their children's participation in school. In order to understand the intersections between globalization and the kitchen table work of families, our research must attend to the social relations of ruling as they are coordinated textually.

Texts and Accountability

Since internationally developed curricula such as *Open Court* are coordinated with the accountability reforms in public education, particularly standardized testing, what is taught in the classroom must have some connection to the tests. So, too, educational policies, curriculum, and texts are increasingly similar across national boundaries and systems (Levin 2001), what Rizvi has called "convergence" (2004), with an emphasis on account-ability linked to learning outcomes.

Open Court Reading is published by Science Research Associates, Inc. (SRA), a division of the McGraw-Hill Companies. *Open Court Reading* is used widely in low-performing urban schools like the ones the chil-dren in our stories attend. As an approved and recommended reading series for school adoption, the *Open Court Reading* series generates mil-lions of dollars in sales for SRA/McGraw-Hill. Finding the same reading series in classrooms in Toronto as well as Los Angeles suggests an active role for corporate publishers in the planning, production, and distribu-tion of a standardized curriculum. The education industry's involvement in accountability reform seems to be expanding as the industry gears up to provide products and services to "meet the challenges" of accountability reform (Walsh 2003). For example, capitalizing on the compliance provi-sions in the NCLB law, companies are marketing such services as tutoring (supplemental education services) and voice-messaging systems that can assist school districts in the United States as they try to raise test scores of low-performing students by notifying parents of absences and meet test-taker percentages by announcing standardized testing dates (Borja 2004; Walsh 2003).

The standardized-testing requirements of accountability reform provide lucrative opportunities for educational publishers, as well. In California, students are required to take the CAT-6/TerraNova, Second Edition, stan-dardized test. CTB/McGraw-Hill develops and sells the TerraNova/CAT assessment systems, complete with reporting software that meets state and national accountability requirements. The California testing contract is worth millions for CTB/McGraw-Hill. The McGraw-Hill Web site states that, as part of its worldwide mission, McGraw-Hill plans to expand its global publishing operations and increase its penetration of the global edu-cation market. It is not alone. Major educational publishers are all pushing to claim a share of the global education industry. At a 2002 presentation where she answered a question about Pearson Publishing's growth strategy for the education market, Pearson's CEO, Marjorie Scardino, said:

> As you know we and McGraw-Hill have about 24% each of the school pub-lishing market, Harcourt has about 18% and Houghton Mifflin are around 12%. So we have a pretty big school business. We don't have a very big supplemental business. As more and more states strive to help each child learn to read and calculate at grade level, which is the objective of the Bush

Bill [NCLB], they need more supplemental materials because the core curriculum materials aren't doing their job. So supplemental is one area for us to grow. Testing is certainly another. Schools don't have a P&L [profit and loss], they only have student performance. So the only way they can figure out if they're getting a return on their investment in students is to test and that's a requirement of the [NCLB] as well. We're the biggest testing company in America. The American testing industry is about a $400 million dollar business, and we reckon that the Bush money is going to double the size of that testing business over time.

She continued:

If you think that the aim is to teach each and every child, the only way you're going to be able to do that is to test each and every child and figure out when he stops learning. You need a lot of information to figure out how to help him, how does he learn best, what are his deficiencies, what are his particular problems, health problems or whatever, and then fashion a program for him. That's the long term future of education where we think we will make a lot of money. We can do this because we have enterprise solutions for schools, we have testing and data collection, and we have school materials.

When asked about the growth prospects for education internationally she responded: "International is a variable feast. I'd say right now that North Asia and Canada are fantastic, doing very well; great growth prospects." (Quotations are taken from the press release of Scardino's presentation at the Lehman Brothers European Media Seminar on September 16, 2002; downloaded from the Pearson Web site).

The education publishing industry may be consolidated further into a new Big Three (Trotter & Manzo 2007). The Houghton Mifflin Company, which once held 12 percent of the market, hopes to purchase Harcourt Education from the London-based Reed Elsevier Group, which would vault Houghton Mifflin to the lead in education publishing, with a 33 percent share of the K-12 market. Such a consolidation would mean that three corporations, producing more than 80 percent of K-12 textbooks, would control the global education industry.

The educational industry's confidence that it has the "enterprise solutions" to meet the learning needs of students will further the development of new institutional technologies—technologies of accountability that could minimize educators' professional knowledge and discretion, a hallmark of classroom teaching, in favor of globally marketed standardized curriculum and corresponding assessment systems.

Parents' Work for Standardization and Testing

Current educational reforms are constructed to mold the work of the classroom to conform to the goals of educational policies. Standardized testing and measures for ensuring educational accountability have been the primary vehicles for top-down control of local school activities. These educational measures are thoroughly textual, constructing a bureaucratic record of classroom teaching and student performance that extends to the school-family relationship by way of such texts as report cards and students' score reports for standardized tests. Implicit in the reporting of student performance to parents is the notion that parents will aid the school in improving students' academic achievement. However, educational initiatives cannot require parental involvement in their children's education. The often-identified disjuncture between families and schools (Lareau 1989, 2003; Lightfoot 1978; Sharp and Green 1975) can be breached only by parents' voluntary participation.

The push toward greater accountability is couched in the rhetoric of preparing children to be productive members in a global society. How these changes appear in the everyday lives of parents with children in school needs to be examined more closely. As parents are asked increasingly to share responsibility for meeting the demands of accountability reform, parents' work on behalf of their children's schooling and the family-school relationship will necessarily change. Parents will require new and different knowledges (Filer and Pollard 2000) and new forms of cultural and social capital. Parents are confronted with the new technologies of accountability as achievement data are produced by government-mandated accountability systems and school curricula are modified to raise standardized test scores. Parents will increasingly be asked to manage new forms of participation that accompany and support these changes—to take up the discourse of shared responsibility.

As our introductory stories indicate, we are conducting two research projects, one in Toronto and one in Los Angeles, that focus on parents' educational work. We are particularly interested in the ways that parents are drawn into the institutional technologies of accountability as they help their children meet academic standards and perform successfully on standardized tests—in other words, how the new technologies of accountability, in part defined by a global educational enterprise, may be changing the nature of parents' participation in educational work at home. In this chapter, however, we focus on the Los Angeles study to illustrate the extended textually mediated social relation coordinating parents' educational work in the home with state-level instructions to parents on how to help their children succeed in school and with the globally organized interests of educational publishing corporations.

Each of the mothers interviewed in the Los Angeles study assumed some kind of leadership role at her child's school site and had access to information not available to most parents about how schools work and what was taking place in classrooms. For example, the mothers understood the standardizing effects of the *Open Court* curriculum. Cynthia, a white and working-class mother, said:

> It actually gets a little crazy with the whole *Open Court* thing—is that, you know, a kid in California can go to X school, Y school, Z school and transfer three times in a year and be on chapter 5 at his first school. And when he goes to—moves to the next school, they're ending chapter 5, going on to chapter 6. And then if he moves again, they're going on to chapter 7 and that there's consistency—you know, everybody in the state on the same page on the same day.

Georgia, an African American mother, made the same observation.

> I actually volunteer in the classes, so I got firsthand as far as seeing how there's a lesson every day, and you can go to any one of our first-grade classes, for example, and teachers should pretty much be right on track as far as the same—doing the same material the other teachers are doing.

And some saw the impact that the curriculum was having on teachers' professional discretion. A Latina and working-class mother, Aida, commented:

> I think it takes out the flexibility, because it's rigorous. You go from A to B, from B to C, to C to D, and there's not enough time in between. And where the teacher, if they need to do something on their own imagination, it's

not within that pattern of the *Open Court*. . . . *Open Court* is so structured that I think that's where a lot of teachers feel that they can't use it with their own way of, you know, teaching.

Regardless of what these mothers may individually think about standardized curriculum and standardized testing, they are participating in the home-based educational work, discussed in the next section, that is coordinated with the classroom-mandated and increasingly standardized educational work of schools.

A Home-Learning Economy

While much of the work parents take up at home involves traditional home-based educational practices such as helping with homework, reading to children, and seeing to proper bedtimes, a new form of involvement is taking shape—helping children prepare for successful performance on standardized tests. Nowhere is this more evident than in the proliferation of first-grade through high school test-preparation materials that are now available for parents' purchase. Major publishing corporations are selling books for different states' standardized tests and for the various grade levels tested. For example, McGraw-Hill publishes its Spectrum series for standardized test preparation for grades 1 through 8 (Foreman, Cohen, et al. 2001). These books are easily found on Internet searches and in the large bookstore chains. The mothers Lois interviewed in Los Angeles shared how they use these books to help their children prepare for testing. Two African American mothers, Lana and Georgia, describe how their kitchen table work supports the school's accountability policy, which in turn is coordinated with the market goals of global educational publishers. Lana said:

And, you know, I was always like, "Okay. So what else can I teach them that they're not learning? Or what else can I teach them to keep them learning this?" And I would always just be in Lakeshore or Toys-R-Us, you know—in the back where the books were, or either Barnes and Noble . . . and there's a little bookstore called Neeley's Bookstore. And they had a lot of like—you remember a long time ago we had the SRA [previous pedagogical strategy adopted by the County]? Okay. Well, the *Open Court* has a new concept. But I went to Neeley's, and I got a certain—this certain little system. It was almost like SRAs. And it taught them to read. If you go to Lakeshore, like with her in the second grade, I got their second-grade level Lakeshore studying for the Stanford 9, CAT 6. And I would have my kids—like during the summer this year, she'll start studying the third grade.

Lana uses a test-preparation book to build her daughter's reading and testing skills.

Every day of the week they read. But three days a week, we do synonyms, you know, because even at my age, taking tests, they always ask you what's similar, you know. And there's some similarities. And my daughter took one yesterday. Let me show you [pointing to page in test-prep workbook]. She took a similarity test yesterday. These are the kind of tests that I give her, to teach her about similarities.

Georgia also mentioned purchasing materials that help prepare her children for testing, especially her first-grade daughter.

With my younger one, we play a lot of games. I buy a lot of material. I buy the booklets at Lakeshore. I have a chalkboard at home, a calendar like they have at school, the whole nine yards. You walk into my son's room; the border around the room is the cursive writing, the ABC, around the room. I mean I buy so many materials, it's ridiculous. But it actually—it's to benefit my children. You have to help them. Because maybe they did get it, but not enough to actually stay in here [pointing to her forehead]. But like when my daughter comes home, we're literally going over it. I mean I'm giving her other examples. If she has a word, she's like, "Oh, Mommy, I know what that word means." I'm like, "Oh, but you know what? That word also means something else. Do you know what else that word means?" I mean—and that has broadened her vocabulary by doing that. But as far as helping them, I think just what we do at the beginning of the year actually helps them, and they're ready by the time they take those tests.

Both of these mothers went to a teacher supply store, Lakeshore, to purchase the standardized test-preparation workbooks and other schooling materials they used in their homes. These mothers not only were engaged in activities at home that mirror the work that takes place in schools, they also were providing supplemental educational work that has been tradition-

Figure 2.1. Marketing Learning Materials in the United States and Canada.
*Sources: Lakeshore Learning Materials, Carson, California (http://www.lakeshorelearning.com)
and Wintergreen Learning Materials, Concord, Ontario (http://wintergreen.ca).*

ally the domain of professional educators. Moreover, by shopping for their home educational supplies at Lakeshore, they were unknowingly aligning their work at home with their children to the global distribution of educational materials. Lakeshore Learning Materials operates thirty-three stores in twelve states in the United States. The company also has an equivalent operation in Canada: Wintergreen Learning Materials. The Lakeshore and the Wintergreen Web sites are linked, and the Web sites include catalogues for purchasing various classroom supplies and teaching materials. Except for the company name, the covers for the learning materials catalogue are identical.

Standardization has crossed borders, and publishing companies are marketing the same products for schools, teachers, and parents in Los Angeles that they market in Toronto. As accountability and standardization coordinate the local family-school relation, these new institutional technologies also textually mediate the family's educational work and the organizational goals of global educational corporations. Our data do not support the claim that the kind of work Georgia and Lana do is widespread among parents; it is likely not—these are actively involved mothers. Still, we can suggest that the interinstitutional relations we see are linked to the social and economic transformation of public education.

For the past two decades, educational institutions have actively supported a growing movement to involve parents more fully in helping their children be successful in school. Traditional forms of involvement were aimed at improving children's grades or behavior, but seldom was parent involvement directly employed to help raise standardized test scores. With the passage of laws such as the No Child Left Behind Act of 2001 in the United States and the Government of Ontario's Bill 160: The Education Quality Act, which use standardized test scores to hold schools accountable, "high stakes" were attached to testing outcomes—schools would be labeled as poor performing, could have funding reduced, or might be "reconstituted" by the removal of ineffective school personnel. Parents' educational work at home, especially when it translates to children's receiving higher scores on standardized tests, can provide critical assistance to low-performing schools. As parents engage with the work of the classroom in the family home, they help produce the high test scores that meet the government mandates for school accountability. When parents purchase and use the test-preparation booklets, we see the coordination of parents' educational work at home and the accountability work of the school in response to the assessment system designed, marketed, and distributed by global publishing corporations—the same publishers that market classroom curricula internationally. The accountability technology we describe, reaching deep into the family home, to the kitchen table, is among the new institutional technologies that will continue to change the nature of the family-school relationship.

Conclusion

Exploring the textually mediated links from and through parents' work in support of their children's academic performance in school and on standardized tests, we bring into view the intersections and disjunctures between different parents' work on behalf of their children's schooling and how the parents are drawn into local, state, and national political and economic priorities that are embedded in standardization and accountability. Schools today rely even more heavily on the work of parents. With the advent of the new curriculum, standardized testing, and reduction of educational support services, mothering and fathering for schooling becomes even more crucial for the child's success.

We began this chapter with an analysis of the institutional technologies that are reshaping the public sector and human services today, and education in particular. We briefly showed how policy convergence or policy borrowing across national and systemic boundaries has brought accountability programs such as standardized testing to such diverse settings as Los Angeles and Toronto, among others. Historically, the exchange of family and school information through texts has been facilitated between local educators and parents. The new technologies of accountability, such as standardized testing, alter this process and assume new kinds of involvement from parents. To participate effectively in these new technologies of accountability, parents must have advanced English reading and comprehension skills; an understanding of schools' curriculum, instruction, and assessment practices; an awareness of the broader goals of accountability reform; and class-based resources, such as money to purchase materials (books and supplemental teaching materials), easy access to newer and faster computers, knowledge of public facilities such as libraries, and flexible time schedules that allow them to do the prescribed activities. In the diverse urban contexts of Los Angeles and Toronto, the implications of these kinds of assumptions have the effect of privileging families that are able to release the mother's time to support her children's education, that are English-speaking, and that are more educated.

In order to understand the relationship between schools and parents' kitchen table work, we cast our research net beyond the local school system. Along with many other educational researchers, we are interested in the ways that parents and educators are coparticipants in the activities of schooling. At the same time, we are aware of the ongoing large-scale educational changes that sweep through educational systems, altering the everyday work of all the participants—administrators, teachers, and parents—and that these changes are situated in an increasingly globalizing economy. These international, often global, social relations of ruling are essential for understanding the ways that education continues as an engine of inequality (Smith 2000), despite the efforts of many well-meaning people in many different educational venues.

NOTES

We would like to thank Tim Diamond, Marie Campbell, Dorothy Smith, and Gillian Walker, who were involved in the development of some sections of this chapter for a research proposal. Additional parts of this chapter were presented as part of a symposium session at the American Educational Research Association meeting, San Diego, April 12–16, 2004. The authors would like to thank Yvette Daniel for her comments on the symposium papers.

1. The Canadian Achievement Test, the CAT-3, is developed by the Canadian Test Centre and is not the same test as the California Achievement Test, the CAT-6, although they have many similar features. In Ontario, the Educational Quality and Accountability Office (EQAO) has instituted standardized testing in grades 3, 6, and 10. In Los Angeles, standardized testing occurs at each grade level, including the new grade 12 exit exam, a high-stakes test that determines access to institutions of higher learning.

[3]

The Promises and Realities of U.S.
Microenterprise Development

NANCY C. JURIK

Editor's Introduction

Conceptual currencies circulating among policymakers are also taken up in the vocabularies of program development and funding. They enter and shape plans not only for public education and welfare but also in the community-based and activist organizations that seek funding from the state. In this chapter, Nancy Jurik reports on her case study of a microlending program envisioned by local activists as a response to poverty in their region. The analysis begins with her own participation in the conceptualization and establishment of the program and suggests that the microenterprise model appealed to funders because of its fit with the dominant policy ideas of the moment, including a rhetoric of individual empowerment and the accountability of a business model.

Using a national survey of similar programs, Jurik found that many organizations shifted their goals and activities over time in order to align their programs with the ideas and expectations of funders; her analysis helps to show how this kind of cooptation can happen despite the intentions of program staff. In the microlending case, the staff knew the real-life obstacles their clients faced in getting businesses going—obstacles that extended beyond business into their daily lives and the realities of family commitments and structural discrimination. But the program model relied on an abstracted view of a microentrepreneur who needed only business training to succeed. And the bottom-line accountability that was so attractive to funders pushed the staff to narrow rather than broaden the assistance provided.

One striking feature of Jurik's account is how U.S. activists borrowed the microlending approach from poverty programs in developing countries as the withdrawal of public welfare expenditures in their region put increasing pressure on existing strategies for providing income support. Such borrowing points, here and for further analysis, toward the web of language and program ideas that links activists and their funders across borders (for other cases, see Naples and Desai 2002), drawing activists into the bottom-line strategizing that has come to dominate policymaking.

* * *

Over the past two decades, policymakers have become enamored of micro-enterprise development as an avenue for alleviating poverty and promoting economic development in marginalized communities. Microenterprises are defined as very small businesses that are owner operated, involve small amounts of startup capital (i.e., less than $20,000), and employ fewer than five employees. Microenterprise development programs (hereafter referred to as MDPs) aim to provide training and small loans to clients—especially to poor women and men of color—to help them start and operate their own microenterprises. The enthusiasm for microenterprise development is exemplified by the awarding of the 2006 Nobel Peace Prize to Muhammed Yunus and the Grameen Bank for pioneering work in lending to the poor (Dugger 2006).

Globally, MDPs like the Grameen have been associated with the empow-erment of both clients and their communities (Counts 1996). For many, empowerment is a critical concept in discourses surrounding the new economy and connotes self-reliance and incorporation into market spheres (Jurik, Cavender, and Cowgill 2006). The peer lending methods developed by some of the more famous MDPs like the Grameen are often identified as a chief source of such empowerment. Peer lending organizes clients into borrowers' circles—groups of up to eight clients that review one another's business plans, decide who gets loans, set loan amounts (within program guidelines), and encourage loan repayment. If circle member loans are not paid, no further loans are issued until the bad loan(s) are paid off. The circle members also provide support for one another in business planning and operation. In addition to its empowerment potential, many peer-lend-ing MDPs boasted a 90 percent or better rate of repayment on their loans to clients (Balkin 1993).

Conditions in the new economy have encouraged the widespread iden-tification of microenterprises as a viable avenue for boosting family in-come. These conditions include the increasing insecurity faced by workers because of industrial restructuring; government fiscal crises; global compe-tition for cheap labor; layoffs; and the growth of contingent work. Declin-ing government investments in employment, social service, and safety-net programs have encouraged the heightened involvement of nongovernmental organizations (NGOs) in social welfare and economic development. Indeed, NGOs have been a driving force in the worldwide growth of MDPs (Poster and Salime 2002).

MDPs were first popularized in southern hemisphere or so-called developing nations, but they also attracted attention in the United States during the decade preceding welfare reform legislation. MDPs promised to promote self-sufficiency among the poor instead of "welfare dependency." There are now more than three hundred such programs in the United States (Walker and Blair 2002).

MDPs aim to address poverty and underemployment issues in a manner that is consistent with today's popular faith in market-driven solutions for social problems (Blau 1999). MDPs are consistent with neoliberal trends that the sociologist Jill Quadagno (1999) describes as a policy shift from the U.S. welfare state to the "capital investment welfare state." This change entails the restructuring of public benefits to better reflect the operating principles of the private sector and a renewed emphasis on individual rather than collective responsibility for wellbeing. MDPs are also praised as an avenue for assisting women who want to combine paid work and child-care responsibilities. Moreover, because of their business orientation, MDPs also promise to emphasize businesslike standards in their operations and thereby avoid heavy government involvement and the "inefficient" operational practices associated with government programs (Morduch 2000). MDPs are consistent with "new privatization" discourses that call for government and nonprofits to operate in a manner consistent with idealized principles of private-sector efficiency and cost-effectiveness (Jurik 2004: 2). Thus, MDPs seem like an ideal solution for alleviating the insecurities of the new economy, a solution that is consistent with neoliberal ideologies that call for minimal government and the increased integration of everyone and everything into the marketplace (McMichael 2000).

To date, most literature on MDPs focuses on programs in southern-hemisphere nations, and the relatively fewer studies of U.S. programs have emphasized advocacy over critical assessment (Clark and Kays 1995; Servon 1999). This chapter is drawn from a larger study of microenterprise development programs located in the United States (Jurik 2005). My research in this area was inspired by involvement in the planning and establishment of an MDP, which I will refer to as MicroEnterprise, Incorporated (ME), that was located in a large western U.S. metropolitan area. I utilized an institutional ethnography approach to understand the social organization of U.S. microenterprise development (see Smith 1987; DeVault 1999). My data on the ME program were supplemented by interviews with a variety of other U.S. MDP providers. This study revealed a conflict between MPD program missions to help economically marginalized clients operate profitable microenterprises and demands that staff keep program operating costs to a minimum. Despite their many accomplishments, ME and other U.S. MDPs made significant changes over the course of their operations. These changes reinforce the alignment of MDPs with discourses popular in the New Economy. Although most of these changes were important for organizational survival, they often contradicted the visions of poverty alleviation and collective empowerment held by ME founders and many MDP proponents worldwide. Ultimately, there was a disjuncture between the lives of economically marginalized clients and MDP proponent discourse that promised both services to the poor and program cost effectiveness (Bhatt, Painter, and Tang 2002).

Methods

In this research, I relied on an institutional ethnography approach to unravel the connections between the everyday experiences of program participants (staff and clients) and the ruling regimes of the New Economy. Institutional ethnography begins with concrete, everyday experiences of local-setting participants and identifies problematic issues or disjunctures that they face. It then encourages researchers to move beyond local routines and face-to-face interactions to ask the question "Where did these experiences come from?" The aim behind this question is to uncover how extralocal contexts inform and shape local practices and contradictions (DeVault 1999; Smith 1987).

Accordingly, I began with my own experiences in the microenterprise development field and explored the routine practices of ME staff, board members, and clients in program planning sessions, training classes, and borrower's circles. With the help of Julie Cowgill and several other research assistants, I gathered data on the ME program and its funders and partnering social service providers. In addition to obtaining data on the ME program, we also interviewed practitioners from a purposively selected national sample of fifty other U.S. MDPs (see Cowgill and Jurik 2005; Jurik 2005: 78–119).

This research revealed a series of dilemmas that practitioners and clients confronted in trying to meet the goals of their programs. Outlining the disjuncture between MDP goals and actual program operations became the initial focus of my inquiry. I then explored the roots of this problematic by examining connections among programs and between local programs and larger national-international contexts. I examined the historical context of MDP origins and diffusion in southern-hemisphere and U.S. contexts and mapped the links between local U.S. MDP practice and various extralocal institutional arrangements in government, business, and other social service agencies (Campbell and Gregor 2002; Smith 1987).

Formation of ME Program and Its Links to the Larger International Context

ME's origins illustrate the links between this local program and its national and global economic context. More than twelve years ago, I was invited to attend a meeting of individuals who wanted to begin a self-employment lending program for poor and low-income women in their community. The steering committee charged with planning the program included women who were community volunteers, civic leaders, social service workers, and academics. Several of the committee leaders had heard about microenterprise lending at a national conference on hunger where speakers argued that even very small loans to support self-employment projects among the poor could promote self-sufficiency and significantly reduce world hunger.[1] One of the committee members even traveled to Bangladesh to visit the Grameen Bank, one of the world's most famous MDPs (see Counts 1996). She was convinced that important components of the Grameen model would work for a program in our region. At the meeting I attended, she argued the need to provide both business training and loans to poor women in the city. She also articulated the early guiding mission of the program—that it would focus on immigrant women who operated small, informal enterprises out of their homes to help support their families.

The steering committee wanted to utilize the peer lending model developed by the Grameen and other famous MDPs, including some programs already operating in the United States. Some members of the steering committee also hoped that the bonding among borrowers' group members would lead to collective buying plans for clients' businesses or collective political action within their communities.

I joined the steering committee and coordinated a needs assessment study for the proposed MDP. This study included an analysis of the economic conditions of the region in which the program would be located, interviews with established MDPs around the United States, and interviews with local service providers about the perceived need for an MDP in the area.

The local community in which the ME program was located illustrates many of the conditions of the New Economy. This western region was troubled by continuing layoffs and persistent unemployment even during a period that was widely proclaimed to be one of national economic recovery and local economic boom. Large numbers of undocumented immigrants and unemployed workers from other parts of the nation were moving into the area looking for work. The new jobs that were generated fell disproportionately in low-wage service employment sectors and lacked health benefits. Local wage levels failed to keep pace with rapid increases in the area's cost of living. The number of families living near or below the poverty line was increasing. Ironically, these conditions of economic insecurity were accompanied by national rhetoric that demanded cuts in welfare spending, demands that enjoyed strong vocal support from citizenry and politicians in ME's region (Jurik 2005).

A little more than two years later, the steering committee's work led to the establishment of the ME program, which has been in operation for more than ten years and has helped well more than a thousand individuals to start and expand microenterprises, primarily in the areas of small-scale sales, manufacturing, and personal and professional services enterprises. In the mid-1990s, ME began offering four and ten-week business training classes depending on the client's level of business experience. It offered from $500 to $1,500 for first loans and up to $6,000 for later loans. Despite myriad successes, ME experienced a number of tensions in fulfilling contradictory program goals. The problems that it experienced were consistent with those reported by other U.S. MDP providers (Jurik 2005: 78–119).

Contradictions of Microenterpise Development

The experiences of the ME program and the reported experiences of other U.S. MDPs suggest that in practice, the logic of microenterprise development requires the balancing of often conflicting organizational goals and extralocal demands. On the one hand are MDP promises to alleviate poverty by extending self-employment opportunities to poor, welfare, and otherwise marginalized clients, and, in some programs, by empowering clients through participation in lending and other management decision making. On the other hand, funders expect MDPs to provide services to large numbers of clients, show business successes, and keep loan loss rates and operating costs to a minimum. These funder expectations exist because small lending programs in the U.S. and developing countries that began in the 1950s and 1960s fell into disrepute; they involved large government subsidies and often reported very poor rates of repayment. The new generation of microenterprise lending programs promises to avoid such costly mistakes and inefficient management (Adams and Von Pishke 1992; Morduch 1999). In fact, many proponents argue that today's MDPs can cover most or all of their program costs with revenue from training and lending services (Daley-Harris ed. 2002).

Such expectations of businesslike management and program cost-effectiveness pose dilemmas for MDP practitioners. Additionally, microloans have quickly attained a reputation as a quick fix for poverty and stagnant local economies (Bates and Servon 1996). As a result, many funding sources have been anxious to provide lending dollars to "get loans out on the street to those who need them" but were unwilling to cover program operations expenditures for training and other support services. Funders anticipate that the high repayment rate on peer loans so often cited by MDP boosters will provide a sufficient source of revenue to cover program operations (Jurik 2005). Thus, MDP practitioners constantly find themselves struggling to cover operations costs, and this need, in turn, subjects them to the often changing demands of funding sources. Although some MDPs carefully scrutinize new funding opportunities to maintain consistency with program-identified objectives, most practitioners report that they find themselves modifying program goals, target populations, training, and loan modalities to conform to funding trends and specific grant requirements.

In its planning stages, ME made several changes in the program to increase its appeal to potential funders. It altered the proposed program name so that the word "women" did not appear in the title as was originally planned. However, funders cautioned that mentioning women in the title might discourage men and even smack of reverse discrimination.[2] Because potential funding sources had expressed concern about the cost-effectiveness of providing any services beyond basic business training, ME narrowed the program focus to center on business training and not to deal with issues related to transportation and child care that might be of concern to disadvantaged clients. Funders also recommended that it would be less expensive to train nonpoverty-level clients to start businesses. Thus,

ME shifted its target population to focus on low-income as well as poverty-level clients. It is notable that, despite advice from funders to the contrary, ME's leadership persisted in its aim *not to exclude* poverty-level clients or welfare recipients who applied to the program. However, this commitment on the part of ME leaders and similar commitments made by other MDP providers were repeatedly challenged by expectations that they produce observable success outcomes and simultaneously maintain an aura of cost-effective and businesslike program operations.

The remainder of this chapter focuses on ME's experiences with its first client cohort and the changes that it made to the organization afterward. These sections illustrate the ways in which extralocal funding pressures and the realities of poor and low-income clients' lives forced compromises and imposed limitations on the program's goal of serving the truly marginalized.

ME's First Client Training Cohort

The types of clients served in ME's first cohort and the types of problems they experienced in the training classes are an example of the disjuncture between MDP program operating discourse and the lives of poor and low-income clients. In response to their experiences with the first client cohort, ME staff and leadership made significant changes in the ME program—changes that marked a significant deviation from the initial program goals and from the popular image of MDPs so often presented by advocates and media.

Those attending ME's first training classes, in 1995, were reflective of the program's original target population—poor and low-income white women and persons of color. In the first cohort, the typical ME client was a woman of color who had a high-school-level education or less and a household income that met HUD low-income standards for the region. About one-third of these clients had gross incomes at or below the poverty level. Between 8 and 12 percent had received some form of public assistance (e.g., food stamps, AFDC) during the year prior to their entry into the program. Five percent were disabled, and more than one-third of the clients were single parents. Most training clients had not yet started a business (see Jurik 2005 for further details on these data).

Most of the businesses planned by ME clients were small, labor-intensive ventures. The largest percentage fell in the sales category followed by child care or assisted living, travel, computer, personal, and other service ventures. Some examples from ME's first client training cohort illustrate the nature of these planned businesses. Laura, a Latina, had worked as a waitress, cook, and manager of small restaurants. After her former employer went out of business, she decided to open her own restaurant. Joey, an African American man, had always worked in food services and wanted to open a mobile vending business. Most clients (63 percent) planned to operate their businesses either within or from their homes. For example, Betty, an African American woman who worked in child care, wanted to open her own home-based child-care facility. She hoped to combine this paid enterprise with caring for her own small children.

Members of the classes described experiences with a variety of problems common to poor and low-income people in the New Economy: unemployment, underemployment, disability, health issues, family-care conflicts, transportation difficulties, and legal problems. For example, an African American woman who had worked at a variety of low-income service jobs and as a salesperson for Tupperware-type companies said:

> Well, I find that the jobs here in [this state] take your self-esteem away from you in terms of pay as well as policy. (Marge)

ME classes were well attended and positively evaluated by clients, but the passage of the first cohort through the ME program also suggested a significant gap between ME program resources to help create successful businesses and client needs. Clients complained about the lack of instructor quality and commitment to the training. In part, problems with instructors stemmed from significant federal budget cuts to the Small Business Development Center that was subcontracted to offer ME's classes. The cuts, which occurred shortly before ME classes began, strained resources and burdened instructors with additional and unexpected responsibilities. Instructors were also part time and poorly paid. Some were distracted and ill prepared.

In addition, the instructors adopted a traditional orientation to business training that was ostensibly "neutral," that is, not focused on the gender, race, and class dynamics in business life (also see Ehlers and Main 1998). Instructors and staff viewed it as a sign of respect to treat ME clients' microenterprises as they would any other business venture, and they treated even small entrepreneurs as they might treat larger entrepreneurs. As a result, courses were insufficiently tailored to the needs of very small businesses; some sessions focused on issues that related primarily to large businesses.

Despite their efforts to be race and class "neutral," instructors sometimes exhibited race- and class-laden assumptions that offended clients. One evening, an instructor was discussing a woman's business idea. She planned to sell art that was produced in her neighborhood, a low-income community with a large concentration of African Americans. The instructor suggested that items the woman planned to sell would be more accurately described as "crafts." The client responded:

> It is art. Art is more than just what white people sell up in Northland [a richer area of town known for its art galleries]. (Carole)

Further unconscious racial bias was evident in the array of predominantly white and upper-middle-class speakers who were invited to ME workshops. Class members were dissatisfied with the guest speakers. They said that the topics were not well coordinated with course subject matter and that speakers' social class and business size did not reflect the realities of their business and life experiences. A client criticized one speaker who was a wealthy woman who was starting a business with financing from her ex-spouse:

> She talked about how she and a friend went out and put flyers on a car in their *mink coats* when her business was starting out. How can I relate to that? At my level, I could take the coat, hock it, and that's my start-up capital. (Ben)

The speakers focused on individual achievement, financial success, and dreams of bootstrap capitalism—starting with little or no capital and building million-dollar businesses. When clients requested a speaker who was a person of color, instructors brought in a Latino man who described how he was poor when he began business but become fabulously wealthy in a short time. A recurrent theme was that if an individual was "committed enough" and "willing to work very hard," he or she could have business success. One class member described the problem:

> The speakers need to identify with the group at large . . . we need speakers who have been in business three to five years, who could talk about the true nuts and bolts. I felt the people in business for fifteen years or more didn't understand as well and have forgotten what it's like to start up, to be a single woman starting a business with no savings. (Naomi)

It was especially significant, given the racial, ethnic, class, and gender makeup of the group, that barriers of racism and sexism in business were never addressed by instructors or guest speakers. One client repeatedly criticized the training and counseling for failing to address strategies that women of color in small businesses could employ to circumvent barriers of sexism, racism, and business size that disadvantaged them in competing for government contracts.

Neither the structural conditions that disadvantage small-scale entrepreneurs in the U.S. economy nor strategies for coping with structural challenges were included in ME training courses. Such discussions were typically viewed by both instructional and ME staff as beyond the purview of business training.

Some clients experienced difficulties comprehending the course material. Such problems were indicative of the challenge involved in offering self-employment training to disadvantaged individuals. The greatest problems of this sort were experienced by older women with low levels of formal education. Some of these women suggested that the length of time for classes be expanded for those who felt "rusty in the education world." They were often hesitant to ask questions during classes because they felt that they were "behind" the progress of other students. ME resources were simply too limited to offer multiple training sessions for students with varying capabilities.

Another problem was attrition rates for clients with limited resources. Clients who did not have access to dependable transportation were sometimes late or absent from class. One client, Marge, said that the area's poor public transportation forced her to spend several hours and go through multiple bus transfers to attend meetings. For some, chronic health problems contributed to attrition or a slow rate of progress. These problems are consistent with issues reported in studies of welfare-to-work clients such as those discussed by Ridzi and Solomon in their chapters in this volume. Despite the ostensible targeting of socially and economically marginalized individuals, definitions of success in these programs favor normative conceptions of the disembodied worker. Embodied workers—those who are disabled, sick, or extremely poor and single mothers and fathers—come fettered with obligations that may require more flexibility than such personal-responsibility-centered programs are prepared to accommodate.

Some of ME's women clients had problems locating dependable child care. One mother asked to bring her child to class one evening, but ME rules did not permit this. Although such problems might plague any group of students, poor and low-income clients were particularly vulnerable to life problems that interfered with their work and/or training activities. During training sessions, clients were advised to start small, perhaps to begin operations out of their homes. Discouraged by this advice, Marcia, a homeless woman, said, "How can I start a home-based business when I don't even have a home?" Low-income individuals targeted for MDP training often have problems of illness, housing, child care, and transportation in their lives. A client described Marcia's plight:

> She lived in a shelter and was told by vocational rehab that she had to get a job. When she got a job, it was at night. . . . [S]he worked two weeks and got sick and has been sick ever since. . . . She's known for two years that she's had breast cancer and couldn't have it treated since she had no money. (Jane)

The experiences of ME clients point out the inadequacy of basic business training programs that fail to provide additional support services for poor clients. These problems were exacerbated by participants' efforts to start businesses and repay ME loans.

Lending Problems and Program Changes

The problems that ME experienced with training increased during the lending stages and led to significant alterations in the ME program's target populations, lending procedures, and the autonomy granted to borrower's circles. Within six months after the first cohort had received loans, almost half had either made numerous late payments or defaulted on their loans. ME board and staff were extremely concerned that such loan repayment problems would jeopardize the program's legitimacy and, accordingly, its prospects for future funding from corporate, governmental, and nonprofit sources. Interestingly, thereafter, that first cohort became a constant reference point for program modifications. After the first cohort, ME made significant changes in the program. Staff members concluded that very-low-income and poverty-level clients did not own sufficient resources— either financial or social—to run successful businesses without substantial additional program expenditures for training and support services (e.g., child care, transportation). Like many experts (e.g., Bates and Servon 1996), practitioners perceived that, without this added support, poor clients were less likely to repay business loans. Yet, intensive training raised operations costs and undermined sustainability efforts (Bhatt et al. 2002).

A hallmark of the MDP movement—peer lending and borrowers' circles—also came under scrutiny. Despite claims that peer lending fostered increased client responsibility and empowerment, the idea of client participation in lending decisions made funders nervous. Staff also came to believe that the circles' supportive functions were interfering with the participants' critical assessments of business plans prior to loan approval. Circle autonomy made it more complicated for staff to influence lending decisions, and trying to foster effective circles while maintaining this autonomy was seen as too time consuming for staff and therefore too expensive for the program.

MDP builders believed they were at a crossroads and that important changes were needed to reduce the potential for loan losses and thereby ensure the program's cost-effectiveness and continuity. They adjusted ME's program priorities, target population, and borrowers'-circle structure to increase program success outcomes (i.e., establishing client businesses) and demonstrate cost-effectiveness (i.e., minimizing loan defaults and operations expenses). Staff efforts in this regard are consistent with New Economy ideologies that suggest that nonprofits should run in "cost-effective" ways that mirror the practices of successful private businesses (Jurik 2004). Rather than emphasize to the community the need for additional services when targeting the poor, ME opted to select clients that were more business-ready and less fettered by educational, economic, and family needs.

Because they feared too many lending losses, ME program leaders began to increase their emphasis on the training parts of the program. A board member said:

> We need to de-emphasize lending to our business owners. We must communicate to them in our orientations and all our literature that ME is, first and foremost, a training program. Lending is not our main activity. That is the carrot that gets them here, but once they're here, our focus has got to be on training, not lending. (Patrice)

Second, the board and staff resolved to emphasize the business-oriented aspects of the program in order to distance ME from welfare-type programming and more strongly emphasize loan repayment. One staff member explained:

> We have to communicate to our funding sources and clients that ME is a business program. These loans are not entitlements. They are business loans that must be repaid. (Karen)

Another staff member distinguished ME's objectives from those of welfare programs:

> There are good social welfare programs, some educate people, help them get a job. . . . We educate them and help them run their own business, so they don't have to worry about standing in a line somewhere to get a check. (Sheryl)

Third, staff increased its screening of program clients, particularly prior to the borrowing stages. The screening of clients was guided by staff expectations about each client's prospects for success.

ME staff developed typologies of "successful clients or true entrepreneurs" and "successful circles" (see Cowgill and Jurik 2005). Staff constructions of "successful clients and circles" were closely interwoven with images of professionalism and business rationality and with the interests of bureaucratic expediency. Staff constructions were also strongly influenced by the pervasive negative images of welfare recipients in contemporary U.S. society (Jurik 2005; Naples 1997).

However, despite these best efforts, each ME strategy to resolve the conflicts between MDP promises and the needs of economically marginalized clients often led to further contradictions. For example, once staff started to screen clients, many clients who had completed training expressed anger at not being permitted to move on to the lending stages. Second, it appeared that screening also significantly decreased the percentage of low-income clients, which fell to a low of 51 percent by the fifth year of operations. Since much of the funding from banks and other sources was tied to ME's record of service to a client population of which a majority was considered low income, this decline was viewed with concern.

ME's efforts to alter its orientation and to target clientele created new contradictions in the program. Interest on loans was viewed as an important source of program revenue and cost-effectiveness in the MDP field (Bhatt et al. 2002). Thus, reducing loan activity was at best a short-term strategy for shoring up loan losses. Moreover, just about the time that ME had effectively redefined itself to be primarily a training program, it received a large U.S. Small Business Administration grant with lending and operations dollars. The amount of operations funding that ME could receive from this grant was tied to the amount of dollars that it loaned. So, in order to take advantage of a rare opportunity to garner new operations funds, ME had to quickly redirect its program focus back toward lending, all the while fearing increased defaults as a result.

In addition, once the staff increased control over the borrowers' circles, cohesion and interest in the circles dropped considerably. Although some circles always presented management problems for staff, the declining significance of the role played by circles exacerbated clients' disinterest in them once loans were made.

Thus, over time, the ME program scaled up its target clientele, emphasized its business rather than social service orientation, tightened and then expanded lending activities, and significantly encroached on the autonomy of borrowers' circles. These changes created additional contradictions in that many funding opportunities were tied to the offering of services to poor and very-low-income clients. Also, borrowers' circles had been touted as a significant source of empowerment and pressure for client loan repayment. These contradictions were not unique to the ME program but rather reflected the dilemmas faced by most other U.S. MDP providers (Bhatt et al. 2002). They also mirrored pressures on other nonprofits in the New Economy to model themselves after ideals associated with the operations of for-profit businesses (Jurik 2004). The raison d' être of these programs is to serve the economically marginalized, yet the expectations for program accountability are neutral and fail to take into account what is needed to serve this population.

Conclusion

By using an institutional ethnography approach to examine the practice of U.S. microenterprise development, this study has identified a disjuncture between MDP organizational logic and the everyday lives of the disadvantaged clients MDPs promise to serve. The growth and popularity of MDPs are integrally linked to life in the New Economy. Images of poverty alleviation and empowerment through self-sufficiency, the destruction of welfare dependency, and heightened demands for businesslike cost-effectiveness are discourses that firmly connect MDPs to the neoliberal ideals that dominate this era.

MDPs are one type of postwelfare social service organization. In the years of attack that led up to "welfare reform" and in the decade since its passage, MDPs have been portrayed as an alternative to welfare and as a solution to the persistent unemployment and underemployment so characteristic of the New Economy. MDPs have been praised for empowering marginalized individuals. This empowerment discourse mostly refers to the integration of clients into the market economy. Although some MDPs promise to give clients control over training and lending processes, U.S. programs have tended to erode this power over time (Jurik 2005). MDPs also purport to function more like businesses than traditional social welfare programs and to avoid efforts to resocialize or morally assess clients. Because so many MDPs are independent, nonprofit service providers, they furthered hopes of a more innovative, less bureaucratic, local and nongovernmental service sector. MDPs promise to ease the insecurities that come with the New Economy, while at the same time minimizing the role of government and the costs of the safety net. However, my data demonstrate that this discourse is disconnected from the material lives of economically marginalized individuals and their families. MDP success ideals still rely on normative conceptions of the disembodied worker.

Although MDPs provide important services to many clients who start and operate their own businesses, the programs fall short of their ideals. MDPs are in caught in a web of conflicting organizational demands. Fundraising and accountability demands pressure staff to exclude more disadvantaged clients. Such screening undermines MDPs' promises to address issues of poverty in the New Economy. At the same time, MDPs' claims to serve poor and low-income clients are important for accessing funds demarcated for such populations (e.g., welfare-to-work funding).

Many clients experience training and lending opportunities in MDPs that might otherwise not have been available to them. Even if only as a method for augmenting wage income, microenterprises are important to many families in today's economy (Sherraden, Sanders, and Sherraden 2004). However, claims that MDPs alleviate poverty and can serve as alternatives to welfare and other safety-net programs bolster MDPs' claims to welfare-related funding and stifle the creation of programs that might more truly address the problems of the poor (Howells 2000; Rogaly 1996).

MDP program training discourse ignores the structural and societal barriers to small business (such as racism, sexism, and a regulatory environment that disadvantages small businesses) (Ehlers and Main 1998). If these barriers are ignored, marginalized individuals who fail to "lift" themselves up out of poverty through microenterprise will be viewed as insufficiently motivated—people whom policymakers can feel justified in ignoring.

NOTES

1. During the first Bush administration, strong support for microenterprise development came from the U.S. House Select Committee on Hunger under the leadership of Representative Tony Hall. Hall was influenced by President George Bush's political agenda and by his own commitment to avoid "liberal" food provision programs. Hall moved the Hunger Committee agenda away from food provision and toward microenterprise development. MDP practitioners spoke to many activist groups fighting hunger worldwide. They argued that food programs were temporary and costly remedies and identified microenterprise development as the best avenue for ending poverty and hunger and promoting self-sufficiency among the U.S. poor (Rodriguez 1995: 103).

2. Note the adoption of reverse-discrimination rhetoric to challenge the overt targeting of women by the ME program. Although this language was popularized in battles against affirmative action programs in government, it is now used throughout society, even in the case of nonprofit organizations that have historically identified special and limited target populations for their services.

4

Work, Disability, and Social Inclusion
The Promise and Problematics of EU Disability Policy

RANNVEIG TRAUSTADÓTTIR

Editor's Introduction

Like those in other liberation movements, disability activists have fought for social inclusion and the right to define their own realities, contesting medical definitions of their "difference" and seeking access to work and the independence it can provide. In this chapter, Rannveig Traustadóttir considers work and employment policies in the European countries, in the context of both disability activism and economic restructuring. As the institutional ethnography approach would recommend, she begins with the goals and experiences of young people in Iceland who are unemployed—some categorized as people with disabilities and some not. The differences between these groups are surprising and begin to challenge the assumptions written into employment policies for both groups. A further analysis of the disability label and statistical data on the incidence of disability suggests that working conditions actually create a substantial portion of what comes to be known as disability, especially in later life, and that the flexible labor strategies of restructuring may be increasing the incidence of some kinds of disabilities.

Traustadóttir's discussion of policymaking in the European Union gives a sense of how activists are using such transnational venues to forge commitments to equity and inclusion. It is also telling, however, that even in western European nations with a strong history of social welfare support, trends toward labor-market restructuring and fiscal discipline are creating barriers to the implementation of progressive policies. Disability rights advocates have made considerable progress in contesting the medical notion of defective personhood; now they must also contest the idea of economic inevitability (Beresford and Holden 2000).

Traustadóttir's discussion also highlights one of the key contradictions of economic restructuring, which is brought into sharp relief when we consider the circumstances of people with disabilities but is relevant across a range of work and family circumstances. Both employers and the state are shifting more risk and responsibility to working people and their families, but these strategies eventually run up against people's obdurate needs for sustenance and the inevitable limitations of our varied human capacities to respond individually to those needs. As employers attempt to shed responsibility for meeting human needs, states bear increasing burdens and also adopt strategies designed to minimize collective supports. The construction of a separate track of disability policy may work in part to conceal this general contradiction, as well as allowing policymakers to evade questions about how our societies will take collective responsibility for the well-being of all workers—who are never disembodied and rarely unencumbered.

* * *

> Every day we are reminded that, for everybody, work is a defining feature of human existence. It is the means of sustaining life and of meeting basic needs. But it is also an activity through which individuals affirm their own identity, both to themselves and to those around them. It is crucial to individual choice, to the welfare of families and to the stability of societies.
> —Juan Somavia, ILO Director General, June 2001

Many observers would enthusiastically endorse Juan Somavia's statement that begins by emphasizing the importance of work for individuals and ends by asserting its importance for "the stability of societies." He asserts that work is important "for everybody," in language that evokes a sense of inclusiveness. Yet, we know that in practice, work is characterized by inequalities and exclusions, many of which have come to seem "natural." In the capitalist welfare states, it has been taken for granted that most disabled people have limited work opportunities and must often rely on benefits for their income. This chapter considers how policymakers and disability activists in Europe are addressing issues of work and employment, with particular attention to how their efforts unfold within a larger international context of economic restructuring.

Our research group in Iceland has been engaged in a long-term study of several "marginalized" groups, including disabled people, and I begin with some findings from those studies, in order to give a sense of the concrete, material lives of the people such policies are meant to address. One of the key issues for disabled people is how to sustain themselves through work— or other source of income. Employment issues have also been a strong part of activism undertaken by the disabled people's movement in Iceland, as in Europe in general. As a result, questions about employment policies have entered the agenda of our research. In the discussion that follows, I present findings from one of our studies in this area and then examine the broader picture of disability and employment in Europe and the European disability policies that form a broader context for the situation in Iceland. I also consider the influence of disability activism and a new understanding of disability on policy development. I conclude by discussing gaps and contradictions in the intersection of disability policy with a broader economic landscape.

Work and Disability in Young People's Lives

In order to illuminate the actual lives of young people who find themselves outside the labor market, I will present some of the findings from a qualitative study of young unemployed people in Iceland, including both disabled and nondisabled people between eighteen and twenty-five years old. This was a small-scale study carried out in 2003 and 2004 as a part of a larger research project that focused on the lives of disabled people in Iceland.[1] Participants were recruited through two agencies; one was an unemployment office serving both disabled and nondisabled people in the Reykjavik capital area, and the other was a supported employment agency serving disabled people. Data were collected primarily through interviews with the young people, but one staff member from the unemployment office and one from the supported work agency were also interviewed (DeVault and McCoy 2001). Besides collecting data through open-ended interviews, we conducted participant observations at both agencies. Following the method of institutional ethnography, we started our inquiry with the lived experiences and everyday lives of young unemployed people (Smith 1987). Our aim was to understand, from their standpoint, how they had come to be unemployed and bring into view the economic relations and policies influencing their lives (Campbell and Manicom 1995; Smith 1990a).

The findings suggest that there were both significant differences and similarities in the lives of unemployed young people with and without disabilities. A key finding for the group of disabled people was that, despite their impairments, all of them could work and wanted to work. Their desire to work was not rooted solely in economic need; all received income (albeit low) through disability benefits. They often spoke of these benefits as "our salary," but they complained of social isolation, boredom, and the feeling of being excluded from society. Thus, unemployment for this group was not primarily an economic problem but was important socially and psychologically. These young people were quite knowledgeable about their rights as disabled people, but not about their rights as unemployed people. In fact, they seemed not to think of themselves as a part of the wider labor market. They had great difficulties finding work, through both the general and the specialized employment offices. Their problem in finding paid work was compounded by the provisions of disability pension programs. These programs functioned as a barrier to work because pensions were reduced significantly if the young people found a job and received an income. It could also be difficult to get back into pension programs if salaries were inadequate or jobs disappeared. The young disabled people saw these as unjust policies that stood in the way of their efforts to work and be active citizens.

When we turned to the group of nondisabled people, we expected quite different situations, and we did find differences, but ones that surprised us. We had assumed we would meet young unemployed people who were eager to find work. What we found, however, was that only a small segment of this group was in fact actively seeking jobs. Those who were looking for work saw themselves as good workers and were confident they would find employment within a short timeframe. For them, unemployment was temporary, and they had been unemployed for a short time due to circumstances such as moving to a new town. What surprised us was that the majority of the young nondisabled people who participated in the study either couldn't work or did not want to work. Many faced a variety of problems, such as alcohol and drug addiction, and mental health issues; for them, it was a full-time job just to manage everyday life. People in this group had limited work experiences and were not sure if or when they would be able to work. There was also a relatively small group of women who had young children and few job skills. The work available to these young women gave such limited income that they couldn't obtain child care that would make paid employment feasible. They saw their unemployment as temporary, lasting while their children were young, and were confident they would be able to find a job when they were "ready" to work. The young nondisabled

people held their lives together by accessing income through unemployment benefits; they were knowledgeable about ways to avoid being offered
work, in order to stay on benefits, and they talked about these strategies
with the interviewer. The kinds of problems we saw in this group—especially the addiction and mental health problems—led us to speculate that if
they had been older, or if the benefit schemes available had been different,
some would likely have shifted to disability benefits.

What both groups had in common were low levels of education, limited
work experiences, and issues related to health and disability, all of which
make it difficult to gain access to the open labor market. It should be noted
that this was a small study, which makes it difficult to draw conclusions
about young unemployed people in general. However, there is also no particular reason to assume that the young people who participated in the
study were different from the larger group of unemployed young people in
Iceland at the time. What is perhaps most important is that these findings
raise important questions about work and disability, not least profound
questions about the category "disability"—a category that seems to dissolve
as we consider these young people's lived experiences. Their connections
to the labor force seem driven not primarily by their capacities but by their
locations in distinct groups labeled "disabled" and "nondisabled" and by
the policies that produce these categories and shape their lives once they
are assigned to one category or another.

Disabled People and Employment in Europe

The findings from Iceland are consistent with data on employment and
disability in Europe more generally. In that broader context, they raise
questions as well about the relatively progressive disability policies adopted
by the European Union[2] (EU), many of which focus specifically on issues
of employment (European Commission 2001a, 2002). Despite these policies and the fact that employment for disabled people has been at the heart
of many EU disability policies, unemployment rates for disabled people remain stubbornly high in Europe. In fact, disabled people are considered
to be one of the most disadvantaged groups in Europe when it comes to
labor force participation (European Commission 2000a). The employment
rates of disabled people are considerably lower than the employment rates
of nondisabled people in Europe. While the employment rate of nondisabled people in the EU is on the average about 70 percent, the average for

disabled people is about 40 percent, with only 25 percent of severely disabled people and around 50 percent of moderately disabled people being employed. In general, disabled women have lower employment rates than disabled men (European Commission 2002). In the United Kingdom, for example, disabled people are six times more likely to be unemployed than nondisabled people, and in France, unemployment increased 194 percent among disabled people since the mid-1990, while it rose 23 percent in the population at large during the same period (Priestley 2003).

Most countries offer special employment programs for disabled people, but, while these are important for some groups, in particular groups of people with severe impairments, they don't seem to have a large-scale impact on the overall employment among disabled people (Grammenos 2003). Disability-rights advocates point out that the low employment rate of disabled people is a result of the systematic exclusion of disabled people from the labor market. They argue that the only way to overcome this discrimination and exclusion is to make changes in the organization of work, workplaces, and society as a whole, in order to enable disabled people to participate in employment and be full members of society (Barnes and Mercer 2005).

There is no single accepted method to estimate the number of disabled people in Western societies, but most countries use one, or both, of two methods. The first consists of questionnaire surveys asking people about limitations on their daily activities as a result of illness or disability. Data gathered by this approach can be analyzed for various situations and subgroups, and relationships of various variables to living standards and participation in the labor market and society in general can be estimated. This approach is most widely used in Western countries (Burkhauser et al. 2002; Ólafsson 2005).

The second method is to count the number of people who are registered as disabled and receive disability benefits. The shortcomings of this approach are that countries do not define and rate disability according to the same standards, and rules about entitlements to disability benefits differ between countries. In addition, disability benefit systems have different functions in European countries. In some countries, disability benefits play a major role compared to illness benefit schemes, unemployment benefits, and income support from municipalities. In other countries, disability benefits play a minor role compared to other income schemes. Given these disparities, counting disability benefit recipients is not a reliable measure of the number of disabled people in a given society (European Commission 2001a; Ólafsson 2005). Research from the European Union and from OECD[3] (Organization for Economic Cooperation and Development) use both types of data but rely usually more heavily on survey data to analyze the number of disabled people and their living conditions (European Commission 2001a; OECD 2003a, 2003b).

The two types of data described often produce different results. Survey data tend to indicate a higher prevalence of disability than data on disability-benefit recipients. The reason is that a number of people have limitations due to illness or disability but do not receive disability benefits. Different surveys also find different prevalence of disability within the same society as a result of difference in the way questions are worded or varying definitions of disability. Because of these and other factors, disability rates vary greatly in the European countries so that it is difficult to compare numbers on the prevalence of disabilities in different countries. Most European documents report the percentage of disabled people to be between 10 and 15 percent on the average (people with physical or mental impairments because of illness, accidents, or birth defects) (Council of Europe 2006; European Commission 2001a), but there are wide variations among countries and age groups. An OECD study reports similar numbers in eighteen OECD countries (OECD 2003c). Despite the variation in disability rates in Europe, it is safe to conclude that disabled people make up a large proportion of the population; the total number of disabled people in Europe is estimated to be about 50 million (European Disability Forum 2002; Workability Europe 2006/2007). The number of disabled people has been rising in Western countries for the past twenty-five years or so. This has led to widespread concerns about the economic strain caused by increasing welfare spending. To respond to these concerns, new policies aimed at restricting access to benefits have been introduced, accompanied by policy measures intended to encourage and support the labor-market participation of disabled people. As a result, growth rates of disabled people have slowed down in many countries (Grammenos 2003; OECD 2003a).

There are significant differences among European countries with respect to many disability issues, such as how resources are allocated to disability services and benefits, how accessible and generous the benefits and service schemes are, the amount of resources used to promote employment for disabled people, and the proportion of disabled people who have paid work. Some countries have recently moved in the direction of separating people's disability status and employment status, thereby making it possible to stay on benefits while receiving income from work. In Denmark and Sweden, where disabled people can receive earnings from both pension and wages, active labor-market participation is higher than in most other European countries (Hvinden and Halvorsen 2003; OECD 2003b).

Studies of disability rates and benefits in Europe suggest that easy access to disability benefits increases disability rates and that disability benefits are used more if access to other out-of-work benefits is restricted or low. Thus, uses of disability benefits are clearly related to availability of other kinds of assistance. These studies also indicate that efforts to assist disabled people to return to work are either lacking or not very successful (OECD 2003b). Despite significant efforts in many countries to rehabilitate and re-integrate disabled people into the labor force, very few disabled individuals are actually able to leave benefits for paid work. In fact, a recent OECD study in twenty countries found that none of these countries had a success-ful employment policy for disabled people. While some used innovative measures based on policies emphasizing economic and social integration, these were few and affected only a small number of disabled people (OECD 2003b). Employment and disability rates are connected in several ways, and there is a close relation between employment rates of disabled people and those of nondisabled people. When unemployment rates are high in gen-eral, disabled people are more severely affected than nondisabled people. Similarly, when there is low or no unemployment or a shortage of work-ers, disabled people are more likely to be employed. This suggests that gen-eral labor-market forces have a strong impact on disabled people and that general policies to promote employment also increase employment of spe-cial groups such as disabled people (European Commission 2000a, 2001a; OECD 2003b).

Such findings raise questions about why the number of disabled people continues to rise in most countries and set the backdrop for considering the efforts of European disability activists and the EU emphasis on progressive disability policies. Can these policies support the efforts of disability activ-ists and others interested in progressive employment initiatives to address the concerns of disabled workers in a changing economy? How likely is it that these progressive policies will be implemented? These are questions taken up in the remainder of the chapter.

Causes of Disability

Disabled people are a very heterogeneous group, and, contrary to what most people believe, only a small proportion of disabled people are impaired from birth (9 percent). The most common cause of disability is illness or accidents that occur during the life course, either acute illness or accidents (52 percent) or long-term health problems caused by accidents or diseases (28 percent). The remaining 11 percent are disabled due to temporary health issues and other causes (OECD 2003a). Most of these illnesses and accidents occur while people are of working age, suggesting that preventative measures regarding accidents, stress, and physical and mental strain, along with comprehensive public health care, are actions that can be effective in lowering the prevalence of disability. The risk of disability grows with age. In fact, the vast majority of disabled people in Europe are more than forty-five years of age (European Commission 2002; OECD 2003b; Ólafsson 2005; Priestley 2003). At the same time, unemployment among young disabled people is a concern in many countries (Grammenos 2003; Roggero et al. 2006).

EU studies have examined how much of chronic illness and disability is caused by work accidents and occupation related diseases (Grammenos 2003). Some studies have found a rapid growth in work-related illnesses. Others indicate a general tendency toward fewer recognized work accidents and occupation-related illnesses, but the studies note that this could reflect recent national policies in many countries that restrict access to disability pensions. The incidence of reported work-related accidents, illnesses, and impairments varies among countries. For example, in Belgium, on the average, about 22 percent of chronic illnesses and disabilities result from occupational diseases and accidents. These numbers differ according to age and sex, among other things, with 32 percent of disabled men declaring work accidents and occupational disease as the cause of their condition, and the numbers rise for people between forty-five and fifty-four years of age; 38 percent of disabled people in this age range list work accidents (28.4 percent) and occupation-related illness (9.4 percent) as the cause of their condition (Grammenos 2003). Many diseases are stress-related, muscular, and cardiovascular. Mental and psychological problems are on the rise; they are the reason for up to a third of disability benefit payments in OECD countries (OECD 2003b). Taken together, these data suggest that the labor market is causing disability—that is, that the rigors of paid work "use people up" and place them in conditions that lead to illness and impairment. Overall, the labor market seems to "create" a significant segment of disability and the large social expenditures associated with disability.

So-called labor-market flexibility has been identified as a significant factor in the rate of physical accidents and in the rising rates of mental health problems. Flexibility has, among other things, increased the number of temporary employees, and studies have found that they usually have poorer working conditions than permanent workers and are therefore more likely to suffer work-related accidents and illnesses. Temporary workers are also more often exposed to discomfort, intense noise, repetitive movements, and short, repetitive tasks (European Foundation for the Improvement of Living and Working Conditions 1999). In Spain, for example, a rise in work injuries of almost 10 percent has coincided with increased employment flexibility (Grammenos 2003). Total quality management, job rotation, and autonomous work teams are also believed to be harmful to workplace health and safety, and negative effects of the increased intensity of work have been found in European countries (European Foundation for the Improvement of Living and Working Conditions 1999).

Most companies do not pay for the social, health, and economic consequences of bad and harmful working conditions. In most countries, the disability premium or contributions paid by employers do not depend on the number of work accidents in their own companies. Only recently have some European countries imposed financial costs on companies with high rates of accidents, for example, France and the Netherlands (Grammenos 2003).

The Development of EU Disability Policy

There has been a growing interest in disabled people among EU policymakers. Various policy issues have prompted this interest, in particular the serious concerns that have arisen in the social policy field regarding the cost of income-replacement schemes such as disability pensions and disability benefits and the cost of health insurance. Those charged with planning EU health policy in the future also require better knowledge of the present health-care situation to support estimates of the needs for future care and related services. In addition, an emphasis on preventing social exclusion and growing shortages of workers in many areas of the labor market have invigorated efforts made within labor-market policy regarding the adaptation of workplaces and the activation and rehabilitation of nonworking disabled people. Finally, disabled people are one of the target groups covered by EU antidiscrimination policies. These issues are among those that constitute the background for the increase in policies directed at disabled people within the European Union (European Commission 2001a).

It is sometimes unclear what the term "European disability policy" means. It can refer to the European Union policies (or those of other European bodies such as the European Council or the European Commission) or to the totality of the relevant policies of EU member states and other European countries. In addition to policies aimed specifically at disabled people, many other policies have intended or unintended consequences for the welfare and living conditions of disabled people, and their inclusion in society. In fact, both at the EU level and in many European countries, there has been an emphasis on moving away from separate policies and segregated services for disabled people. Instead, the emphasis has been on "mainstreaming" or "sector responsibility," meaning that all sectors of public services and administration should take responsibility for disabled people as citizens (European Commission 2005; Grammenos 2003; Hvinden and Halvorsen 2003). I use the term "European disability policy" when referring to EU-level policies and relevant policies in Europe more generally. If it is relevant to distinguish between these, I do so.

There was not much attention to disability issues in the European Economic Community, the EU predecessor established in 1957, and no mention of disability in the Treaty of Maastricht, the founding treaty of EU, in 1992. Between the early 1980s and the mid-1990s, EU efforts in the field of disability were primarily through action programs focused on the exchange of experience and the dissemination of innovative programs and ideas to promote good practice (Hvinden and Halvorsen 2003). In 1993, however, the social inclusion of disabled people became a European issue in response to the United Nations *Standard Rules on Equalization of Opportunities for Persons with Disabilities* (United Nations 1993). Since the mid-1990s, the EU has developed a new, broad disability strategy aimed at influencing both the policies and the practices of member states. The *Communication of the Commission on Equality of Opportunity for People with Impairment* in 1996 was a turning point (European Commission 1996). The document was endorsed as a Recommendation by the Council of Ministers the same year. Key elements of these new policies were the provision of equal opportunities for disabled people, nondiscrimination, mainstreaming, use of a rights-based approach, social inclusion, full participation, and identification and removal of barriers to equal opportunities and participation. These remain the cornerstones of EU disability policies (Brown 2004; Hvinden and Halvorsen 2003; Maudient 2003).

The Treaty of Amsterdam, in 1997, strengthened efforts to combat discrimination. Article 13 of the Treaty, which covers disabled people, provides the European Community with powers to take action to combat discrimination on grounds of sex, racial or ethnic origin, religion or belief, disability, age, or sexual orientation (Grammenos 2003). On the basis of this treaty, the Council launched an action plan to combat discrimination (2001–2006), an ambitious plan to combat a wide range of forms of discrimination, including that based on disability (Council of European Union 2000a). Another significant development in disability policy was a Council Directive in 2000 outlining a framework for equal treatment in employment and occupation. This policy was not directed solely at disabled people, but there are numerous references to disability and measures to enable disabled people to gain access to, participate in, and advance in employment (Council of European Union 2000b). Social exclusion has been a priority on the EU social policy agenda in general. This is also an issue that has been a particular problem for disabled people. It was therefore important for disabled people when the European Commission accepted a Communication in 2000 titled *Towards a Barrier-Free Europe for People with Disabilities* (European Commission 2000b).

Two strong threads can be identified in EU disability policies: first, a focus on adult employment and related issues; second, a movement toward a more general rights-based approach (Maudient 2003; O'Reilly 2003; Priestley 2003). Increasingly, policymakers are conceiving "citizenship" in terms of work and access to an open labor market. However, this notion of the "working citizen" or "contributing citizen" has also led to trends in some European and OECD countries toward requiring people who receive benefits to participate in employment or vocational rehabilitation. This is sometimes framed as "mutual obligation," whereby society is seen as obligated to support disabled people and disabled people should likewise be expected to contribute their share. Some have suggested that receipt of benefits should be conditional on participation in employment or vocational rehabilitation and that a failure to participate in the labor market should result in benefit sanctions (Hyde 2000; OECD 2003c).

I have emphasized the way disability policies and strategies have been developed by collective European policies and institutions. Now, I would like to turn to the influence of disabled activists and disabled people's movements on the formulation of priorities in European disability policy. Disabled people have organized themselves at the European level for more than twenty years. The European Region of Disabled People's International (DPI Europe) has been the strongest actor representing thirty-six countries, the vast majority of the countries in Europe. Disabled people's representation at the EU level is also formalized within the European Disability Forum, EDF, which includes national councils in all EU member states, plus Norway and Iceland.

Disabled people's movements have had critical influence on the development of disability policies in Europe. These policies have been informed by and responsive to the priorities and agendas set forth by disabled people's organizations and advocacy. One example of political activism that influenced and shaped the direction of European policy was the European Congress of Disabled People, held in Madrid in March 2002. It was an important meeting of six hundred disability activists and policymakers from thirty-four countries and resulted in the Madrid Declaration, developed jointly by the European Disability Forum, the Spanish Presidency of the EU, and the European Commission (European Disability Forum 2002). The Declaration is a progressive document that identifies disability as an issue of discrimination and calls for rights, not charity, the self-determination of disabled people, attention to diversities among disabled people, and work toward the broad goal of an inclusive European society for all. Importantly, the Declaration makes explicit the ingredients needed to achieve inclusion, in the formulation "nondiscrimination + positive action = social inclusion." The Declaration also established eight priorities for action: (1) antidiscrimination legislation, (2) challenges to disabling cultural values and attitudes, (3) services that promote independent living, (4) support to families, (5) special attention to the needs of disabled women, (6) mainstreaming of disability issues and policies, (7) employment as central to social inclusion, and (8) participation of disabled people on all levels of decision making: "nothing about us without us." Reviewing the priorities in the Madrid Declaration, one sees that there are strong similarities between the disabled people's agenda and EU disability policies, at least in the language used (European Disability Forum 2002).

The shift in European disability policies has been heavily influenced by a new way of understanding disability. This change originated in many sources but is most often associated with the so-called British social model of disability, first articulated by the disabled people's movement in the mid-1970s and developed largely by disabled academics in Britain (Barnes, Oliver, and Barton 2002; Oliver 1996). The British social model is critical of dominant approaches to disability and disability policy, characterized by a biomedical and individual view that frames disability as a personal tragedy. Social modelists distinguish between *impairment* (functional limitation arising from a physical, mental, or sensory condition) and *disability* (which they see as arising only from discriminatory social attitudes and environmental barriers). This understanding of disability draws attention to social barriers, instead of individual impairments, and allows activists to assert that "we are disabled by society, not by our bodies." The British social model of disability is but one of the many social approaches to disability now being developed by scholars in disability studies internationally, for example in the Nordic countries (Gustavsson et al. 2005) and the United States (Davis 1997). In fact, one of the main changes in the field of disability over the past two decades has been the shift from viewing disability as an individual tragedy and deviance to a more social understanding that emphasizes the critical influence of social, cultural, and environmental issues on disabled people's lives.

Although there is a great deal of controversy among scholars and activists about the details and implications of the British social model—primarily around questions about the extent to which impairments and barriers matter—there is no question that the British social model and associated disability activism have had a major impact on the terms of the discursive and policy landscape (Shakespeare 2006). EU policies—with their recognition of socially produced barriers and their emphasis on nondiscrimination—certainly reflect the influence of a social understanding of disability. These policies also represent a very significant commitment to the social inclusion of all citizens, and they view open employment and participation in paid work as a key to inclusion.

Before moving on to discuss the implementation of these policies, it is important to note that it is complicated to talk about "Europe" or even "the European Union." There is an idea of "one Europe," but Europe consists of many and diverse countries, including the older EU member states, newer member states, applicant countries, and European countries that are not part of the EU. European countries have different histories of development and governance; they include the western European nation-states (former colonial powers and postwar partners); the Nordic countries, with their distinctive cultural links and a heritage of strong welfare systems; the southern countries, which have experienced slower economic growth and public welfare development; and the former Eastern bloc countries. The diverse histories and state configurations of these nations influence the development of their employment and welfare policies for all citizens, including their provisions for disabled people. Despite local differences and varying national priorities, there is clearly an increasing awareness of the situation of disabled people and attention to disability issues in Europe. Recent survey data indicates that 58 percent of Europeans know someone who is disabled (including about one in four who had a family member with a disability), and eight Europeans in ten feel at ease in the presence of disabled people. Seventy-five percent believe that access to public facilities is difficult for people with common impairments, and, while 57 percent think that access has improved in the past ten years, 97 percent think that more should be done to improve integration (European Commission 2001b).

EU disability policies are progressive and will increasingly frame the possibilities of disability equality and the interventions that support or undermine the European goal of equality and justice for all. The European Union has moved toward a philosophical and political vision of an inclusive European society, in which the social inclusion of disabled people figures directly. Policymakers, researchers, and activists will need to engage not only with a critical examination of policy and regulations but also with their implementation, and the social forces that influence whether and how these policies will be implemented. The next section deals with the implementation of EU disability policies.

Implementation of Progressive Policies

The EU progressive disability policies are relatively new, and it remains to be seen how successfully they will be implemented in the member states and in other European countries. A consideration of these policy ideas in the context of economic restructuring is a sobering prospect. In this section, I offer general observations about some of the trends and contradictions that seem likely to mediate the implementation of disability and employment policies. "Welfare reform" is a phrase that has different meanings in Europe and in the United States, where we have seen a major restructuring and retrenchment of public assistance. But concerns with global economic competitiveness and fiscal pressures are felt in Europe, too, and these may increasingly limit the possibilities for an inclusive society, despite progressive European policies that emphasize an open and barrier-free society for all.

In light of ongoing labor market restructuring, it is important to note that some of the policies aimed at or affecting disabled people of working age are part of broader economic strategies aimed at creating conditions favorable to capital accumulation. Other policies are specifically aimed at disabled people. These policies are also affected by concerns about the perceived negative impact of state welfare provisions on economic efficiency. Thus, despite the disability-friendly policy statements now in place on a European level and in many European countries, these policies are generally designed around two main imperatives. As "fiscal policy," they are designed to reduce, to the extent possible, the size and scope of the social security budget. As "labor-market policy," they are designed to reinforce a work ethic, labor productivity, and economic competitiveness. In both aspects, disability policies are increasingly being shaped in ways that benefit companies and the state first, rather than disabled people. Labor-market deregulation and "flexibility" can be devastating for disabled people. They bring increasing pressures on all workers, and disabled people often find it more difficult than others to respond to those pressures; at the same time, deregulation often means that employers have more freedom simply to let people go. Furthermore, the introduction of measures to reinforce work (or "workfare") into social assistance programs for disabled people, a measure that among other things requires unemployed people to work for their benefits, has led some scholars to suggest the development of an active "reserve army" of unemployed people, including disabled people (Hyde 2000).

The experiences of disabled people may be useful to highlight features and trends of economic restructuring and a so-called New Economy. They are perspectives that may illuminate the problems and paradoxes of work organized for the "disembodied" or "unencumbered" worker, precisely because it is often quite difficult, given the obduracy of the body, to think of disabled people in these terms. And, despite trends toward a focus on social barriers, the insistent cultural focus on the individual and the impairment continues to be a part of the dominant disability discourse, making the context and processes of employment invisible. But, from the standpoints of disabled workers, we can see that the way work is organized is a problem.

Overall, I wish to suggest that an exploration of disabled people's everyday lives, European disability policies, disability activism, and new understandings of disability in the context of new labor-market realities reveals many contradictions, conflicts, and gaps. We see, for example, a labor market that "creates" disabled people (through work-related accidents and ill-nesses) but takes no responsibility for them. We see policies that emphasize social inclusion, nondiscrimination, and human rights on the one hand and large groups of people excluded from open employment, isolated in segregated employment, unemployed, or hidden away on benefits on the other. Gaps remain in the policies, especially with respect to particular barriers that face disabled women and other groups of disabled people, such as immigrants and the members of ethnic groups, who face distinctive circumstances and social barriers.

Despite the new understanding of disability that rejects disability as an individual problem and draws attention to social barriers, employment policies—like other disability policies—continue to be informed by an individualized and medicalized view of disability. This traditional view explains economic disadvantage in terms of individual impairment and locates the solution in adapting and rehabilitating the individual. Adopting solutions based on fixing individuals leaves problems in the organization of work and workplaces unaddressed. As a result, the marginal status of disabled people is reproduced, despite the policy emphasis on equality and social inclusion. Finally, one of the contradictions in this arena lies in the different interests of employers and the state. Getting people off social benefits makes economic sense for the state, but employers do not necessarily see the profit in it. Thus, EU social policies that promote the participation of disabled people in the labor market are not strongly supported by employers. The potential for productive intervention, however, lies in the deepening crisis produced by simply shifting, rather than addressing, the sustenance needs of such a substantial portion of the population.

A closer look at the EU disability policies may reveal why it has proven so difficult to implement them in the member states. Policy analysts distinguish between two different kinds of policies: *redistribution* and *regulation* policies (Hvinden and Halvorsen 2003). Redistributive policies are usually financed by tax provisions and redistribute resources such as health, education, social and employment services, and income transfer, among citizens. Regulative policies, on the other hand, involve public efforts to influence the behavior of the citizens and include health, safety, building, and work environment regulations. These policies may also involve efforts to influence nongovernmental organizations through financing incentives, tax regulations, legal initiatives, negotiations, or persuasion.

In general, regulative policies have not been very effective in improving the lives of disabled people, for example in removing barriers to employment participation. Most regulations have been formulated as recommendations, and sanctions against those who do not follow them are weak or nonexistent. Another major problem with regulation policies is a general lack of knowledge about these regulations and their implications among disabled people, the disabled people's movements, and among employers, unions, lawyers, architects, and city planners. Thus, the potential of regulation policies is yet to be realized. Most EU disability policies are regulative and suffer the same problems as other regulative policies: they offer general and vague formulations open to different interpretation, they are not binding or obligatory, and they lack supervisory agencies and systematic follow-up.

In contrast to EU policies, many national policies in Europe have been redistributive. These are increasingly challenged as being too expensive and as leading to economic dependency among benefit recipients, and many observers have called for cuts in existing programs and tighter rules for eligibility. Others have criticized national disability policies, not least employment policies, for being ineffective and badly coordinated. The EU's focus on regulation rather than redistribution is related to the emphasis on creating a European market exchange that fosters the free movement of labor, capital, goods, and services. The emphasis on Europe as one open market is strong, and the EU strives to remove all restrictions on the free flow of all aspects of economic life.

The EU attempts to coordinate member states' disability policies, but most member states resent the prospect of the EU's making rules in areas that have traditionally been on the national or municipal level. The EU is not a federation state but a union of member states that place emphasis on their sovereignty and independence (Geyer 2000; Hantraris 2000; Newman 1977). Thus, it is unlikely that member states will accept anything but regulatory provisions from the EU in the foreseeable future.

Efforts by the EU to introduce progressive disability policies are for the most part restricted to regulatory approaches that may be challenged, avoided, and questioned by member states or powerful interest organizations within each country. Despite their problematic implementation, the EU's disability policies have been successful in bringing disability to the European agenda, have made issues of disability more visible, and have started a process of promoting a more equal and accessible Europe for disabled people with emphasis on nondiscrimination, universal design, human rights, and a rights-based approach to disability provisions. However, the everyday reality in European countries regarding the situation of disabled people creates a complex situation where the regulatory character of EU policies may render them ineffective in the face of other, more powerful political and economic forces for change.

Conclusion

Europe has many resources and a strong foundation for effective employment practices for disabled people. However, the vision of "a European welfare state based on values of solidarity and justice" and "a society open and accessible to all" is not reflected in the everyday lives of many—perhaps most—disabled people in Europe, including the young unemployed Icelandic people discussed earlier. I do not mean to suggest that all disabled people in Europe lead sad, tragic, and difficult lives—far from it. Yet, social exclusion and discrimination still shape the everyday lives and experiences of many disabled European citizens.

Considering disability policies in a wider economic context allows us to map some of the various policy threads that intersect and diverge. For example, while some (disability) policies seem to be directed primarily at the relatively small group of people with severe impairments, other (economic) policies seem directed primarily at nondisabled people who are economically privileged. We might notice and wonder about the convergence between the demands of disability activists for an open labor market and meaningful work and the efforts of welfare reformers to cut budgets, restrict access to benefits, and promote work discipline. Overall, we might consider whether the powers of the economy are strong enough to override the progressive EU policy efforts to ensure disability equality.

NOTES

1. I would like to thank Adalbjörg Traustadóttir, who worked on the study as a part of her MPA degree in the Department of Political Science, Faculty of Social Sciences, University of Iceland.

2. The European Union (EU) celebrates its fiftieth anniversary in 2007. Its historical roots lie in World War II. Europeans wanted to prevent such killing and destruction from ever happening again. Soon after the war, however, Europe was divided into East and West. The West European nations created the Council of Europe in 1949, a first step toward cooperation, but six countries wanted more extensive collaboration, and, in 1957, the Treaty of Rome created the European

Economic Community (EEC), or "Common Market." The six founding countries were Belgium, France, Germany, Italy, Luxembourg, and the Netherlands.

The Treaty marking the establishment of the European Union is known as the Maastricht Treaty and was signed in 1992. The Maastricht Treaty brought together the three Communities (Euratom, ECSC, EEC) and institutionalized cooperation in the fields of foreign policy, defense, police, and justice under one umbrella, the European Union. The EEC was renamed, becoming the European Community. The Treaty also created economic and monetary union, established new Community policies (e.g., on education and culture), and increased the powers of the European Parliament. The number of member states of EEC and EU has gradually grown since 1957; in 2007, the EU has twenty-seven member states, with a total population of 490 million people, and three more countries are in the process of applying for EU membership. There are nineteen European countries that are not EU members. However, most of the nonmember countries have wide-reaching collaboration with the EU and take part in many EU projects. For example, nonmember countries such as Iceland and Norway take active part in the EU frameworks for research and higher education.

The European Union (EU) regards itself as a family of democratic European countries, committed to working together for peace and prosperity. It is not a state intended to replace existing states, nor is it simply an organization for international cooperation. The EU is unique in that its member states have set up common institutions to which they delegate some of their sovereignty so that decisions on specific matters of joint interest can be made democratically at a European level. (See the EU Web site at www.europa.eu.)

3. OECD (Organization for Economic Cooperation and Development) is a collaboration of thirty countries, most of which are well-to-do Western countries in Europe and North America, plus Mexico, Australia, New Zealand, Japan and South Korea. Due to OECD's active relationships with an additional seventy countries and numerous NGOs, it has a global reach. OECD describes itself as "an international organisation helping governments tackle the economic, social and governance challenges of a globalised economy" and is well known for its publications and statistics on economics, social issues, education, development, science, and innovation. OECD studies and statistics are widely used internationally. (See the OECD Web site at www.oecd.org.)

PART II

Mobile Bodies

Incorporation Without Inclusion

The two chapters in this section examine the global movement of workers across borders, treating that mobility as the result of intentional strategies developed to address new imperatives of capitalist enterprise, such as the ensemble of practices labeled flexible production. Beginning in different geographical sites and industries—information technology (IT) work at various U.S. locations and food processing in the midwestern states—the authors show how the flexibility in such strategies is built on modes of incorporation that absolve employers and the state of responsibility for the care and reproductive needs of workers.

In each case, the regimes supporting these modes of incorporation involve categorical constructions of labor in the abstract and a disturbing lack of provision for workers' material lives—a phenomenon that Joan Acker (2006) names "nonresponsibility." These strategies are also based on, and sustain, racialized modes of incorporation that sort workers, on the basis of national origin, into positions of relative disadvantage. Indian IT workers gain access only to temporary and contingent work in the United States by virtue of federal visa regulations; the Mexican workers who hold more permanent positions in the Midwest, and who sometimes hold U.S. citizenship, are positioned in other ways as only temporary residents, regardless of their legal status. Thus, these chapters illustrate both corporate and community processes that produce incorporation without inclusion.

5

Flexible Hiring, Immigration, and Indian IT Workers' Experiences of Contract Work in the United States

PAYAL BANERJEE

Editor's Introduction

In managerial thinking and practice, flexibility typically means shedding responsibility for labor. Immigrant labor often provides a basis for strategies aimed at flexibility. Payal Banerjee's analysis, in this chapter, of IT labor contracting points to an evolving, elaborated system that incorporates skilled labor from India, yet keeps workers in tenuous and marginal positions. Banerjee quotes IT analysts who refer to the H1-B visa as the "workhorse" of the industry—in their vocabulary, productive power is located not with the people who travel here to do the work but in the paper text that allows managers to use their labor as needed and then send them elsewhere.

Banerjee's account of the layered system of subcontracting, with its Bodyshops and labor vendors working through consulting firms—a system whose layers and sublayers continue to proliferate—points to the increasing distances from which managing labor now often proceeds. These employees may never meet their employers of record—they are slotted into the system and passed from one middleperson to the next. These mediating enterprises are new social formations that have grown up in the niches of opportunity created by the H1-B visa program. Like the emerging educational enterprises, discussed in chapter 2, that have grown up around demands for accountability in public education, the Bodyshops and labor vendors discussed here connect the managerial ideologies of flexible, just-in-time production with real people on the ground whose work makes it possible to act, organizationally, on the basis of those ideologies.

* * *

This chapter foregrounds how the terms of immigration and flexible labor practices in advanced capitalism shape the experiences of marginalization and disembodiment encountered by Indian information technology (IT) workers on the H-1B visa in the United States. Since the 1970s, the viability of capitalism has depended on the implementation of a variety of neoliberal policies, including the liberalization of trade, capital circulation, and the extensive reorganization of international division of manufacturing and service labor between the first and third worlds (Alexander and Mohanty 1997; Mitter and Rowbotham 1994; Steger 2002). These measures followed closely on the heels of colonial capitalism and resulted in massive economic and labor restructuring, which continue to have critical significance for workers on a transnational scale. Operating under the development guidelines promulgated by organizations like the World Bank and the International Monetary Fund (IMF), many newly independent countries opened their economies to foreign investments and adopted export-oriented economic reforms that heightened the incorporation of third-world labor into global capitalism under highly racialized and gendered terms. Structurally integrated with the global economy, first world countries, such as the United States, experienced the corollaries of these transformations in terms of increasing deindustrialization and shifts toward a service-oriented economy (see Peck 2002; Persuad and Lusane 2000; Sassen 1998; V. Smith 2001). In both geopolitical locations, trade, commerce, and corporate profit maximization have thrived on hyperfragmentation of production, flexible employment, and consistent erosion of labor rights (Acker 1990, 1998, 2003; Bonacich and Appelbaum 2000; Harvey 1989; Persuad and Lusane 2000; Ridzi and Banerjee 2006; Smith 1997; Standing 1999).

Scholarship on these aspects of global restructuring, associated with processes often clustered under rubrics such as post-Fordism or postindustrial capitalism, late capitalism, and the New Economy (in the context of the United States), has captured how employment patterns and experiences of workers have been deeply impacted by the demands of flexibility (Bowring 2002; Clinton 1997; Houseman 2001; V. Smith 2001; Standing 1999). Whether employed at free-trade export-processing zones in the third world or at corporate offices in the service sector in the United States, workers face an employment regime characterized by casualisation of labor through subcontracting, job insecurity, questionable labor rights, inadequate pay and benefits, and utter neglect and insensitivity toward their embodied needs, such as childbearing, caregiving responsibilities, and illnesses (Acker 1990, 1998, 2003; Marchand 1996; Mitter and Rowbotham

1994; Moghadam 1999; Ong 1991). In the United States, the corporate sector has been increasingly relying on accessing labor as services from a wide variety of labor-market intermediaries and temporary-help agencies and from short-term, part-time, on-call, or contract workers (Freeman and Gonos 2005; Houseman 2001; Kalleberg 2000; Theodore and Peck 2002). These trends have typically been attributed to retrenchments in manufacturing and the proliferation of low-skill and low-wage service jobs that are disproportionately filled by women, minorities, and immigrants of color (Hipple 2001; Persuad and Lusane 2000; Sassen 1998; Wiens-Tuers 1998).

Recent literature, however, suggests that employment patterns in the so-called high-skilled and high-wage services sector, including IT, are also rapidly changing in response to companies' heavy reliance on flexible hiring (Barley and Kunda 2004; Benner 2002; Koeber 2002; V. Smith 2001; Zalewski 2005). In their effort to minimize operations costs and to be able to respond quickly to the highs and lows of market demands without incurring large expenses for maintaining large pools of permanent employees, companies are engaging the services of staffing agencies and subcontractors, in-house service providers, consulting companies, Web-based labor brokerage firms, and nonemployee consultants and independent contractors. Given the burgeoning predominance of a range of flexible, contingent, and short-term contractual work arrangements in the high-skill services sector, workers in skilled professional fields are becoming increasingly vulnerable in an employment scene characterized by cycles of unemployment and underemployment, job insecurity, deskilling, lack of career mobility, and reductions in income and benefits (Barley and Kunda 2004; Benner 2002; Carnoy, Castells, and Benner 1997; Koeber 2002; Kunda, Barley, and Evans 2002; Rubery and Grimshaw 2001; V. Smith 2001; Zalewski 2005). Given the significance of immigrant labor in high-skilled technical services in the United States, it becomes important to identify how these workers' legal standing, as constructed by immigration and visa policies, informs their experiences of marginalization in the context of flexible hiring.

Data presented in this chapter are derived from approximately forty in-depth, semistructured interviews conducted with Indian IT professionals at four key sites in the United States between 2002 and 2004. These sites, located around key metropolitan areas in three states in the Northeast and one in the South, hosted multiple large corporations that hired Indian IT workers as temporary workers from multiple labor subcontracting firms. The sample of interviewees was constructed using the snowball method.

Typically, interview sessions varied between one and a half hours to four hours, with the exception of four interviews where interviewees were able to give extended commentaries that lasted between seven to twelve hours over several days. The sample of IT workers included thirty-seven males and three females, whose age ranged from twenty-five to forty years. A disproportionate gender distribution in favor of males characterizes the Indian IT workforce in the United States (U.S. GAO 2000).[1] All interviewees had a bachelor's degree, and more than 50 percent had postgraduate degrees in engineering or management. In addition to these interviews with Indian IT professionals, this study also included visits to corporate locations (clients) where these immigrants worked and interviews with managers and human resources personnel of firms serving as the direct employers of these immigrants. Furthermore, interviews conducted with IT professionals in India and extensive review and analysis of government and policy documents on science and technology policies, immigration, trade in services, and liberalization provided critical insights about the transnational dimensions of labor issues in the United States.

Indian IT Workers and the Construction of Immigrant Status Under the H-1B Visa Program

The rising importance of technology for sustaining virtually every process of the global economy led to the meteoric demand for technically skilled labor and prompted the United States to intensify the recruitment of skilled immigrants for IT occupations since the mid to late-1990s. The H-1B visa program, which enables U.S. employers to hire college-educated, skilled foreign workers for specialty occupations, facilitated the large-scale recruitment of these immigrants as professional and documented workers into the labor market. Although many skilled immigrants are employed in professional fields such as science and engineering, higher education, and business, this visa has become particularly important for hiring immigrants for IT occupations since the late 1990s.

Referred to as the "workhorse of the IT industry" (Ayers and Syfert 2002: 540), the H-1B visa has been a critical enabling factor for the United States, the world's leading exporter and trader in IT-based products and services, to meet its labor needs in profitable terms. It is estimated that about 17 percent of workers employed as computer scientists, computer engineers, systems analysts, and programmers are foreign born, whereas about 10 percent of the total population in the United States is foreign born (a category that includes naturalized citizens, noncitizen permanent residents, and individuals on temporary status, such as student or other visas [Ellis and Lowell 1999]). During the late 1990s, workers on the H-1B visa made up about one-sixth (1/6) of the total IT workforce in the United States (OECD 2002: 2). During 2003, 2004, and 2005, the number of H-1B petitions from companies that offered employment to foreign nationals and needed to process their visas exceeded the annual quota (U.S. GAO 2003). Within the group of immigrant IT professionals in the H-1B skilled workers category, Indian nationals have constituted an overwhelming majority (Lowell 2000). In 2001, about half of all H-1B workers were from India (U.S. DHS 2003). In 1999, 60 percent of all H-1B visas went to immigrants hired for the IT field, and about 75 percent of all immigrant IT workers on H-1B visas were from India (U.S. GAO 2000). In general, these trends have continued over the years.

For immigrant IT workers on the H-1B, advanced capitalism's logic and operation of flexible hiring have engendered a specific form of vulnerability and marginalization. One of the most critical features of the H-1B is that it is an employment and employer-dependent visa, and individual immigrants hired on it have no personal claim to it. When an employer decides to hire a skilled worker who is not a permanent resident or citizen, it has to petition to appropriate departments of the state to procure an H-1B visa to enable this employee to work in the United States. Consequently, these employees' ability to work and reside in the United States under the visa coincides with their employment, and their status in the country depends entirely on their being employed with the company authorized by the state to hold their visas. Since their status under the H-1B is employer-dependent, these workers lose their right to work and live in the United States if they are fired, and they become liable to deportation unless they find employment with another company that is willing to transfer their visa under the new employer's name. The H-1B is issued for three years and may be renewed for three more following a petition for extension. There is, however, no assurance that the person hired on an H-1B will remain eligible to work or be able to maintain status continuously for the initial three years; if employment is terminated during this time, these workers lose their legal status. For nonresident immigrant workers hired under the H-1B, these stipulations have made employment, work authorization, and legal status codependent and have necessitated uninterrupted job tenure with their visa-holding employers.

These visa stipulations have impacted immigrant IT workers on the H-1B in two critical ways. First, given how the visa defines the status of these immigrants, these workers become entirely dependent on their visa-holding employers for both their work and their immigration status in the United States. Needless to say, this form of socially constructed dependence on employers severely compromises these immigrants' bargaining power and heightens their vulnerability in an employment regime already fraught with chronic job insecurity associated with project-based work and flexible hiring.

Second, the H-1B visa's requirement that non-U.S. workers be directly hired by U.S. employers has also contributed to their exploitation and disproportionate concentration as contract workers employed by labor vendors in the lower tiers of subcontracting (Banerjee 2006). Typically, companies in the United States fulfill their labor needs for IT services and products by engaging the services of consulting companies and labor vendors that manage and execute the project and also oversee the deployment of contract workers from multiple labor vendors. Driven by the mandate of flexible hiring, consulting firms, like their clients, have minimized direct hiring. This disinclination to employ permanent workers poses a problem for inducting individuals who must have *an employer* to process and hold their H-1B visas. The corporate sector in the United States has come out of this quandary by delegating the large-scale recruitment and employment of non-U.S. workers to a subset of companies among labor vendors that supply contract workers. These vendors, often referred to as Bodyshops, serve as the direct employers of immigrants and process their visas so that companies in the United States can access this labor force without having to assume any responsibilities for this immigrant workforce. These subcontractors exist almost exclusively to facilitate the incorporation of skilled workers from India who need employer- and employment-based work authorization in the United States, that is, the H-1B visa. As such, these companies have been instrumental in maintaining the viability of flexible hiring and labor subcontracting indispensable to the corporate sector. This research provides ample evidence to suggest that Indian IT workers, lacking any independent work and legal status under the H-1B, become completely dependent on employers that will hire them, that is, subcontractors or Bodyshops, and in the process are restricted from pursuing employment options available to citizens or permanent residents. Employed primarily by subcontractors, workers on the H-1B are typically further removed from clients than their citizen and permanent-resident counterparts (who are most likely to be directly employed by the clients or their consulting firms).

Creating Flexible Workers: The Questions of Dependence, Powerlessness, and Transience

Within the context of how work is organized as temporary and contingent for contract workers employed with labor vendors, the terms of the H-1B visa have made immigrant IT workers especially vulnerable to exploitation. As the previous section explains, employers of Indian IT workers are most likely to be labor vendors or Bodyshops whose primary function is to process visas for these immigrants so that they may be accessed as contract workers by consulting firms for their clients' projects in exchange for hourly pay. Since legal status, work authorization, and livelihood overlap and depend on being employed with their H-1B–holding entities, these immigrants have to ensure that they generate enough income for their employers and behave in ways that do not put them at risk of being fired. Vishal, an Indian IT professional in his late twenties who is employed by a Bodyshop, described how the wage system works in subcontracting and how being on the H-1B contributes to these immigrants' anxieties about unemployment:

> The way it works is that the client has a certain billing rate for you, the contract worker. They are paying a fixed amount for me to the company in the middle. This company keeps a certain amount as commission and gives the rest to my employer, which then keeps a certain amount before I get my salary. So now I get 60 percent of the billing rate and they keep 40 percent. Whether I will be fired or not depends on whether I am generating revenues for my immediate employer. If I am not working for a client, then I am not making any money for him, so he can fire me anytime. And, if they fire me, then there goes my visa!

This wage distribution system, where contract workers earn their livelihood on the basis of labor rendered through their placement with clients, is more or less typical in IT. Immigrants on the H1-B, however, are more likely than U.S. citizens to be employed as contract workers and earn less, as their subcontracting employers are two or more steps removed from the client (Banerjee 2006). As the number of intermediary companies increases between the client and the contract worker, the employees' salary decreases because of commissions deducted by each entity in the successive layers. A recent study based on data from the U.S. Department of Labor determined that although workers on the H-1B visa are supposed to be paid the prevailing market wages, IT workers on this visa earn about $13,000 less per year on an average than their U.S. counterparts in similar occupational categories and geographical areas (Miano 2005).

Vishal's explanation also reveals a critical point about how immigrants' experience of this commission system extends beyond the question of salary, given the fact that these workers' immigration status is deeply enmeshed with their ability to work for clients and generate revenues continuously so that their employment-based visa status can be preserved. Sunil, an IT professional employed on the H-1B with an Atlanta-based Bodyshop, talked about being "worried" and under continuous pressure about his job and visa status in the following terms:

> Even when I am on a client's project, I worry about where and how the next project is coming. Since these contracts are short term anyway, you are lucky if you find something that is like longer than a few months, you constantly think about how to get the next project. You cannot sit back and relax and say, okay, I have this project now. Even before one project is over, you are back on the market looking for another one. If you don't find a project, your employer will not keep you, you will get out of status, and so the pressure is definitely on you.

For this population on H-1B visas, not having a project thus not only equals financial difficulties but also represents the threat of losing immigration status. To avoid being "out of status," these immigrants take it upon themselves, as their own responsibility, to search for clients and projects so that they may continue to generate profits for their employers. Krish, another immigrant worker on the H-1B, explained this further in the following terms:

> See, when I am out of a project, I am not generating any money, as there is no client to pay my hourly wages. Now, my employers look for projects to place me. But, I cannot rely on them. What if they are not looking hard enough or not looking properly and cannot find me a project? In that case, after a short time, I will be the one fired, right? So, what I do is I do not wait for my employer to find me a client. I conduct a search on my own.

Even in instances where employers cooperate and participate in the quest for clients, the immigrants still assume the bulk of the responsibility because they have far more at stake than their employers in terms of preserving their employment status to maintain their legal standing under the H-1B. Interviewees had also experienced instances where their employers, aware of their position as immigrants on the H-1B who "cannot afford" to get fired, completely shifted the task of finding clients to the workers. Hari, an IT professional on the H-1B, recounted how he had to assume the responsibility of finding his projects in his career as a contract worker.

> Out of all the projects I have worked on, my employer has only found me one, the first one when I was hired. After that, I have had to take the initiative and search for all my other projects. I have no choice, for if I am not working, I don't make any money for my employer. That guy can fire me and I will be out of status. I cannot afford that, so I go on and look and look, until I find something. When I find a client or project, I tell my employer where it is and which company it is with and if they approve, I go and work there.

The experiences of the majority of Indian IT workers on H-1B visas in the United States illustrate how intersections between visa policies and the practice of flexible employment in the late-capitalist period have shifted the weight of individual responsibility—of staying employed and on legal status—onto individual immigrants. The following statement, from Sunil, serves as a representative narrative on behalf of immigrant IT workers on the H-1B visa:

> In fact, all the projects that I got in the U.S., I got on my own. . . . Then I was keen about finding my own projects and completing the whole [process] on my own, and I found a company . . . I somehow found out about that company. And every negotiation, everything, I did. All the monetary negotiation, what would be the hourly rate, I had done everything there.

Sunil's experience, like those of many other immigrant contract workers like him, shows, first, how their employers are increasingly becoming ceremonial entities, except for their role in fulfilling immigration-related formalities demanded by the state, and second, how these workers are having to perform tasks formerly undertaken by employers. Immigrants' descriptions of their interactions with employers revealed the minimalist nature of their interactions. In the vast majority of the cases, the immigrants had not even met the labor vendors or Bodyshops that employed them. Vivek, for example, said:

> When I flew in from India, I went straight to the client's site in Virginia. Then, from there, I went to another client and so on and on. I have never seen my employer. This guy lives in New Jersey and we communicate through email and phone.

In a similar fashion, Ravi said:

> I guess my employer has some kind of an office in Atlanta. I talk to him and all. But I have never been there, and there is no point anyway, because my work is always at the clients' locations.

During his work experience with his Bodyshop employer, Anil had only one brief meeting with another administrative staff member from his company.

> The only time I met someone from the employer's office was when I was joining a client that day and this person had come to deliver me some papers. We did not talk for more than five minutes, she came, gave me the papers from the hall and left. As far as my interaction with the Bodyshop is concerned, it's limited to visa-related issues, paying my salary, and things like that. As long as I am on a project and they are getting their commission, that's all there is.

These experiences show how the subcontracting firms' day-to-day interaction with employees is often nonexistent and how employers absolve themselves of the responsibility for providing steady work for their employees.

These detachments notwithstanding, immigrants feel the enormity of their employers' presence and importance, given the critical role these companies play in "holding" their H-1B visas. Brij, an Indian IT worker hired by a labor vendor, described this in the following manner:

> Since these guys hold our visas, we are pretty much tied to them. Okay, legally I can change employers, but even that employer has to hold my visa. So, no matter what, you are bound by some company.

Many interviewees used expressions such as being "tied" or "bound" to their visa-holding employers. Since the question of maintaining or "staying in status" on the H-1B overlaps with being "bound" to their employers, these immigrants, in sharp contrast to U.S. citizens and permanent residents, are placed in a relationship of dependence and subordination to their employers. Suresh, another contract worker, felt that employers could "govern" immigrants on the H-1B:

> On a H-1B you are bound by somebody, there is a body that governs you, I will put it that way.

Employers' ability to exploit their visa-dependent workers emerges from the terms of the H-1B, which contribute to the asymmetry of power between employers and their immigrant employees. As contract workers on an employment-based visa, these immigrants become particularly vulnerable in an employment regime where work is contractual and temporary and the availability of projects intermittent, with significant time gaps between successive assignments. Vinay described the anxieties about legal status and livelihood that immigrant workers undergo when on the bench, that is, when these workers are without a project.

> The pressure is immense and it comes from many angles. Well, first, if you are out of a project for too long, they begin to slash your salary as you are not making any money for them. First they cut the pay in half or something, but beyond a month or two, don't expect anything. If you are lucky, they will keep you on benefits, if you have them that is. The longer you are without a project the more you worry that they will give you the sack. And if that happens, your visa goes and you are out of status. In that situation, you take any project. You take a bad [billing] rate, you move to a project in another state, you do what you can to keep your job. You cannot bargain really.

Desperate to protect their employment and visa status when their bargaining power has already been weakened, these immigrants concede to paying larger commissions on the wages and accept "any project" that comes their way. Abhi's experience bears testimony to how these immigrants lose bargaining power and also shows how employers wield significant control over their employees' decisions about accepting clients' projects:

I had a very tough time. I was on bench for three months, August, September, and October. I started to look for projects on my own towards the end. I tried. Finally I had two offers . . . but my company didn't agree. My company didn't like the rates they were offering. So the contact person for this project said that they will pay something like $30 per hour that would go directly to the company. But my company didn't like that rate. They wanted much more. I needed a project badly, right. I even asked my employer to cut down my salary, take whatever cut of the billing rate they wanted, but they didn't agree.

The circumstances of being on the bench make immigrant contract workers eager to accept any project to resume work and avert a possible layoff. Their employers, however, can veto these decisions in an effort to extract higher commissions or wait for a better-paying client. Needless to say, these strategies go against the legal and economic interests of the employees, who try to change their employer's decisions by volunteering to take salary cuts and to accept higher commissions paid out of their billing rates. Since immigrants on the H-1B are by definition employees of their visa-holding companies, they cannot accept or work on a client's project unless their employers approve and agree to enter into a formal agreement with the company managing the labor contract for the client. Employers often take advantage of this power. Interviewees reported how some employers explicitly state that they will allow immigrant contract workers to accept a project if they agree to increase the commission.

Given these issues, Indian IT workers on the H-1B described their bench periods as one of the most negative and demoralizing aspects of their experience. Seldom hired at the upper level of firms (large firms or consulting companies), this particular group of workers is most likely to be the employees of the labor-supplying companies and work on short-term contracts that last anywhere from a month to several months. Because of the predominance of this type of temporary contractual work in these workers' professional lives, their experience of being on the bench recurs frequently. Palash, who endured a bench that extended over seven months, mentioned how the fear of losing legal status was one of his biggest concerns:

It was very depressing, but the biggest fear was the legal fear, about the visa.

Abhi, who had been on the bench twice in one year, underscored the mental anguish that immigrants experience while on the bench:

> I must say that when guys like us who are on the H1-B sit on the bench without any job, it is a mental torture, it is a mental harassment. . . . That stage cannot be described unless and until somebody really is in that position, be in exactly that situation, be in exactly that type of frame of mind to realize what someone is going through . . . it is really a trauma.

Given these vulnerabilities, immigrants do everything within their capacity to stay employed and, in the process, subject themselves to considerable hardships and unstable terms of work. Although U.S. citizens and permanent residents working in IT also encounter job insecurities in the New Economy, they are not subjected to the vulnerabilities, subordination, and consequent exploitation that result from the specific condition of being in the United States on fragile immigration status.

Left with little latitude in terms of being selective about projects, these immigrants structure their personal lives around the demands of available projects. Frequent relocations across the country for temporary contracts, including some that last for only a month, have led many of these immigrants to lead seminomadic lives. In the short period from 1999 to 2002, Krish, an IT worker on the H-1B, worked on seven projects at different clients' sites spanning the states of Georgia, Oregon, Kentucky, Maryland, Massachusetts, and New Jersey. After finishing his master's degree, Sanjay got his first job with a subcontractor in 2002. Within one year, he had moved from Virginia, to California, to Washington, D.C., and again to California to work at four different clients' sites. During this period, he was on the bench three times. To minimize his living costs when without a project, Sanjay would come back to Pennsylvania to live with friends while he searched for a new project. While on his third bench, he said:

> I don't know how long I will be here in Pennsylvania. I am between projects now, so I may have to leave any day, wherever the new project is.

These contract workers have to be prepared to pack and leave for client destinations on short notices. To Aneesh, frequent relocations seemed to characterize "the life of an H-1B consultant":

I have moved seven times in the last three and a half years! That is the life of an H-1B consultant! You work from project to project to project and move from one place to another, within a matter of six months, three months, two months whatever. You are lucky if you get anything longer than a six-month project.

While some participants were fortunate in being able to find clients within a certain geographical radius and set up homes, most had no permanent residence and typically shuttled from state to state every few months. According to Krish, single men are better able to respond to these demands:

When I was not married, it was easier. I could just move like that, and if I didn't find a place right away, I could somehow manage. Before, I could share an apartment with other bachelors or rent unfurnished places. I didn't care for myself. Now that I have my wife, I can't do that.

Immigrants with families, specifically those with children, found these terms extremely difficult to cope with. Krish explained how he and his wife, Shobha, have not been able to settle down as a result of his frequent relocations:

We have not bought anything. No big furniture, TV. They don't reimburse our moving, so it costs too much to hire movers or a big truck. I rent furnished apartments, but there too I lose lots of money every time, because I have to break the lease in three months or four months and go somewhere else.

Like Krish and Shobha, Rajnish and his family had moved eight times in three years across multiple states. Fatigued from these repeated dislocations, they arrived at the decision that Rajnish's wife, Mala, would live in Atlanta in a small apartment with the young girls while Rajnish put up with his sojourns at client sites. Other couples and families of contract workers have also been forced to live with few possessions and to defer setting up households according to their personal wishes.

Conclusion

The narratives presented in this chapter illustrate how the intersections between the terms of the H-1B visa and the mandate of flexible hiring have
informed the deeply gendered and racialized disembodiment of immigrant
labor. The state, as the legislator and adjudicator of immigration law/H-1B
policy, has constructed these immigrants' sociolegal dependence on employers in a manner that denies these workers the autonomy to enter the
labor market or live in the United States without being affiliated with an
employer. It is also alarming to note how employers, made indispensable
by the H-1B visa stipulations, are ever-present in the lives of immigrants
as status grantors and commission collectors while taking little or no responsibility for responding to the professional or embodied needs of their
employees. As a result, these immigrants are exposed to perpetual anxieties about their legal standing and livelihood, which heighten their docility
and subservience to the corporate sector as a whole. Furthermore, neither
the clients and subcontractors (who bring immigrants to the United States)
nor the state (responsible for enabling this labor incorporation through
the H-1B visa program) has extended the necessary provisions that might
address these immigrants' personal, social, or professional well-being. On
the contrary, employers and the state have collaborated to undermine immigrants' legal status, independence, and bargaining power so that they
may be positioned as a pool of exploitable labor ideal for flexible hiring.
The larger institutional apparatus constituted by the state and the corporate
sector has thus privatized and individualized immigrants' problems and
compelled this community to overcome the disembodying challenges of
flexible accumulation on its own.

NOTE

1. To compensate for the lack of more women's voices, I spent several days with
one female participant to sketch a short life history based on her experiences.

[6]

Economic Restructuring and the Social Regulation of Citizenship in the Heartland

NANCY A. NAPLES

Editor's Introduction

Nancy Naples reports on a community study focused on the recruitment of Mexican and Mexican American workers to new enterprises in two small U.S. towns. She points to a line of fault in their experience: they are asked to contribute economically in the United States but are too often denied full membership in their communities. In order to explore "how it happens" that way, Naples adopts an expanded conceptualization of citizenship as an ongoing accomplishment. Her perspective illustrates the interrelated community regulatory processes through which citizenship is activated and the kinds of barriers these new residents encounter as they navigate multiple institutional arenas outside their workplaces. The study relies on the ethnographic methods of community study and brings an institutional ethnographic sensibility to the analysis and discussion here, pointing to the ways that ruling relations are "woven through and across different institutions" in the community. The analysis points to numerous sites that would reward more focused institutional ethnography: the schools and government offices where migrants encounter agents of the state, local churches and businesses, and police work in parks and other public areas of the community. In each site, encounters between long-time and new residents are shaped by the standard operating procedures of these institutional sites and also by discursive constructions of "real Americans" and others, presumed permanent and temporary residents.

Naples's analysis makes clear that the official texts of citizenship—important as they are—can provide only a step toward full inclusion in community life. Citizenship, like any other textual status, is activated through situated and embodied processes of interaction. Language and racial identities are often implicated in those processes. And both long-term and new residents

are active in producing experiences of inclusion or exclusion, sometimes con-
sciously and often in ways that make it seem that "these things just happen"
(Jackson 1995).

* * *

This chapter centers the experiences of Mexican immigrants, Mexican American migrants, and white European American residents in rural Iowa and argues for a broadened definition of the state that captures the multiple arenas through which these residents are incorporated into the U.S. economy, society, and polity (and how community processes, migratory patterns, and resistance strategies may inhibit incorporation). This process of incorporation occurs at the local community level and involves ongoing social regulatory activities that circumscribe the ways in which new residents can make claims as permanent members of specific locales. These local social regulatory activities and interactions construct the racialized, gendered, and class-specific grounds upon which Mexicans and Mexican Americans can earn a living wage, access social provisions, and gain a political voice to protect their status as legitimate members of the local polity.

The history of Mexicans and Mexican Americans in the United States is influenced by a complex pattern of colonization, proletarianization, agricultural industrialization, and disparate migratory flows. Economic restructuring contributes to a shifting international division of labor that is reshaping the racial-ethnic composition of communities across the United States. Mexicans have been particularly hard hit by the processes of displacement and wage depreciation in regions across their country. As a consequence of their displacement from other regions coupled with the development of low-wage food-processing and related industries in the rural Midwest, Latinos are forming a growing proportion of migrants to the Midwest (Stanley 1994). As a result, rural communities in the Midwest with a traditionally white European American population have been forced to confront their own racism and manage ethnic tensions previously seen as the problems of urban areas or rural communities in the South, Southwest, and West. While much has been written about the experiences and incorporation of Mexicans and Mexican Americans in the West or Southwest (Acuna 1981; Boswell and Jorjani 1988; Chavez 1992; Fernández-Kelly 1983; Douglas Massey 1987; Montejano 1987; Robinson 1993; Thomas 1985), less is known about the more recent immigration and migration of Mexicans and Mexican Americans in the rural Midwest (see Fink 1998; Lamphere, Stepick, and Grenier 1994). Ethnographic attention to the experiences of incorporation for immigrants and migrants to the rural Midwest provides an opportunity explore the complex ways citizenship is achieved as well as contested.

Citizenship is achieved in particular local contexts and is an ongoing accomplishment that cannot be understood by an exclusive focus on law and INS policy. The local social regulatory practices reveal the complex and contradictory ways different individuals and groups are incorporated into the wider polity and how gender, race, and class are woven in and through these practices. I use the term "citizenship" in a broader sense than is typical in studies of immigration and migration to examine ways in which citizens and others with legal standing in the United States achieve legitimate status as full members of specific geographic communities (also see Coutin 2000). Therefore, I view citizenship claims beyond T. H. Marshall's (1965) conceptualization of civil, political, and social rights to include how newcomers make claims on the social, civic, and physical spaces and other features of particular locales. Following the feminist geographer Doreen Massey (1994: 138–139), I define "localities" as "*constructions* out of the intersections and interactions of concrete social relations and social processes." With this situated approach, it is possible to analyze how global economic and political processes, national and state policy, and local practices and social interactions work together in complex and sometimes contradictory ways to *regulate citizenship*.

My intersectional approach is especially indebted to Dorothy Smith's (1987, 1990a) institutional ethnographic approach that avoids reifying systems of oppressions and argues for a contextualized and historicized angle of vision.[1] I initially did not construct my community-based research on the migration of Mexicans and Mexican Americans to rural Iowa through the lens of institutional ethnography. However, as I deepened my engagement in the field and analyzed the initial interviews, I became increasingly aware of the benefits that an institutional ethnographic lens would provide for understanding the relationship between the local experiences of new migrants and other residents of the rural communities and the larger economic, political, and social processes that shaped their experiences. I must also confess that my early reading of institutional ethnography did not include an understanding of how this approach could be applied to a community study that did not focus exclusively on one or more specific institutions such as health, social welfare, or education. Fortunately, I began to revise my view of institutional ethnography to include a sensitivity to Smith's (2005) broader understanding of institutions, which differed from the bounded view typically described in the sociological literature. As she explains in her most recent book, the terms "institutions" and "institutional" are used to "identify the intersection and COORDINATION [*sic*] of more than one relational mode of ruling" (ibid.). Although Smith defines institutions as "organized around a distinctive function, such as education, health care, and so on," ruling relations are woven through and across different institutions in such a way that a community-based study is well positioned to capture the ways in which these relations are organized within and across different institutions and how they influence the everyday lives of local residents. As Smith explains:

> The institutional is to be discovered in motion, and its distinctive modes of generalizing coordination are themselves being brought into being in people's local doings in particular sites and at particular times. (Ibid.)

The longitudinal study is especially well positioned to capture how the more abstract and socially constructed problems of migration, immigration, and economic restructuring impact the organization of different community-based practices that, in turn, are themselves changed over time as a result of local responses to these social changes.

The specific analysis presented here is based on a twelve-year ethnographic study in Midtown, a pseudonym for a small town in rural Iowa where a local food-processing plant expanded in 1990. As a consequence of active recruitment by the plant owners and informal networking, Mexican and Mexican American workers and their families migrated to the town.[2] The increased presence of Mexicans and Mexican Americans as permanent residents altered the ethnic composition of this formerly ethnically homogenous town. The economic and demographic changes provided the basis for a longitudinal ethnographic study of the relationship between economic restructuring and social restructuring of class, gender, and race-ethnicity. By placing the analysis within a community context, I explore the relationship between citizenship practices and the market, state and local social institutions, and informal community interactions. By shifting the standpoint to the everyday life experiences of immigrants, migrants, and others who are the targets of state interventions, I am able to bring certain less visible features of state activity and the contradictions of this activity into view. This embedded intersectional approach sharpens the view of the multiple sites through which state agents and nonstate or extended agents of the state contribute to the *social regulation of citizenship*. As a result, my approach reveals the complex processes that influence the *social regulation of citizenship*, processes that are invisible in other modes of analysis.[3]

Defining Citizenship

Who deserves entry to the United States, and how is "deservingness" constructed through the implementation of immigration policy? The boundaries between legality and illegality, as well as the construction of appropriate identities associated with legality, are an everyday accomplishment involving complicated interactions among applicants, advocates, lawyers, judges, and numerous other actors who are often hidden from view in the formal proceedings used to assess deservingness. Using an ethnographic lens, Susan Coutin (2000) explores "how . . . undocumented immigration and illegal sojourn redefine not only the nation but citizenship, movement, and existence itself" (8). As Coutin emphasizes, "These boundary-creating interactions also contribute to the 'othering' of many who have been born into or achieved the status of citizen or legal resident" (see, e.g., Park 1998; Perea 1996). Using an ethnographic lens, Coutin (2000) explores "how . . . undocumented immigration and illegal sojourn redefine not only the nation but citizenship, movement, and existence itself" (8). Inspired by Foucault's (1972) methodology, she investigates "how law produces citizens, illegal aliens, legal permanent residents, legal immigration, illicit travel, and even territories and the state" (10). Coutin concludes that, "like borderlands, the space of illegality produces innovative strategies and practices" (46; Anzaldúa 1987; Flores and Benmayor 1997). Coutin (1993: 228) asserts that:

> [R]esistance is an ongoing part of social life. If society is continually constructed through human action (which is itself a product of society), and if these actions have the potential to reinforce or deconstruct particular power relations, then acts that are as seemingly trivial as furnishing proof of work authorization to an employer or not requiring identity documents of one's baby-sitter have political implications. Like their implications, the effects of such actions may not be immediately apparent.

In her study of how immigrants who are applying for various forms of legalization are disciplined through legal proceedings and by legal agents,

Coutin draws on Mindie Lazarus-Black's (1997) conceptualization of "rites of domination" (107). While this construct is most relevant to Coutin's focus on how immigrants must symbolically and materially position themselves with regard to the legal practices and rituals associated with achieving legal residency, my goal is to foreground the informal and less visible ways that new residents come to feel part of a community, regardless of legal standing. In fact, I argue, even those who have achieved formal citizenship may not be able to enact their rights in different community settings (Naples 1996).

In this regard, the conceptualization of "cultural citizenship" offers a useful framework for expanding our approach to citizenship practices that go beyond the more limited legal dimension (Flores and Benmayor 1997). Blanca Silvestrini (1997: 44) defines "cultural citizenship" as "the ways people organize their values, their beliefs about their rights, and their practices based on their sense of cultural belonging rather than on their formal status as citizens of a nation." This notion of "cultural citizenship" parallels, to some extent, Coutin's understanding of Salvadorans' legal consciousness, yet goes beyond the limits of legal discourse and encounters with the law to incorporate more collectivist understandings and practices. Furthermore, as Renato Rosaldo (1997: 37) explains, "the dominant claims of universal citizenship assume a propertied white male subject and usually blind themselves to their exclusion and marginalizations of people who differ in gender, race, sexuality, and age." Writing about the experiences of Asian immigrants, Lisa Lowe (1996: 162) observes that "the American contract of citizenship is quite evidently contradictory; if it proposes the state as the unified body in which all equal subjects are granted membership, it simultaneously asks that differences—of race, class, gender, and locality—be subordinated in order to qualify for membership in that democratic body" (also see Roberts 1997).

In a recent study of Indian immigrants in Chicago, Sharmila Rudrappa (2004: 147) builds on Lowe's analysis and further highlights the "racialized content of American citizenship." She argues that "citizenship is centrally about the rights that accrue to us because we have this national membership" (9). Referring to T. H. Marshall's (1965) discussion of social rights, which include the rights to "economic welfare and security to live the life of a civilized being according to the standards prevailing in the society" (quoted in Rudrappa 2004: 9), Rudrappa argues that "two realms of citizenship . . . are inextricably tied together—the cultures of American citizenship and the social rights associated with citizenship" (11). My analysis of the social regulation of citizenship provides further evidence for the importance of viewing citizenship as a practice and a cultural resource that is dependent as much on cultural practices and community ethos as on legal standing.

Defining the Social Regulation of Citizenship

Social regulation of citizenship involves the control of citizenship through the interaction of three dimensions: (1) formal social policies and institutional practices (e.g., immigration, law enforcement, education, health-care, and social welfare policies and practices); (2) informal social practices and local associational activities (e.g., access to housing, recreation, and other sites of community-based association) and (3) discursive fields, which define who has legitimate claim to the identity of *citizen*.[4] The social regulation of citizenship generates contradictions that are most evident when local practices and everyday life events are examined. Furthermore, those who have formal citizenship and legal residency but are denied access to social rights that are due them and other features of community membership also resist local social control efforts in a variety of ways that are revealed when we shift the standpoint to the experiences of diverse community members.

Citizenship defined as the right to vote and the "opportunity to earn" (Shklar 1991: 3) captures the contradictory place of Mexicans and Mexican Americans in U.S. society today (also see Thomas 1985). For many who have the right to vote, their right to earn is firmly circumscribed by the segmentation and segregation of the labor market and by discrimination and other racist practices in employment and community settings. For those who have attained the right to earn, their incorporation as full members of specific locales is circumscribed by informal social regulatory community-based processes.[5] This study reveals the often hidden processes by which citizenship is constructed, experienced, and resisted in sites that are outside the formal state institutions that regulate these forms of political identity. My intersectional approach to the analysis of local citizenship practices also reveals the contradictions of formal state institutional policies and practices (also see Naples 2003).

I demonstrate how the processes that regulate citizenship are embedded in numerous aspects of civic and public life. Processes of social regulation are evident in everyday interactions with local police, state licensing agencies (e.g., the motor vehicle bureau), housing policies and practices, health-care and social services agencies, educational institutions, and parks and recreation facilities, among other formal and informal arenas of social life. Formal and informal agents representing these different spheres actively extend the reach of the state as a controlling force in the lives of the new residents. Everyday interactions with formal and informal agents also have contradictory effects for newcomers, as well as for longer-term residents. Furthermore, these contradictory tendencies are experienced differently by residents depending on (a) modes of incorporation; (b) intersection of gender, race, and class; (c) facility with English; (d) "legal" status; and (e) the history, culture, and political economy of the particular locale. I use the term "politics of location" (Rich 1986) to highlight the contradictions of settlement, mobility, communication, and association in a particular place.[6]

First, access to housing and employment is directly related to one's ability to secure settlement and to socially reproduce oneself and one's family, which, in turn, can be firmly circumscribed by patterns of exclusion and marginality in both residency and income. For example, as Robert Bullard and Charles Lee (1994: 1) point out, emphasizing the experience of African Americans, "Apartheid-type housing and development policies have resulted in limited mobility, reduced neighborhood options, decreased residential choices, and diminished job opportunities for millions of Americans." However, access to other community-based sites such as recreation, churches, and laundry facilities also shapes one's sense of settlement and social reproductive capacity.

Second, social regulation of mobility is directly related to achievement of full citizenship "in terms both of identity and space" and "has been in some cultural contexts a crucial means of subordination" (Doreen Massey 1994, 178). The feminist critique of the split between the so-called private or domestic sphere and the public sphere illustrates how this spatial dimension can shape citizenship (also see Pateman 1988). As Doreen Massey (1994: 179) explains: "The attempt to confine women to the domestic sphere was both a specifically spatial control and, through that, a social control on identity." Critical race theorists have also stressed the significance of mobility for achieving full citizenship (see Bullard, Grigsby, and Lee 1994; Goldberg 1993). In my expanded view of community-based sites that contribute to the social regulation of citizenship, I include opportunity to travel from one space to another, as well as the opportunity to secure the means for travel, such as a driver's license and insurance.

Third, the politics of language and translation also circumscribe one's freedom of expression, as well as one's ability to obtain basic services and secure legal rights. Lack of access to effective translation or bilingual services circumscribes some residents' ability to utilize these services and thereby impedes their ability to protect their legal rights as well as to participate in the broader social and civic life of the local community.

Fourth, regulation of association and social relationships inhibits the achievement of citizenship or full membership in a political and social space. Local community practices can inhibit free association on the basis of these dimensions. Furthermore, community regulation of association, dating and sexuality, and emotional expression are experienced differently by men and women. They also have different consequences for different community members according to their race-ethnicity and their socioeconomic class. In this way, citizenship practices are gendered and racialized and feature class differentiation.

Finally, the social regulation of settlement, mobility, communication, and association are accomplished through everyday social interactions that reveal the contradictions of the social regulation of citizenship.

Shifting the Standpoint on the State

In order to explore the processes by which nonwhite residents are incorporated into rural communities, I began an ethnographic investigation of two towns in rural Iowa in 1990, just before a food-processing plant in one of the towns expanded. Each town had a population of approximately 1,250 residents. The percentage of nonwhite residents at this time was negligible. The owners of the plant recruited Latino workers from Mexico and Texas, among other regions in the United States, to fill the low-wage jobs. By 1996, almost 15 percent of the towns' population was Latino. I continued to document the social changes until December 2002. I conducted the research with the help of six research assistants. In sum, we conducted twenty field trips that ranged from one week to three weeks in duration. The two towns were chosen for this study on the basis of the following criteria: distance from a regional center, decline in farm and business ownership, increasing rate of poverty between 1970 and 1985 when contrasted with the state as a whole, presence of low-wage industrial employment, and active economic development commissions.

Data include both ethnographic observations and in-depth interviews. Ethnographic data include observation of numerous community events during twenty field trips that spanned the twelve years of investigation. These events include school board, city council, and economic development committee meetings, church and other community events, and informal gatherings. In addition, open-ended responses to in-depth interviews were used to identify the salient experiences of community workers and other relevant community residents. These data consist of (1) interviews with a subset of Mexican, Mexican American, and white European American community workers; (2) interviews with other community residents who are well placed to comment on the effectiveness of the community workers, including clergy, educators, public officials, and other community leaders; and (3) interviews with additional Mexican and Mexican American residents in order to assess their perspectives on race relations and what influence the community workers have had in their daily life experiences. For ease of presentation, I use the terms "Latino" and "Anglo" interchangeably with "Mexican and Mexican American" and "white European American," respectively, although both terms have very specific racial-ethnic meaning that may not capture accurately the specificity of the Mexican and Mexican American residents or the diversity within the white population in Midtown.

Two interview schedules were designed. The first, focused on the community workers, explored their motivation for community work, their varying perceptions of their role in the community, their goals, and their perceived effectiveness. The second, focused on assessing the wider community's reaction to their efforts, especially toward the Mexican and Mexican American residents, included a section on experiences with and perceptions of the community workers' bridging activities. The second interview schedule also gathered background family and demographic information, migration patterns, household survival strategies, family relationships, support network, evaluation of economic development and community process, and experiences of discrimination. More than two hundred community members have been interviewed at least one time, while a subset of community residents were reinterviewed annually over the twelve years of field work. All interviews and field data were transcribed and analyzed using N*Vivo, a qualitative software product developed by QSR International. The process of transcribing field notes and interviews and using the software program to help organize the data provided the opportunity, as

Smith (2005: 143) explains, to "assemble people's accounts to locate a social organization in which their experiences, as told to us, are embedded but not wholly visible." The data generated for the study are utilized as progressive accounts that help make visible the "connections, links, hookups, and the various forms of coordination that tie [different actors'] doings into those of others" (ibid.). In this study of social restructuring in rural Iowa, I was especially interested in linking the experiences of the new migrants to those of the other residents and to the institutional practices that were manifest in their different accounts.

Following a discussion of the local social regulation of citizenship, I explore the informal social regulatory processes in terms of the politics of settlement, mobility, communication, and social interaction. I conclude with a discussion of how these class-based, racialized, and gendered patterns contributed to the social regulation of citizenship in rural Iowa.

The Local Social Regulation of Citizenship

Resistance to the civic, social, and relational incorporation of Mexican and Mexican American residents in Midtown is firmly entrenched in the housing practices, provision of health and social services, and translation services, as well as in the social regulation of interpersonal relationships, especially teenagers' associational and dating behavior. These community-based social regulatory processes led to limited contact between Latino and non-Latino residents, shaped interactions among police, educators, service providers, and Latino clients, and compromised associational possibilities and relationships among residents in a variety of settings.

Community-based constructions of, and responses to, racism and ethnic tension vary across different parts of the United States. New Latino residents to the rural Midwest rarely have access to advocacy organizations and other formal groups established in other locales to protect the rights of workers or community residents who experience discrimination, harassment, or lack of access to vital health and social services. Since most long-term residents in these towns hold onto a firm distinction between those who belong and those who are considered outsiders to the community, "newcomers" frequently face a great deal of resistance when they begin to make claims in different arenas (see Naples 1996). One significant way outsiderness is constructed is through visual markers such as one's race-ethnicity. This racial-ethnic differentiation inevitably places anyone who does not (visually, at least) appear to share the same racial-ethnic background at the margins of small-town life. Class position, language, and associational patterns such as marital status and household structure are also markers of belongingness in rural Iowa.

The widely held belief in agrarian ideology serves as a powerful discursive frame that informs the social regulation of citizenship in rural Iowa. Agrarian ideology refers to a privileging of family farmers, especially those who adhere to a traditional gender division of labor and who have a multigenerational history in the region (Fink 1992). This formulation of community identity and belonging makes it difficult for anyone who moves into the region for work in a factory or other low-wage nonfarm employment to become an accepted part of the community (see Naples 1994). Those residents who do not own farms in the community but play central professional roles such as doctor, educator, or clergy are also granted a high status within the community, a consequence of class relations within these small towns. Those who perform nonfarm work at minimum wage or who are receiving public assistance are therefore further marginalized within the somewhat collectively held class-based ethos of the rural Midwestern town (see Naples 1994, 1997).

The privileged position of the middle class farm household with the traditional gender division of labor masks the many inequalities that have long characterized rural Midwestern communities. These patterns of class, gender, residency, and race-based inequalities serve as the grounds for denying "membership" in the community to those from non-farm working class backgrounds or who are single mothers or who have recently taken up residence as well as anyone else constructed as "an outsider." Those who dare to speak out against inequality and discrimination are further marginalized (see Naples 1997). Many more keep silent for fear of reprisals from their neighbors who are invested in seeing only the positive benefits of rural life (also see Fitchen 1991). Consequently, agrarian ideology serves as a social regulatory frame that inhibits the full incorporation of many white European-American residents, as well as Mexicans and Mexican Americans.

As a consequence of these powerful processes, those within the marginalized segments of the town may never acquire the designation of legitimate community member (see Naples 1996). However, certain changes in the political environment may create the grounds for shifts in designations that result in reincorporating some newcomers or disenfranchising other, longer-term residents. For example, when the Immigration and Naturalization Service (INS) raided Midtown, some of the longer-term residents began to incorporate as "community members" the Latinos who held legal residency or citizenship status but were picked up in a raid and detained at the regional INS office, in Omaha. Further, as the composition of the Latino community shifted from predominantly single male workers to two-parent families, Anglo residents softened somewhat in the negative attitudes they expressed, although mistrust of Latinos' long-term commitment to Midtown remained strong. White European American residents often commented, "Well, many have strong family values." In keeping with the privileging of a heterosexual two-parent family form, when longer-term residents are divorced or turn to welfare for economic support, they frequently experience alienation from the perceived "community-at-large." Ironically, this heteronormal construction of family serves as one dimension upon which Mexican and Mexican American residents find acceptance

Regulating Settlement

The politics of location are especially revealing of the contradictory features of social regulatory practices. Here class, race, and gender all intersect to enhance the process of marginalization that accompanied the migration of Mexicans and Mexican Americans to Midtown. Lack of affordable housing was one of the most consistently mentioned problems in the community. The mayor, city councilmen, and social service providers, as well as almost every other resident interviewed, stressed that Midtown did not have an adequate supply of affordable housing. Furthermore, they did not see how the town could absorb the new workers who were earning the minimum wage in the food-processing plant and could not afford to pay for the limited housing in the community. Owners of rental property took advantage of the housing shortage to increase rents and alter rental practices. In response to this perceived need, the economic development corporation worked to establish an apartment complex financed by the Farmers' Home Administration (FmHA) that would provide low- to moderate-income housing for sixteen families.

In the meantime, some workers commuted up to fifty miles to work in the plant. A number of residents were concerned about the problems posed by workers from out-of-town who do not have a sense of "pride in the community." However, when workers and their families were able to find housing in the community, a process of segregation and discrimination was put firmly in place. The director of the local social services agency reported that when a low-income family qualified for a housing subsidy, landlords often refused to make the required repairs to their buildings in order to pass HUD inspection: "[S]ome of them [eligible for HUD assistance] . . . found a house but then the landlord refuses to do anything to pass inspection and so there it is, they're stuck again." Furthermore, she reported that, in response to the expansion at the plant, some residents were buying housing and charging "outrageous prices for rent." For example, she explained:

> They have some trailers down here in the trailer court. I mean, they're new trailers—but they're talking $400.00 a month rent and they're furnished and everything, but, still if you work at [the plant] up here for [minimum wage], there's no way they can afford that.

Some landlords also took advantage of some workers' need to share housing with one or more other families. Rather than charge a flat monthly rent, some owners were charging the Mexican and Mexican American renters a monthly fee per adult in the home.

Half of the Mexican and Mexican American workers and their families found rental housing in the trailer park. The trailer park was located on the edge of town and provided housing primarily for low-income families. Some members of the community believed that the trailer park was the home for unemployed people who are "not really desiring of a job." Others saw it as a place where there were a lot of problems connected with a supposed low-income "lifestyle." As one white community resident explained: "It's just the traditional, the minimum-wage workers, that's their lifestyle and that's really what you expect." However, the owners of the trailers did little to correct problems renters found with their homes, and the quality of the housing in the trailers continued to deteriorate over the course of our field work. Sister Theresa, one of the two Catholic nuns who commute to Midtown and provide support for low-income residents, complained about the bad condition of the trailers: "Some of those trailers should be burned down. When you go in there, it is just like you are almost outside." Another informant explained:

> I think if you went down and wanted to rent one, they would probably rent you one. . . . They are in bad shape. They have the water shut off to them now. . . . But there has never been any upkeep on those trailers at all. Nothing. . . . . There were holes in the floors and ceilings. They are just terrible.

The economic development groups in Midtown and the neighboring town of Southtown have placed housing high on their agenda. However, the director of the local Housing Authority who is charged with facilitating the development of low-income housing reported having trouble finding landlords who will take the low-income rental certificates:

> I am having trouble . . . trying to get property owners, landlords to register with our office, that way, if someone comes in, not a property manager, but we can give them a list of people to contact. So far, that is a slow process. I think they are afraid that we will try to force them into doing things. I don't know. . . . There are some vacant houses that I have contacted the owners to try to get them to turn those into rentals and they don't want to bother. They would rather just leave them sit than do anything with them. It is frustrating. Someone drives around and sees an empty house, there is an empty house but there is not much we can do unless the owners themselves decide to do something.

The housing segregation and discrimination furthered the social regulatory process and broadened the stigma placed on all low-income residents. The interaction between state and federal programs to assist those living in poverty and community processes to exploit and marginalize these residents left many Mexican and Mexican American families with few housing options and household arrangements available to them (also see Bullard, Grigsby, and Lee 1994). Ironically, commuting to their jobs at the plant, as well as sharing limited housing with several adults or extended family members, served as markers of their marginality, as well as of a presumed lack of commitment to the local community. In this way, the social regulation of settlement served to sustain the belief held by many Anglo residents that the Latinos were not interested in full incorporation into the town. Regardless of the newcomers' desired or expected longevity in the town, the new residents were treated by many longer-term community members as temporary residents who were expected to move on within a short period of time. Regardless of their citizenship status, many also viewed them as "illegal" residents. The informal regulatory practices further circumscribed the new residents' access to the social rights associated with community membership and citizenship. These practices furthered the out-migration of many Latinos and contributed to turnover in the plant and the town that had a negative effect on both the new migrants and longer-term residents.

Regulating Mobility

Many Mexican and Mexican American residents interviewed complained that their mobility and their access to the small number of public spaces were circumscribed by their fear of unpleasant interactions with white residents. As the number of Latino youth increased, Anglo community members worried about importation of urban problems such as gang activity, use of drugs, and interracial violence. After one incident where a fight broke out between a Latino and an Anglo teenager, the high school and the park became objects for white ethnic community concerns and police surveillance. The police chief explained: "We have had some racial tensions and some racial problems at school and basically we just put officers over there to make sure there is no violence or anything like that." He explained that the school officials called in the police when the fight broke out. He said that he now sends police officers over to the school "towards the end of the school day when people are getting out and then we monitor the traffic and the parking lot." He believes that their presence will deter further outbreaks of violence.

Since there are few places for young people to congregate after school, both Latino and Anglo youth gravitate toward the park. During the summer of 1998, a fight broke out between an Anglo teenager and a Latino youth that led to widespread fear about the so-called racial tensions in the community. While most European American adult residents we spoke to about the incident in the park blamed the Latino youth, both Anglo and Latino youth told a more nuanced story. One Anglo teenager, Tim Brown, explained:

> a sophomore beat up a Mexican kid because he drove by . . . the park and the Mexican threw a ball at his car or something and he pulled in and was asking him why he did it and the Mexican kid got up in his face and he spit in it and that was it. He just knocked him out and that was pretty much all there was. He didn't get into any trouble because the Mexican kid started it by throwing the ball at his car, which is how it is.

This incident seemed to ignite the fears of many white North European American residents that the Mexican and Mexican American youth were engaging in "gang activity." Many parents forbade their children to go to the park. In an interview in 1998, Tim Brown explained that, as a result of the park incident, white residents felt run out of the park. From the accounts we received by Anglo and Latino youth, this perception reflects Anglo fear of the growing Latino presence in the town. According to Tim,

> During the summer, it used to be that we'd go up to the park and play basketball all the time, but really the park in the summertime now is pretty much all Mexicans and they have pretty much run all the white kids out of playing basketball, but we still do some. It has changed that way because there are a lot more now than there ever was and when they get a big group there, there is more racism against white people than there would be there by themselves.

Of course, the Latino teenagers tell a somewhat different story about the park incident and other interactions with Anglo community members. They define the Anglos' reaction to their presence in the park as a result of racism and their dislike of Mexicans and Mexican Americans. Ironically, Anglo fear of the Latino youth contributed to their circumscribing their own children's mobility and use of the park. Here we see another illustration of the contradiction of social regulatory practices.

State licensing agencies also play a key social regulatory role. One of the main sites in this regard is the Department of Motor Vehicles (DMV). Public transportation is generally unavailable in rural communities. Consequently, most residents require access to motor vehicles for getting to work, shopping for groceries, attending church services, visiting health clinics, and so on. Consequently, the DMV plays a central role in providing the means by which residents of rural communities can sustain their lives. Obtaining a legal driver's license is even more essential for the Mexicans and Mexican Americans, who are often stopped by local police with little or no cause. However, even those who possess legal birth certificates and working papers report further problems when they apply for a license to drive.

Anna Ortega's experience illustrates the problem. Ortega, who is a bilingual U.S. citizen, was successful in her fight to protect other Mexican Americans from discrimination by DMV officials. She effectively mobilized the political power of the Mexican American community in her hometown of Laredo. Ortega reports:

> [The DMV] tried to take away the U.S. citizenship cards from the Tejanos. I had to bring the judge over and complain. I had to call Immigration. I even had to call the mayor of Laredo, Texas, to tell him what was going on

here—that they were picking up our birth certificates saying that they were fake and that we were illegal aliens.

Ortega's story highlights the value of two key resources for the migrants to Midtown: English-language proficiency and ongoing links between the migrant and settled Mexican American community in other areas of the United States. The links between residents in Midtown and Mexicans and Mexican Americans in other parts of the United States as well as in Mexico illustrate the maintenance of a transnational community. Residents of Midtown draw on their national and transnational community for information on other job possibilities, immigration law, and other forms of less tangible support. They, in turn, provide financial assistance, among other resources, to family and former neighbors living in other parts of the United States and Mexico (see, e.g., Espiritu 1992; Ethnic and Racial Studies 1999).

This observation points out the significance of cross-border constructions of community and their significance for the cultural and social citizenship of migrants. Here, it is important to recognize "the cultures of American citizenship," as Rudrappa (2004: 5) does in her study of Indian immigrants. She explains that "as a cultural concept, citizenship refers to sets of practices citizens follow to constitute themselves as a nation." She draws on Christian Joppke's (1998) analysis in *Immigration Challenges the Nation-State*:

> that nation-states are fundamentally constituted on the principle of sedentariness, that is, the fixity of a population in a geographical territory. Yet, immigrants challenge this principle of sedentariness and the idea of the geographically bound nation-state because they are transnational subjects. (Rudrappa 2004: 5)

Analyses of cultural citizenship practices must also attend to the ways that relations across regions within the United States pose a challenge to the idea of a bounded community that is often used to construct the difference between rural and urban, between the Midwest and other parts of the United States, and between communities, like Laredo, that have varied histories, demography, and racial-ethnic cultural practices that reflect diversity and those, like Midtown, that have long histories of almost exclusively white community membership. This point becomes even more evident when we shift attention to the informal practices that contribute to the regulation of communication and association. In some communities across the United States, Spanish is the dominant language, and, in many other communities, interracial relationships are far from rare; however, in rural Iowa these features of difference were frequently met with fear and contributed to additional practices designed to socially regulate the interactions among and between Latinos and other residents.

Regulating Communication and Association

During field trips to Midtown in 1991, white North European American residents were especially vocal about the Mexicans' and Mexican Americans' lack of English-language proficiency. Many believed that it was simultaneously a sign that these "newcomers" did not want to be a part of the community and a reflection of a lack of educational ability. On the other hand, key community actors initially resisted the idea that they should provide English as a Second Language (ESL) courses or hire a Spanish teacher for the local high school. Each of these strategies would cost the town money, and, they argued, the Mexicans and Mexican Americans were not going to remain long in Midtown.

Progressive clergy who initially spoke out in support of the new residents were frequently chastised by parishioners who wanted to deny the community's racism, ethnic tensions, or poverty. Steps taken by local officials to address the specific needs of non-English speaking residents, such as the hiring of translators for emergency services or ESL teachers for "limited English proficient" students, were all too often compromised by the limited Spanish proficiency of the translators and ESL teachers. Maryann Manor, the wife of one of the ministers, was among the community residents who attempted to address the problem (which she defined as a mutual inability to communicate). She spoke a little Spanish. She organized a study group for other community members who wanted to learn the language. Manor reported that she and two other community members approached the plant owners with the idea of offering an ESL course to the workers at the factory, but the owners refused the offer.

Workers stated that the plant did not employ a translator. The management called upon bilingual employees to help them communicate with non-English-speaking workers. In 1991, Erin Landers explained why they had not translated the employee handbook and how the workers learned about the plant's policies and employee benefits:

[B]ecause it is fourteen pages long, compressed print. Yeah. So what we do there, when they are hired, when I interview them I go over the things that are in the handbook so they are aware of our policies and benefits and, you know, all of their requirements. Ah, and if they don't speak good enough English then I have somebody that is bilingual help me to translate that and that works real well.

However, some of the workers interviewed who did not speak English reported that they were unable to understand how their pay was calculated or the procedures for overtime. Workers who knew more English helped their coworkers, as Efren Palacios explains:

Your companions who are more advanced and know some English [explain the rules, the contract, and so on]. There is one guy who works with me and who helps. There is always a companion who is there to help. If there is a Mexican who needs help with filling out an application, someone goes and tells a companion and they go to help with the application.

Lack of English proficiency compromised the workers' ability to advocate for their rights in the workplace. When asked what the workers did if they had a complaint, Palacios explained: "Well no, no one complains. No one knows who to go to or any of that." Most of the Mexicans and Mexican Americans also discussed the ways that lack of English proficiency left them vulnerable in their daily interactions with non-Spanish-speaking members of the community. Manuel Gomez explained: "We don't know English. We don't know how to read it or speak it so as to defend ourselves."

Several Mexicans interviewed believed that neither the interpreter nor the ESL teacher (who also acts as an interpreter when called upon by city officials) provided accurate translation. Carlos Medina explained:

Everyone knows that I don't like the way they interpret. I tell them what I can and what I can't, well so be it. I don't want them to say something else. Because I know they say one thing and one understands that they're not saying it the way it is. If I say it, I'm going to say it like this, even if it's not good, but you're saying it the way you want it said. They, no, they say other things that aren't so. Friends of mine have told me that they told them to say one thing and that they said something else. And they said, "hey! that's not what I said" so they know it's not right. I don't like them to interpret.

During the period 1992–1994, one bilingual community worker from Texas who lived in Midtown was not used as an interpreter by the city because, Medina believes, he was of Mexican descent "'cause the police think . . . he'll help the Mexicans."

Public officials claim that there are few capable bilingual residents who can serve as translators and ESL teachers and that the limited pool forces them to choose less than adequate personnel. Others insist that the services are more than adequate, while still others resent the need to provide such services. However, bilingual Latino residents claim that the translators typically hired by public agencies do not communicate effectively with Spanish-speaking residents and often make significant mistakes when interpreting to public officials and health care and service providers. Depending on the context, these mistakes are of more or less consequence, with the most serious problems occurring when these translators are used in court. The provision of ESL classes has improved since this 1994 field trip. However, a shortage of competent ESL teachers and translators who are trusted by the Latino residents was evident as recently as December 2002.

Language is a crucial site of contestation in which long-term residents and newcomers negotiate their relationships to the community and to each other. This process of negotiation goes beyond the limits to communication that language differences pose. In fact, many white North European residents react with fear to the Latinos who speak Spanish among themselves in public spaces. A teenager, Martha Glass, reported:

> If they [the Latinos] are at the park or something and they are talking in Spanish, they [the police] go up to them and they say that they are saying that they are going to do something. This one kid, he waves to the cops to say hi, and is pulled over and they started yelling at him for doing that. At the park, if the Hispanics are talking and standing around, people think they are talking about them.

Martha articulated this fear herself when she described her reaction to a group of Latino high school students talking among themselves in Spanish. Although she does not speak Spanish, she assumed that these young people were talking about her and her friends: "Some of the Hispanics are kind of rude sometimes and they are talking in Spanish about us and I told them if they wanted to say something, they should say it to my face or don't say it all and they came over and started yelling at us."

The struggle over language and communication ran through interactions with employers, coworkers, city employees, and other community residents. Not surprisingly, language barriers and cultural differences posed key challenges to the school personnel. School officials and teachers often reacted with fear when Latino students spoke to each other in Spanish. A number of high school students reported that Latinos have been suspended for speaking Spanish in school. As the examples illustrate, community members who were in positions of power frequently tried to control the mode of expression and association of the young Latino residents. These attempts were especially directed at controlling gender and race relations. They also had some contradictory consequences for white European American residents.

The social regulatory practices that shaped the possibility for achieving citizenship and full membership in Midtown included surveillance and informal regulation of gender, class, and racial-ethnic relations. Interracial dating was particularly disturbing to those interested in maintaining the divisions between segments of the community with different class and racial-ethnic backgrounds. Concerns about interracial dating and marriage were articulated by educators, social workers, parents, and clergy. Joan Lamm, who had been a teacher in Midtown High for six years, summed up her fears as follows:

> Culture differences are real interesting too because, um, the man's approach to women in Mexico is much different than it is here. And it's very confusing to the high school students. . . . Well, you will find groups of Spanish-speaking boys talking together about the girls [and the girls] . . . are flattered by this, but actually . . . [the boys] are not speaking in a flattering way, okay. So they, I don't know, they have a tendency that they're real charming to the girls, but they're not. The approach is not the same as an American boy's would be and sometimes the girls are a little confused and hurt by this.

Lamm, who did not speak Spanish, feared that the young boys were saying "things in Spanish that would translate to whore or slut, or things that were derogatory." The fear of Latino male sexuality and aggression formed a powerful discursive subtext in the interviews with white North European American women residents. Anglo community members viewed Latino men through the stereotyped notion of "machismo," which is said to be characterized by, among other things, "extreme verbal and bodily expression of aggression toward other men, frequent drunkenness, and sexual aggression and dominance" (Hondagneu-Sotelo and Messner 1994), thus contributing to their surprise when Latino adolescents and men did not exhibit these qualities.

Rarely did the white European American residents mention the Mexican and Mexican American women. In keeping with the stereotypical construction of "machismo/marianismo," many white residents constructed Mexican women as "submissive, maternal, and virginal" (Cantú forthcoming). Furthermore, because of the recruitment strategies of the plant owners and the gendered migratory pattern of Mexican and Mexican American labor, the first wave of workers consisted of men between the ages of sixteen and forty. During the second wave, a number of women migrated to work in the plant or to accompany their husbands. The third wave includes a larger percentage of families, made up of men and women and their children. As a consequence of the migratory time sequencing and the gender division of household labor, the men are more visible to the wider community. Furthermore, several other factors contribute to the Latinas' public invisibility at this stage of migration. These factors are related to the patterns of settlement, mobility, and communication mentioned earlier. For example, many of these women did not have access to transportation, nor does Midtown offer the food products they desired. Families pooled resources and traveled weekly to Des Moines, two and one-half hours away, to purchase groceries from a store that stocks Mexican food and other Mexican products. Lack of facility with English also contributed to their limited interaction with other community members.

Initial research indicated only reluctant attempts in the early 1990s to deal with the perceived differences. Many white European American residents contrasted the ideal-typical traditional resident with the newcomers. And, of course, the Latinos were viewed as not measuring up for a variety of reasons. The racism and classism implicit in many comments about the Mexicans and Mexican Americans was couched in discussions of the white residents' fear of a rise in the cost of education and social services, a growing underclass, and increased crime (also see Hagan and Palloni 1999). By the end of the 1990s, a number of significant shifts had taken place. Since a growing proportion of Latinos were remaining in the town for longer periods than was typical in the early 1990s, their presence was now viewed as a permanent feature of the community. Furthermore, as the Latino children entered the schools, they formed friendships with Anglo children, thus breaking down divisions between residents of different racial-ethnic backgrounds.

The regulation of association across gender, race-ethnicity, and class contoured the social construction of citizenship in this local context. As a consequence, social regulation of dating, sexuality, and emotional expression were experienced differently by men and women and were further differentiated by race-ethnicity and class. Of course, these patterns were also fluid, shifting over time, and were shaped by the modes of incorporation and racialization processes that were part and parcel of economic and social restructuring. The process of racialization is a dynamic one that influences the social regulation of citizenship and shapes the everyday lives of both Latino and non-Latino residents in Midtown. As Ali Rattansi (2005) observes, "[t]he reproduction of race and nation occurs, then, through the workings of the state and myriad social interactions in a wide range of social fields, sites, and institutional contexts" (p. 287). The racialization processes contributed to the social construction of citizenship in Midtown and intersected with notions of the ideal citizen that were further contoured by agrarian ideology and economic restructuring. Rattansi further argues that:

> Patriarchal forms, sexualized relations, classes, gendered, and sexualized racisms, nationalisms, ethnic attachments, differing structural characteristics of national states, all play contextually variable roles in influencing the character of social life. (Rattansi 2005: 288)

An institutional ethnographic approach provides the analytic lens to help us map out how these different structuring characteristics work to coordinate "people's activities, their work in the generous sense" (Smith 2005: 211).

Conclusion

Rather than viewing the state as a static and concrete entity with fixed and bounded policy arenas and citizenship as a formal legal category, this analysis defines the state and the social regulation of citizenship in dynamic relationship with those who are targets of specific state interventions (also see Haney 1996). The Latino and Anglo residents whose perspectives form the basis for this analysis experience the state as fluid, ever-changing, and woven throughout their social lives. The identity of citizen is also constructed in relational terms. For example, even Latino community members with formal citizenship rights feel themselves marginalized by informal social regulatory processes of racialization. As Anna Ortega, a U.S. citizen who moved from Laredo to Midtown, explained:

> But a lot of the Americans think that because we're brown everybody comes from Mexico and it's not like that you know. Because you can be Mexican, Hispanic, and you can come from Texas; you can come from Chicago. . . . You can be born and raised in California. . . . [They think]: "They're from Mexico. They're all illegals."

As I note in my discussion of the "outsider phenomenon" in rural Iowa (Naples 1997: 97), Ortega distinguished herself from the white North European American residents whom she defined as "Americans." Community social regulatory processes create a boundary between "real Americans" (read: white European Americans) and other Americans. These boundaries are maintained by ideological constructions, as well as by material practices, institutional arrangements, and cultural patterns. Those who do not fit the narrow definition of "American" feel themselves outside the category despite their legal status as citizens.

An embedded intersectional analysis provides a view into the complex processes that are part and parcel of citizenship yet are obscured when we start our exploration from places far from the ground. A socially embedded exploration can deepen our understanding of how migrants and other nonwhite racial-ethnic groups are incorporated into the economic, social, political, and cultural life of diverse communities. This analysis reveals how the social regulation of citizenship changes over time and is influenced by the extent to which diverse community members serve to extend the reach of the state by legitimating or denying community membership to "newcomers." By highlighting the politics of settlement, mobility, communication, and association, I also revealed the contradictions in social regulatory practices.

The power to control settlement is one of the most potent strategies for circumscribing citizenship claims and other modes of incorporation (see Doreen Massey 1994; Rose 1993). It also masks the interdependence of dominant groups with those kept on the margins. bell hooks (1990) highlights this contradiction in analyzing the dynamics of domination and resistance in the segregated community in which she grew up. Hooks also reminds us that such marginalized places can also serve as sites of resistance and "a space for radical openness which allows the creation of a counter-hegemonic politics" (hooks 1990 summarized by Rose 1993: 156; also see Evans 1979; Fraser 1989). Despite the potential of such physical marginalization to provoke radical challenge to the dominant class and racial-ethnic group, the diversity of the Mexican and Mexican American community, different migratory patterns, and out-migration of many workers and their families undermined the radical potential of their marginalized status.

An institutional ethnographic approach reveals the contradictions of the locally contoured social regulation of citizenship. Such an approach will enrich future analyses by contextualizing the means by which different racial-ethnic groups negotiate their incorporation into particular locales. Attention to gender, racial, and class subtexts of these social regulatory practices will advance our understanding of how "relations of ruling" are woven through and reinscribed as well as resisted in everyday life (Smith 1987).

NOTES

1. An institutional ethnographic approach further responds to postcolonial feminist cautions against viewing the formulation of the "global-local as a monolithic formation," which "may also erase the existence of multiple expressions of 'local' identities and concerns and multiple globalities" (Grewal and Kaplan 1994: 11). Inderpal Grewal and Caren Kaplan (1994: 13) suggest "the term 'transnational' to problematize a purely locational politics of global-local or center-periphery."

2. Some of the Mexican workers are recent immigrants from several towns in Mexico, and others are long-term residents of the United States. Consequently, I will refer to these workers as Mexican and Mexican American. None of the white residents referred to the new residents as "Chicanos," including the Mexican American community worker and missionary who was working with the "Hispanic population" [sic] in Midtown. The only terms heard throughout the field work were "Mexican" and "Hispanic." In fact, white European American residents did not differentiate between Mexicans and Mexican American residents, referring to all individuals of Mexican descent as Mexicans or Hispanics.

3. Recent works by feminist social geographers are offering new ways to conceptualize the relationship between gender and place (see, e.g., Doreen Massey 1994; Momsen and Townsend 1987; Rocheleau, Thomas-Slayter, and Wangari 1996; Rose 1993).

4. Here I draw on the Foucaultian definition of discourse, which holds that discourse itself "is a practice, it is structured, and it has real effects" (Ferguson 1994: 18) and, more important, it is not the property of individual actors. Foucault argues that "[t]he key to power is not overt domination of one group by another, but the acceptance by all that there exists 'an ideal, continuous, smooth text that runs

beneath the multiplicity of contradictions, and resolves them in the calm unity of coherent thought'" (Foucault 1972: 155, quoted in Worrall 1990: 8–9). Analysis of the social regulation of citizenship highlights how citizenship is accomplished as a discursive strategy as well as a legal status.

5. As Lisa Lowe (1996: 2) argues, "the collectively forged images, histories, and narratives that place, displace, and replace individuals in relation to the national polity—powerfully shapes who the citizenry is, where they dwell, what they re-member, and what they forget."

6. As Caren Kaplan (1996/2000: 25) explains, "the term 'politics of loca-tion'—particularly in Euro-American feminist criticism—depends upon *several* contradictory but linked discourses of displacement. The notions of a politics of location argues that identities are formed through an attachment to a specific site—national, cultural, gender, racial, ethnic, class, sexual, and so on—and that site must be seen to be partial and not a standard or norm." The term was first used by Adrienne Rich (1986) in her exploration of the limits of feminism and her critique of the totalizing construct of "woman" and racism and homophobia in the U.S. women's movement.

PART III

The Fictional Worlds
of "Unencumbered Workers"

In the United States, welfare reformers have put forward a discourse of personal responsibility in an attempt to bring welfare recipients into line with a mode of work and family organization seen as typical of contemporary "working families." Their view was written into the text of the 1996 legislation establishing work requirements and time-limited assistance, and since then the activities of front-line workers in local agencies have been reorganized in accord with those mandates. The first two chapters in this section explore that reorganization, pointing to considerable gaps between the abstract visions of the policy makers and the real circumstances of low-wage women workers. The third chapter focuses on the work of college and university professors—a very different kind of job and mode of work organization where internalized ideologies of personal responsibility may be as important as institutional enforcement. A final chapter in this section discusses the imperatives of personal responsibility from the perspective of deafblind college students preparing for employment and looking ahead at their prospects for full social inclusion.

In each of these settings, people are pressured to fit themselves to increasingly detached and disembodied versions of work and life, whether imposed or internalized. The consequences are quite different, of course, in these different settings, placing some workers in positions of relative privilege and others—often those with the heaviest responsibilities for others and the greatest bodily challenges—in the harshest of material circumstances.

[7]

Training for Low-Wage Work
TANF Recipients Preparing for Health-Care Work

BRENDA SOLOMON

Editor's Introduction

*The political debate that led to welfare restructuring in the United States
shifted the grounds of discussion, over a number of years, by successfully constructing the use of public assistance as an undesirable "dependency" (Naples
1997); thus, the new TANF program was designed to move recipients into
paid employment. In this chapter, Brenda Solomon explores a job training
program that served welfare-reliant women in New York State in the early
days of the reforms. She highlights the role of the front-line trainer, who not
only teaches nursing skills but also helps the women work themselves up as
responsible and committed to paid work, screening her students along the
way (perhaps inadvertently) for employability.*

*Employability is a key term in the TANF program, but Solomon's analysis
suggests that it is deployed in the policy discourse, and even in front-line implementation, as a textual construct tied only tenuously to the actual circumstances of those it purports to describe. In this case, training opportuities are
tied to local labor markets, which are gendered; men are less employable than
women, simply by virtue of the low-wage jobs available in the area. In addition, welfare-to-work policies locate employability in the individual, assuming that any client should be able to operate as an unencumbered employee.
Yet, most of the women in the program have the multiple responsibilities for
others that are so important in low-income communities—and these responsibilities are not easily shifted to the men in these households. Finally, assessments of employability seem to assume reasonable health and capacities for
work, ignoring the chronic problems often associated with poverty.*

Solomon's analysis also explores the complex role of the front-line trainer. Her activities are guided by the official texts of implementation—a curriculum tied to professional standards of nursing work and the rules that govern eligibility for the program and standards for its completion. But her work is also guided by her familiarity with broader discourses that have set the terms of her students' participation, the discourses of personal responsibility that come to seem like common sense. Front-line workers learn to speak intelligibly to their clients, but they speak as well (and with powerful consequences) in the voice of employers and the state—the voices of ruling.

* * *

In the following pages, relying heavily on the accounts of women I met while writing an ethnography about welfare-to-work training, I discuss the relationship between a welfare-bound policy of personal responsibility and the actualities of women's lives. I use Dorothy E. Smith's (1987, 1990a, b) method of institutional ethnography to make connections between everyday life or taken-for-granted local actions and larger social practices or organizing texts and policies. As Marie Campbell (2002) points out, "the question that an institutional ethnographer wants to answer is: 'what organization of the world maintains the position that these people live and suffer from, and how can my research offer insight into that?'" (4). To answer this question, I take direction particularly from the works of Marjorie L. DeVault (1991, 1999) and Timothy Diamond (1992). From everyday accounts of parents' family food preparation, DeVault (1999) draws attention to the gender and class order of unpaid family care. Similarly, Diamond (1992) underscores the ways everyday activities of care in a nursing home conform to administrative logics of medicine and capitalism. In my ethnography, I link the experiences of women I met in a welfare-to-work training program to a system of work and reward that maintains the social exclusion of poor women and their families, and I show how the ideology of personal responsibility inscribed as social welfare policy in the United States forms welfare training. First, I consider how the ideology of personal responsibility drives funding and a program of job readiness for low-waged women workers. Then, I look at the ways it arranges women recipients' program participation. Next, I review how personal responsibility sets the terms by which front-line workers carry out a policy of welfare-to-work with women recipients. Finally, I examine the ways that resistance by recipients inadvertently conforms to a logic of personal responsibility. I conclude by briefly discussing how women have been divided by welfare and work against one another to their collective disadvantage.

An Ideology of Personal Responsibility Drives the Funding
and Implementation of Job Training for Low-Waged Work

In 1996, when I decided to study close up several iterations of a welfare-
to-work nursing assistant program, the Personal Responsibility and Work
Opportunity Reconciliation Act (PRWORA) had just been signed into law.
Among other revisions, the act replaced the long-standing Aid to Families
with Dependent Children (AFDC) program with Temporary Assistance
for Needy Families (TANF). According to proponents of the so-called reforms, TANF would correct the mistakes of AFDC. In short, it would undo
welfare recipients' dependency on government. In contrast to guaranteed
cash assistance realized under AFDC, TANF would limit cash assistance
and expand job readiness and work mandates. Under PRWORA, monetary
help is temporary, and programs support "allowable work activities" such
as job-readiness training, assistance with employment searches, and services to help recipients start and stay on the job (Edin, Harris, and Sandefur 1998: 36).

The Department of Social Services of the county in which I conducted
my ethnography had used its share of the state's TANF block grant to ar-
range for short-term occupational training, intensive case management,
and job-search assistance, provided by other established educational institutions and programs. The training program that I studied, like many
welfare-to-work programs throughout the country, had been operating
for some time. It ran for ten weeks: five weeks of classroom study and five
weeks of hands-on experience in a nursing home. There was a curriculum,
a textbook, homework, tests, and, for time spent in the nursing home, a
uniform. It was located within the county's Division of Continuing Education and supplied nursing assistants to the three nursing homes and several home-health-aide programs in the area. Few of the trainees paid out
of pocket for the program. Most were supported by government training
funds such as those available through the Department of Labor. However,
because of the incremental policy shifts that underscored job readiness and
culminated in the Act of 1996, while I was studying the program, most of
its trainees were referred by TANF caseworkers and supported by TANF
funds. It is difficult to account for the method that TANF caseworkers used
to select TANF recipients for nursing-assistant training. However, word in
the training program and reports from various caseworkers suggested that
the "higher functioning" applicants were directed to the program.

The changes put in place by the Act of 1996 reflected, in part, a larger shift in work-family responsibility across the country. Simply, a call for poor mothers to take personal responsibility for the care of their children's economic welfare as well as their everyday caretaking needs occurred as more nonwelfare American mothers were managing both work and family obligations. Proponents of PRWORA claimed that the legislation asked nothing more of women who received assistance than to match the practices of seemingly more productive families that did not receive assistance. Still, missing from these claims is an account of the everyday practices of the working mother. While many more affluent American women worked in the labor market, it was not always the case that they were working full time or away from home (Besharov 1995). As these women left home for work, it is likely that they relied on extended-family supports and paid services to make their choice tenable. Some women worked to meet their career goals, others to make up for falling wages earned by their male partners (Levitan et al. 1987/1993), and some simply to supplement their male partners' wages in a seemingly insatiable quest to advance family material worth, status, and influence. Despite the difficulties encountered by these more affluent women surrounding the demands of employment and family, it was commonly assumed that their families remained their priority, that they strongly considered the wishes of their male partners, and that they would choose not to work if their children's welfare were compromised. These were not the prerogatives of poor women as they were called to meet the terms of a welfare-bound ideology of personal responsibility.

An Ideology of Personal Responsibility Drives Women's Participation in TANF

As the terms of TANF were making their way into everyday practices of welfare offices state by state across the country, former AFDC recipients were introduced to the time limits of cash assistance and the mandates of work requirements. It was during this time of transition that I entered the first of three nursing-assistant training program cycles that I studied. Over the course of three programs, I met a nurse trainer whom I call Mrs. Thomas and twenty-eight nursing-assistant trainees, all women and most accommodating work requirements of TANF. I found the women trainees eager to learn and to meet the educational demands of nursing-assistant work. As I have written elsewhere (Solomon 2003), they reminded me of myself.

They viewed education as an opportunity to challenge themselves as they had not before; they saw the classroom as a space to consider possibilities beyond their current circumstances and the likely resulting employment as a welcomed step toward economic security. Similar to what I had experienced when I began new adventures in education, many doubted their ability and perseverance; they were concerned that their shortcomings would be revealed and that they might not find the economic rewards promised by educational advancement. Generally, they expressed a desire to talk back to a larger story about them that disapprovingly rendered them as "welfare mothers." They wanted to show that they were not lazy, dishonest, and unscrupulous and rather were smart and capable, trustworthy and stalwart. As I was told regularly, "We're not like they say we are." They had a great deal more to overcome than I had to meet their educational goals, and much more at stake if they didn't. This is what I found separated me from the women I studied—not our will or our ability but the ways that our lives were steeped in and defined by contrasting economic and social advantage. Although I had known this to be the case, as I sat among these women, I saw up close how the fragile differences between us operated with command and pervasive effect. In part, this effect placed me in a university classroom to meet the demands of doctoral work and them in a nursing-assistant training program to meet the mandates of welfare-to-work. As I see it, similarities and differences such as those between the trainees and me have been manipulated to form the basis for a welfare policy of personal responsibility.

As I said earlier, it is commonly accepted that the demand for personal responsibility asks women on welfare to do no more than what many more advantaged women are doing: work and raise a family. With or without regard for the excessive demands made of them, enough women have actually taken up the work of both caretaker at home and worker in the labor market to make these dual roles normative. Yet, what is largely overlooked in legislative accounts of mother-workers is all that it takes for poor women to do the same as other, more affluent women. While mothers across social and economic lines share similar concerns and responsibilities, especially with regard to their children and families, poor women commonly have even more concerns and responsibilities than their better-off counterparts and far fewer resources to meet those concerns and responsibilities. This was the challenge that faced the women trainees I met: how to meet mothering and work demands as socially and economically advantaged mother-workers do, and do so from multiburdened circumstances with inadequate and compromised resources (Solomon 2001).

To explain, I must talk about the everyday lives of the trainees I met—the demands of family and home they had to negotiate to get to training or work and the ways that service provisions failed to identify and fill the gaps between more affluent and poor mothers' lives. First, consider the least visible work tasks of the women trainees I met: those performed before they arrived at the training program each day. Several explained how they were "up before the birds" making breakfast and lunch and starting dinner. They also talked about the day and night care of ill children that mediated their sleep schedules so that they "never *really* sleep." Several of the women I met, like many other poor women, had children with special needs. In many cases, the children were born with complications and conditions common to poor families that required ongoing care throughout their lives (Duncan, Brooks-Gunn, and Klebanov 1994; Margolis, Greenber, and Keyes 1992; Oliker 1995; and Parker, Greer, and Zuckerman 1988). African American children, who typically suffer even greater economic hardship than their white low-income counterparts, are at even greater risk (Ellwood 1988). Several women explained that, because they cared for their children day in and out, they could intuit their needs. Since they had to leave home each day to meet work requirements, the few who could left their special-needs children with a trusted friend or sister. Of course, when the women used family and friends for child care, they were usually expected to return the favor, and this bartering put even more demands on their time (Edin and Lein 1997). The rest of the women had to leave their children in day-care facilities that were generally ill equipped to respond to their children's health complications. These women explained how, over the course of a day, their minds would wander to concerns about how their children were faring without them, especially if they knew one of them was particularly out of sorts that day. As one woman told me, "I'm here but as soon as I get a chance I'm thinkin' about my kid. No one knows what he needs like I do."

One source of help that only a few women relied on regularly, and typically only for short periods of time or in a pinch, was their male partners. While care of children was an obvious concern that TANF addressed, though often inadequately, through day-care provisions, the program largely ignored the women's male partners. Most of the men in the lives of the women I met were unemployed and/or disabled. Their frustration and anger with their own job losses and inability to find work were exacerbated by the women's work requirements. Even when the men were part of the household of record, it was often their women partners who were deemed by welfare officials to be more employable, a result of the greater availability locally of low-wage jobs gender-typed as female. Thus, while the historical arrangement of work would have males considered for employment over their female counterparts, jobs such as nursing-assistant work, commonly compared with mothering or caretaking, were among the better jobs in the low-wage job market. While several of the women's male partners expressed a desire to be the breadwinner, none of them wanted to be a nursing assistant. As a result, there was an understanding between the TANF caseworkers and the couples with whom they met; the women were best suited for the work the caseworker had to offer.

Despite the character of the jobs these women were preparing for, it seemed that the women's employment of any sort regularly proved threatening to their male partners. As one woman put it, "I try not to throw it in his face. I try to make it as if nothing has changed but he's mad and that's all there is to it!" The incidence of domestic violence associated with welfare women's employment requirements appears to be a persistent problem for welfare-to-work women, though researchers find that it is sometimes overlooked or viewed skeptically by welfare-to-work caseworkers, (Kurz 1998; Pearson, Thoennes, and Griswold 1999; Raphael 1999; Sable et al. 1999; and Scott, London, and Edin 2000). As I saw tensions play out for the women I met, it was as if the government had forfeited poor men's place in the gendered order of work. Ignoring the resulting frustration and shame for these men, the program created difficulties for women with their male partners and provided no resources to help the family to meet those difficulties.

Like their children and also because of the uncertainty and hardship common to poverty, the men often suffered from some form of physical ailment or disability that accounted for their employment difficulties. Many of the women I met also had some sort of emotional, mental, or physical health care need (Albert and King 1999; Lens 2002). While critics argued early on in the welfare-to-work debate for such assurances as child support, medical protections, and jobs for welfare women that could support families (Ellwood 1988: 178), a recent report of the U.S. General Accounting Office (2001) found that 44 percent of TANF recipients had a physical or mental impairment that affected their ability to work. And researchers have reported that these physical and mental impairments, such as those experienced within the families I met, limited the mothers' attempts to leave welfare for work (Brandon and Hogan 2004). Even so, as the women trainees I met were about to enter the labor force, their ability to meet the demands of home and employer were irregularly assessed. For example, one woman with a major psychiatric disorder found it more difficult to manage her health care needs while at work. Without state guidance, whether she received support or not depended upon the discretion of her caseworker; although the woman's work requirements were eventually reduced, some caseworkers took an active role in meeting her needs while others did not.

In addition to these family health concerns, most of the women I met had not lived in their current residence for more than a year. Trouble with neighbors, increases in rent, structural failures, and neglect of housing kept them moving from poor housing unit to poor housing unit (Olson and Pavetti 1996). Others have reported on the greater likelihood of fire, burglary and landlord neglect that interferes with poor people's ability to get and keep a job (Oliker 1995). Several of the women I met found themselves in the middle of their neighbors' domestic disputes as a result of which other women would seek refuge in their homes. Likewise, they were regularly counted on to look after other children in their neighborhood. Of course, these obligations did not evaporate as the women began attending welfare-to-work training. Rather, they had to be negotiated alongside work training—and homework.

Adding to these difficulties, in the small city where the women I met lived, public transportation was spotty. There were few bus stops, and buses ran only during the day. Jan L. Hagen and Irene Lurie (1994), from their three-year JOB implementation study of ten states, reported transportation to be one of the major barriers to client program participation. They noted that the concern was not just with the availability of transportation services but also with program allocations for transportation. Hagen and Lurie (1994) also indicated that, while the problem was most severe in rural areas, it was a prominent issue in small cities, in areas just outside major cities, and even in metropolitan areas where employment at times was most available in suburban areas. Despite efforts by TANF to address transportation issues, distance from employment confounds women's ability to leave welfare for work, adds to their job expenses, and further depresses their earnings (Ong and Blumenberg 1998).

Many of the women trainees whom I met wondered how many other women there were in the county who would have liked to be in the nursing-assistant training program but just could not possibly get there. As it was, the women who did find a way back and forth each day had their share of problems. Few could rely on public transportation. For instance, one woman opted to ride her bike to and from the training program and later to the houses where she was a home health aide. Those who did use public transportation often had to walk quite a distance before they reached a bus stop. Since most had to get their own kids off to school before they could leave for the training program, they were in a time crunch and had to find rides with friends or family or, as a last resort, call a taxi. Often enough, catching a ride had more than monetary consequences. For instance, one woman's grandfather drove her back and forth each day. However, when he became ill, in addition to losing her ride, she had to help with his physical care. Another woman, unable to drive herself, got a ride each day with her husband, who reportedly disapproved of her efforts to get a job. Yet he was suspicious of her activities and drove erratically to scare her. Another woman took a ride from a neighbor. In addition to having to pay for the ride, she felt beholden to the neighbor and helped her out (more than she would have liked) with child care. When the neighbor's car broke down, the trainee walked several miles to the program, which was located on the outskirts of town and just off a well-traveled road with few pedestrian walkways.

The multiple responsibilities these women had to manage to meet a public policy of responsibility were beyond policymakers' understanding and thus were underaddressed in their legislation. While needs typical of more advantaged women workers, such as day care and medical care, were written into policy, the numerous responsibilities and needs particular to women living in poverty were largely unrecognized and overlooked. Because the program failed to account for these, the women I met were further disadvantaged and the complex care of their families threatened. Even so, most of the women I met managed to meet work-family demands as outlined by TANF. Their successful transition from welfare to work translated into cheap labor for the medical industry. Working for low wages, at unusual hours, without room for advancement, and with inadequate benefits, especially without provisions for time off to care for sick children (Brooks and Buckner 1996; Hagen and Davis 1995; Heymann and Earle 1999), the women I met occupied the lowest position within the medical hierarchy. As nursing assistants in nursing homes, the women performed low-wage work that often replaced another women's unpaid caring labor—likely a more affluent working daughter's care for her ailing parents or in-laws. Welfare-to-work formed the terms on which women of welfare status could be made into "a special labour market category" (Ng 1990: 97), commodifying their labor to meet the gap in caring labor realized as better-off women worked in the labor market. That is, the poor women's work allowed other, likely more advantaged women to continue in their jobs.

An Ideology of Personal Responsibility Drives the Front-Line Trainer's Activities

For the women I met, an ideology of personal responsibility arranged not only everyday life at home and the need to get to work but also what happened in training and on the job. For instance, it accounted for the work of the nurse-trainer, Mrs. Thomas: what she had to do to help the women meet training requirements and obtain employment. Simply, Mrs. Thomas was supposed to ready the women for nursing-assistant work. Yet, by her report and my observation, the curriculum she was handed did not provide an adequate bridge between welfare and work. In Mrs. Thomas's words, "This [the nursing-assistant training textbook] has everything they need to know and it shows them how to do it too. That's important. But, [she laughs and shakes her head] it doesn't help them figure out how they're going to get to work every day—how to manage their lives to be nursing assistants and mothers." Thus, like the trainees, Mrs. Thomas had to do more than what was accounted for in her job to be successful and produce successful trainees. One way she did this was by creating what I have described elsewhere as informal feathers of the formal training day (Solomon 2003). That is, Mrs. Thomas used a day's worth of training not only to school the women in nursing-assistant work, as was expected, but also to school them in the successful practices of working mothers. She encouraged them to express their hopes and fears and conspired with them around the family and child care they had to do to get to work. If some were close to meeting training requirements but falling a bit short, Mrs. Thomas met with them after a day of training to help. She let women make up missed days for commonplace absences to care for their sick children. She helped women figure out how to handle their disgruntled boyfriends and unresponsive landlords. However, as helpful as Mrs. Thomas could be, she had her limits.

Considering the time and resources available, Mrs. Thomas assisted women whose problems were closest to what was familiar to her and to what she could accept. While, for the most part, I do not believe these choices were conscious ones, she put effort where it would most likely be met with success. As Kamini Maraj Grahame (1998) points out from her study of job training for immigrant women, "women who appear to already have the cultural resources of an American middle class, or appear able to develop those with a little help, are more likely to be seen as potential successes" (89). In this way, the women whose lives could be brought in line with those with more financial resources had a better chance of being successful nursing assistants and were regularly rewarded with Mrs. Thomas's attention.

To make it, with or without Mrs. Thomas's aid, the women had to figure out how to respond to a work world arranged by the affluent without the resources that the affluent take for granted to get by. As I saw it, somehow the women had to rid themselves of the demands of poor women or meet those demands with minimal impact to the training program and, later, their jobs. They either had to stop caring for extended family and friends or care only for those who could offer support in return. I watched as many of the women ran themselves ragged trying to attend to the increasingly complex demands that filled their lives. I thought of the term "supermom" and how it had been used to capture the extraordinary ways that working women do it all and yet how it failed to capture the extrasuper demands put upon the poor women I met. In many ways, Mrs. Thomas appeared to understand the injustices that faced the women in her training program. She regularly summed up her position by saying, "I'm always for the underdog." Still, her personal white, middle-class standpoint, along with her position as professional nurse trainer, directed her not to bring government and professional programs into line with the women's lives but, rather, to bring the women into compliance with government and the professions. While in many ways Mrs. Thomas demonstrated that she was for the underdog, it also seemed that she failed to acknowledge the full extent of how the women I met strained to "do it all." To honor a system of family and work that was based on the lives of those with greater social and material resources, the women commonly had to separate themselves from the ways they understood and had always carried out responsibility to themselves and others; in some cases, women had to forfeit long-standing relationships and cherished practices altogether.

The reward for mimicking middle-class practices and for adopting some sort of posture consistent with a middle-class model was to avoid the ridicule often directed at women on welfare. As others have found (Fraser and Gordon 1994; Nelson 2002; Reid 2003; Stuber and Kronebusch 2004), when women exit welfare, they distance themselves from the punitive mea-

sures and harsh characterizations associated with it and regularly feel tre-
mendous relief. Even though their work performances were not rewarded
with livable wages, to be spared the critical treatment extended to so-called
welfare moms was a major weight off the shoulders of the women I met.
Their desire to distance themselves from welfare at almost any cost fit with
the needs for low-wage women workers to carry out the undesirable, back-
breaking caretaking work of the nursing-home industry.

An Ideology of Personal Responsibility Drives Resistance by Women and Front-Line Workers

Another, and final, way that the ideology of personal responsibility entered into everyday life and arranged the terrain of welfare-to-work was in
the ways that women like the twenty-eight trainees I met were able to resist
its rule. I found that the ideology of personal responsibility led the women
I met to challenge its demands in three ways: one, by drawing from traditional family values; two, by calling the practices of more affluent working
women into question; and three, by extending the claims of personal responsibility.

For instance, some of the women enlisted traditional family values and
reported that they wished to stay home and raise their children or that
their children with special needs particularly needed their mothers. As one
woman simply told me, "My children need me more than the people in
the nursing home need me." Her concerns were similar to those raised by
other women leaving welfare for work reported in other studies (Burtless
1997; Butler and Seguino 1998; Loprest 1999; Parrot 1998; and Pearlmutter
and Bartle 2000). The women I met who made claims against the demand
that they provide family care *and* shoulder economic responsibility did so
by enlisting the traditional value of a mother's primary job to her children.
They were able to argue that the extent of family care they needed to perform was enough to prioritize it *over* economic responsibility.

Some of the women also drew on traditional family values to state their
continued commitment to their overlooked and undervalued partners.
They professed their will to stay with their men despite their shortcomings
and to acknowledge their male partners' frustration with regard to being
denied or unable to provide for their families. In some cases, the women
understood that their partners' mistreatment of them was connected to the
state's mistreatment of their partners. As one woman explained, "He is a

good person but what do you expect from someone who believes it should be him, and not me, out there getting a job and then, you know, they [the welfare agency] have nothing for him?" Notably, while the women customarily stood by their men, none of the women I met went so far as to suggest that their male partners, rather than themselves, should actually be the primary breadwinners for their families. I believe the women were grateful for the financial sway employment offered them.

From my observations in the nursing home and from later interviews with the women as they worked in the nursing-home industry, even as some of the women's family values-based claims were met with empathy, the empathy extended to them by the trainer, other aides, and, later, employers did not alter the expectations surrounding their family-work responsibilities.

Another way that women were able to talk back to an ideology of personal responsibility was by challenging more affluent working women— those to whom they were most compared and in close proximity. After all, the poor women I met were vilified by a policy that, at once, contrasted them to and exalted better-off working moms. A policy of personal responsibility put in place and encouraged this contrast and comparison. It positioned affluent women against poor women. It also employed more advantaged women in the grooming of poor women for employment.

This talking back could be seen in the exchanges between some of the women in the training program and Mrs. Thomas. It was Mrs. Thomas who encouraged them to leave their unsupportive male partners, took points off for the use of improper English and misspellings, and was unwilling to work with them for missing too much time for family crises. It was Mrs. Thomas who showed them how to dress and act to meet the social expectations of a world of work as they entered jobs that did not offer wages or benefits to support their continued efforts to meet those expectations. Many of the women expressed their displeasure with Mrs. Thomas's assumptions about what they needed or should let go of. They understood her demands in terms of her personal "pet peeves" and not in terms of the inventions of the welfare state or the medical industry (Solomon 2003).

It was also the case that many of the women mumbled under their breath or spoke over one another at the break table about working for "the man" and white dominance, or how they were being exploited by welfare and substandard working conditions in the nursing home. Yet their busy family-work days did not put them in easy contact with legislators and heads of government service or nursing homes. Rather, their concerns were more immediately directed at and responded to by front-line workers in welfare and nursing, largely working women. While they were more affluent than the trainees, the women who worked with trainees were in less-than-lucrative jobs. Instead, the collective labor of the trainees and front-line workers who carried out welfare policy, like Mrs. Thomas, kept economic power in place. Policy ideology placed poor and more advantaged women at odds with one another; policy implementation placed them in close proximity to one another. These arrangements helped to focus their attention on the actions and inactions of particular women and off the ways that women were collectively being used and disadvantaged within a system of work and reward.

Sadly, I found that the most effective way women were able to contest the policy of personal responsibility was by invoking its ideology and extending narratives of individual deficits. That is, the women were sometimes motivated to declare that their individual problems were worse than welfare policy assumed—so much so that they were unable or unfit to work. They could resist welfare-to-work mandates by drawing attention to incompetences that might place them beyond the reach of the program. Thus, an accepted way to avoid the demands made of them was for the women to demonstrate personal *irresponsibility* to an extent that would exempt them from policy demands. For instance, some claims of mental illness and family dysfunction could keep work demands at bay. While some women have been able to extend time limits or keep from meeting job requirements altogether, as a result of these practices the most vulnerable and challenged women are left in the welfare system (Albelda 2002; Nightingale 2001). As Schram (2000) explains, such an outcome, in turn, may strengthen the idea that welfare use is "a product of personal characteristics, habits, and conditions rather than of political and economic structures and processes" and, even more, "appears to justify a paternalistic approach" (81) toward recipients. It seems extremely troubling that the most immediate and effective way for women to resist the policy's rule was to engage in claims that would ultimately further pathologize themselves and their families.

Conclusion

One year after their graduation from the nursing-assistant program, I was able to locate only eighteen of the twenty-eight women. Fourteen of those I spoke with were in health-care-related jobs. Six of the women were full-time nursing assistants, one was a full-time home health aide, two others were part-time nursing assistants, three were on disability due to nursing-assistant work-related injuries, and two were on maternity leave from nursing-assistant jobs. Another one of the women had completed a Licensed Practical Nurse program. Three more were working in non-health-related jobs (Solomon 2001).

Most of the women with whom I spoke seemed confident and strong—and from their reports they needed to be. Largely, they were no better off financially than when they had been on welfare. The costs associated with work absorbed any gains they might have made, or more. Those who were about to use up their sick time to care for ailing children found their jobs on the line. For some, money owed to landlords and creditors were at a tipping point. While three of the women were on disability, others complained of the physical strain of lifting patients and the risks involved in contact with patients' body fluids. Most stated that their efforts to keep up with their children's needs and the demands of their employment had made it nearly impossible for them to get a good night's (or day's) sleep. And, as confident and strong as I may have found them, the hardships they reported had taken their toll.

Remarkably, despite the difficulties they described, most reported that they were glad to be off welfare and away from the scrutiny that welfare drew to them. They told me that being off welfare was worth the difficulties they faced each day—at least no one was looking over their shoulder or telling them what to do. What little money they had was theirs, and they did not have to be grateful to anyone for it; as one woman put it, "It's my money and no one can tell me what to do with it." They often added a few words of appreciation for Mrs. Thomas. Most believed that, as difficult as she could be at times, it was, after all, Mrs. Thomas who had helped them get to where they were. And, again, most of them believed that they were better off. While the trainees had moved on, after one year, Mrs. Thomas was where the women had left her: still training nursing assistants. Yet I remember her remark to the women that one day, in the not-too-distant future, she would likely end up in one of the homes that the women worked in, and, of course, she hoped they would remember her well.

It is likely that women's dual role in the labor market and in the family, along with the comparison between welfare-reliant and working women, will continue to shape both women's lives and welfare policy for some time. What is more striking are the questions and comparisons that have been neglected in public debate and in subsequent reforms. For instance, how is it that a policy of personal responsibility focuses only on women's behaviors and fails to call into question long-standing practices that consistently advantage men? How does a policy focused on women obscure the divisions between poor, disproportionately Black and Latino men and better off, disproportionately white men? And, finally, how might a policy of personal responsibility hold the most wealthy accountable to the state?

Thinking about the formulations of personal responsibility that accept and promote women's disadvantage and serve the wealthiest at the expense of those with fewest resources leads me to a final consideration of resistance among the women in the training program and with Mrs. Thomas. Given how the training was set up and run, there were limits to Mrs. Thomas's resistance. For instance, if she had done extra work with the women not to bring them into the fold of working mothers but to help them organize against practices that further exploit them, she would likely have put at risk her professional position and status. She would also have jeopardized the trainees' opportunities to meet welfare-to-work guidelines and become employed, goals they sought and worked for. With little if anything at all to fall back on, if the women in the training program were to resist welfare policy to an extent that called their commitment to employment into question, their immediate subsistence would be threatened. While resistance is possible, there is a great deal at stake in resisting ways that do not further the goals of personal responsibility or fit the patterns that ultimately reinscribe women's subservient role in domestic and labor market affairs.

The ideology of personal responsibility and its expression in welfare policy works to keep those in poverty, poor women particularly, the subject of analysis. It forfeits poor men altogether. It serves to pressure more affluent women into meeting the complex demands of family and work in order to maintain their man's privilege at home and at least an illusion of their own privilege in the labor market. Such policy should be resisted, but not in ways that further exploit poor women or separate women from underpaid and poor men, as personal responsibility accomplishes. It should be resisted in ways that are formed from women and underpaid and unemployed men's common exploitation, on terms that best serve their interests.

Over and over again, the women I met remarked how the most important yet unexpected outcome of the welfare-to-work training program for them was the alliances they formed with other women. Such alliances could be extended toward accomplishing not a responsibility defined by government and the interests of the most privileged members of the society but rather a responsibility to what might after all best sustain underpaid and poor workers, especially women. Certainly, the women I met deserve nothing less.

[8]

Women's Lives, Welfare's Time Limits

ELLEN K. SCOTT AND ANDREW S. LONDON

Editor's Introduction

Debates over welfare reform in the United States did not end with the passage of new legislation; reformers, advocates, and researchers continue to argue over the likely costs and benefits of new arrangements, especially potential dangers of time-limited benefits. In this chapter, Ellen Scott and Andrew London report on research they conducted in one of several multicity longitudinal research projects designed to assess the effects of restructuring as it proceeded. In their ethnographic component, they deployed a critical qualitative interview method to follow recipients as new provisions took effect. Here, they examine the stories of fifteen women who hit time limits and therefore lost assistance they had relied on. Although the researchers did not begin with an institutional ethnographic focus on the texts of this policy change, their account provides a striking and essential contrast to policy and media reports that emphasize the official measure of success, reductions in the welfare rolls. In addition, these women's stories carry traces of the textual administration of reform: the image of the "ticking clock," the warnings they receive in advance of cutoffs, the plans made by their "self-sufficiency coaches," and the official assessments of risk that do not recognize their needs.

While the chapter is built around the women's stories, one can see as well the ongoing transformation within the welfare regime of fundamental ideas about state responsibilities for protecting and supporting vulnerable groups, especially children and their parents. That shift can be seen in the conduct and interpretation of the county's child safety review: it is clear that clients need help, but they're not officially "at risk." One former recipient, herself doing relatively well (though in the kind of low-wage job typical for those moving off welfare), wondered why it is not possible to offer those in need "that little added push that we need." And the final story in this chapter, which shows how a precarious arrangement can begin to fray and then cascade into disaster, suggests how critical just a little help can be

* * *

> The logic behind the rhetoric is impeccable—if assistance is actually hurting the poor by creating dependence, then denying it is not cruel but compassionate.
> —Somers and Block (2005: 265)

The crowning achievement of the neoliberal restructuring of the American welfare state, the passage of the Personal Responsibility and Work Opportunity Reconciliation Act (PRWORA), in 1996, represented the triumph of the linked ideological tenets of individualism and market fundamentalism (Kingfisher 2002; Morgen and Maskovsky 2003; O'Connor 2001; Somers and Block 2005). For more than one hundred years, policymakers and researchers in the United States have debated whether poverty is a product of structural inequality and labor market exploitation or of individual failing and behavioral weakness (Katz 1989). Always dominant in this debate, the behaviorists finally won when the PRWORA passed with bipartisan support. A neoconservative logic of individualism—the view that poverty is a problem of cultural deficits and lack of motivation rather than of an unequal distribution of power and wealth—became largely uncontested in policy arenas (O'Connor 2001).

In this era of welfare reform, "dependency," as it had been constructed in popular, political, and legislative discourse (Fraser and Gordon 1994; Misra, Moller, and Karides 2003; Naples 1997), rather than poverty and hardship, was constructed as the problem that needed to be solved; welfare reliance diminished the motivation to work for pay and thereby to be self-sufficient (Kingfisher 2002). Women's unpaid carework was rendered invisible (Cancian and Oliker 2000; Cancian, Kurz, London, Reviere, and Tuominen 2002), and politicians and the public adopted in mutually reinforcing ways a "rhetoric of perversity" to criticize and ultimately dismantle the welfare system; the very system that was intended to reduce poverty or mitigate some of its most negative consequences was believed to cause laziness and dependence and "thus inexorably exacerbate[d] the very social ills that [it] was meant to cure" (Somers and Block 2005: 265). Within this context, the limited notion of "personal responsibility" conceived by many policymakers and researchers became the "conceptual currency" of welfare reform; as such, it became the ideological engine driving programmatic restructuring, staff training and reward, and interactions with welfare-reliant women (see the chapters by Solomon and Ridzi in this volume), as well as, sometimes, the frame through which women came to think about themselves and their own choices and experiences in relation to family, work, and welfare. Promoting the disembodied worker notion of "personal responsibility" that predominated in welfare reform-related texts and discourses provided policymakers and welfare administrators a culturally acceptable means to reorder poor women's apparently disordered priorities, practices, and relationships to the state without having to take responsibility for addressing their actual, embodied lives and circumstances. It also helped to ensure an adequate supply of domestic, low-wage workers, which the New Economy increasingly demands (Marchevsky and Theoharis 2006)

Within this neoconservative ideological framework, time-limited, temporary assistance to needy families (TANF), as the new welfare regime is called, became normalized. The logic of perversity and the demand that welfare recipients become self-sufficient through their wage labor became cemented in the policy debates and, ultimately, implemented in TANF programs (see, for example, Ridzi 2004; Ridzi and London 2006). No one with the power—with "epistemic privilege" (Somers and Block 2005)—to be effectively heard in these debates and change their course challenged the dominant ideas therein. Ignoring the exigencies of the low-wage labor market, this public narrative often also actively ignored or denied the enormity of the problems in the lives of some people forced thereby to rely on welfare (London, Scott, and Hunter 2002; Polit, London, and Martinez 2001; Scott, London, and Myers 2002). The hegemonic political discourse erased from view the life stories of those who might contradict the claims that the welfare system produced dependency and laziness and that welfare reform had been an unmitigated success with few negative consequences (Marchevsky and Theoharis 2006). Women's lived experiences, knowledge, and claims for the right to living wages, health-care coverage, and resources to care for themselves and their children were generally excluded, marginalized, or rendered secondary to other concerns in both the policy debates about welfare reform and the evaluations of TANF programs that followed (Christopher 2004; Mink 1998).

In this chapter, we examine the consequences of time limits and the loss of access to part of the public safety net for women who relied on cash welfare and resided in some of the most disadvantaged neighborhoods in Cleveland, Ohio. Using data from in-depth, qualitative interviews with welfare-reliant women, we interrogate the claim that welfare reform and time limits were an unmitigated success.[1] Interviewed in an open-ended, conversational manner many times between 1998 and 2001, fourteen[2] of the thirty-eight women in our sample were cut off of cash benefits when they hit Cleveland's initial thirty-six-month time limit in October 2000 or shortly thereafter. From these interviews, we obtain a sense of their complex life circumstances and the varied ways they managed to survive when they initially lost cash assistance. As their stories reveal, in some instances they were able to make a meager living in inadequate jobs, while in others they relied on family and friends. Yet some of these women found neither work nor family upon whom they could rely. Their stories are devastating. All of these stories contest the dominant claims that time limits do no harm and help to facilitate a positive transformation among the urban poor in the United States. By centering these women's experiences, we are able to describe some of the overwhelming circumstances in which "personal responsibility" and "self-sufficiency" may not be enough and the injustice of time-limiting access to cash benefits and a minimal safety net for some of the most disadvantaged and vulnerable people in our society. We are also, along with the other authors included in this volume, able to contribute to a larger institutional ethnographic project of mapping the ideological contours and discursive technologies of the new economic regime, which emphasizes competitiveness, accountability, personal responsibility, and work as empowerment, demanding more from workers while systematically marginalizing their human needs.

Welfare's Time Limits

Time limits to the receipt of cash benefits constitute one of the most significant changes embedded in the new welfare system. No longer can income-eligible households receive cash benefits continuously until the youngest child turns eighteen. Rather, the new federal welfare regulations dictate a five-year lifetime limit and allow states or counties to either opt for shorter time limits or extend eligibility using their own resources (General Accounting Office 2002). As of early 2002, most states had time limits that result in termination of families' welfare benefits (Bloom, Farrell, Fink, and Adams-Ciardullo 2002): twenty-three states had a sixty-month termination time limit, and seventeen states had a shorter termination time limit. In addition, eight states and the District of Columbia had a time limit that reduces benefits or changes the form of benefits after the limit is reached, and two states had no time limit. Because the latter two categories include large states like California, Michigan, and New York, they constitute nearly half of the national welfare caseload. Bloom et al. (2002: ES-1) note that "[A] central theme that emerges . . . is that time limits are far more complex than they seem. This complexity is evident in the states' diverse policy choices, the way time limits are implemented at the local level, and the difficulties in interpreting data and studies about time limits." They estimate that 231,000 families had reached either the sixty-month federal time limit (54,000) or a shorter state time limit (176,000) as of the end of 2001. However, it was not precisely clear how many of these families had their cases closed or their benefits reduced due to time limits because of the complexities noted earlier.

There has been a proliferation of state and local policy evaluations that focus in whole or in part on the effects of time limits. These include studies in California (Crow and Anderson 2004); Connecticut (Bloom, Scrivener, Michalopoulos, Morris, Hendra, Adams-Ciardullo, and Walter 2002); Florida (Bloom, Kemple, Morris, Scrivener, Verma, and Hendra 2000; Brock, Kwakye, Polyné, Richburg-Hayes, Seith, Stepick, and Stepick 2004); Massachusetts (Massachusetts Department of Transitional Assistance 2000); Ohio (Bania, Coulton, Lalich, Martin, Newburn, and Pasqualone 2001; Brock, Coulton, London, Polit, Richburg-Hayes, Scott, and Verma 2002); Virginia (Gordon, Kauff, Kuhns, and Loeffler 2002); and Wisconsin (Gooden and Doolittle 2001). One study explicitly examines the effects of time limits and make-work-pay strategies on children's well-being (Gennetian and Morris 2003). Because a detailed, critical review of these reports is beyond the scope of this chapter, we focus specifically on describing how the time limit was implemented in Cleveland, Ohio, the site of our study, and women's initial experiences in the aftermath of its implementation.

According to Brock et al. (2002), in Ohio, responsibility for administering "Ohio Works First" (OWF), the state TANF program, was devolved to the county level. In Cuyahoga County (Cleveland), Ohio, OWF administrators implemented a thirty-six-month time limit with eligibility for an additional twenty-four months of cash assistance following twenty-four months of nonreceipt. From the inception of welfare reform in Cleveland, officials made it very clear that they had every intention of implementing the thirty-six-month time limit, which would commence beginning in October 2000, for all households that had received cash benefits continuously since October 1997. Beginning in October 1997, welfare recipients received monthly letters informing them of the "time left on their clocks," and welfare offices were decorated with huge wall clocks with the inscription "Your Clock Is Ticking." There was no mistaking that welfare officials were serious about the time limit. Further, they did not intend to issue exemptions, regardless of circumstances, despite the fact that federal regulations permitted the exemption of 20 percent of the monthly caseload.

Just prior to the implementation of the first time-limit OWF benefit terminations, in October 2000, the Welfare Department established new services meant to cushion the blow that would result from families' loss of their primary source of income. Caseworkers, renamed "self-sufficiency coaches" at the outset of the implementation of Cleveland's welfare reform, were instructed to conduct in-person or phone interviews with all families facing an imminent time limit. In these interviews, self-sufficiency coaches were expected to confirm that recipients understood that their cash benefits were about to end and to ensure that families continued to receive Food Stamps, Medicaid, and child-care subsidies for pre-school-age children. Some families were assisted in making applications for emergency funds for rent, utilities, appliances, a car, or other employment-related expenses. Additionally, workers were expected to confirm that recipients had a plan regarding how they were going to replace the income from cash benefits. In the spirit of the legislative mandate that recipients take "personal responsibility" for their lives, workers asked clients to write a statement that spelled out their plan for supporting their families.

Two new emergency programs provided caseworkers with some alternatives if recipients faced being cut off cash benefits and had no other options: one was a job search and subsidized employment program, and the other provided six months of additional cash assistance for individuals with particular barriers to employment (e.g., teen parents who had infants and who were finishing an educational program, individuals who were caring for a disabled child or relative, or those who were physically or mentally ill). Yet recipients had no expectation that such programs would be available to them, and caseworkers were highly discouraged from using these programs.[3] The message was clear: the time limit was real and virtually unavoidable if women remained on the welfare rolls.

To ensure that their radical effort to reduce caseloads through strict adherence to a thirty-six-month time limit did not harm children unduly, OWF administrators also implemented a child safety review process whenever clients did not attend their pre-time-limit interviews or did not appear to have sufficient income to replace their cash assistance. In the first year after the time limit went into effect, approximately 1,900 families were referred for in-home child safety reviews, which were conducted by social service workers from community-based agencies. According to county staff, "the vast majorities of families who were contacted did not appear to be at risk of severe problems like homelessness or child abuse or neglect, though they often needed economic supports and other services" (Brock et al. 2002: Sum-11).

In the end, in the year following October 2000, four thousand people, most of whom were single mothers with children, were cut off cash benefits in Cleveland. An additional 433 participated in the job search program, and 155 participated in the emergency program to extend cash benefits.

Women's Lives

As a focus on women's lives and experiences makes clear, there were many welfare-reliant women and families who could have benefited from continued assistance for periods longer than thirty-six months and who were harmed by the loss of cash assistance. Yet, the fact that the time limit was aggressively implemented with little recourse to emergency programs and extensions of cash assistance even when people had compelling need suggests that the question of harm had shifted dramatically in the years subsequent to welfare reform. What might previously have been considered harm no longer seemed to raise the ire of our public officials. The concern for children and parents living in poverty and the limited sense of collective responsibility expressed in AFDC's entitlement, which vaguely acknowledged the multiple structural causes of poverty, gave way to a draconian, individualist explanation that placed responsibility squarely on the shoulders of the recipients with little or no regard for inadequate school systems, racial and gender discrimination, the economic conditions of urban neighborhoods, or the physical and mental consequences of long-term poverty.

Data from the Urban Change survey (Brock et al. 2002) provide some indication of the circumstances of the women in Cleveland who were terminated from cash assistance because of the thirty-six-month time limit and the degree to which they were more disadvantaged than women who were not at immediate risk of reaching the time limit (i.e., those who had more than twelve months of cash benefit eligibility remaining in 2001). Overall, 15 percent of the women in the sample were terminated from

OWF cash assistance because of the time limit. Although all of the women were single mothers between eighteen and forty-five years of age who were on AFDC and who were living in neighborhoods of concentrated poverty and welfare receipt when they were sampled randomly from administrative records in May 1995, the women who ultimately hit the time limit in October 2000 or shortly thereafter were less likely than the women who had considerable time left on their clocks to have a high school diploma or GED as of May 1995 (36.9 percent versus 61.7 percent) and more likely to have been on welfare for eighteen or more months out of the prior twenty-four months (90.3 percent versus 82.8 percent). However, the two groups did not differ with respect to whether they had worked for pay in the prior year.

The Urban Change survey data also provide comparative, descriptive information about the employment patterns, experiences, challenges, and material circumstances of women who were terminated from welfare and those who had more than a year of eligibility left as of the 2001 interview. Women who hit the time limit had worked in fewer months in the prior forty-eight months (18.0 versus 31.5 months on average); were less likely to be working at the time of the 2001 interview (59.2 percent versus 76.9 percent); were more likely to be neither working nor on welfare (38.8 percent versus 15.2 percent); were more likely to have a child with an illness or disability (32.4 percent versus 18.4 percent); and were more likely to face three or more out of eleven barriers to employment (69.9 percent versus 37.9 percent) than those with twelve or more months of eligibility remaining. Despite the high levels of barriers they faced, 96 percent of the women who were terminated because of the time limit had worked for pay at some point during the forty-eight-month period prior to the 2001 interview. Among those who had ever worked during that forty-eight-month period, the women who hit the time limit had lower average hourly wages at the current/most recent job than those with substantial remaining eligibility ($7.31 versus $9.14), lower average weekly earnings ($257.32 versus $355.78), and a lower likelihood of having a job that offered medical benefits (14.3 percent versus 50.9 percent). A much higher proportion of the women who hit the time limit were also living in poverty in 2001 (78.3 percent versus 40.8 percent). Partly as a result of their high levels of poverty and low earnings, a much higher proportion of women who had hit the time limit retained Food Stamps (92.2 percent versus 33.5 percent) and Medicaid for themselves (87.3 percent versus 34.7 percent) than did women who had twelve or more months of eligibility remaining on their thirty-six-month time clock.

Comparisons such as these cannot be interpreted as evidence that the time limit per se was responsible for the relative disadvantage faced by those who hit the time limit. Rather, as Bania et al. (2001: 2) note: "the imposition of time limits has served as a sorting mechanism, resulting in the most employment-ready welfare recipients leaving welfare prior to hitting time limits, and the most challenged exiting upon hitting their limits." Nevertheless, these data help illustrate the extent to which the loss of a guaranteed cash assistance safety net may add to the burdens and disadvantages faced by some of our most vulnerable fellow citizens. That this is indeed the case is exemplified further by the lived experiences of the women who participated in the longitudinal, qualitative interview portion of the Urban Change Study in Cleveland.

Nearly 40 percent (15/38) of the women we interviewed from 1997/1998 to 2001 for the qualitative interview portion of the Urban Change Study in Cleveland said they were cut off cash benefits when they hit the time limit. With the exception of one person who seemed confused about the reason for the loss of her cash benefits, all of the women we spoke with understood the time limit and expected the loss of cash welfare when they were finally terminated.[4] They reported receiving letters monthly about their welfare status, and some said that they had phone or in-person conversations with caseworkers about the imminent termination of benefits. However, beyond warning recipients that they would lose cash benefits, our respondents reported that the Welfare Department made no interventions when the time limit neared, even when families had no clear source of alternative support. The Welfare Department in Cleveland did an exceptional job of providing advance warning that families would lose their cash benefits, and it managed a smooth process of promptly terminating families when they had received cash for thirty-six months. However, emergency programs for the most part were not utilized, even when families faced dire circumstances. Most former recipients, however, continued to receive Medicaid (12/15) and Food Stamps (9/15). Some continued to receive child-care subsidies, as well.

Of the fifteen women who hit the time limit, seven continued in or subsequently found employment, while eight did not. All but one had multiple problems that are often considered to be barriers to employment, including low educational attainment and their own or their children's mental and physical health problems. Some had very serious health problems. Most had histories of domestic violence. A few had histories of drug or alcohol addiction. Almost 75 percent had a pre-school-age child during the time of the study. Most were living in poverty, but none had access to the cash assistance safety net for twenty-four months. Below, we tell some of their stories.

The employment circumstances of the women who moved (eventually) from welfare to work after they hit the time limit were not promising. Their jobs exemplified those available to workers with low educational attainment and few skills in the new, restructured, deindustrialized, global economy: they were low-wage, mostly service-sector jobs that lacked benefits and stability. These were the jobs that welfare-to-work training program administrators expected them to get in order to demonstrate their individual responsibility (Solomon, chapter 7). For example, at the outset of the study, Martha, an African American woman and the mother of four, had recently left her husband of seventeen years, who had abused her physically and emotionally. Over the course of the subsequent several years, she struggled to care for her youngest two children, who had serious behavioral problems related to ADHD, and to meet the mandates of welfare reform. She moved from job to job, working in a beauty supply store, then in a seasonal job in the concessions stand of a sports stadium, and finally in her job as a home health aide. Among the seven women who were working post-time-limit, Martha had one of the best employment outcomes, even though she was only earning eight dollars an hour as a home health aide and had no benefits. She did, however, continue to receive Medicaid and income from SSI for two children who had ADHD. Martha was happy to be working rather than relying on welfare, although it was difficult to make ends meet and she was exhausted from the physical demands of the job. She liked being paid every two weeks and thought her family was better off financially; however, she made twice monthly trips to her church food pantry in order to provide adequate food for her family.

When Marcy, an African American woman who was twenty-two years old when we first met her, hit the time limit, she moved into a job with low wages but excellent health benefits. She worked as a food server for a large hotel chain, earning $2.55 an hour plus tips, which amounted to $276 a week in a good week. All of Marcy's three pre-school-age children had asthma, but Marcy was lucky to have a boss who was willing to accommodate her absences. She said:

I told my boss when he first hired me: "I'm reliable and dependable. I want my job, I care about my job. But my job is not more important than my kids." . . . He said: "I understand that." You know, the job I had before that, they couldn't understand that. I had to quit my job because my daughter went into the hospital and had to stay in there because she had an asthma attack real bad. They [staff at the hospital] were like: "You have a job?" [I said:] "No I don't. Not no more. 'Cause I quit."

Her daughter was hospitalized three times in the first year of the study. During the last year of the study, Marcy's mother had a stroke, which required her to use a wheelchair, and her father-in-law had three heart attacks and finally died during the period in which we were conducting the last interview. He owned the building in which she and her children lived, so there was some question about whether she would be able to stay there. Although Marcy thought that her life was better after she found work, particularly because work gave her life more meaning, she continued to face serious material hardship: she lost her phone at several points during the study, and she had her electricity cut off numerous times, including during the last year we interviewed her. Marcy earned $1,100 per month and depended on child-care vouchers, which she estimated to be worth $1,600 per month. In reflecting on her need for the child-care vouchers, she commented:

They wonder why can't nobody prosper? We all have to stay down because when we need help or when we have the help or when God see that we tryin' to help ourselves we still can't get that little added push that we need.

Three of the seven women who were working when we interviewed them one year after they were cut off cash benefits were in considerably more precarious employment circumstances than Martha and Marcy. For example, Sarah, an African American mother of five-year-old twins in her custody, finally found work two months before we interviewed her for the final time. She earned six dollars an hour working in a factory that produced athletic banners. However, this job was only a three-month job, which she found through a temporary agency. She applied for many jobs before she found this job and reported that when she was about to be cut off of cash benefits because of the time limit, she asked her caseworker to help her find a job:

She started giving me all this stuff [for big companies] and you must have experience—a diploma or something. Now, she wanted me to go and apply for this. I said, "Ms., you see the qualifications on there, it says: high school diploma, GED equivalency, and um experience. I don't have experience and I don't have a high school diploma." [She said:] "You could still go put in the application." [I said:] What is the use of going to put the application in? They're not gonna look at it because I don't have a high school diploma and no experience. And she gets mad about that.

Somehow the reality of Sarah's life—that she was unlikely to be employed due to deficits in what many researchers and policymakers would call her "human capital"—seemed to be something her caseworker was unwilling to acknowledge and address, perhaps because it would have made harder her mandated obligation to move people from welfare to work in the post-welfare-reform era.

Of the eight women who hit the time limit and were not working in the formal labor market when we last interviewed them, five had family assistance. Three women did not, and their stories were quite distressing. Next, we briefly present some of Flossie, Glenda, and Hallie's stories to illustrate post-time-limit reliance on family and network support, and then we conclude by presenting in detail the stories of two women who had almost no family assistance, were not working, and had been cut off cash benefits when they hit the time limit.

Flossie, a thirty-three-year-old African American woman with two children, ages nine and four years at the time of the 2001 interview, managed to make ends meet because she lived in low-income housing and received financial assistance from both her mother and her boyfriend, who was the father of the children and lived with her. They still received Food Stamps and Medicaid. She was applying for SSI for her diabetes and asthma.

After being terminated from welfare because of the time limit, Glenda, a twenty-eight-year-old African American woman with five children (she had custody of two of them, two were in the custody of her parents who lived upstairs, and one was adopted when an infant), lived in an apartment owned by her parents and was doing light housework for a number of elderly people in her neighborhood. She still received Food Stamps and Medicaid. During the years since welfare reform was implemented, she had moved in and out of numerous jobs, all for very brief periods, unable to sustain employment for a range of reasons—unreliable child care, unreliable transportation, pregnancy and the need to care for a newborn, inability to find child care, job termination for not producing fast enough on an assembly line (which may be related to curvature of the spine that causes her legs to go numb), severe migraines, and a car accident. Her relationship with her parents, particularly her father, was volatile, but she had no other place to live, and she earned only about sixty dollars a month cleaning. She and her father argued daily, and he called her names, belittled her, and sometimes became violent. Glenda reported that he had physically abused her as a child, but she never talked about how she felt about that or living with him as an adult.

Hallie, a white woman who was twenty-five years old and had one child when we first met her, briefly worked at multiple jobs during the time we interviewed her. However, she was unable to sustain employment. Her educational attainment was very low—she made it only through the sixth grade. She said she had learning disabilities and had been in a special classroom. She also reported that she and her sisters had been physically and sexually abused by their alcoholic father. Despite the history of abuse, she was living with her parents when we last spoke with her. She was quite uncertain that she would ever be able to sustain employment, and she adamantly objected to marriage. When asked if she had ever been married, she responded: "Nope, don't believe in it. If you can't live together, then you shouldn't be together. Why have a piece of paper and a ring on your finger to prove anything? For the man to say I own you? Oh no. I'm against that." Her opinion about marriage never wavered during the four years in which we interviewed her. While we suspected it might have something to do with the abuse in her childhood, she never made that connection. Like Glenda, she also never discussed how she tolerated living with her father again as an adult when she could not support herself.

Three women who were terminated from cash assistance because of the time limit neither found work in the formal labor market nor had family on whom they could rely. State involvement was reduced to removing children from families, or it disappeared entirely in families where the children were older. These women faced multiple barriers to employment. Although *all* our cases do not paint a terrible portrait of the costs of denying state support, these stories reveal that in some instances the worst-case scenario did occur.

At the time of the last interview, Kathy, a white woman, was fifty-three. Her youngest child had recently turned eighteen, so she would have been cut off cash benefits anyway. Nonetheless, she was cut off because of the time limit, not because her child had aged out. Kathy had been married for nineteen years and had not worked for eighteen of those years, since the time her daughter was born. Her daughter is "borderline retarded," as Kathy put it, but she had been denied SSI since they started applying in 1996. Kathy's husband worked off and on. When Kathy's cash benefits and Food Stamps were terminated, her husband found a job working as a security guard. They barely made it on his wages. He lost that job and then was employed in "spot labor," as she put it. There were times when they had no money and turned to their church for food. She didn't question the loss of her Food Stamps, assuming that this was automatic when she lost her cash benefits.

Kathy was separated from her husband when our interviewer last met with her. She reported: "He was [working at a security job], and one night when he went in to work, he just decided not to show up and take off. He got on a Greyhound bus and took off. He went to southern Ohio to live with his kids, found a job there, and stayed." He did not send her a single dime after he left. Kathy had no source of financial support. Kathy searched for work with no luck. She worked in a factory for a week, earning six dollars per hour. However, the bus got her there late, and when she couldn't find another way there, she was fired. Although she believed that there were jobs available, she did not expect to find a good job, given her age and her low educational attainment:

> I don't apply for anything that requires a special amount of education or anything because I know I can't do it. It's best to do it that way. You know what your limitations are and you don't go looking for a job that you know if they hire you that you're gonna stand there and say I don't understand how to do this.

Kathy told us that when she couldn't find work, she ended up sending her daughter to live with her other daughter and husband:

> I, well actually I had to kinda send her there, well she didn't mind. I said: 'Honey, would you, you might have to live with your sister for awhile because my utilities might be getting shut off' and I didn't want to have her in the house too. . . . I wouldn't want to have her and me in the house and the gas is off, the electric is off, it would be hard enough for me to stay there. So I thought, my financial situation is, is really dreadful, so it's a good thing that I really am living all alone.

Kathy constantly reiterated that she is alone now. "I'm just an older person all alone now" was her constant refrain.

Kathy described in detail her post-time-limit struggle to survive. She said, "[I am] just doing whatever I can, for survival. I've been getting food from relatives, getting a little bit of money here and there, whatever I could do. I feel like an animal trying to survive in the woods." She did eventually indicate that she had gone to welfare for Food Stamps, but they wanted her to come back in two weeks. She described her embarrassment at having to "borrow, beg, borrow, beg," as she put it. She said:

> I really don't like to do that [ask for help] and make people get the impression, even like my family, "God every time this woman needs something she thinks it's just gonna be handed to her." And you know, sometimes it's embarrassing, but sometimes I've been pushed in a corner so bad that I, I had to practically beg for something and it, you know, it makes you feel like a jerk. I mean, oh geez, like a coupla weeks ago, when I was just almost starving upstairs, I just went and called my one brother and he came over with two bags of food and loaned me ten dollars.

She concluded by blaming herself for her financial circumstances: "If I'd made different choices, stayed in school, maybe I wouldn't be in this place; probably the bad financial situation is basically my own fault due to bad decisions."

The final story we present is that of Katie, a twenty-two-year-old white woman with three children when we first met her. Her story is very complicated and represents another very extreme example of how the loss of the public safety net can contribute to devastation in women's lives.

Katie's mother was murdered when Katie was three years old; she was raised primarily by her grandparents, but Katie also spent three years in foster care after her grandmother died. Her father had been in prison on child molestation charges for eight years when we first met Katie; Katie disclosed severe childhood sexual abuse in our final round of interviews with her. Katie dropped out of high school in tenth grade. She had her first child when she was fifteen years old. She lived with the father of this child until she was seven months pregnant but left him to live with her sister when he began abusing her. Subsequently, Katie had two more children by another man, who was also abusive to her. As detailed later, Katie got into yet another abusive relationship, maybe two, during the course of the study. While Kathy's story illustrates the struggles of an older women with low educational attainment and no labor-market experience, Katie's story illustrates the struggles of a young woman with a history of child abuse, low educational attainment, little labor-market experience, and a long, on-going history of relationships with violent men, all of which culminated in the loss of her children to child protective services, extreme drug use, and work in an escort service to feed her drug habit and survive.

When we first met her, she had just left a battered-women's shelter and was living with a friend she had met there. Katie described a history of severe and ongoing violence with the father of her two younger children. When she went to the shelter, she was pregnant with his third child. Despite the fact that she had previously always objected to abortion, she decided to have an abortion because she feared another child would further tie her to the man she was trying to leave. Shortly after we first interviewed Katie, in 1998, she became involved with another man and became pregnant yet again. She, her boyfriend, Juan, and her three kids lived briefly with his mother and then found their own apartment. That was where she was living when we interviewed her a second time.

At the second interview, done in the summer of 1999, Katie said that she had not worked in the previous year. She participated in a job-training program in the fall of 1998 and had applied for some jobs in retail. However, because of her pregnancy and the birth of her fourth child, in April, she was allowed to defer her participation in the job-training program. She planned to re-enroll in job training when the baby was six months old, and she talked about wanting to get her GED, which she saw as crucial to her ability to find decent employment. During the year, she and Juan had argued a lot, mostly about his unemployment, and he began to be abusive toward her. At one point she called 911, and Juan was arrested. They separated, but Katie expressed extreme ambivalence about leaving him and said she was still in love with him. They ended up getting back together, and Juan found a job. But neither Juan's work nor their reconciliation lasted. In the spring of 2000, Katie reported that they had again been fighting a lot, and he had been in and out of the house. Ultimately, he ended up back in jail on domestic-violence charges.

Katie told our interviewer that she had decided that she needed to "take care of herself." She reported: "I was tired of sitting at home and then every couple of months they was mailing me letters and it says my thirty-six months, my clock is ticking. I thought it was a form of embarrassment. . . . They were totally downgrading me. . . . So, I was like, let me at least try to get a GED so that way I can get a job." Katie contacted her caseworker; she got Katie into a job-training program, and all four children into the same daycare center (they were all under five years old). Katie entered a training program in a local hotel and was offered a job there, cleaning rooms. Her caseworker arranged for Katie to get her driver's license renewed, tapped into emergency funds that allowed Katie to purchase a used car so that she could get her kids to day care and get to work on time. The system seemed to be helping Katie, and Katie felt that, compared to her situation during the past year, her life was finally coming together: "I'm not so dependent on welfare, I'm trying to live without it. Last year, I was, I had nothing. You know, I had no car, I had no money, I had no nothing. I think that's changed a lot. Last year I was messed up. This year is much easier." Katie was still receiving cash benefits but anticipated they would be reduced and eventually cut off with the coming thirty-six-month time limit approaching in October 2000.

For about a year, Katie kept things together, despite her ongoing relationship with Juan, who was in and out of jail and seriously addicted to alcohol and crack cocaine, often dealing out of their home. His violence persisted: she told of times he had pulled a knife and threatened her, of a time when he broke into the house by punching through a glass window, causing glass to fly all over the room where Katie and the children were sitting, and then threw furniture and broke things, and of times when he'd pushed her or punched her. Still, she loved her work, trusted the children's day care, and managed to keep going to her job.

Katie's downturn began in the fall of 2000. Her car broke down, and she did not have the several hundred dollars required to fix it. She had an open case with child protective services because of the drug use in the home, and they had threatened to take the children if she did not live apart from Juan. She lived in various places, with a cousin and off and on with Juan. Her cash benefits were cut off, as expected, when she hit her thirty-six-month time limit. Then we lost track of her for almost a year, despite repeated attempts to contact her. When we found her again, in the summer, her life had essentially fallen apart. In a field note, our interviewer reported that she looked terrible: "emaciated, hair disheveled, agitated, distracted, black circles under her eyes, so unlike she ever was earlier in the study. She seemed just so unhappy from the inside out. Before, she was always chatty and joking, even when she was complaining about her life." She had developed a severe addiction to crack, despite the fact that she did not appear to be using at all in the previous years of the study. We think that when the fragments of her life started to fray, she abruptly and dramatically fell apart, especially because she had no one to turn to who could offer her some safe harbor from the incredible difficulties she faced.

Katie reported that she had moved constantly during the prior year, sometimes to escape Juan, sometimes due to evictions. She lived in condemned buildings. She worked for much of the year in her job, and she began working in an escort service in order to maintain her worsening drug habit. Eventually she lost her job and began to live with her drug supplier in what she described as a crack house. She exchanged sex for drugs with him, and he began abusing her, quite severely. Child Protective Services put her children into the care of their fathers, or sometimes other relatives, although for a long time she struggled to keep her eldest daughter with her. Katie suffered severe health consequences from the crack addiction and ended up in the emergency room and, finally, in a detox program. She went back to the crack, and the new dealer-boyfriend, when she got out of detox.

As of the fourth interview, conducted in the late summer of 2001, a caseworker had given Katie a year to detox and get back on Section 8 and get her kids back but said that after a year the kids would be put up for adoption. Katie was determined to find a way to regain control over her life and get her children back. But she was desperate, our interviewer said. She had no one to turn to. She partially blamed the time limit for her incredible slide into this abyss. She felt that if she had been able to turn back to welfare temporarily, she might have been able to stabilize in her own apartment and be less dependent on the men in her life who were themselves drug addicted, abusive, and very much a part of this terrible downturn.

Conclusion

Some of the fifteen women in our sample who hit the time limit did manage to find very low-wage, sometimes temporary employment; others relied on network members to provide them with minimal financial assistance, at least for the time being. For some women in our sample, the time limit brought the worst of times—true desperation, the turn to informal sector employment, including sex work, and the loss of utilities, housing, children, and dignity and self-respect. All the women in our sample who hit the time limit faced severe barriers to employment that predated the latest round of welfare reforms and had emerged from childhoods and teenage lives of disadvantage that were beyond their control. For those who did find employment when they hit the time limit, it is entirely unclear how long they were able to sustain it. We stopped interviewing these women in 2001, so we don't know whether the worst of times came for others in our sample. There was no predicting whether some of the others who hit the time limit would join Kathy and Katie at the bottom, given their multiple barriers to employment, their precarious job situations, and the worsening economy.

Welfare reformers tout the benefits of the self-sufficiency they presume will result from implementing work requirements and time limits. But listening closely to these women, who have been reliant on welfare and are subject to its time limits, we must ask whether we are neglecting and abandoning some of our fellow citizens who are most in need of social support. What could self-sufficiency mean for women like Kathy and Katie and even some of the other women we've described whose lives teeter on the edge of desperation? Is laziness really the problem, dependence really the evil some imagine it to be? What does self-sufficiency mean in the context of a low-wage labor market, no universal health care, and periods of high unemployment in which, we can imagine, some of these women would be the first to lose their precarious positions in their service-sector employment? With no national commitment to guaranteed employment, a living wage, and universal health care, is this a sustainable, meaningful self-sufficiency?

These stories also reveal another level of the triumph of individualism: not only do policymakers and the general public buy the discourse of individualism and an ideology that blames the welfare recipient for her plight, but so, too, do welfare recipients accept the premises of this discourse and ideology. For example, Kathy blames herself for her financial circumstances, stating they result from her bad choices. Here, Kathy articulates the culture-of-poverty view that she has not pursued educational and employment opportunities that would have meant a better life. She repeats the logic that it is her laziness and poor judgment that account for her situation—not the structural conditions of the labor market that she and her husband face, not the structure of gendered family relations that encourage women to drop out of the labor market and depend on their husbands until their husbands leave (often long before a child turns eighteen), not the circumstances of her childhood that may have contributed to her low educational attainment—abandonment by her father, growing up with her single mother in conditions of poverty. Kathy was not the only woman in our sample who blamed herself for her circumstances, having bought, apparently, the cultural logics predominant in the media, welfare offices, policy debates, and on the street.

When we last met Marcy, she reflected on the changes in welfare reform and told the interviewer:

> I hope that when they go through these interviews that they see how [welfare] affects people and how people really feel about it and maybe they could make a change so like in the near future . . . it'd be available to people and that they can use it, like, if they need it. I can understand that some people do it [rely on welfare] because they can, but it's hurting the people that really need it [to limit welfare] regardless of whether they did it for three years, maybe a lot of them may need it a little longer than that. You know, you don't understand their situation completely and you never could until you walked a mile in their shoes.

Marcy clearly gets what neoliberal, neoconservative welfare reformers do not. Neoliberalism framed the restructuring of the American welfare state such that we have truly ended welfare as we knew it: no longer are families entitled to financial support if they are income eligible and have children under the age of eighteen. With the triumph of individualism and market fundamentalism, cash assistance is now time limited, and we have lost this country's only safety net for poor people. Policymakers and the public have become convinced that the welfare system itself creates "dependence" and laziness that in turn prevent work and "self-sufficiency." However, the life stories and experiences of those affected by time limits challenge that definition of the situation and the policies that emerge from it. We must continue to bring their stories forward and advocate for redefining the situation; we must seek meaningful policies that address welfare-reliant women's lived experiences and the structural causes of poverty and inequality that shape their, and all of our, lives.

We conclude with a methodological note. Unlike most of the contributors to this volume, we did not employ an institutional ethnographic approach in our larger study or in writing this chapter. That is, we did not specifically aim to "bring into view the local moments of articulation of the extra-local relations of restructuring" (Griffith 2001: 88) that are the foci of institutional ethnographic studies (see DeVault and McCoy 2001). Nevertheless, in this chapter, by focusing on women's lives and welfare's time limits with our more traditional qualitative interview data and analyzing these data with attention to the ideological discourses that are operating at the interface of welfare reform and the New Economy, we are able to contribute in substantial ways to the collective institutional ethnographic project of mapping "the regime—the 'connective tissue' located in text—that is realigning practice in the myriad sites of everyday work and life" (DeVault this volume).

Like institutional ethnographers, we started with women's lives and a critical perspective on the structures constraining them. When we looked at the world from the perspective of low-income women facing the mandates of welfare reform—that is, in Marcy's words, when we walked a mile in their shoes—we got a clear sense of the ways in which the relations of ruling in the new economic regime define their lives. Unlike an institutional ethnographic study (Smith 1987, 1999), our critical ethnographic approach did not rely specifically on the analysis of textual products of this regime that conveys the relations of ruling that mediate and structure women's daily lives. We did not conduct interviews and observe within sites in ways that would allow us to "point toward next steps in an ongoing, cumulative inquiry into translocal processes" (DeVault and McCoy 2001: 753), as institutional ethnographers usually do.

Despite these differences in approach, we knew something about the texts from the Welfare Department, like letters forewarning women they were approaching the time limit on welfare receipt, and we learned something about women's reactions to these warnings from our interview data. Had we conducted an institutional ethnographic examination of time limits, we would likely have defined a more specific extralocal problematic and collected data to interrogate it with more attention to both local circumstances and connections to broader institutional and extralocal social relations. In that instance, we likely would have interviewed caseworkers and welfare officials, observed in welfare offices, and reviewed the reams of paper, faxes, and electronic communications flowing from and within the offices during this period.

Still, even though we did not approach our research in that way, our indepth interviews and the anecdotal discussions of these texts confirm and reflect the findings from concurrent institutional ethnographic studies of welfare reform also published in this volume. We still get a sense of the nuanced ideological web woven by the textual products of the mutually reinforcing welfare and new economic regimes operating during this time and the power of that ideology to "capture" women in its institutional talons. Discourses of self-sufficiency and personal responsibility—the reigning ideological frames disseminated at this time—pervaded our interview data.

Thus, the findings from both more traditional, critical qualitative studies (see also Marchevsky and Theoharis 2006) and institutional ethnography concur and confirm the ways in which the notions of "personal responsibility" and "self-sufficiency" have become the "conceptual currency" of welfare reform. This institutional discourse framed the redefinition of programmatic structures and staff interactions with welfare recipients. Indeed, it framed the manner in which many women came to think about themselves and their own choices and experiences in relation to family, work, and welfare.

NOTES

This project was supported by MDRC's Project on Devolution and Urban Change and the Next Generation Project (which is funded by the David and Lucile Packard Foundation, the William T. Grant Foundation, and the MacArthur Foundation), and the Joyce Foundation. We thank the following people for their critical work conducting interviews and coding the data: Lorna Dilley, Kristy Harris, Ralonda Ellis-Hill, Karen Fierer, Vicki Hunter, Leondra Mitchell, Samieka Mitchell, Kagendo Mutua, Laura Nichols, Liz Piatt, Marnie Salupo, and Sarah Spain. We also thank Allison Hurst for her initial analysis of some of the data used in this paper. Finally, we would like to thank the women who chose to share their stories with us.

1. These data were collected under the auspices of MDRC's Project on Devolution and Urban Change. Details regarding how the sample was obtained and the interviews were conducted are available elsewhere (e.g., London, Scott, Edin, and Hunter 2004; Scott, Edin, London, and Kissane 2004; Scott, London, and Hurst 2005).

2. An additional respondent stopped receiving cash benefits about the time she should have reached the thirty-six-month time limit, but she did not attribute this clearly to having been cut off because of the time limit. In our analysis, we include her case because we believe she was cut off cash benefits because of the time limit. Thus, we consider fifteen of our thirty-eight respondents, or almost 40 percent of our sample, to be in this category.

3. See London, Scott, and Hunter (2002) for examples of women who were caring for children with chronic health problems and were told explicitly that they could not obtain an exemption or extension.

4. This may in part result from the fact that our interviewers repeatedly asked women how much time they had left on their time clocks over the course of the study. However, it may also result from the emphasis staff placed on communicating this message, since, in 1998 and 2001, 93.8 percent and 96.6 percent, respectively, of Urban Change survey respondents reported that they were aware of the

time limit. These results contrast sharply with findings from the 2002 National Survey of America's Families (Zedlewski and Holland 2003) that indicate that there may be considerable confusion about time limits in other areas: nationally, 37 percent of recipients lacked information about when their benefits would end, and 50 percent of those with two or more barriers to employment lacked information about time limits.

[9]

Personal Responsibility in Professional Work
The Academic "Star" as Ideological Code

CATHERINE RICHARDS SOLOMON

Editor's Introduction

*The discursive motors of restructuring are hierarchically nested—there are
ideas that become reigning principles of the era, more specific conversations
about the issues of particular institutional arenas ("quality," for example,
in health care or "outcomes," in education), and then the particular textual
mechanisms that organize people's activities (Smith 2005). In some lines of
work, control is exercised through direct measurement of performance, and
new electronic technologies seem to have increased the precision of such control, as well as extending it into the professions, such as education (chapter 2)
and social work (Parada 2002). In higher education, administrators are increasingly held to account for expenditures and pushed toward more precise
assessment of outcomes (McCoy 1998). The work of tenured faculty members
still appears to be protected from such overt control, yet changes in the landscape of academic work seem perhaps to be leading toward a polarized pro-
fessoriate, divided between the privileged few and a large pool of part-time
and contingent teaching labor (Jacobs 2004).*

*This chapter takes as its point of entry the talk of young faculty members
beginning careers in this context and follows traces of these social relations
that appear in their talk (Smith 1987). These professors, working in research
universities, continue to benefit from organizational arrangements that provide not only relatively high salaries but also stability and employer-based
health and other services. But pressures to hold onto these jobs encourage
these workers to subordinate their family and personal lives to professional
activities (and these decisions are understood as justifying the privileges they
are accorded in comparison to other workers). Solomon noticed, as she analyzed her interview data, a vocabulary of the academic "star" that recurred so*

frequently in the talk that it seemed to operate as an organizer of these work-
ers' thinking and practice. Drawing from Smith's concept of an "ideological
code" (1999), her discussion suggests that, for some academics, the rhetoric
of a star system provides an ideological touchstone and rationale for choices
about work and family commitments. But these professors' talk does more
than simply help them make sense of their context; it also constructs their
choices as individual ones and serves to naturalize an emerging two-track
labor system, making it seem the inevitable result of stardom or its absence.

* * *

The so-called New Economy has brought increasing uncertainty and risk
for many workers. But as manufacturing workers see their jobs moving
elsewhere and high-tech workers watch their bubble burst, it seems that
high-status professional workers are shielded from these ideologies of personal responsibility and risk. This chapter suggests, however, that the imperatives of personal responsibility simply appear in a different, perhaps
subtler form. Academic work has always had an entrepreneurial aspect,
reflected in the autonomy of faculty to shape and build their intellectual
careers. The transformations of the New Economy, however, seem to be
stratifying the academic workforce (Jacobs 2004). Scholars who want to retain the privileges of intellectual autonomy must choose to work to a high
standard. Such choices are highlighted as more women enter the academic
labor force (and other professional jobs), so that both women and men on
university faculties must organize lives that include both work and family.

The focus of this chapter is on the ideological code of the "star" in academe, as an organizer of these apparently individual choices. Talk of the
star references a standard of success that infuses the career and family talk
of assistant professors. It shapes their understanding of scholarship production, of work habits, of work/family policies, and of the choices they feel
are necessary to be a successful scholar in today's professorial occupation.
This model is taken up (or resisted) as a representation of the ideal worker
in academe, one who sacrifices involvement in personal life activities and
family life to have a successful professional life. Stars set the standard for
professional, and personal, behavior of academics. But professors are not
passive receivers of this code. They use it to understand their actions, the
actions of others, and the accomplishments necessary to ensure their space,
and its associated occupational privilege, in academe.

In this chapter, I explore the interlocking components of the ideological
code of the star. I also show its organizing power in the everyday experiences of untenured but tenure-track assistant professors at two research

universities. The star code shapes the decisions that these men and women made about how much to work, what they believed they had to do to be successful in their work lives, and whether and how to use their universities' work/family policies. Throughout the chapter, I also situate this ideological code in the context of the ruling relations of universities, a context that is evolving from a reliance on public supports to greater private sponsorship.

Data and Methods

The focus of this chapter is this language of stardom, treated as an ideological code (Smith 1999). An ideological code is "analogous to a genetic code" in that it "orders and organizes texts across discursive sites, concerting discourse focused on divergent topics and sites, often having divergent audiences, and variously hooked into policy and political practices" (Smith 1993: 51). Although an ideological code may use certain words, such as "star," it is not "a *definite form of words* [but] a constant generator of procedures for selecting syntax, categories, and vocabulary in . . . the production of talk" (Smith 1993: 52; emphasis added). Thus, the ideological code of star does not necessarily manifest in the use of certain words or terms or only in certain locations. It is an understanding of a type of scholar that infuses the career talk of professors and appears in various writings about professional life of academics (e.g., *The Chronicle of Higher Education*).

Data for this chapter are from a larger project that focused on untenured assistant professors' work/life management (Solomon 2004). Participants work in two large research universities in the northeast, Hilltop University and Valley University (both pseudonyms). Hilltop University is a private research university where assistant professors made up 27 percent of full-time faculty. Valley University is a public university with about the same percentage of assistant professors. I conducted semistructured in-depth interviews with thirty-seven assistant professors. Of these, nineteen were women and eighteen were men; thirty were white, five were Asian-American, and two were African American; and twenty-one were parents and sixteen were nonparents. Participants were randomly selected and were asked a variety of questions about their work lives (e.g., schedules, work responsibilities, tenure expectations, work/family policies), as well as their personal lives (e.g., family life, leisure activities, and child-care arrangements if applicable). Pseudonyms are used for all participants, and any identifying information has been changed or omitted to protect participants' confidentiality. Because I interviewed participants at research universities, the data are probably most reflective of the lived experiences of professors at such institutions.

Data analysis. Results from this larger study (Solomon 2004), for which I used a more conventional ethnographic approach, demonstrated that professors immensely enjoyed the autonomy and flexibility that accompanied their career. At the same time, however, they felt expected to live up to a high standard of productivity and dedication to their careers. Some professors accommodated this expectation, giving work priority over other aspects of their lives. Others resisted it by drawing protective boundaries around nonwork activities (including spending time with family) to protect them from the demands of work. Whichever approach was used, efficiency and discipline were two work habits employed to either meet the high standards or to keep nonwork activities as a priority. For this analysis, I adopted institutional ethnography to focus on the ideological code of star, as the vocabulary of the star system seemed to present one piece of the picture that could be analyzed using some tools of institutional ethnography. I paid particular attention to instances where participants used the word "star," described stardom, or employed an understanding of stardom that influenced choices they reported making at home and at work. This language of star occurred naturally in participants' talk without any direct prompting, and this was true for respondents who resisted or accommodated work demands. Quotations used in this chapter are the best illustrations of a theme or comment; they represent multiple occurrences in the data.

Stardom and Its Effects

Individuals who exemplify the pinnacle of professional success in academe are often referred to as "stars" (Arnone 2003; Baron 2003; Fain 2005; Fish 2003; Hochschild 1975: 61; Lloyd 2004; Mangan 2003; Tenner 2004). As ideological codes do not always rely on a particular term (Smith 1999), stars are also referred to as "the best" (Jacobs 2004: 15), the "giants in the field" (Bailyn 1993: 51), or ones "who rise to the top" (Hochschild 1975: 50). These labels indicate that such scholars have outstanding records and reputations. Such accomplishments are seen to exceed "normal" standards for success, including tenure. Surpassing such standards makes professors seem "out of this world" exceptional, and so they are seen as somewhat disconnected, bigger, and *above* others (even towering above, as in reference to "giants" in a field). They are the cream of the crop. The word "star" portrays them as beyond the reach of other academics and, perhaps, disembodied from the everyday responsibilities of personal life, such as family caregiving. In this sense, stars are the ultimate disembodied workers (Acker 1990), individuals who have few, if any, distractions from their nonwork lives. In this section, I outline the distinguishing characteristics and behaviors of the ideological code of stardom, ones that signal a person's star status to others. In addition, because an ideological code is a "social organizer" (Smith 1999: 175) in that it organizes what people say and what they do, I illustrate how this ideological code sets parameters for professors' work and family decisions and shapes their understanding of their behavior at work and at home.

Publications. One necessity for stardom is an exceptional rate of publication. Scholars are evaluated on their publication rate, but usually only of certain texts (e.g., peer-reviewed articles and books; Bailyn 1993; Hochschild 1975; Lloyd 2004). Because fields differ in what they consider exceptionally high rates (e.g., a book and six peer-reviewed articles before tenure might be high for one field, whereas in another this might not qualify), it's not easy for assistant professors to assess how much is enough. The standard is also implicitly tied to school requirements for tenure. For example, Mick was in his second year and had a book and a "landmark" article published in a "top journal." He said that he was pretty sure that he would get tenure "assuming [he] continues to breathe" and thought he looked like a star to others. Thus, the number of publications that makes one a star (and thus enables one to easily get tenure) is contingent on the particular field and institution.

Participants frequently mentioned the number of publications that they thought stars had. For example, Josh said, "There's no reference point [for how well I'm doing] because of the way our field works. It's not often talked about. The only people you hear about are the people who submit fifteen [articles] a year and they're the stars. If you want to be a star then you have to be at that level." Publishing at high rates is a necessity for stardom, but publishing in top-tier journals or with prestigious publishers (seen as quality outlets for one's work) is a boost to that status (Lloyd 2004). Steve mentioned this when he said:

> I think the research expectations that these two important people in my department have with me is they expect I will be publishing in the *top* journals and presenting at the *top* conferences. (Emphasis added)

As Steve suggested, the pressure to publish in the "top" places (i.e., the best places) reinforces the hierarchy among scholars and the competitiveness to be the one whose name appears in those top places (Bailyn 1993; Hochschild 1975). Professors routinely compared themselves to and seemingly competed with those they saw as stars. Mick shared how he compared his own publication rate to that of others (supposedly stars): "I am hearing those people out there in the world. The people like me at [Incredibly Famous University] who are *producing a certain amount* and thus *implicitly defining what I should be doing* if I am to be among them" (emphasis added).

One reason why professors may feel they have to compete with stars is the decreasing availability of tenure-track slots. Institutions are increasing the number of adjunct, part-time, and non-tenure-track instructors (Aronowitz 2000; Giroux 2001; Mohanty 2003; Poovey 2001) and are experiencing decreasing public funding. All of these changes in the composition of university faculty place untenured tenure-track assistant professors (particularly those at research universities) in a coveted, yet vulnerable position. To maintain their position of privilege in academia, they are faced with the pressure to be a star, as stardom assures them of being able to maintain their position and occupational flexibility in a field with a shrinking number of tenure-track positions, positions that offer the promise of job security.

However, not everyone strove to have publication records that would lead to star status. For reasons usually related to family life, some professors said they focused on just getting tenure or doing work that they enjoyed:

> For me, my personality, I don't really care about the prestige of being the top of the field. I just want to do well and have a comfortable living. The problem I had in the fall, and this is just something to deal with, is that there is one person who's sort of the star of the department and potentially of the school in terms of research productivity . . . and it's one of those things at first I felt like I had to deal with or I had to comp—not compete but live up to that role model. Then as I thought a little more [I thought] well, no, because that role model is far exceeding tenure expectations. (Josh)

> Right now my attitude is I'm gonna do what I'm gonna do and I'm only going to get done what I'm gonna get done and I'm not gonna sacrifice

spending time with my children. I'm not gonna get divorced over it. If I get divorced, it will be over something else. (Samantha)

These participants define for themselves a standard of work that seems more reasonable or that permits a more balanced life between work and home. What is striking is that their talk is still organized by the language of stardom, which constructs their resistance as individual choice.

Awards and grants. In addition to producing a great deal of scholarship, and scholarship in all of the top places, stars collect accolades for their research (Hochschild 1975; Lloyd 2004). They win awards for their articles or books and grants or fellowships for ongoing or future research projects. These awards and fellowships are signifiers that stars do research on the cutting edge of a field that will garner them future awards and monies. Obtaining funding is especially a mark of star status in fields in which research funding is hard to come by. Steve described how this worked with one of his graduate school friends when he said, "My God, he's got, I don't know, a $500,000 grant to do something. And in [field], you don't get grants that big very much. We have small grants and he's just publishing all the time." The words that Steve used to describe his friend's situation ("My God," "we have small grants," "all the time") illustrate how stars have the power to inspire feelings of awe. He starts off with "My God," invoking a sense of wonder about his friend's accomplishments. He implicitly compares his friend to others and himself in the field ("he" and "we"), compares his friend's "big" grant to others' "small" grants, and compares his friend's publication rate ("all the time") to an unspoken but implied slower rate of publication. In an occupation where status is important, getting big grants is better than getting small grants, and having one's name appear in journals "all the time" is better than appearing some of the time. This language reinforces the ideological code of stardom and separates his friend from a larger group that Steve sees himself as part of.

Prestige. One benefit of getting awards, fellowships, or grants is that they increase one's visibility in the field and act as a form of self-promotion to build a reputation (Hochschild 1975). Essentially, it increases a professor's prestige. This search for prestige works to the benefit of both the university and the individual. Being well known in one's field is important for the individual because universities want to hire stars for the name recognition factor (Aronowitz 2000; Arnone 2003; Fain 2005; Fish 2003; Hochschild 1975; Mangan 2003; Slaughter and Leslie 1997). Universities want stars, or those with star potential, because stars increase universities' prestige level (Aronowitz 2000; Polster and Newson 1998; Slaughter and Leslie 1997; Wilson 2005). Prestigious universities attract more money from state governments and from private sources (Aronowitz 2000; Giroux 2001; Slaughter and Leslie 1997). The more universities can rely on the latter for funding, the less they have to rely on dwindling state education budgets (Giroux 2001; Mohanty 2003; Poovey 2001). Thus, administrators look for individuals who have the "best" records, compete with other universities to hire them, and offer excellent packages to stars or potential stars in hopes of hiring them (Arnone 2003; Baron 2003; Fish 2003).

As professionals, professors are supposed to be able to work without supervision and without outside control (Burrage and Torstendahl 1990; Evetts 2003; Leicht and Fennell 2001; Vollmer 1966). To overtly control the behavior of professors challenges the very nature of professionalism. Thus, universities seek ways to implicitly control professors' behavior and output for maximum profit and prestige. The ideological code of stars serves this purpose, as "no one seems to be imposing anything on anybody else; people pick up an ideological code from . . . hearing or watching; and replicate it in their own talk" (Smith 1999: 175). Thus, it appears that professors themselves are the ones creating such high standards for success; in fact, they are taking up and participating in a broader discourse that serves as an implicit means of controlling or managing professors' work behaviors.

At research universities, star status brings with it larger salaries, reduced teaching loads, graduate-student research assistants, large startup grants for research, and even the hiring of spouses. Being a star does work to the benefit of the university, but it also benefits individuals because it grants them a lot of privileges that others may not get and ensures career mobility as universities continue to seek out stars. In the next section, I explore the ways that individuals position themselves in relation to this ideological code and how it organizes their work within the institution.

Taking Up the Code of the Star

Participants' descriptions of their decisions about the job market and their job-market experiences reflect the influence of this ideological code on the hiring process and individuals' career decisions. Mick described why he stayed in graduate school an extra year and how this benefited his career:

Mick: I was very much done and I think somewhat more polished than maybe your typical Ph.D. candidate when I came out on the market the next year and did pretty well.

CRS: How did you mean you're more—?

Mick: I'm a strong believer in staying in grad school until—coming out on the market as strong as possible. The problem is, people who get jobs on the sort of randomness even when they're not quite done sort of thing, they start out as a professor without ever having really polished up their dissertation. If you're in a discipline like [mine] where you need to publish that as a book, what you've essentially just done is given away the luxury of having another year as a grad student. So I've seen a *bunch* of friends who were lucky enough, as they thought at the time, to get a job early on and then it just seems like it put them permanently on a more difficult track in the sense that their dissertation-slash-book never quite got to be as good as everybody thought it was going to be when they were given the job. Whereas, certainly I think in my case, and a couple of other people I know who felt like they had had enough time in grad school for that second really serious polishing of their dissertation, you can hit the ground running once you get the job. I sent my dissertation off to publishers in the fall when I got here and it's coming out next year, which makes me look like *a superstar*. [Emphasis added]

This excerpt shows how Mick delayed graduating for an additional year to be *better* than others who were not quite "as good as everybody thought" they were going to be. He made a conscious choice to stay in graduate school in order to increase the chances that he would "look like a super-star."

This excerpt from Kendra's interview illustrates the influence of the ideological code of star on the hiring process, and her awareness of its benefits.

CRS: How did you negotiate only teaching one class [every semester] for three years?

Kendra: They offered it to me. [Laughs] Yeah, they want me to be very research active. . . . I think I've been really fortunate because even other faculty [who] started after me didn't get that kind of a deal. I don't know, honestly. Again I didn't negotiate it, they offered it to me.

CRS: Why do you think that they offered [you] that sort of package?

Kendra: I think that they knew that I had a number of different offers and I think that I have a fairly good record and I think that they're interested in increasing the research visibility of the college. That's been a goal and so I think that they really wanted to provide me with an attractive package that would make me consider Hilltop because I had offers from schools that were ranked more highly, where I'd get better graduate students and things like that.

CRS: What do you mean by you had a good record?

Kendra: [Where I got my Ph.D.] is one of the top 10 [specialty field] departments. That was absolutely a bonus. My research field bridges—it's at the interface of [area] and [area] and that's becoming a really hot field. I think that I interview well and I think that I had good recommendation letters and I have a good publication record. So I think all those combined.

Specific facts about Kendra's education and publication record were interpreted by the hiring committee and university administrators as suggesting that she had star potential. First of all, she was sought after by other schools, thus marking her as a valuable commodity that Hilltop should try to attract. Second, she had a "good record," which is a catch-all phrase that includes some of the defining star features: a Ph.D. from an elite institution and department, lots of publications, and innovative research. Because Kendra had star potential and could, in the eyes of university administrators and her colleagues, increase the "research visibility of the college" (and therefore the prestige of the university and its potential to attract funding), she was offered a teaching load that was half the normal load. The ability to get such special treatment is highly sought after at research universities such as the ones in this study because it gives faculty time for research, which can increase star status further. Indeed, job advice disseminated to graduate students encourages them to develop a good curriculum vitae, one with presentations, awards, grants, fellowships, and publications, to help them present a star persona to prospective employers.

These experiences highlight one professional arena (the job market) in which the concrete practices of academe reinforce and help professors internalize the ideological code of stardom. Professors, both those looking for jobs and those with jobs, account for themselves in texts in a variety of ways. As Kendra's and Mick's statements demonstrate, curriculum vitae (CV) and letters of recommendation present a certain account of a job applicant's career. CVs continue through professors' careers to be the standard text by which individuals are evaluated and judged. Annual CV updates, by which faculty gradually build up textual accounts of themselves, are used by administrators to make decisions for market-based salary increases, courseload reductions, and sometimes the assignment of graduate research assistants. Tenure and review committees use CVs (and the accompanying folders of other texts such as scholarship pieces and letters of recommendation) as the basis for decisions about tenure and promotion. The CV, as a text that supports or proves stardom, also has consequences beyond one's institution. For example, many granting agencies (particularly the larger government ones) look for a textual record (present in CVs or other places) of previous grant proposals, previously awarded grants, and scholarly pieces that arose out of previous grant monies when reviewing grant proposals. CVs are also standard texts used for many professional organizational rewards, particularly career awards that honor individuals for careers of distinguished scholarly contributions to their field. These academic practices demonstrate how star is a flexible ideological code that can refer to the local (i.e., institutional) level and/or the national level. Whichever level such discourse occurs on, it is supported by specific texts and particular concrete academic practices.

Working long and hard. To be such a prestigious and coveted scholar, one must invest long hours working on scholarship. Working long and hard hours is necessary because professors have to find time to write, to revise, and to submit manuscripts for publication in addition to their teaching, advising, and service duties. For example, Josh said, "There is one person who's sort of the star of the department and potentially of the school in terms of research productivity. They're also working enormous hours, they're here every weekend, they're working most nights."

Stars' production of scholarship has to be constant. That is, they have to continue publishing to keep their coveted position in their field. For example, Kendra described how she felt she was expected to produce exceptional scholarship on a constant pace to keep her status. She shared, "There's no real, *wow*, you're so great kind of thing. It's one thing after the other but you're *expected to keep producing* those things one after the other" (emphasis added). Being a star is a tenuous status. Because there is no permanency to stardom and few star slots available (Bailyn 1993; Hochschild 1975), scholars must work to preserve their status at the top. To do otherwise might mean losing one's position to someone else. This expectation of long and hard work hours is evident in how participants described their work habits.

> Professors tend to be workaholics. . . . I literally work all the time and so I don't like that. I wish that you could just stop and just go on vacation and you just say, okay for two weeks or for a week or whatever long the vacation is, like my friends do. . . . For a week, I'm not doing anything. I always feel compelled to take work in my suitcase. You're going to a beach, right? You're taking work in your suitcase, you know? [Laughs] I can't help it. (Samantha)

> Whenever you take time off and you do things, you're always feeling guilty. It's like having an exam the next day and not having studied for it. That's the continuous feeling you live under. (Jafar)

Participants mentioned how important it was for them to be efficient when they were working, reflecting the language of professionalism and, ultimately, stardom that stresses organization, efficiency, and productivity (Burrage and Torstendahl 1990; Epstein 1981; Evetts 2003; Hertz 1986; Leicht and Fennell 2001; Vollmer 1966).

> I am just very attentive to what I'm doing. I make lists of what I need to accomplish that day and I do that in both settings. At home I've got a list and at work I have a list. Like tonight I will know exactly what I am doing tomorrow, barring anything unusual happening, of course, any emergencies. But I know at what point in the day I'm doing different things. I'm extremely organized and structured, both for the work setting and for the home setting, and I try not to mix the two very much. (Jenny)

Working this way was supported as the ideal when participants spoke disparagingly about not being efficient, organized, or disciplined enough.

> I got to say this year is a crisis management year. [Chuckles] I'm trying to find that balance. I'm not at the place where I really can set my priorities. I do have to take things pretty much as they come and just meet the deadlines and just hope that after the summer I can see things a little more clearly, I'm in a groove a little more, and I can set a *rational* program for myself. At this point I really do feel like I'm just taking things as they

come. . . . I don't think I've hit a point yet where I could *rationally* prioritize. (Miranda, emphasis added)

I don't think there are enough hours in a day. I feel like I should manage
my time better, that if I were really *good* at this I would not find myself at
the end of the morning having read my emails and cleaned up the kitchen.
[Laughs] [It] feels like, why can't I use my time better? I should have written three pages for a paper and been reading the text that I'm going to
teach this afternoon . . . what have I done? I've done my correspondence.
I think that's probably true, I could manage my time a lot better. (Leigh,
emphasis added)

When participants felt that they were not making the most efficient decisions or working efficiently, they reprimanded themselves. They expressed
feelings of guilt that point to their efforts to live up to a star standard of work
behavior. Underneath the frustrations over their work habits was an underlying message that upheld the ideal of a star status. Participants implicitly
compared themselves to the star standard, to an imagined someone who
was always on task and had an organized plan, the consummate professor
(Moore 1970; Pavalko 1971); they implicitly argued through their self-dis-
paraging comments that this model was *the* way to work. But because these
participants were not "rationally prioritizing" or felt they were not "good" at
working efficiently, they saw themselves as failing to live up to this ideal.

Some faculty said they refused to uphold this aspect of star status. These
professors saw being a star as requiring a sacrifice of time with family, a
sacrifice some participants were not willing to make. Instead, they put a
cap on their hours to invest time in other, usually family-related, activities.
For example, Morgan said, "The main reason [I don't work on the week-
ends is just I want to stay married [laughs], and right now [my wife] really
needs me on those two days. We need to spend time together and I need to
take care of the baby and give her a little time away from the baby."

Personal life, including family, comes second. Stars are able to constantly
produce scholarship and to win awards because they work long, hard
hours. But working such hours means that they have little or no personal
life. Stars were routinely portrayed in this light, as these quotations demonstrate.

There is one person who's sort of the star of the department and potentially
of the school in terms of research productivity . . . [he] has a much differ-

ent view of personal life. Their personal life wasn't anywhere near, by their own admission, anywhere near what he want[s] it to be and [he is] focused almost exclusively on work. (Josh)

The reference group of the people that *I'm trying to be* when I'm sitting in this chair are the great scholars. Many of whom are completely insane and have no life or no children or ignore them entirely or whatever. (Mick)

Because stars are perceived this way, participants frequently mentioned that minimizing personal life was a necessary sacrifice to achieve star status.

I feel like I'm working really hard and it's really draining on my personal life. I mean it's really good for me to be engaged [in my field] and to be part of a very active [professional] community, which this department really is involved in. And it's good for me to go to the conferences, it's good for me to give talks, it's good for me to do all of these things that are incredibly time consuming. (Annemarie)

It is hard to take time off, I think . . . because if you take time off it means you're just not doing what you need to do. It's not like anything stops or whatever. It's still there and you're just not doing it now. So okay, I'm going to go on vacation, which means I'm not going to do my school work for a while . . . because you never get done. . . . The vacation is always a negotiated time. It's not like you have vacation time. It's always time that you're pulling away from other stuff. (Sebastian)

Part of minimizing personal and family life included postponing having children until star status, or at least tenure, was (more) secure. Many participants refused to give in to this expectation, however, as Meg described:

I just decided that I was old enough to have a kid and I should, if I was going to have a kid, to actually start. [Laughs] I *never* thought I'm going to wait until I get tenure to have kids. That never entered my mind. I thought if I don't get tenure because I have a kid, then I don't get tenure because I have a kid, but I have a kid. [Laughs]. But I never had that thought. . . . [This professional seminar I went to] was actually really discouraging because there were all these women who were about 10 years older going "Well, you have to wait until you have tenure" and we're like, "Well we're not gonna so" [We laugh]. Yeah, so it was really actually a stressful experience. [Laughs]

Thus, one of the perceived sacrifices that stars (and those around them) were making was to put personal and family life on hold until success had been achieved.

Some professors said they were not going to adhere to this aspect of the ideological code, however. For example, Josh decided not to compete with the star in his department; he said, "It [having a star in my department] started out as a stressor but then really turned into a positive check—that's not the way to go" because

> I know [my wife and I] both don't want to wake up 25 years down the line saying, "Why are we in this? Are we married just because we have kids now?" And so I think this finding quality time and quality things to do, early on in a relationship, is important to build a foundation and if I'm working or she's working all the time, it's destroying rather than building.

Note, again, that he understands his strategy as an individual choice to reject the star model.

Given the changes in university structure, sacrificing personal time for one's career, at least until tenure is won, seems like an economically rational choice to ensure job stability. Relying on and sustaining the ideological code of stardom and the attendant sacrifice pushes professors (surely not all, but many) to strive for that status for fear that they will lose their position and be relegated to the un- or underemployed ranks of adjunct or temporary faculty. For faculty at research universities, this outcome may be understood as a death knell, as such positions not only offer no benefits, job security, or adequate salary but also do not allow the time to do research (unless one is supported by a financially well-to-do partner). Because most faculty are socialized to place research above everything else about being a faculty member and internalize the identity of "researcher," losing the ability to engage in such activities means losing a part of one's identity and the possibility of being seen as successful in one's field, even for those who resist the ideological code of star.

Use of university work/family policies. The ideological code of stardom affected participants' choices and experiences with parental-leave policies, particularly that at Hilltop, which is among the more progressive policies offered at universities. Because stars minimize their involvement in nonwork and family-life activities and work long hard hours, the implied expectation is that they will not or *should* not have a need for such policies. Hilltop University had three policies relevant to professors' family responsibilities: extension of the tenure probationary period, parental leave upon the request of parents, and maternity leave. The university allowed for two one-year extensions during the five pretenure years for any tenure-track professor, male or female, who became a parent through the birth or adoption of children less than seven years of age. The parental-leave policy allowed for a semester of half-duty: either a reduction of one course *or* up to one-half of a semester without any duties. This leave was paid and had to be taken within twelve months of the birth or an adoption of a child. Both men and women were eligible to take this leave, as long as they were the primary caregiver for their child. Academic couples who wished to take this leave could do so during different semesters. The maternity-leave policy at Hilltop (considered part of the medical disability policy) allowed for a woman to take between six and eight weeks of paid leave due to medical disability as prescribed by her doctor or midwife. A woman could combine the maternity and parental leaves if her maternity leave extended at least four weeks into a semester. By combining these policies, a woman could receive a full semester off from teaching duties at full pay. Valley's policy was minimal compared to Hilltop's (offering only six to eight weeks of paid maternity leave as "temporary disability" under its sick-leave policy), but it still offered a paid leave for the birth of a child, which many employers in the United States do not (Galinsky 2001). That these universities offered their faculty more than most other workers, especially in the case of Hilltop, puts these men and women among an elite class of employees in the United States.

The ideological code of stars, with its requirement of working long and hard and minimizing personal life, influenced the ways in which faculty at Hilltop used its progressive work/family policies. Specifically, professors who took advantage of the policies felt a little guilty about using them for fear of inconveniencing department colleagues. For example, Mick delayed taking parental leave because he worried about how his colleagues might react to his withdrawal from teaching a certain class, even though it would have been easier for his family if he had not delayed it. He said:

> [My wife's] serious work period hit [after my son was born] and I had arranged for parental leave but didn't—well the parental leave happened in the spring and not the fall which would have been much, much better. It

would have been much better to have done the parental leave that fall because he was a really little baby and she was working a whole lot. But I
guess by the time she got pregnant and it occurred to me to ask for parental leave. . . . I was scheduled to teach two classes that would have been
very difficult for the department to get me out of. One that they didn't have
anybody else to teach was the core [topics] graduate seminar. I also love to
teach it so I didn't want to get out of that. But then I had also signed up to
teach this interdisciplinary . . . course. It's this team-taught thing that they
have a hell of a time recruiting people for and you have to commit to a
whole year. I had committed to that a little before she got pregnant and if I
had pulled out of that all hell would have broken loose. So anyway, I ended
up taking my parental leave in the spring, which made the fall pretty crazy
. . . [because] between the two of us we couldn't really cover taking care of
the baby as we liked to.

Mick's own enjoyment of his work (he "loved" to teach this certain
class) and his concerns over his status in the department shaped his plans
for when he took the parental leave. In other words, there were external
and internal occupational reasons why he adjusted his family life for his
work life. By delaying when he took the leave until it was easier for his colleagues, he was demonstrating the primacy of work over family life and
reinforcing star status. Similarly, stardom influenced Meg's experience on
leave. She described how her chair was very supportive of her leave-taking
and worked to counteract the ideological code of stardom:

The person who was the chair of the department at the time, he worked
really hard to make sure that I understood—he made it really clear that parental leave was intended to be *that* and so I wasn't coming back so I could
make up for all the stuff that I had missed when I was away.

Even though Meg felt her chair was supportive of her when she was on
leave, she also told me that she came in several times during that period to
catch up on work. Coming in to work while on leave illustrates her attachment to her work and perhaps how she had internalized the ideological
code of star.

Charles's perception of his department's culture affected the way he
thought about taking leave in the future. He compared taking parental
leave to the exchange program in his department. He described how being
involved with the exchange program seemed to hurt a professor's status in

the department and the chance of getting tenure. He wondered if taking a semester of parental leave would have the same effect. He said:

> The school has a very strong [exchange] program in [foreign city] . . . a lot of faculty members go there, teach for a year, [and] come back. You realize when you are on the tenure track that if you do that [and] take a year, even though they claim that they stop your clock, you're not here. When you're not here, you really are missing out on a lot of conversations. You're missing out on building one's identity within the school. So I would think that if you take a year [on] some kind of leave that it would be in the same spirit, unless you're tenured or unless you're established within the faculty. It's something I could not *not* do [take parental leave]. But at the same time . . . I know this discourages many of our faculty to go to [foreign city] when they're on tenure track because politically you're missing out on a lot of action that's going on around here. People tend to forget [chuckles] who you are. When you come back they're like, 'Oh you.' Really all that you struggle to build on is, not lost, but it's not—I guess you lost some of that momentum, which I would think would be worrisome. It's interesting to note that most of the people who have gotten tenure in the last six or seven years, none of them ever went to [foreign city]. Like they all got the message, they all figured it out. I think that message has been passed on to the new hires. Now I think everybody is pretty much on the same page there too.

Charles's statement also demonstrates the power of the star ideological code. Part of being a star is being well known, and taking parental leave hinders one's ability to be well known, even at the department level. Even though the study-abroad program was for a year and the parental leave for only for a semester (and not in another country), *any* time away from his department might be perceived as a sign that he was less than dedicated to his job and might negatively affect his status in his department. Even though progressive policies are in place at Hilltop, they do not fully mitigate the pressure of the ideological code of stardom. The fact that young faculty talk about the requirements of stardom when discussing family-life policies suggests that the ideological code may override such policy initiatives and points to the need to address this ideology of success.

Unattainable status. No matter what participants had achieved, there was always a nagging sense that they were not stars. There was always something amiss about their record of publication or their ability to produce in the future. Comparisons of their records to those of others made these feelings of inadequacy almost unavoidable, as there was always someone with a better record. Mike shared this about his award:

Mike: When I look at [the other people's Web sites], I feel very small. I feel like a fake. [Laughs]

CRS: Because?

Mike: Because when you look at it they have a much [more] developed idea about things, which I am trying to develop and I'm not really well developed. I'm still searching for that kind of concise description about myself. That makes me feel uneasy about this part of things because when you look at others and they have a lot of collaborations and their work and publication and all this kind of thing, it's pretty nice.

Even though Mike had won a fellowship for his research (one for which a colleague had recommended him) and he thought that he was "at the forefront" of his field, he felt like a fake. He was a fake because there were others who were more productive, more advanced in their research, and who had more collaborations. The reason that definitive stardom is ultimately unattainable is because there is no limit to what a professor is expected to achieve. As Amy said:

So then it's like, [says loud] oh more is better! I would only feel okay if I had 25 [publications], but then I would hear that somebody else had 35 and I'd be like, it's not enough! I think that it's kind of a universal across untenured professors feeling, this free-floating anxiety, like I'm not doing enough, I have to do more.

Internalizing the External

Instead of seeing this ideological code as externally generated by the ruling relations of academe, most of these professors attributed the pressure to be a star to their individual personalities. That is, they presented themselves as internally driven to be stars, exclusive of any demands placed on them by their profession.

That's actually not I think real particular to me [to want to be a star] because there's sort of a self-selection that the people who make it into a lot of tenure track jobs, get there because they have this *internal pathology* that they are driven to do considerably more than they actually need to do. (Mick, emphasis added)

This drive to be the best, I think that's more my father in me. He always told me whatever you do, you have to be the best at it that you can be. I don't think anything that people here say or do affects that. But I think that the overall [occupation] of professors—you have to be that kind of person because [of] these kind of fleeting accomplishments. (Kendra)

As these statements illustrate, professors' personalities were seen as the driving force behind the desire to be stars, not occupational expectations. Though it could be that a certain personality type is attracted to academic professions, I argue that it goes further than particular individual tendencies. Professors do not perceive this code as externally generated for two possible reasons. One reason is that the nature of professionalism necessitates a certain vision of one's career and career decisions as self-controlled. The second reason could be that professors are expected to act as entrepreneurs in academe, seen by others and themselves as self-promoters and free agents.

Professionalism. As others have shown, traits that appear to be aspects of personality are often occupational norms and values that are internalized as professionals are socialized into an occupation (Blair-Loy 2003; Cooper 2002; Dryburgh 1999; Moore 1970; Simpson 1972; Traweek 1988). One aspect of professionalism is the "acceptance of norms and standards" of one's profession (Moore 1970: 8). These internalized standards then guide professionals' work behavior and attitudes toward work (Moore 1970; Pavalko 1971). For example, male computer programmers view their own internal drives as the reason they work intense hours, rather than the need to meet industry standards that emphasize being the first one out with products and on the cutting edge of software design (Cooper 2002). Like computer programmers, assistant professors in this study seemed to have internalized the ideological code of stardom to such a degree that they considered it part of their personality. Few of these professors regarded the ideological code of stardom as generated by universities or the ruling relations of their occupation. For example, Kendra had recently cut back her work hours to have Saturday off to make more time for nonwork activities. Yet she found it hard to do this:

I really think that it's hard for me to cut back because *I've always wanted* that kind of outside validation and I'm learning that that's not the most important thing. That that's not what's making me happy and my relationships with other people and being happy myself, like really working on being happy and liking who I am, are making me far more happy. But I'll say that and that's what I want for me. But I'll say it's also people in academia *base their opinion of you of what's on paper* and things like that. That *I still fall into that mode* like, oh, if I don't publish these papers everyone's going to think I'm a bad researcher or something. (Emphasis added)

Although Kendra saw the intensity of her work style as mostly her fault for thinking of stardom as *the* standard for success, she also acknowledged that professors *are* judged by others on their accomplishments—by texts that show the number and perceived quality of publications, their awards, and their fellowships and grants. As previously mentioned, one's promotion to associate and full professorship, as well as the granting of tenure, rests on peer evaluation of these texts. Prospective employers and funding agencies look for a record of accomplishment before selecting scholars for jobs or grants. Thus, professors must achieve a certain status if they want maximum career mobility and flexibility. The drive to achieve is not solely an effect of personality.

Nature of academe. At research universities, professors engage in activities to promote *themselves*, through publishing, presenting at conferences, getting grants, and so forth (Fain 2005; Gersick, Bartunek, and Dutton 2000; Hochschild 1975; Tenner 2004), not solely to promote their university. Although all these activities indirectly benefit universities by conferring prestige and grant money, they also serve to increase the market value of the individual professors. When professors increase their own market value, they become valuable to the university for which they work and to other universities, which might pay them a higher salary, give them more prestige, or provide work in a preferred region of country. Thus, the pressure to be a star can be seen as internally generated because professors want to increase their individual value to have maximum career mobility. Because both universities and faculty benefit from the code of star, it is not conceived of as a burdensome work demand that university administrators impose on faculty. Instead, it is seen as a "fact" of scholarly life.

Conclusion

The ideological code of stardom is one that serves the interest of both universities and individuals in increasing professors' levels of funding and prestige. This code is taken up and used by professors as they make decisions about how much to publish, how much to work, how to search for prestige, what kind of personal and family life to have, and whether and how to use parental-leave policies. It organizes their thoughts and options for their career paths, with some choosing to use it as a career guide and others using it as an "anti-role model," one that they choose not to follow in favor of other definitions of success. Whether professors follow it or not, it shapes the thinking of professors, administrators, and others about what success in academe requires and what it looks like. This code is made up of comparisons (of publication rates, of work habits, and of prestige), competition (for grants, for the best publication rate, and for prestige), and sacrifice (long work hours, minimal personal and family life, minimal, if any, use of parental-leave policies). Even decisions to not follow the code reify its existence as *the* standard of behavior and thus reproduce it as a professional icon.

Although it could be argued that professors can choose whether to accept the ideological code of star (and some definitely chose not to), it is not *solely* a personal choice, because the system operates in conjunction with the code. Universities want to hire and keep stars, funding agencies want to give money to people who have proven they can deliver results, people want to hear stars speak at conferences, and, thus, professors are implicitly expected to buy into this ideological code or risk not being part of the academic game. Those individuals who resist using this code as a measure for their success are then tracked into different career paths (those with less prestige and fewer professional rewards) that can be viewed as "lesser" by some.

Given contemporary changes in academia, with the decreasing number of tenure track slots, controversy over the existence of tenure, decreasing funding for research in certain fields, and stretched state education budgets (Aronowitz 2000; Slaughter and Leslie 1997), the concern these professors felt about not trying to be a star is not surprising. They were responding to a changing occupation and realized that their position as tenure-track professors was becoming increasingly hard to attain as universities rely more on adjunct or fixed-term instructors (Aronowitz 2000; Mohanty 2003).

Given these structural changes in the makeup of universities and the fact that universities are increasingly using high rates of publication for tenure evaluation (Slaughter and Leslie 1997), these professors feel, with some reason, that they must succeed at becoming stars in order to keep their jobs. To achieve such status is to ensure or solidify one's value in a tight job market. Thus, it makes sense that these professors would take on the responsibility not only of working long hard hours but also of creating a personal and family life that interferes very little with their work life.

But professors do not take up this ideological code of the star solely because of a fear of losing their jobs. There is also the satisfaction of being involved with scholarship and the privileges afforded them by their occupation. These privileges exceed what many other workers have access to, such as high salaries, occupational prestige, health benefits, autonomy, flexibility, and paid parental leave. Working hard and trying to be a star helps professors maintain these privileges. There are great incentives to do so, and the seemingly temporary sacrifices to ensure a stable job with privileges may seem a small price to pay.

"Use What You Have, Be Thankful You Have It"

Work and the Promise of Social Inclusion for Students with Disabilities

KATRINA ARNDT

Editor's Introduction

Katrina Arndt examines the imperatives of personal responsibility from the perspective of college students who are deafblind and preparing for future employment. The experiences of people with disabilities in the early twenty-first century reflect the successes of disability rights movements—at least in Western industrial democracies; one effect of this activism has been the opening of new opportunities and a significant increase in the college attendance of students with disabilities. The watchwords of disability activism have been inclusion (especially in education) and independence, which activists have conceptualized as autonomous decision making, in contexts designed to minimize barriers to participation. Many people with disabilities have the capacities and desire to participate in the labor force; they wish to be independent and responsible. However (as Traustadóttir cautioned in chapter 4), in an era of shrinking expenditure for social assistance, it remains unclear whether such participation will be possible, and on what terms.

Arndt's larger study of her participants' college experiences explores how they manage identities as deafblind individuals in a setting designed for students who are audiologically deaf, with a lively and robust Deaf culture. As members of an institutional community where they are seen as different by virtue of their visual impairments, the students must work to educate others about their disabilities and the kinds of assistance they need. They receive effective assistance from college staff but often struggle for inclusion in the social life of the college—in part, they believe, because other students do not understand their impairment and how it affects their lives. Such struggles, and the extra work of communicating with others about how they might be included, will surely follow them into future workplaces.

The analysis here focuses on a single student's internship, in order to explore the kinds of issues that may arise in the transition from school to work. The single narrative that provides the basis for this discussion is an idiosyncratic one, to be sure; but so is the story of every worker and perhaps especially every worker with a particular sensory impairment. And college internships are not real jobs and may often (for any student) lack the challenge and satisfaction of longer-term employment. Still, Arndt's discussion suggests that, as more young people with severe impairments move from college into jobs, they will likely confront the two-sided (and paradoxical) dominant construction of access. On the one hand, access is treated as an individual matter, to be taken up and managed by the person who needs assistance; on the other, it is seen as a matter to be decided institutionally, in ways that too often set aside the person's own grounded knowledge of his or her capacities and preferred types of support.

* * *

People with disabilities have faced substantial difficulties in accessing education and have experienced much higher unemployment than non-disabled citizens. In recent years, opportunities for higher education have increased dramatically, yet it remains uncertain whether obtaining a higher education will translate into more successful transitions to employment for these students. While increasing numbers of students with disabilities are entering college, it is less clear that the college experience is an effective route to employment or to the social inclusion that work might promise.

Higher education is increasingly perceived to be essential for success in the workplace. Of the twenty fastest growing occupations in the United States, twelve require postsecondary education (Bureau of Labor Statistics 2006). However, people with disabilities may not benefit from higher education in the same ways that people without disability labels do.

At this historical moment in the United States, the disability rights movement has affected attitudes about disability, bringing changes in policy and practice for people with disabilities. Prominent successes include more accessible transportation and the establishment of the right of all children to receive a free and appropriate public education (Longmore 2003: 154), as well as the passage of the Americans with Disabilities Act, which emphasizes accommodation for people with disabilities (Thomson 1997: 49). These changes resist a medical model of disability and the construction of professional authority as overruling the authority of the person. The medical model perceives disability as wrong and aberrant—as a clinical problem that needs treatment by the medical profession to remedy. Disability activists argue that this ideology is damaging to people with disabilities. Linton (1998) notes: "The disability studies' and disability rights movement's position is critical of the domination of the medical definition and views it as a major stumbling block to the reinterpretation of disability as a political category and to the social changes that could follow such a shift" (p. 11).

There is also an increasing emphasis on education as the key to employment and employment as key to full citizenship for all. These developments pull young people with disabilities into higher education and promise fuller inclusion. But their experiences in college are not always so positive; those experiences suggest that social inclusion does not follow directly or automatically from work or participation in college life (see Arndt 2005) but may often require more and different kinds of social support.

Recent programs in the United States that support the employment of people with disabilities include those established by the Workforce Investment Act of 1998 (see Cohen, Timmons, and Fesko 2005) and the Ticket to Work and Work Incentives Improvement Act of 1999 (see Capella-McDonnall 2005; Mitchell and Zampitella-Freese 2003). The Workforce Investment Act is designed to provide a "one-stop" delivery system that facilitates relationships among education, workforce, and disability services and emphasizes interagency collaboration (Cohen, Timmons, and Fesko 2005: 221). The Ticket to Work provides vocational rehabilitation services to people with disabilities who receive federal support (Capella-McDonnall 2005).

It will be important to track the experiences of those using such programs and to examine their on-the-ground operation. Will these kinds of support assist people with disabilities to participate more fully in their communities? What kinds of jobs will they find? Traustadóttir's discussion of disability policy and programs in EU countries (chapter 4 this volume) suggests that these programs may not produce the smooth access to employment and social connection that they promise; she sees "policies emphasizing social inclusion (and some very good policies) on the one hand, and on the other, large groups of people excluded from open employment, isolated in segregated employment, unemployed, or hidden away on benefits." Access may be supported by the language and mission of programs and acts such as those reviewed, but the daily reality of accommodation and access are highly personal and idiosyncratic. What is illustrated in the examples discussed later in this chapter is the perspective of a young worker with disabilities. His sense was that accommodations were provided without his supervisors really attending to his input, and then he was left on his own. The agency staff exercised a form of professional dominance, perhaps prioritizing the routine practices of the institution over Hurcane's individual needs. As a result, the work of inclusion was left entirely to Hurcane.

Despite the hope and expectation that employment itself can produce social inclusion, the experiences of students and workers with disabilities point to the limits of this notion and to the need to consider work and life more holistically. Work as a vehicle for relationship and connection is an implicit goal for many who enter the workplace. The reality for people with disabilities, however, does not always include opportunities for social connection.

Data for this chapter are drawn from a larger interview study of college students who are deaf or hard of hearing and have some visual impairment. The study site was one of only a few U.S. colleges for students who are deaf and thus represents a context in which D/deaf[1] students are much better supported than elsewhere (though support for those who have visual impairments as well is more uneven; see Arndt 2005). All of the student participants accessed services from the college to help them handle their visual impairment and were recruited through a general email I sent to all students receiving such services. That qualitative study included eleven students and nineteen interviews; students were interviewed between one and four times over a twenty-two-month period. Interviews were open ended, and topics covered in interviews were directed by students and included experiences at work and class, educational history, interactions with others, and management of vision loss.

Interviews were conducted in the language and modality of the students' choice. These included American Sign Language (ASL), Signed English, spoken English, and a combination of all three. I conducted interviews and transcribed the videotapes into an English transcript myself; I managed communication issues by meeting with students before the initial interview to develop rapport and become familiar with the student's signing style. In the interviews, I asked for clarifications as needed.

Findings from that larger study revolved around the work that students engaged in related to establishing their identity, accessing services, and educating people about their disability. Their social relationships were a primary concern for many students. They had to work hard to keep up in class and to manage the complexity of arranging the assistance they needed; several found that keeping up with their coursework was so time consuming that they had little time left for socializing.

As students worked to access services, they encountered supports and barriers. Some students had very positive experiences as they requested and received supports such as note takers and interpreters, while others had a more challenging time securing the supports they needed to be successful. A related type of unpaid work is the work students did to educate people. Because deafblindness is rare, it was common for students in this study to encounter people who were not familiar with deafblindness and who needed to be educated about how to interact with someone who is deafblind.

A final type of work students participated in is the work of developing and maintaining relationships. In this study, students had a variety of coping mechanisms related to relationships. This is not unfamiliar work; all people work to begin, maintain, and even end relationships. The added work for students in this study includes teaching others about deafblindness and managing relationships that may feel unequal because of one person's limited driving ability or need for sighted guides, slower communication, or dependence on others for information about the environment.

The college staff who engaged with the students did important work by helping them access the supports they needed, and the students were skilled in navigating the college and services. But even in the presumably welcoming setting of this college campus, students who are deafblind had to educate others about their particular sensory problems and needs. Their work would not end when they moved from a college to a work environment. Challenges students might face in the workforce, whether in a segregated or inclusive setting, continue to include identity work, dealing with requesting and managing support, and navigating social relationships.

One participant, Hurcane (a pseudonym), talked at length about his experiences with a cooperative work placement that was part of the degree requirements at his institution, and my analysis here is based on his account of that placement. Hurcane is legally deafblind. Deafblindness is a rare disability and one that significantly affects access to information, communication with others, and engagement with people and things in the environment (Aitken, Buultjens, Clark, Eyre, and Pease 2000: 3). Olsen estimates that in the United States there are 70,000 people who are deafblind (2003: 2). Hurcane's impairments are called cortical deafness and blindness; his vision and hearing are both inconsistent because his brain cannot always interpret the information it receives. As a result, sometimes he can see or hear and at other times he cannot. He speaks to express himself and also uses sign language with tracking or tactile sign supported by speech to access what others say to him.

What emerged from Hurcane's comments about his cooperative work experience was a "line of fault" (Smith 1987) between his expectation that performing the job would bring respect and integration in the workplace and the realities of his internship. While such disjunctures are not uncommon even in internships for typical college students, the particular lineaments of Hurcane's experience suggest an even greater disconnect for a student with a sensory impairment. By tracing out this line of fault and considering how Hurcane's work experience went wrong for him, I point to some of the routine practices of the workplace that may limit the social inclusion of many workers with disabilities.

Hurcane's experience may be emblematic of internships in that he was not well supported or well integrated into the permanent workforce at his job site. That may be a typical internship experience, but because coordinating his support is so complex, the range of opportunities provided to him is probably much reduced compared to that of his typical college peers—and therefore each experience becomes laden with more import and meaning. So a bad experience may not be as easy to dismiss and move past. On the other hand, it may be that this experience was one that tested Hurcane's resourcefulness and advocacy skills and was useful in that way.

Co-op Experience

At Hurcane's college, students were required to participate in at least two quarters of work experience, called a co-op placement. For some students, co-ops that were initially unpaid were opportunities to showcase skills and compete for jobs. Some students got their first jobs after graduation at their co-op placement. Hurcane was placed at an agency that provides services for people with visual impairments as an unpaid experience. That Hurcane was expected, as were all students at his college, to participate in an internship was of particular interest. As a young adult with a severe disability, he was entering an inclusive setting, a fairly new phenomenon in the United States.

Over the course of several interviews, Hurcane complained about his experiences at the agency. One narrative in particular caught my attention, and it is that experience that I consider here in three parts. Each part explores his lived experience and the challenges he faced. First, I review the difficulties he had in using the bus system to travel to and from work. Second, I explore what he said about the work tasks and the work space he was assigned. Finally, I examine the disconnect between Hurcane's expectations and the agency's provisions and responses to his needs and hopes—for a work experience that would provide opportunities to develop work skills, as well as for social connection on the job.

"I kept getting told I was supposed to pay extra money. The bus driver told me."

The co-op was to provide transportation and did so by giving Hurcane a bus pass. He was assured that he did not have to pay anything. Hurcane traveled from the college campus into the city and crossed a zone line to do so. He needed to pay a flat rate—covered by the bus pass—and an additional fifty cents for changing zones for each ride. The problem was that the co-op did not give him the right bus pass; it gave him one for the local area that did not cover leaving a particular zone. As a result, Hurcane had to pay a total of a dollar for the additional fare each day. He explains:

> I had a bus pass for a month. A regular bus pass. It's not cheap, it's very expensive, so I'm told. I learned later that to get from Sunnyside College to downtown where the bus normally goes, it costs not a dollar twenty-five but a dollar seventy five. The bus pass only covers a dollar twenty five. So I had to pay fifty cents. They [co-op] should have mentioned something about the extra fee. They didn't mention anything. And where am I supposed to get the money to pay for the bus? They are not paying me, they only said they'd give me a bus pass. And they gave me no warning of this. It didn't happen right away. It happened in like the second week when people were telling me I had to pay the fifty cents. I didn't understand. No one told me. And when I asked, they checked several times and said there should be no charge. There should be no extra money. But, I kept getting told I was supposed to pay extra money. The bus driver told me. And I told the co-op, and they said "this shouldn't happen." Then they finally found out that I have to pay fifty cents more.

Hurcane was not wealthy, so that five dollars a week was more than an inconvenience. He had to deal with the bus driver who told him about the extra charge, which was embarrassing and frustrating. When Hurcane tried to get support from the co-op, it took some time to figure out that Hurcane was right, they were wrong, and he did need to pay. There is clearly a gap between the plan for work experience and the details of its implementation. The plan recognized that Hurcane needs transportation to work and provided for that transportation. But the standard bus pass envisioned by the plan was not the extended pass that he needed.

This seems a simple mistake and one that could be easily corrected. However, his reports about the problem were discounted and perhaps minimized, and it seems that supervisors at the agency responded reluctantly, at a pace that meant Hurcane had to endure two weeks of being asked about the additional fee and managing that difficulty on his own. An alternate and perhaps more reasonable solution would have been to give him petty cash or a new bus card while sorting it out. Instead, Hurcane was left feeling that the agency was not upholding its part of the employment bargain.

Scott (1991) conducted a study of organizations designed to serve people who are blind and examined the "blindness problem" in America (p. 2). He commented: "The personal conceptions that blinded persons have about the nature of their problems are in sharp contrast with beliefs that workers for the blind share about the problems of blindness" (p. 77). The effects of this contrast play out in Hurcane's experiences; his real problem with the bus card may not have been perceived to be problematic by the workers at the agency. It may be that in this situation the staff at the cooperative were initially more willing to trust the plan than to listen to Hurcane's account of his needs. Such was his perception, at any rate.

Hurcane felt devalued by the place he hoped would provide work opportunities for him. He received support for transportation to work, but only minimally and in ways that seemed to him grudging and reluctant. While this kind of experience may not indicate any ill will on the part of his employer, it may be indicative of the general character of accommodation. That is, those who administer the internship program and supervise in the workplace may often have ideas of what's appropriate, and it's not easy to revise those ideas. But Hurcane is really the one who can speak with authority about what he needs.

"Half the time I was working at the agency I wasn't even doing any work."

Once at work, Hurcane found that his position did not have a job description. This is sometimes the case in internships; in this case, a task was identified for him to complete, but little supervision or guidance was provided. Hurcane struggled with the evolving role he had at the agency. He compared his co-op with an earlier work experience that had been more successful: "the . . . job description is set up already. It's there, it's ready, that means you don't have to develop it as you go along. That's the problem with my co-op; they had to develop it as you go along."

The task Hurcane was assigned at the agency was to check phone numbers and update an existing contact manual. This task could be part of a job description related to public relations, outreach, or publicity; on the other hand, it could be a one-time job given to a short-term employee, which may have been the case in Hurcane's situation. That would be reasonable, given that Hurcane was doing a short-term stint. But his comparison of this experience with his previous work experience suggests the significance of a job description. Because there was no job description, Hurcane understood that he did not hold a position but simply worked at tasks that seemed designed to be given to a short-term intern. Again, this may be a common experience for a college student in a short-term job. But the ambiguity of his position seemed to contribute to Hurcane's sense that he was slotted into a make-work task, rather than included as a member of the organization's workforce.

In addition to having a task that was unclear, Hurcane received little supervision and feedback. The result was his feeling that the work he was asked to do was not meaningful and that his presence in the agency was not important. He commented:

Half the time I was working at the agency I wasn't even doing any work. 'Cause I was kind of lost. I mean I was not given any direction. Nobody was asking me how my work was going. Don't you want somebody to check in on you and stuff and see how you're doing in your work? Nobody was doing that. And I thought well, this is so easy to get away with, so why bother if no one is going to check in on me. I played games on the computer, backgammon, gin. Passed the time.

Though Hurcane was placed with the agency to gain "real-world" experience, his work was not treated as essential or meaningful, for him or the agency. One might comment that Hurcane needed direction and guidance about when to ask for supervision and support. If he chose to play video games for hours at a time, it may be that no one noticed or commented because he was at his desk. He did not benefit from the experience in rich ways, in part because of his lack of initiative in asking for clarifications and support. The communication problems I discuss later may have contributed to a situation in which neither Hurcane nor his supervisors did the work required to ensure that he understood his role and the significance of his work within the organization.

In addition to feeling that he could play computer games at work, he complained that the space he was assigned was less than ideal:

> My work environment kind of sucked. Where I was working was actually in the kid's room. Kind of . . . part evaluation room and part play room. They have a lot of toys in there and that means they have kids coming in there sometimes in the summer. And this room is very spacious. It's not small like office size.

Hurcane was not considered a permanent or "real" employee and was housed accordingly, in a space that was "part evaluation room and part play room." He might have been provided with a work environment and supports conducive to his communication needs. He references the fact that the room was "very spacious"; given that he has difficulty discriminating what he hears and needs a quiet environment to focus on his work, this was a significant barrier to completing his tasks. In addition, he was interrupted at times by "kids coming in," another distraction that is not typical in the workplace.

While he was placed in an agency dedicated to serving people with visual impairments, the staff was not sure how to communicate with Hurcane and seemed not to value the work he was doing. It may be that a task was designed for him that was not essential, and as a result staff was not vested in ensuring the quality of his work. The result for Hurcane was a lonely experience marking time. He did not have a clear idea of what his job was and did not feel connected to his colleagues. Traustadóttir notes (this volume): "in practice, work is characterized by inequalities and exclusions, many of which come to seem 'natural.'" Exclusions for Hurcane were related both to his work task and to opportunities for socialization; as a result, he was left isolated and lonely. This internship was an opportunity to gain experience in open employment. As such, it was vitally important that he feel and experience success to buoy his confidence in the benefits of the workplace. Without a belief that there were benefits to such employment, how could he be expected to pursue further openings?

"I asked if I could have the program I prefer. They said 'use what you have, be thankful you have it.'"

Advances in technology provide many new kinds of assistance for those with sensory impairments, yet requests for such supports are often treated as extraordinary demands, so their potential remains unfulfilled. In this case, the agency made a cursory effort to accommodate Hurcane's communication needs. It did not provide effective assistance and, in response to his requests for consultation, argued that he should be grateful for what little it did provide. The agency seemed to feel little responsibility for attending to Hurcane's own sense of what he needed in the workplace. In this section, I examine three aspects of this part of the story: first, Hurcane's perspective on the agency; then his attempts to obtain effective supports; and, finally, a larger issue of communication and inclusion.

Overall, these problems are shaped first by a longstanding division of jurisdiction associated with discrete disability categories and the difficulties brought forward by individuals like Hurcane, whose impairments cross categories in complex ways. Speaking of his overall situation at the agency, he commented: "They didn't have a lot of information. Not all of the staff were aware [of my communication needs]. Some of them are, but not everyone. The problem is that it is more . . . hearing oriented for the blind and visually impaired." That is, the agency was one designed to provide supports for people who are blind and visually impaired. Managing interactions or supports for people with hearing impairments was not a typical consideration for this setting; as a result, the staff was not always well versed in how to support Hurcane's communication needs related to his deafness.

As a student intern, Hurcane had developed modes of accessing material that worked well for him, and he had the skills necessary to do the work assigned to him. He was ready to consult with his supervisors about how he could best complete the work. But his supervisors were not ready to hear from him:

> They had information on contacts for people for disabilities, in this book for people who are deaf and hard of hearing. It got really frustrating because it was hard to read to get through it, and it was very confusing. I had to adapt to computers and software that I was not comfortable with. A different kind of magnification software which I did not enjoy very much. I asked if I could have the program I prefer. They said "use what you have, be thankful you have it."

As with the bus pass, the agency provided "support"—that is, it made a special arrangement designed to help an abstract "person with visual impairment" access his work materials. But the particular mode of assistive technology provided was not appropriate for Hurcane. The lack of responsibility or follow-through he experienced suggests that the agency was not responsive to maintaining or adjusting supports once initially provided.

The communication problems that Hurcane encountered in doing his work also affected his integration into the workplace more generally. Hurcane expected that the work setting would be a place for meeting new people. He was frustrated and commented:

> I expected communication at my co-op. Being able to talk to the people I work with there. Communication was kind of . . . limited. They had some nice people there at my co-op, but there was not a lot of communication. For example, when I was eating lunch, I was always by myself. When I ate at [previous internship site][2] lunch, breakfast, there I was always eating with a group of people that I know and having conversation. There at co-op, what? Nothing.

The role of the workplace in Hurcane's mind included being a place to meet people and develop social relationships, while the agency's conception of its responsibility to him probably did not include providing any supports for developing social relationships. The disconnect illustrates varying conceptions of the role of work; is work purely a place to perform a function for the employer, or does the role of work include being a place both to contribute to the company and to develop relationships?

People who are deafblind often experience isolation in general (Lieberman and MacVicar 2003; McInnes 1999; Sauerberger 1995). One study of transition-age youth who are deafblind found that 50 percent of participants had no friends other than family members and paid service providers (Petroff 1999). Factors that lead to isolation and having few social relationships are several and include the difficulty of finding people who are willing to spend time and energy communicating with someone who is deafblind. People who are deafblind are "much more heavily reliant on other people to assist them in interpreting their environment" (Riggio 1992: 68). This reliance may present a barrier to initial and evolving social connections in the workplace if colleagues perceive it to be burdensome or difficult. If that is the case, colleagues might simply avoid a co-worker who is deafblind to avoid the work of navigating that complexity. Yet these kinds of work must be accomplished if people with sensory disabilities are to participate in paid labor and especially if they are offered the promise of social inclusion through work.

Analysis

Just an internship—often frustrating, less than ideal. I have examined a single student's experience, and a student with an unusual impairment at that; I cannot assume that the experience is typical. But this small slice of experience provides a point of entry for considering some of the institutional arrangements that may make it difficult for many college students with disabilities to move into work settings and some of the limits, for people with disabilities, of ideological constructions that present a job as the centerpiece of social inclusion. The assumption that having a college degree will be sufficient to aid graduates with disabilities in gaining employment may be too simple. Unemployment for people with disabilities is high; one estimate is that more than 70 percent of people with disabilities are unemployed (Harris 1998: 5). Roy, Dimigen, and Taylor (1998) similarly report that 70 percent of Americans with visual impairments are unemployed.

A major issue in thinking about disability is the reality that many nondisabled people fear becoming disabled themselves (Thomson 1997: 12). One way of managing this fear is to relegate disability to a marginal status or to relegate it to experts. Historically, in the United States, the medical profession accepted the role of expert and conceptualized people with disabilities as sick (Charlton 1998: 10), as exotic and aggrandized (Bogdan 1988: 97), and as freaks (Thomson 1997: 11). As such, they have been denied full citizenship in human society. Disability studies struggles to change the way society thinks and responds to people with disabilities, supporting the individual right of self-determination for all people. The utility of the medical model, for the nondisabled, lies in positioning disability as an issue that can be relegated to medicine, ignored by the general population, and contained.

A result of medicalizing disability is that it allows people to view disability as so different from the norm that special considerations, programs, and services must be designed and pressed into service. Thus, segregated workplaces or enclaves where people with disabilities work with nondisabled people in mainstream settings have historically often been the primary employment options for people with disabilities. However, over the past forty years there has been "gradual and steady progress away from segregation of persons with disabilities toward policies and practices that fostered inclusion into the mainstream of society" (Wehman and Revell, 2005: 84). For example, the U.S. Rehabilitation Act Amendments of 1986 included provisions related to supported employment and specifically emphasized integrated settings (Metzel, Foley, and Butterworth 2005).

However, there is concern that, while these programs are designed to support the employment of some people with disabilities, they may not be effective for people who are blind or visually impaired (Capella-McDonnall 2005). Extending that analysis, it seems reasonable to think that, for people who are deafblind, finding employment in the mainstream is particularly challenging. The issue continues to be one of designing supports and services that are tailored to the needs of an individual in a particular setting. The gaps Traustadóttir mentions between disability policies related to work (chapter 4 this volume) and people with disabilities certainly apply here.

In Hurcane's situation, deafblindness was not well understood or accommodated. In 1979, Yoken commented: "A primary shortcoming of rehabilitation services for deaf-blind people is the lack of specific training for the counselor or social worker entering the field" (p. 2). A lack of specific training remains problematic today, as deafblindness is a low-incidence disability. The literature has consistently maintained that deafblindness is not generally understood (McInnes 1999; McInnes and Treffrey 1982; Sauerberger 1995), and efforts must be made to inform people who are deafblind and their communities about what it is and about its implications. It is considered "one of the severest disabilities known to human beings" (Sauerberger 1995: vii), and a very complex one to understand or support. The result for many people who are deafblind is unemployment and a lack of service providers who are knowledgeable about supporting a deafblind person in the workplace.

In the field of deafblindness, some institutions are working to minimize the struggle of accessing services. In New York State, for example, the Commission for the Blind and Visually Handicapped (CBVH) and the Office of Vocational and Educational Services for Individuals with Disabilities (VESID), along with the state Department of Education, developed a joint policy that states:

> While there are proportionately few individuals who are deaf/blind, their needs are complex and are exacerbated, not resolved, by fragmented ser-

vice delivery. Our mutual experience shows that where the expertise of both CBVH and VESID programs are delivered collaboratively, individuals who are deaf/blind experience significantly improved access to services and have much greater opportunities for success. (VESID 1999)

This collaborative effort is responsive to the needs of people who are deafblind and recognizes the ways that interacting with a single agency that may not have expertise related to deafblindness can be challenging. For a more detailed review, see Metzel, Foley, and Butterworth (2005) for their qualitative analysis of six state-level interagency agreements.

The alternative to an abstract, categorical understanding of disability would surely be one that takes a more collaborative approach in which professionals could recognize the person's knowledge of his or her capacities. Unfortunately, the difficulties Hurcane faced in his internship are echoed throughout the professional service system. For example, Patti Lago-Avery, who is deafblind, attended the Deafblind International Conference in 2004 and later wrote an article about her experiences for *The Deaf-Blind American*, a publication of the American Association of the Deaf-Blind (AADB). Lago-Avery commented:

> When deaf-blind individuals tried to give feedback regarding accessibility issues for this conference we were told this is a conference for professionals who worked with deaf-blind people. I found this very insulting as a deaf-blind person, but more so as a professional who works in the field of deaf-blindness. We have many wonderful professionals in the USA who are deaf-blind and who work in the field of deaf-blindness. It is like we are being told that our knowledge and expertise are not welcome. (Lago-Avery 2004: 30–31)

Because of the assumption that professionals in the field are all hearing and sighted, an offensive and exclusive attitude emerged that people who are deafblind cannot hold jobs that include supporting people who are deafblind. Accessibility at the this conference was poor for people who are deafblind. Lighting and sound systems were inadequate; in addition, the interpreters used Canadian sign language and no American Sign Language interpreters were available, limiting Lago-Avery's access to presentations.

The comment Lago-Avery made about the poor accommodations for people who are deafblind is emblematic of the model under which some in the field of deafblindness continue to operate. There is a medical construct that professionals—doctors, educators—use that makes them the only appropriate bodies to investigate how a person who is deafblind should be taught and should live.

Hurcane's experience also points to some of the limits of a rhetoric that makes work the key to social inclusion, without adequate attention to the specific contexts of the worker and the job. Hurcane experienced very little supervision or support, was made to work in a playroom, and was given assistive technology that he did not know well and was not comfortable using. He did not feel valued as an employee and commented that he would have liked to have colleagues to eat with. One reason for his isolation at co-op may have been that his colleagues were not knowledgeable about his communication needs. Hurcane's visual impairment had an enormous impact on his ability to engage with others socially. Not being able to see others curtailed the possibility of striking up conversations with others unless they chose to approach and make themselves known.

The students who participated in my study described the many kinds of work they did to facilitate their own participation in the classroom and social circles of their college campus. The social model of disability seems to imply that this work of inclusion should be shared, but in most work settings it is placed squarely on the shoulders of those who are "different." Such a division of responsibility is upheld by larger cultural notions of independence. The American ideal of rugged independence is a myth, but a very powerful one; students in this study internalized it. It may be that for people with disabilities the need to prove independence is more present than it is for people without disabilities; the fear of being seen as a drain or a burden is a real one for Americans with disabilities, given our postindustrial emphasis on independence and self-reliance. Russell notes: "the emerging market society meant that disabled people who were perceived to be of no use to the competitive profit cycle would be excluded from work . . . generally all disabled people came to be viewed as "unfit." . . . the phenomena of 'disability' itself came to be defined in relation to a capitalist labor market" (Russell 1998: 60–61). The result is often a "be thankful for whatever we give you" attitude in the workplace.

The transition to work may be difficult for all college students, especially in an increasingly uncertain economy. Like many others, Hurcane saw his internship as an important part of his transition and hoped he would be "lucky":

Some people are lucky. They go for co-op and end up working for the company right after having the same co-op there. You have to be very lucky to get that.

But there is more than luck at work in shaping his experience. His frequent references to previous work (which was at a center specifically for people who are deafblind) suggest that we may be seeing a channeling process at work—that this kind of experience may lead some students to feel that being segregated into a work agency specifically designed around a particular disability label is preferable to working in any other setting as a way to achieve social inclusion. At that center, work experiences for deafblind students might include opportunities for socialization and access to technology tailored to their capacities. But such settings would leave people with disabilities on the margins of their communities and vulnerable to the politics of funding such facilities.

The analysis here is far from complete or definitive, but it does raise questions about the place of individuals with sensory impairments in the emergent economic regimes. Will higher education pay off in better employment? Who will shoulder the work of access and inclusion, especially for those with relatively uncommon impairments? What will it take to create genuine bridges between the separate worlds of disability categories and the work worlds of the nondisabled?

NOTES

I wish to thank Dr. Marj DeVault for her support and encouragement.

1. Brueggemann (2004: 1–2) notes: "The debates—and confusion—over when, where, and how to use 'Deaf' or 'deaf' have been considerable. Some scholars argue that the use of 'Deaf' (capitalized) emphasizes the idea that deaf people have a unique culture and a shared language, whereas 'deaf' (lower case) only conveys the medical/audiological designation of a condition . . . the fact remains that most of the time, authors—and readers—are still confused about which one is right (or wrong) in any given instance."

2. Hurcane's previous work experience was in a setting specific to deafblindness.

PART IV

Fiscal Discipline
The Texts of Public-Sector Budget Cutting

The drive to reduce social welfare expenditures has been an undercurrent in many of the preceding analyses. The chapters in this section examine more closely some of the virtual strategies of a new public management, involving new forms of budgeting that affect both workers in the public sector and the clients they serve. These analyses show how budget cutting is woven into the rhetorics of empowerment and choice that have developed alongside moves to shrink public support.

The managerial strategies these authors examine have been developed by public administrators working with the conceptual currencies of accountability and quality management, borrowed from production and introduced into public-sector management and work. Often, they artfully combine a concern for rising expenditures with responses to expressions of need (through a vocabulary of client- or consumer-focused decision making, for example). The promise is that efficiencies of tighter control and market-driven contracting will bring reduced expenditures and better-quality services. But that promise depends on a virtual reality of abstracted clients, clearly defined tasks, and disembodied workers; the daily realities of service delivery are quite different.

These analyses explore management that operates in a textual world, producing what Campbell (in chapter 13) identifies as a "not seeing/not caring" about the real people at work who provide and receive care. In their textual forms, the programs offer "consumer-directed," "student-focused," and "client-centered" decision making, but, in their simultaneous drive to achieve "more bang for the buck," they also bring systematic subversions of these desired goals.

[11]

Exploring Problematics of the Personal-Responsibility Welfare State

Issues of Family and Caregiving in Welfare-to-Work and Medicaid Consumer-Directed Care Programs

FRANK RIDZI

Editor's Introduction

Frank Ridzi's analysis picks up the theme (from chapter 8) of textualized planning in the administration of social welfare, demonstrating an implementation of personal responsibility that shifts responsibility for managing scarce resources to clients. In the two U.S. programs he studies, clients are encouraged to become contractors of caregiving labor, thus placing them in the difficult position of securing and managing efficiency in a gendered and historically underpaid field of work. Within the logic of neoliberalism, it makes sense to look toward market solutions for caregiving needs. Middle-class families find such solutions, the reasoning goes, and those with fewer resources should have similar choices. But that reasoning leaves in place a low-wage caregiving workforce—often made up, literally, of the same low-wage workers who need government assistance to meet their own families' care needs.

In other work (2003), Ridzi has analyzed the implementation of this same county's welfare-to-work program, looking closely at the processes through which cases are opened, plans are made, and clients are slotted into various levels and types of work requirement and service provisions. He shows there that, in the work of intake, welfare staff work with clients to produce a case folder containing multiple documents that together make up an implied narrative about the client and her circumstances (c.f. Pence and Mchahon 2003). In this chapter, he focuses on difficulties that may arise as clients struggle to implement such plans—difficulties that bring into view some of the missing elements in the official narratives of these cases. The analysis reveals the faulty assumptions built into these textualized plans, where caregiving labor is calculated in hours alone, without regard for the particular person who gives care or the one who needs it.

* * *

As legislators and policymakers work to reinvent the U.S. social welfare state at the turn of the millennium, the promotion of "personal responsibility" has emerged as a widely accepted discursive theme. The notion is central to a range of new initiatives, including personal retirement accounts to replace social security, individualized medical savings accounts to replace Medicare, and efforts to enforce child-support collections more actively. In these and related areas, welfare-state proposals, demonstrations, and legislation have sent the message that personal responsibility is a central principle in welfare-service delivery. This chapter employs an institutional ethnographic approach to explore how these new understandings of "personal responsibility" are understood and put together on a daily basis for women participating in aspects of two of the U.S. welfare state's most visible aid programs—Temporary Assistance for Needy Families (TANF), and Medicaid Consumer-Directed Care (CDC).

In each of these programs, "personal responsibility" is conceived, "textualized" (see chapter 1), and brought to bear on women's lives as a way of ordering their interactions with the state—and ultimately as a way of reordering their family/household lives. In this context, the idea of "personal responsibility" is what Dorothy Smith and other institutional ethnographers would term a "conceptual currency"; it is a phrase linked discursively with ideas of client empowerment and self-sufficiency to forge a discourse that draws clients into an organizational logic, fosters consensus with a new regime among staff, and coordinates their interactions in the local sites of front-line policymaking. It is a discourse that sounds reasonable and makes sense in the textual and virtual forms of policy documents and the logics of implementation but often fails to make sense in the context of clients' actual lives.

In exploring how "personal responsibility" plays out in the lives of TANF and Medicaid CDC clients, I begin with an overview of the TANF and Medicaid CDC programs in the locations of study and methods used. Then I explore fair hearing processes and their texts to explicate how personal responsibility is conceived and enforced in ways that reorganize the family and household in accordance with new state policies and the mandates of fiscal restraint.

The Programs: New York's Family Assistance and Consumer-Directed Personal Assistance Program

The conceptual currency of "personal responsibility" is perhaps most clearly visible in the hallmark federal Personal Responsibility and Work Opportunity Reconciliation Act of 1996 (PRWORA), which ended the means-tested entitlement to Aid to Families with Dependent Children (AFDC), the nation's primary cash-assistance welfare program and required work in exchange for benefits. Under Temporary Assistance for Needy Families (TANF), the program created by PRWORA to replace AFDC, states were delegated the authority and responsibility to establish rewards and punishments ("carrots" and "sticks," in the everyday language of program implementation) to encourage personal responsibility to work among clients and within a federal legislative framework.

The federal legislation framed the welfare reform as responding to a perceived "crisis" in the ability of low-income families to perform many of their public functions, due to family structure and an overall lack of acceptance of the "responsibility" to do these jobs. Its first lines express Congress's consideration of the public goods that families provide as "the foundation of a successful society" that "promotes the interests of children." Children are seen as public goods, to be cared for by parents who embody "responsible fatherhood and motherhood" so that they may become successful and productive members of society. States are directed to expend their block-grant funding in ways that contribute to the following goals:

1. Provide assistance to needy families so that children may be cared for in their own homes or in the homes of relatives;
2. End the dependence of needy parents on government benefits by promoting job preparation, work, and marriage;
3. Prevent and reduce the incidence of out-of-wedlock pregnancies and establish annual numerical goals for preventing and reducing the incidence of these pregnancies; and
4. Encourage the formation and maintenance of two-parent families. (SEC. 401. PURPOSE)[1]

New York State's version of TANF, Family Assistance (FA), like most such programs (Hays 2003), has implemented welfare reform in a manner that emphasizes personal responsibility through work. This theme of personal responsibility is also reflected in Medicaid's Consumer-Directed Personal Assistance Program (CDPAP).

Medicaid, another means-tested program, has received a great deal of attention as of late due to rising costs that threaten to push states into fiscal crisis (Behn and Keating 2004). Towering over TANF assistance payouts in 2003 (with outlays of $222.9 billion to 47 million beneficiaries, as compared to TANF's $16.5 billion spent on 5 million recipients), Medicaid is a likely next target for major reform (National Association of State Budget Officers 2001; National Association of State Budget Officers 2003; U.S. Department of Health and Human Services 2000).

Federal legislative reconstruction of social programs often begins with state-level pilot and demonstration programs. With Medicaid, one of the most visible of these programs is the effort toward consumer-directed care (CDC), in which clients are encouraged to assume the personal authority and responsibility to hire, train, manage, and fire their own personal care providers. Appropriated fixed funding in the form of allocatable payroll hours, this usually optional program is advertised as a cost-effective alternative to the more traditional institutional and hospital-based provision of Medicaid services and as a way to address skyrocketing Medicaid long-term nursing home expenditures, which in 1998 accounted for nearly half (46 percent) of all U.S. spending on nursing home care (U.S. Department of Health and Human Services 2000).

In New York State, the push toward consumer-directed health services began with demonstration projects in 1991, followed by the incorporation, in 1995, of a legal mandate that CDPAP be offered in all counties in the state under the 1995 state Social Services Law (Section 81 Chapter 365) (Consumer Directed Choices, Inc.; Consumer Directed Personal Assistance Association of New York State 2001). This program is acclaimed for empowering Medicaid beneficiaries (especially those with long-term care needs) to assume greater autonomy in managing the accommodation of their personal care needs. It also serves the fiscal interests of the welfare state and addresses Medicaid-related budgeting stress (New York State Office of the Governor 2004); states save money by substituting lower CD resource allotments for the higher cost of institutionally provided Medicaid care. The program makes clients responsible for efficiency. Participants are asked to "be responsible for recruiting, hiring, training, supervising and terminating caregivers," as well as "arrang[ing] for back-up coverage when necessary, arrang[ing] and coordinat[ing] other services; and keep[ing] payroll records" (New York State Department of Health 2003). As stated in program literature:

> This program is based on the belief that the majority of consumers know best what their own needs are, and do not require extensive medical intervention.

As with TANF's welfare-to-work program, Medicaid's CDPAP program requires poor beneficiaries to assume new responsibilities and experience new dilemmas in the allocation of limited government resources for their needs.

Method

This chapter presents two case studies derived from observations and interviews at fair-hearings proceedings. Fair hearings are formal arbitration meetings officiated by a representative of the New York State Welfare Commissioner's Office. Held in cases where clients appeal the actions of the counties that administer welfare programs (such as TANF and Medicaid), both county representatives and appellants are provided an opportunity to articulate their positions in the presence of a state hearing officer. Decisions are rendered by mail after review at the state level. I observed fair hearings proceedings for thirty-six clients in six counties in New York State. Of these fair-hearing cases, approximately 50 percent pertained to TANF aid and 65 percent involved Medicaid (these percentages include overlapping cases). My analysis emerges from a larger study that includes observations and interviews with staff in TANF intake and Medicaid offices.[2]

I use the multilayered institutional ethnography approach as an empirical means to connect stated policy objectives with their daily manifestation in women's lives. I consider the fair-hearing appeals of Amy, who is appealing a TANF work sanction, and Betty, who is appealing a Medicaid CDPAP denial of increased aid. Their appeals become contrasting "points of entry" from which to build separate but overlapping maps of the ways in which the activities of a fair-hearing appeal are aligned with relevancies produced by the discourse of "personal responsibility" that is both textualized and implemented in the TANF and Medicaid programs. Key texts that arise within the appeal hearing for each case provide bridges from which to escape the confines of an administrative hearing and explicate the relations of ruling that have been constructed around the conceptual currency of "personal responsibility."

Findings

Policymakers have constructed and presented both the TANF and the Medicaid CDPAP programs as offering empowerment to those who choose to accept personal responsibility. As conceived and textualized, the programs require women to demonstrate their acceptance of personal responsibility by orienting their actions so as to display their compliance with the institutional program of action. Prominent for both Amy and Betty are establishing "plans" for such undertakings as child care and health care and securing "providers" to assist in their implementation. For Amy this comes in the form of an "employability plan"; for Betty, it is a "personal care plan." Complying with these "plans" requires a reorganization of the family and household on the basis of an outsourcing model. The resulting difficulties for clients are exacerbated by their invisibility within the workplace logic of welfare staff.

Case 1: Amy's Appeal of a TANF Work Sanction

Amy is an eighteen-year-old white woman who is struggling to get by with her three year old daughter. Her child's father is not involved in the family, and she lives in a rural suburb of a medium-size city in northern New York State. Part of her survival strategy includes TANF public assistance. Like most recipients, she is required to have an employability plan. For Amy, this includes a full week of GED classes on Monday (seven hours) and a welfare-to-work work experience placement on Tuesday through Friday (thirty-two hours). In return for complying with this work and school schedule, Amy receives a public assistance grant of $380 a month (semi-monthly in $190.50 allotments).

Amy is appealing a sanction that she has received for "failure to comply with employment requirements." This sanction, which will last for 180 days and reduce her monthly benefit to $209, was issued by the county social services department after the time sheet submitted for her GED class indicated that Amy was absent from two classes. This time sheet cued a member of the social services employment team to file a "noncompliance referral." Samantha, the caseworker, reports that a conciliation notice was sent to Amy but that she failed to reply within the required ten-day period (a common occurrence). As a result, Walter, the chief county fair-hearing representative, explains, the agency "was required to pursue a sanction."

Referring to relevant sections of the state's regulations, Samantha explains that a reduction in benefits was calculated by removing Amy's share of the TANF benefit from the family's budget; this sanction will remain in place "until Amy demonstrates that she is willing to comply with employment and training rules" but will not be removed before 180 days have passed, since this is her third instance of noncompliance. Amy was sanctioned two years ago, in 2002, for "failing to keep an appointment" and again last year, in 2003, for "unsatisfactory attendance at a previous employment or work activity." For Amy, the pending loss of $171 per month (reduction from $380 to $209 per month) presents a substantial dilemma. Though she receives an alimony and child support "pass-through" of $50 a month ($25 for her and $25 for her daughter), her rental housing alone (including heat and water) costs $200, leaving her with $59 per month in addition to her food stamps benefits to get her through the next five months.

The hearing begins with a relatively straightforward dialogue designed to establish facts:

Hearing Officer: Please confirm that your name is Amy Smythe.
Amy: Yes.
Hearing Officer: Who else is in your household? A child?
Amy: Yes.
Hearing Officer: And how old?
Amy: Three.
Hearing Officer: How many days did she miss?
Amy's Legal Aid Attorney: [Interjects] May I have her testify?
Hearing Officer: Yes.
Amy's Legal Aid Attorney: You are required to attend both GED classes and Employment Experience, GED on Mondays and Work Experience on Tuesday through Friday?
Amy: Yes.
Amy's Legal Aid Attorney: Have you done all of your employment experience? And are you current?
Amy: Yes.

As the hearing officer moves into questioning Amy's absences and approaches the heart of the hearing's official purpose—establishing Amy's compliance or failure to embody personal responsibility, and whether the agency is correct in sanctioning her—the legal aid attorney deftly interjects. In doing so, he attempts to begin the testimony instead by establishing Amy's strengths as a TANF participant (i.e., full participation in her employment assignments) before addressing the issue of GED absences.[3] Though Amy is present, these institutional representatives are engaged in a contest of texts.

The Central Text. The central text of Amy's case is an attendance sheet produced at the site of her GED classes, but this must be viewed as a subaspect of her overall "employability plan." New York State law requires that districts conduct an employment assessment for all adult recipients. This assessment is used to develop a plan to meet work requirements and to move individuals toward self-sufficiency, taking into account "the individual's education level; basic skills proficiency; child care and other supportive services needs; prior work experience; training and vocational interests; family circumstances, including the special needs of a child in the home" (NYS Department of Labor 2000: 4). Though each plan is personalized, the "employability plan" is also an artifact of the social organization by which welfare-to-work demands certain client behaviors and orchestrates surveillance to determine compliance with them. The GED attendance sheet is one such element of this surveillance, but not the only one. In Amy's case, there is another attendance sheet pertaining to her "work experience" assignment. Together, these two activities make up the heart of Amy's "employability plan," and they also show how Amy's case is linked into a wider effort to define and produce personal responsibility.

The "employability plan" is important not only for clients like Amy; it is also organizationally significant. Local jurisdictions are subject to financial penalties should they fall below federally mandated participation requirements (see Ridzi 2004), which set benchmarks for both the percentage of TANF clients that must be participating in "approved work activities" and the number of weekly hours a client must attend these activities in order to be counted as "participating" (see table 11.1, p. 245). Amy is a single mother and the year is 2004 (when the program continues to operate under 2002 benchmarks pending the stalled congressional reauthorization process of the 1996 PRWORA), so she is required to participate at least thirty hours a week to appear favorably on the welfare-to-work agency spreadsheets as "participating." Since the financial stakes are high, it is common for counties to aim above the minimum for participation (as in the case of Amy, whose weekly participation commitment well exceeds thirty hours); in the words of one administrator, "we aim high so that even when we miss our target, we are still above the state target and won't get penalized."

Amy's participation is furthermore coordinated by the federal and state "countability" of "approved work activities." Her two activities of Work Experience and GED classes are listed as acceptable but not equal for these purposes, since activities pertaining to High School or Equivalent educational attainment can be counted only for hours in excess of twenty (see table 11.2, p. 245). The "Non-Compliance Referral" completed in Amy's case (table 11.3, p. 246) indicates that there are many ways to fall into noncompliance, and each of these possible failures has its own corresponding surveillance and reporting mechanism. Work and other responsibilities not accounted for on this list, however, remain invisible within these institutional mechanics.

The Extended Social Relations. Amy's participation in GED and employment experience activities reflects the "work first" (NYS DOL 2000) approach to personal responsibility that stresses immediate labor-force involvement in return for cash-assistance grants. With this priority in mind, no doubt, Amy's legal aid attorney first points out that her attendance in employment experience activities is satisfactory. Then he calls attention to the behind-the-scenes work that is needed to accomplish her participation:

Amy's Legal Aid Attorney: While you were participating in the employment experiences program, who minded your child?

Amy: My sister, five days a week.

Amy's Legal Aid Attorney: Was she supposed to be paid by the Department of Social Services?

Amy: Yes.

Amy's Legal Aid Attorney: Did you report this to the Department of Social Services?

Amy: Yes.

Amy's Legal Aid Attorney: Did your sister receive pay?

Amy: No

Amy's Legal Aid Attorney: Is she still minding your child?

Amy: No. She quit.

This line of questioning begins to expose an entire subsystem of the work-first welfare regime that is required by the insistence that mothers work full time in the labor market. It is particularly pertinent to Amy's case because it reveals that her attendance record is accomplished not only through her responsibility to the program but also her ability to successfully negotiate subcontracting for child care.

Entering into these arrangements requires beneficiaries to think of themselves as care-giving managers, rather than as direct providers. A TANF staff member explains that this is an intended aspect of welfare reform:

> From day one we're asking them to start thinking about having a provider. Who is going to take care of your children, because eventually [because of the reform] either you're going to go to work or you're going to start the job club.

As part of inculcating this postreform type of responsibility, clients are also told they will need backup providers, as well, for when their children get sick or the sitter suddenly quits or becomes ill and for coverage during summer and school vacations. The framework or script for this subcontracting relationship is institutionalized in child-care plans that TANF applicants must submit. It is also reinforced in interactions with welfare staff such as the job coach in the following excerpt, who emphasizes the critical nature of adequate care-management plans and strategies:

Coach: Well what if your cousin is watching him and he gets sick, what are you gonna do?
Client: I don't have nobody else, I'm all my son's got.
Coach: Well you need to have a plan.

In instances such as these, we see evidence of disjuncture between textual constructions that coincide with the conceptual currency of personal responsibility yet often appear disconnected from clients' actual circumstances when applied in daily processing.

As the immediate managers of care-work subcontracts, those TANF beneficiaries who fail to successfully negotiate risks also assume the repercussions and liabilities. This is evidently the case with Amy, as the ultimate reason for her absence from GED classes is revealed in the course of her testimony:

Amy's Legal Aid Attorney: So why did you miss those two days of GED classes?
Amy: My sister had to go to the emergency room with a broken wrist. I had no gas and no babysitter.

Amy's Legal Aid Attorney: Did you tell anyone?
Amy: No, I should have.

Experiences like Amy's were common in the fair hearings observed for this research. In addition to revealing the ordinary gaps between textual plans and the exigencies of daily lives, they reveal a gendered dynamic at work. Faced with the task of outsourcing care, TANF clients are encouraged to demonstrate personal responsibility by recruiting family members to assist.

Within the TANF program as implemented here, a gendered division of labor is tacitly reproduced. For example, in an orientation meeting, a welfare-to-work staff person instructs a client that female kin may be suitable "staff."

Technical Assistant: Now we have three kinds of providers. One, is the typical daycare. Then we have licensed childcare providers who have been trained and licensed and now their house has become the site of child care giving. And we also have informal childcare such as your mother or sister or something taking care of the kid.

The recruitment of female kin such as the mother or sister that is explicitly recommended frames care as women's work and glosses over the differences between paid care providers and family help subsidized by the program. But the subsidies, like salaries for carework generally, are quite low, and, in Amy's case, payment to her sister was delayed repeatedly—yet Amy is held responsible for lapses in the plan.

Drawing Parallels

It is at this point that we might connect Amy's TANF case and Betty's Medicaid appeal. Given the longer life expectancy for women than for men, Medicaid CDPAP recipients, like TANF recipients, are overwhelmingly female. And, like TANF, CDPAP positions beneficiaries to insert themselves as low-level managers within a predominantly female low-wage labor force. The admonitions to TANF mothers like Amy to ensure that childcare responsibilities are taken care of parallel the messages sent to CDPAP beneficiaries that they must assume the charge of coordinating care work on their own.

CDPAP Administrator: We really tell them [CDPAP participants] right up front that you must, you really need to get a backup because if someone quits, you must have a backup, they really need to because we are not the backup . . . they won't get their services.

The responsibilities of uncompleted or poorly done work fall on the shoulders of CDPAP clients, in much the same way that TANF clients are sanctioned for child-care snafus. A Medicaid employee explains that this is a part of the arrangement that must be accepted by all who choose to participate:

With CDPAP you can choose to have people do things that [traditional] Medicaid homecare can't do, like have people drive. . . . But then the liability goes to the driver, then it's on her insurance, so that's the liability. And with injections, our aides can't do it but they can do it under this program. . . . If they give the wrong needle it's not our responsibility.

The TANF and CDPAP programs are different in many ways, but the point here is to call attention to similar institutional logics and technologies that orient actions taken by staff in both programs. In Betty's case, as in Amy's, we can see connections among a ruling discourse of "responsibility," its textualization in plans and documents of accountability, and the local activities of front-line workers and clients.

Case 2: Betty Challenges Medicaid CDPAP's Denial of Increased Aid

Betty is a sixty-seven-year-old white woman who is having difficulty obtaining home health assistance. She is quadriplegic and lives alone in an apartment in a rural region of New York State. Having been confined to a motorized wheelchair following a car accident nearly twenty years ago, Betty has come to rely on Medicaid as a primary source of sustenance. As a long-term care client, Betty has received services that have ranged from nursing home residency to hospital stays to her present status as a CDPAP participant. In this program, Betty has the responsibility for locating, hiring, training, firing, and supervising personal care providers. According to her "personal care plan," she has been assessed as eligible for level 2 personal care, indicating that her hires can be compensated (according to Betty's scheduling of hours) for level 1 personal care activities (such as housekeeping, laundry, and dishes) as well as level 2 personal care (such as bathing, shampooing, and other activities related to personal hygiene).

Betty comes to the hearing with Eugene, her pro bono legal aid attorney. She is appealing Medicaid's denial of her request for increased home health aide assistance from the twenty-three hours allotted under CDPAP to the twenty-eight hours of care she was receiving under Medicaid long-term care in a nursing home. Betty had moved from the nursing home to a hospital to have surgery on her knee. Upon her release, the department of social services was required to reassess her needs. At that point, she was approved for long-term care (as she was previously enrolled in), but there were no longer any spaces available in local long-term-care facilities. She did not want to return to a nursing home, but there was no space available in any of the area's accessible senior living centers either. As an alternative, Betty was enrolled in the CDPAP program and, subsequent to assessment, approved for twenty-three hours of personal care assistance. The following testimony provided by an adult-services case manager describes the problematic that arose for Betty soon thereafter.

Case Manager: Ms. [Betty] Brewster was approved for long term care, but there was no space available so she was placed and agreed to participate in the CDPAP program. The appellant said she only needed 21 hours of personal care assistance but the county approved her for 23 hours following her assessment. Eight days later she requested additional hours. At the time she still hadn't filled all 23 hours because she was having a hard time filling the positions. It was too soon to re-assess, and there was not yet anything to go by since she was not using her full 23 hours so we could not determine if she needed more.

County Attorney: How did you eventually conduct your re-assessment?

Case Manager: I conducted a home visit. Everything was neat and clean.

County Attorney: Did you have a discussion?

Case Manager: Yes. She expressed having difficulty getting aides because she lives far out in the country. She felt it would be easier if she could offer 3 hours instead of 2 hours to aides each morning. It would be more attractive since they had to drive all the way out there.

County Attorney: What did you tell her?

Case Manager: I told her that the county does not offer extra money for hardship and we discussed other options such as going back to a nursing home or adult care facility and requesting family assistance. She said her family would add any other assistance that she needed.

The Central Text. As with Amy, Betty's case centers on an institutionally produced and activated text. The "personal care plan" is at once the matter of contention and the standard by which accomplishment of personal responsibility is measured. In Betty's estimation the care plan is flawed. She explains:

> I do not feel that the current 23 hours are sufficient because I have to hire people off the street and they are not qualified and to know what to look for on my body. All the time they have to hurry. . . . Even when all the hours have been filled they have to choose between washing me completely and doing housework. . . . I have my current aides until the end of the week but they don't want to work for $6 an hour—or $7 an hour, but after taxes it's $6. I've trained about 150 [providers], no exaggeration, I have had about 20 aides. Many have been interested but won't [take the job] because of low pay.

Betty's complaint is complex: twenty-three hours a week is insufficient, but apparently primarily because she is having a difficult time recruiting workers at the wage she can offer them. If she could recruit satisfactory workers, perhaps twenty-three hours would be enough. The county's representative argues in rebuttal that the hours are computed correctly. Rather, what is at issue is Betty's need to assume full responsibility for arranging providers according to the conditions given in the care plan:

County Representative: In consumer-directed care regulations, it is up to the client to hire and fire and train, not up to the county. The nurse does the number of hours; it is based on the DMS score. It's really a bank account of time. You have all those hours banked so you can use them. You get 23 hours a week averaged over the year so you can short them [your providers] an hour in the future [to make up for extra time you need them to work now].

This senior caseworker aims to justify the county's opposition to granting Betty increased hours. However, ironically, Betty does seem to be thinking responsibly about how to manage, given the low hourly wage she has to work with.

In subsequent cross-examination of county witnesses, the validity of the "personal care plan" itself, as an adequate response to Betty's real-life needs, comes into question. Betty's legal-aid attorney calls upon the nurse caseworker responsible for establishing the appropriate number of hours to be allotted.

Betty's Legal Aid Attorney: For the personal care plan. . . . How was the number of 23 hours arrived at?

Nurse Caseworker: I talk to the client and to caregivers that are present to find out how long it takes to do their personal care, housekeeping etcetera and I personally know some estimates from doing this for a while. Then I use a worksheet for the care plan, as you can see in page 11 [of the document submitted for this appeal], the worksheet shows how the numbers are calculated...

Betty's Legal Aid Attorney: So how did you come up with the 23 hours then? You just talked over this whole thing with the applicant [Betty] and gave her the numbers she asked for and made no adjustments?

Nurse Caseworker: Yes. . . . Her estimated times seemed reasonable. . . .

Betty's Legal Aid Attorney: But what if the client is not right?

Nurse Caseworker: You look at the household every few months and look for deterioration.

In this testimony, it seems that the twenty-three-hour allotment is grounded in a collaborative consultation with the client, but one that loses its collaborative nature once made official.

As the hearing continues, the parties disregard Betty's role in its estimation, and the twenty-three-hour allotment becomes a standard by which the client's assumption of personal supervisory responsibility is measured.

Betty's Legal Aid Attorney: Now at Betty's 2nd request for more hours, did you have any concerns?

Nurse Caseworker: No concerns regarding the home or environment at the time. She [Betty] requested no changes in the care plan. She said she felt the aides at the time did not have enough time to complete what was on the care plan.

Betty's Legal Aid Attorney: You did though?

Nurse Caseworker: Yes, I thought they had enough time...

Betty's Legal Aid Attorney: What would have led you to raise her hours?

Nurse Caseworker: If I had felt there had been any physical deterioration.

Because visible deterioration was the standard by which she could obtain a reassessment of the hours allotted, Betty was forced by the "personal care plan" either to find ways to adjust to the difficult market herself or suffer in the hope that her hours would be increased eventually. Looking further into her interaction with the care plan offers insight into some of the ways in which Betty was directed to live up to what Medicaid CDPAP implementers saw as her "responsibility" to make the care plan work. It also provides a window through which to explore the broader social relations that are implicated within the construction of the "personal care plan."

The Extended Social Relations. Subcontracting of care work is a central premise in both the TANF and the CDPAP programs. For TANF, women are expected to engage in contracting for the purpose of securing child care, while personal-care needs are addressed through similar contracting practices within CDPAP. The positioning of clients within subcontracts situates them as street-level managers of historically female and notoriously low-paid care workers. Under these circumstances, by requiring female welfare recipients to "manage" care providers, these practices create hierarchies between women while at the same time informalizing and deprofessionalizing child care. In this situation, it is not always easy to find adequate and appropriate help or to keep it. Betty's difficulties scheduling her aides are echoed in the ethnographic data gathered in other sites. For example, a welfare mother explains the difficulty she is having to a TANF worker.

Applicant: I'm, all my son's got, I don't got . . . he was in day care but he got kicked out of day care, [explaining] he got a little rough, that's a problem.

Another TANF mother explains:

Applicant: I did have a job and got fired because nobody was watching my kids.

Echoing the recruitment and retention concerns of TANF mothers, a Medicaid administrator explains that CDPAP participants face similar challenges:

Medicaid Administrator: It's hard to hire health care aides. The pay stinks and to get someone you can trust to care in your household and not rip off you and your loved ones just for your family is a plus.

Women who must hire other women to bathe them, cook for them and do housework may also be constrained both by the fact they cannot offer enough hours to make remaining in their employ worthwhile and the fact that the women they can hire often lack adequate training to complete needed tasks in the time that a personal care plan allows them to compensate. This sometimes leads CDPAP participants to supplement their caregiver's pay out of their own savings, even though it is a violation of

Medicaid policy. The pressure placed on CDPAP clients to absorb un-covered costs of needed care work is compounded by the transference of training responsibilities to CDPAP participants and the common practice of allocating Medicaid funds according to estimates of work efficiency on the basis of the assumed capabilities of trained health-care professionals. In reality, however, these "trained professionals" are not available to CDPAP participants. As a result, participants must find creative ways of making ends meet or challenge these assumptions in fair-hearing appeals.

While women can employ the fair-hearing appeals process to challenge the expectations placed on them to manage child and health caregiving in the TANF and CDPAP programs, respectively, this is a road taken less of-ten than might be expected (Gilliom 2001). Furthermore, it is not a path-way likely to bring success. Among the county representatives interviewed, most placed the rate at which their county's actions were affirmed by state arbitrators (in ruling against client appeals) at around 90 percent. Indeed, rather than pursue an appeals process and risk "rocking the boat," perhaps incurring the wrath of local aid administrators, the path of least resistance for TANF and CDPAP participants is to seek the assistance of family and other kin to fill in the gaps in needed care. This recruitment of aid not only occurs frequently; it is encouraged by the wider institution.

As in the TANF program, CDPAP clients are encouraged to recruit fam-ily members to fill in the gaps in care left by inadequate staffing or insuf-ficient funding. Though unspoken in many instances, the gendered nature of family recruitment for personal needs care work is manifest in unques-tioned remarks such as the following suggestion of a nurse caseworker that a client recruit her daughter to assume the workload for which a county did not wish to supply extra funds.

Nurse Caseworker: We decided that there was no reason to increase the hours she was approved for; if she's having difficulty cooking she could ask her daughter and have her make all her meals ahead of time and freeze them and deliver them on the weekend.

These routine practices imply that it is female family members who will be recruited to do the care work (DeVault 1991), offering gendered scripts for clients to emulate in recruiting and maintaining care providers. How-ever, it is not only who is recruited for what types of assistance, but also how different types of assistance are valued that points to the patterns that these programs accommodate and institutionalize.

The Textual Category of "Provider" and the Gendered Valuation of Care Work and Paid Labor

It is mostly women who make up the three groups involved in these care relations: TANF and CDPAP clients, their low-wage subcontractors, and the family members that are recruited to assist with caregiving. As a result, participants in these means-tested programs are particularly vulnerable to a culturally dominant practice of valuing wage labor above unpaid labor. This practice is rooted in a discourse of "working families" that envisions "two-paycheck" couples and that has historically characterized the outsourcing of family work as an escape from the "second shift" available to the more affluent (Ehrenreich and Hochschild 2002). Working within this framework, these programs employ a textual category of "care provider" in ways that gloss over the differences between paid care providers and unpaid family help as they are experienced by these less affluent women. The differential valuation of care work and wage labor is most visible in the contrast that exists between the intense scrutiny devoted to TANF clients' work hours and the discretion involved in the calculation of care work hours within CDPAP.

For TANF participants, wage labor is documented by meticulous accounting of hours worked.

TANF Staff Member: On here [the form] you put 14 to 30 hours and looking at your pay stubs there is 10, 15, 30, 15 hours per week . . . this doesn't show me full time employment.

Client: 30 hours isn't?

TANF Staff Member: Well that was back in the beginning of May . . . based on this here you would be eligible but to be eligible, because you're not employed to your capacity. . . .

Client: But I got full-time sometimes . . . but when it's full-time you [the welfare office] don't help nobody. . . .

TANF Staff Member: So that's what you need 'cause then you help yourself.

In TANF, the state requires clients to account for every hour worked in the paid labor force in order to demonstrate personal responsibility.

Under CDPAP, however, the state holds itself to a much less rigorous accounting of the work that it seeks to reimburse. This is perhaps consistent with the tendency for those dependent upon personal assistants to construct this work as invisible (Rivas 2002), though in this case it serves the state rather than the disabled person. For example, in the following exchange from a fair hearing, the benevolence of a landlord who helped a client make ends meet is knowingly overlooked.

Appellant's Lawyer: If the county was relying on help from family and friends, did the county have a number for those hours in the personal care plan?

Adult Caseworker: No, I don't think they were included.

Appellant's Lawyer: You said you know the landlord was providing services and the county did not attribute/calculate any value to that help?

Adult Caseworker: No. Not to my knowledge.

In another exchange, a medical-needs assessor employed by a county explains the logic, and the incongruity, behind this practice.

Appellant's Lawyer: Did you take into account family support?

Nurse Caseworker: No, I do not take into account any family or outside support, what they do I consider extra. . . .

Appellant's Lawyer: You said you deal with similar cases, people in wheelchairs, et cetera, but they only get 6 hours of aid. So there must be some dissimilarity, 6 versus 23 hours?

Nurse Caseworker: But they have a lot of family support.

Appellant's Lawyer: But you said you don't take family support into account?

While the attorney appears to have scored a point in this exchange, the nurse's approach is on the whole consistent with wider cultural practices that devalue care work relative to paid labor. In the present case, it embodies the most recent front in a decades-old social-welfare thrust to transfer responsibility for bridging gaps between economic constraints and human needs to the individual beneficiaries themselves.

These program efforts find their nonmedical equivalents in TANF and in the welfare reforms that led up to it and that, in the 1980s, redrew the costly contract between the government and the poor so that the state would no longer financially underwrite the labor that mothers perform in the provisioning and caregiving of their own children (Naples 1997). While the state is no longer to subsidize the care that poor mothers provide to their own children, it is, ironically, willing to pay (however meagerly) for women to give care to other people's children.

Conclusion

Social dynamics of dominance and power relations, U.S. history has taught us, are resilient. They resist efforts to change them, transforming over time but in ways that maintain their force within a dynamic society (Collins 1997). Relations of power and domination are also subtle, working in the unquestioned assumption or the taken for granted routine (D. Smith 1987, 1999; V. Smith 1997). Social welfare policies are constructed and implemented within this social milieu and are not unaffected by such relations.

In contrast to their forerunners, the TANF welfare-to-work and Medicaid CDPAP programs can be seen as granting increased personal autonomy to their predominantly female beneficiaries by encouraging the replacement of government dependency and reliance with new ideal statuses of worker and consumer. Citizenship in advanced capitalism has come to be epitomized by the dual identities of tax-paying workers and consumers; these characteristics confer a sense of entitlement and deservingness within the larger political and economic system that stands in stark contrast to the undeserving status that is conveyed to those women who are neither wage earners nor consumers due to fiscal dependence on state aid (Alexander and Mohanty 1997). Previous feminist literature locates means-tested programs such as cash assistance and Medicaid as occupying a low status within a hierarchy of welfare-state programs. Referred to as the second tier (in contrast to those in higher tiers, such as Social Security and Medicare), these programs have historically offered meager benefits and required invasive, punitive and often stigmatizing practices of their predominantly female and disproportionately non-white clients (N. Fraser 1989; Haney and March 2003; Orloff 2001; Valocchi 1994).

By mandating that TANF beneficiaries participate in welfare-to-work job preparation and employment activities and by offering Medicaid recipients the option of enrolling in consumer-directed personal-assistance programs, these means-tested welfare programs encourage beneficiaries to distance themselves from the characteristics of feminized dependency associated with the lower tier of welfare services (N. Fraser and Gordon 1994) and instead take steps to align themselves with the more respected and autonomous clientele of the upper tier. It furthermore invites and compels these poor women to embody a spirit of entrepreneurship that, itself an abiding cultural characteristic of U.S. society, positions personal responsibility as an unassailable moral good (Biggart 1989). This new personal-responsibility approach asks poor women to transition away from traditionally feminized forms of dependence on the state and to embrace statuses that society has masculinized, such as those of an independent, tax-paying worker and consumer (N. Fraser and Gordon 1994). Though this proposed transition appears to abandon gender as an organizing principle of welfare policy, the preceding sections present evidence that this is not the case in practice.

This chapter documents that both the nationally implemented TANF model of welfare-to-work and New York State's innovative Medicaid CD-PAP program impose new household relations in order to ensure that the public role of families to provide for the care of children and ill relatives is carried out. With TANF, standards of personal responsibility complicate the provision of child care by mandating full-time participation in the paid workforce in conjunction with the outsourcing of child care to often minimally trained, low-paid, and comparably poor women (Hays 2003). Personal-responsibility standards simultaneously disregard nonfinancial (in-kind and other) contributions to childrearing that are offered by non-custodial parents by pursuing paternity establishment and child-support enforcement policies that threaten to further alienate single mothers from informal networks of male caregiving (I do not have the space here to thoroughly address this thread of analysis but see Haney and March 2003).

For similarly situated poor Medicaid beneficiaries, the CDPAP program also sets about ensuring that the public work of the family is done in accordance with new relations of ruling. The responsibility required in the CD-PAP program is that of recruiting, training, and hiring from a labor pool of often untrained, mostly poor women to ensure that the care work formerly done by trained professionals is accomplished in efficient and cost-effective fashion (see Sapiro 1990). To attain these arguably unrealistic standards of efficiency, clients are further encouraged to compensate for unmet needs by enlisting the support of family members, typically women, to routinely produce work that is otherwise unaccounted for within the Medicaid structure.

One can find both contradictions and patterns at work within these two manifestations of the emerging personal-responsibility welfare state. There are certainly contradictions in that welfare reform acknowledges women as potential breadwinners, yet overlooks gender-related inequities in the labor market. In addition, the stated CDPAP goal of empowering long-term Medicaid beneficiaries has a reciprocal effect of transferring the burdens of budget-challenging medical-care costs onto local clients who must now accrue invisible debt to family and friends that they recruit to pick up the slack of funding inadequacies.

Amid these contradictions, however, there are patterns, as well. However it is labeled—the capital investment welfare state (Quadagno 1999), the shift to a daddy state (Starobin 1998) or the nonresponsibility welfare state (Acker 2003)—the emerging personal-responsibility welfare state is one that stresses the downloading or delegation of many of its most difficult conundrums to the individual beneficiary, in part by activating a textual category of "provider" that glosses over the differences between paid care providers and unpaid family help. As noted in Naples's (Naples 1997) discussion of the new political consensus that preceded the 1996 welfare reform, an agreement was reached regarding the responsibilities of low-income citizens who seek assistance, but no such agreement was reached as to the responsibilities of the government.

The U.S. welfare state is transforming amid a wider global restructuring, and a so-called New Economy in which leaner government is thought to be the only option for continued national prosperity (Persuad and Lusane 2000). It is not federal, state, and local administrators that must be blamed but rather these globalizing logics that must be analyzed. The dynamics that here are shown to obscure, undervalue, regulate, and restructure care work within the family are a microcosm of a global undervaluation of care work. According to UN Asia Committee estimates (United Nations Social Commission for Asia and the Pacific 2002), close to 50 percent of care work globally is undervalued. The challenge that faces all welfare states is how to address a history of gendered work embedded in social policy while concurrently adapting to new logics of a global economy. We are in a period of transition in the United States. The PRWORA is now reauthorized, and Medicaid reform is imminent. As such, this report is not intended to be definitive and conclusive but is rather a progress assessment that will necessarily be updated; it serves the purpose of illuminating where to look in the future as we continue to monitor ruling relations within the welfare state.

TABLE 11.1

Participation Rate Requirements.

FFY YEAR	All Families Participation Rate	Number of Weekly Hours
1997	25%	20
1998	30%	20
1999	35%	25
2000	40%	30
2001	45%	30
2002	50%	30

SOURCE: Welfare-to-Work Policy and Program Framework, March 2000, Welfare-to-Work Division, NYS Department of Labor; available at http://www.labor.state.ny.us/workforcenypartners/PDFs/wtwppf.pdf.

TABLE 11.2

Countable Activities

Activities	Participation Rate Impact (Countability)		
	TANF All Family	TANF Two Parent Families	Safety Net
Unsubsidized Employment	counts	counts	counts
Subsidized Private-Sector Employment	counts	counts	counts
Subsidized Public-Sector Employment	counts	counts	counts
Work Experience	counts	counts	counts
On-the-Job Training	counts	counts	counts
Job Search	counts but for only 6 weeks per year	counts but for only 6 weeks per year	counts toward hours above 30
Job-Readiness Training	counts but for only 6 weeks per year	counts but for only 6 weeks per year	counts toward hours above 30
Community Service	counts	counts	counts toward hours above 30
Vocational Education	counts but for only 12 months total	counts but for only 12 months total	counts toward hours above 30
Job-Skills Training	counts toward hours above 20	counts toward hours above 30 or 50	counts toward hours above 30
Education Training	counts toward hours above 20	counts toward hours above 30 or 50	counts toward hours above 30

TABLE 11.2 *(Continued)*

Countable Activities

Activities	Participation Rate Impact (Countability)		
	TANF All Family	TANF Two Parent Families	Safety Net
High School or Equivalent	counts toward hours above 20	counts toward hours above 30 or 50	counts toward hours above 30
Child-care Provider for Community Service Participant	counts	counts	counts toward hours above 30
Job Search/Job Readiness (beyond 6-week limit)	does not count	does not count	does not count
Other Local District Activity Not Included Above	does not count	does not count	does not count

SOURCE: Welfare-to-Work Policy and Program Framework, March 2000, Welfare-to-Work Division, NYS Department of Labor; available at http://www.labor.state.ny.us/workforcenypartners/PDFs/wtwppf.pdf.

TABLE 11.3

The "Noncompliance Referral" form completed in Amy's case.

Employment Activities: (Select one)
___ Failed to keep/complete appointment
___ Failed to keep/complete an employment/training appointment
___ Failed to go to an employment/training assignment
___ Failed continuation of employment/Work Activity assignment
___ Failed to keep/complete job search appointment
___ Failed to complete job search
___ Failed to go to a job opening interview
___ Failed to take a job
___ Failed to provide a medical report
___ Failed to provide a medical report (limitations)
___ Failed to keep/complete a medical exam appointment
___ Failed to keep/complete a medical exam appointment (limitations)
___ Failed to work register
___ Failed to provide employment status
___ Failed to actively seek employment and provide proof
___ OTHER, Please explain _____

NOTES

1. This is notably framed in gender-neutral language, even though there is clearly a gender subtext in the sense that single-mother families are seen as the root of the problem.

2. The larger study includes data from conversational interviews with sixty-seven staff members, clients, and administrators (DeVault and McCoy 2000) and field notes taken for more than two hundred hours of observation between 1999 and 2004 (which included observations of intake processing for more than one hundred TANF clients).

3. His intervention here illustrates the importance of having a legal-aid attorney, which, from the evidence amassed in this research, has an unquestionably positive impact for the appellants who are able to secure one.

12

The "Textualized" Student

An Institutional Ethnography of a Funding Policy for Students with Special Needs in Ontario

YVETTE DANIEL

Editor's Introduction

Yvette Daniel demonstrates how, in response to a new process for allocating special-education funding, teachers, administrators, and other professionals in Ontario were drawn into an elaborate work process that resulted in a shift of focus from real students to textualized profiles of need. Discussed as resource-led (as opposed to demand-led) funding, the new process was explicitly aimed at rationing scarce resources. It was also labeled a student-focused program, suggesting through its two names that the new process could deliver more focused and therefore more effective assistance. Like the programs that Ridzi analyzed in the previous chapter, then, this procedure knits together vocabularies that respond to users' interests (e.g., in empowerment, choice, and individual attention) with those of budgetary restraint.

In this case the procedure put in place doesn't work; administrators see too clearly the funding consequences of their paperwork, and they mobilize staff to manipulate the system; as a result, the process is quickly scrapped. Still, in its focus on a failed procedure, Daniel's discussion raises intriguing questions. It underscores the fact that our analyses capture only snapshots of economic and organizational restructuring, processes that unfold and are redesigned over time. While we may identify key moments of change in legislative frameworks and philosophies (the shift to resource-led funding, for example, or passage of welfare-restructuring legislation), these moments do not show the end of the story. Implementation trajectories are more complex and nuanced than many analyses—focused on the making rather than doing of policy—suggest. In addition, Daniel's analysis, like others in this volume, shows us people in particular places actively taking up, responding to, and reshaping policy direc-

tives. Thus, it reminds us that technologies of accountability are not seamless or unassailable. It highlights the adjustments and improvisations of front-line workers as they implement text-based policies; in each moment of practice, they must develop a version of textually prescribed activity that not only responds to guidelines but also fits the circumstance at hand. In many cases, people make those adjustments so skillfully that they are hardly noticeable. But examining moments of subversion or organizational chaos might point to fissures in the edifice of textual power.

The starting point for Daniel's inquiry was her own work process, and this chapter may speak to many in the helping professions who wonder at the transformation of their work—it provides a model for carrying that kind of interrogation beyond individual puzzlement, inspiring strategies with which to question what people know in such settings and how they know it.

* * *

The nomination form was the way we started off—by identifying any child that could, by any leap of the imagination, become a funding claim. It was controversial, but we were told, "Just do it to get them in."

These are the words of one professional who participated in the funding exercise in one of the local boards in Ontario where I conducted this study. The controversial funding policy, Intensive Support Amount (ISA) claims, has now been suspended, and the provincial government is seeking ways to replace it with a revised funding formula. However, this tale must be told, for once we remove "policy from its pedestal" (Ozga 2000) and study the social organization of knowledge (Smith 1987, 1999), we bring "into view the local moments of articulation to the extra-local relations of restructuring" (Griffith 2001: 88) that highlight the lived reality of a policy that started out with claims of making funding more equitable but quickly spun out of control to create a "disembodied" and "decontextualized" student for the purposes of funding. This phenomenon appears to be part of the global reorganization of production that has influenced policy discourse and practice in many service sectors, including education.

The way funding is allocated for children with special needs can be analyzed within this larger infrastructure of changing ideologies, discourses, and practices. My study examines the issue of funding provisions for special education in Ontario against the backdrop of general changes in the system as a whole. Within the larger context, I focus on one particular aspect of accountability embedded in the new funding formula. It is known as "student-focused funding" and was introduced by the Ministry of Education and Training (MET). This new funding formula mandated a complex process of "financing rationing" through layered funding processes made up of several grants. Specifically, I study one feature of funding for special education, the Intensive Support Amount (ISA) claims for students with high needs. The process of making a claim for ISA involved a range of educators, professionals, and others with expertise in the pedagogy and administration of special education. In order to obtain funding, school boards had to adhere to stringent guidelines and protocols established by the provincial Ministry of Education in Ontario. Accountability was implemented by means of rigid eligibility criteria, documentation, and audits.

This study originated from my own experience and standpoint as an administrator in one of the local elementary schools at a time when the ISA claims policy was being implemented. I became an active participant in the process of submitting names of students to the Special Education team. Generally, I assisted Board of Education personnel in preparing files for claims submission. As I engaged in this work, I began to realize the textual nature of the exercise that was organized and dictated by rigorous guidelines and procedures. I began to interrogate the manner in which I was engaged in ruling practices when I thought I was "helping" students. "Ruling, as practiced by professionals, is often done in the interest of even-handed and accountable administration" (Campbell and Manicom 1995: 11). Many other services to students were put on hold as the work of preparing files for ISA claims took precedence in the daily work of the Special Education department.

One central question underscored this research project: how did ruling and authoritative knowledges organize the construction of a student whose educational needs were special enough to make claims on funds set aside for the education of students defined as having special needs? The increasingly textually mediated character of special-needs funding through ISA had "textualized" particular students for funding purposes. In the work of producing an ISA "folder"[1] for funding claims, a "textual" child was constructed through the extensive documentation required for claim purposes. This exercise was a complex work process that separated the textual mode from the lived experience through an intertextual dialogue (Griffith 1984). I wanted to understand how this funding process operated as actual practices of people whose work intersected with the bureaucratic structures of educational institutions.

Dorothy Smith (2002b) claims: "If people at work[2] . . . could examine, by examining the textual forms of organization, how their work is concerted so that it produces the outcome it does, maybe they could find ways of designing it differently." As activists/educators/practitioners, we must take on this challenge by examining our own work processes and the social relations in which they are embedded while searching concomitantly for "progressive change at the level of practice and attitudes" (Pence 1997: 183). This study opens up opportunities to explore the spaces where future research and activism can begin to transform the manner in which needs of children are constructed by educational and bureaucratic institutions.

This chapter has four sections. First, I set the context by providing a brief overview of the ISA funding policy. Next, I discuss the manner in which institutional ethnography enables us to map these textually organized links and brings into view the processes by which educational funding becomes part of the relations of ruling often perceived to be neutrally accountable administrative procedures. In the third section, as part of an institutional ethnography study, I show how the lived realities of people engaged in this work process are shaped by these textually mediated social relations. Last, I conclude with findings and lessons learned by deconstructing these experiences and opening up the possibilities for thinking differently.

The Context: An Overview of the ISA Funding Policy

ISA funding was one aspect of the "student-focused" funding model for education. The ISA process was meant to be a demographic analysis for the purpose of establishing a baseline for funding. This funding model was resource-led; a finite amount allocated by the government was to be distributed to school boards across the province. This shift in funding from a demand-led model (where governments allocate resources in response to the needs) to a resource-led one "has occurred across whole societies in Western countries and reflects one of the societal attitudes which need to be taken into account" (Stakes and Hornby 1997: 6).

There were four categories to the ISA grants, but in this study, I elaborate upon ISA 2 and ISA 3, worth $12,000 and $27,000, respectively, which provided funding for students with high needs as determined by a detailed claims procedure in which a comprehensive claims folder had to be created for each student. The creation of this folder was guided by strict Ministry guidelines called "profiles." The claims process required exhaustive documentation, such as a professional assessment that in most cases involved a diagnosis, a documentation of concerns, a current and fully developed Individual Education Plan (IEP), and a detailed schedule for students to account for the manner in which additional supports were provided. The various "texts" in this process were made to work to construct a child's profile to match the eligibility criteria laid down by Ministry guidelines. The ISA claims process, mainly an "audit of need" (Bines 1995), was revised and refined several times after the government introduced this policy. The eligibility criteria for ISA claims made under each profile were clarified so that school boards and Ministry auditors could have some consistency in interpreting them to make the claims process more equitable.

The nomination form sets in motion a lengthy bureaucratic process. Figure 12.1, Collecting Textual Evidence, is a schema I created to illustrate the work process and the discourse dictated by the language of the Ministry profiles. All the textual work done by various professionals was guided by the criteria outlined in these profiles. As such, it focused on labeling and categorizing students to generate funding. The profiles became the "master documents," and at every stage professionals preparing the claim folders had to ensure that the texts adhered to the profile mandates. These profiles were the filters through which each text had to pass. As one special education consultant remarked:

> If you are going to label a student with Mild Intellectual Disability (MID), then we do need hard data. I wish we could focus less on the formal identification part and put our energies into providing the supports needed. That would be more efficient and worthwhile.

Institutional Ethnography: Text-Mediated Social Relations

Institutional ethnography is being taken up in human-service areas such as health care and social work to examine the production and use of objectified bureaucratic processes that govern our work and experiences. Darville (1995) refers to work with bureaucratic texts as "organizational literacy" that is "concerned with effecting organizational processes" (p. 254). Institutional ethnography is useful in analyzing the ISA policy in which everything rests upon the manner in which the various documents in the claims folder are "written up" (Darville 1995: 254).

Institutional ethnography, as a method of inquiry that shows how actions have roots in social relations, illuminates the connections among the sites and situations of everyday practice and the ruling relations that shape everyday experience. Such linkages and connections are accomplished mainly through a textually mediated social organization that is so pervasive in our lives that we barely notice it. Several institutional ethnographers have studied the textual process of documentation in nursing and health care work, which is crucial for reimbursement of services. Nurses and other health-care workers realize that they have to revise the language they use to summarize a patient's medical condition, and so they become creative.

> There's a kind of work lore, an exchange of knowledge about, "Try reporting it that way," or "This phrase always seems to work." This kind of creative writing of charts and reports is going on among people everywhere. This is a work process. People are doing it and it takes up time. There's a connection among people who share this kind of common situation where they feel that they can't give proper care to their patients unless they do this work of creative charting. (Smith 2002b)

A similar process was involved in producing an ISA file for funding purposes that would pass the centralized audit. Professionals engaged in this work learned what it takes to make a file successful. One coordinating principal for Special Education commented during our discussion:

> The ISA process as it is now does not really demonstrate needs- it demonstrates ability to work the system. And there's this joke going around that ISA stands for "I'll Sign Anything" that will help the case. That was the game we have learned to play and we keep justifying that by arguing that the children will benefit in the long run.

Professionals prepared the various documents that made up an ISA claim. The language used to describe a student as having "high needs" was coordinated with the language used in the realm of special education in the system. In the ISA process, a student with needs was transformed into a category of the prescribed eligibility criteria by a set of textually mediated work processes. One special-education consultant summed up the entire ISA process in one sentence. He remarked, "This exercise of preparing documentation and files has very little to do with the children in reality."

The textual world conceptualized by Smith helps us understand "the textual architecture of routine organizational action" (Campbell and Gregor 2002: 24) that shapes a bureaucratic or professional world of text-mediated action in which power is carried through texts and by the organizational discourse around these texts. When we begin to understand the important role of text-mediated social relations, we can begin to observe how people at different sites, though separated by time and space, are linked through action. Official texts hold considerable power and authority, and "to read is to expose oneself to capture. It is to risk being entered by an organization of language and making it ours" (Smith 1999: 214), and even when we want to withstand the official "ruling text," we find ourselves struggling to resist "institutional capture" (Smith 2002b).

The student-nomination form prepared by the classroom teacher or the special education teacher set in motion a chain of organizational action that was dependent upon the use of language, either written and/or spoken utterances that built organizational versions for a particular course of action. Various professionals who interacted with the nomination form determined what information was necessary to "fit" the child to the particular claims categories (profiles) created by the Ministry. The "successful" folder was the one that contained the required "texts" that followed the prescribed "textual architecture" (Turner 2001) that determined the next steps in the process. The objectivity created through these forms was useful, and, as some of my interview participants admitted, also important, given the limitations of time and resources. Difficult decisions had to be made in a short time, as the future of funding for special education was dependent upon this process. Thus, people became part of an exercise of power and relations of ruling and entered into social relations in this text-mediated world of preparing an ISA claims folder organized through texts across multiple sites and through multiple readings. The process of preparing a successful ISA claim depended upon the capacity and ability of professionals to use the appropriate language of the Ministry profiles in all documentation, especially in Individual Education Plans (IEP) and Confidential Summaries. One of my informants, a social worker, explained how she as a professional was implicated in this relation of ruling dictated by ISA policies and procedures. She remarked:

> Generally, people who have gone through the system do what they are told. And, most of us don't want to get our hands slapped. We have learned how to adapt, and how to jump through the hoops. Most of us who have these

jobs have done fairly well in the system, and that's because we conform to the rules. We try to keep our integrity but we do not rebel. In fact, we teach our kids in school to conform.

Data Collection and Analysis

As stated earlier, the study began with my own work as a school administrator. I attended several workshops to learn about my role and responsibilities in this process. I kept a journal and collected documentation in the form of emails, guidelines, and policy documents that I encountered in the course of my daily work in the school. Opportunities also arose for informal conversations with people over the phone, via email, or in chats over coffee that added to my observations. Every encounter was potential data. Over the course of the year, I gathered information through my own work, interactions with others, and the various texts I encountered. Furthermore, I conducted interviews with sixteen informants, including special education teachers, special education consultants, school social workers, school psychologists, supervising principals, and Ministry auditors.

In institutional ethnography interviews, the purpose of the interview is not only to enable informants to describe a particular event or circumstance but also to "point toward next steps in an ongoing, cumulative inquiry into translocal processes" (DeVault and McCoy 2001: 753). Hence, the interviews involved talking in detail about the textual process of the work of participants, how they activated the text and understood the manner in which the text was taken up at different stages and sites within a highly structured work organization.

Texts move among various sites through people's work at points termed "processing interchanges" (Pence 1997: 60). Pence argues that "the construction of these processing interchanges is coupled with a highly specialized division of labor that accomplishes much of the ideological work of the institution" (p. 60). She explains that "almost all interchanges are structured by the required use of forms, administrative procedures, regulations, or laws which screen, prioritize, shape, and filter the information the worker uses to produce accounts, reports, or documents related to a case" (p. 55). In the ISA claims process, I investigated how professionals at each interchange worked with the various texts (text-action-text) that organized their work and created the compilation of documents integral to making a successful claim. In my interviews I had to pay careful attention to these "processing interchanges" of the work setting, the practices, and the documents (whether in paper or electronic forms) that make up an "institutional technology" (Pence 1997). My interviews were informal and open-ended, allowing informants to talk about their work and, through this talk, making connections to others doing the work of preparing ISA claims. One interview led to another in a snowballing effect as people gave me names and contacts to pursue. Some turned out to be more useful than others, as can be expected with such work.

In my interviews, I was cognizant of the use of institutional language. As an insider to the educational bureaucracy and the ISA process, I, too, was proficient in the discourse of the institution. People used institutional concepts to communicate efficiently in their work. Indeed, as an institutional ethnographer, I learned to explicate the concepts used, such as when someone said, "But he is 3.2" meaning "he fits into Profile 3, Level 2 for ISA claim," or "she is MID [Mild Intellectual Disability]," "the IEP had to be modified," and similar examples of institutional discourse that "conceal the very practices IE aims to discover and describe" (DeVault and McCoy 2002: 768). Such professional discourse became one of the hazards of research. Informants describing their work in this manner saw their version as the only correct one. Sometimes informants submerge what they actually do by glossing it over, speaking of it in terms given in policy or in rules. Pence (1997) calls such accounts "ideological." However, such accounts do not reveal what actually happens (Campbell and Gregor 2002).

Institutional ethnographers check their knowledge of the topic as it develops and evolves (Campbell and Gregor 2002). Like all ethnography, the analysis does not begin nor does it end once the data collection has been completed. In order to analyze texts, we go beyond the "surface of the text[3] as focus" (Smith 1987:4) to examine them as constituents of social relations[4] as the subject reads and works with the texts to uncover the organizing capacity inherent in them (Smith 1987). We have to examine the many layers of activity, for example, when the teacher or principal fills out the nomination form for an ISA claim. The aim is not just to collect and describe these accounts but to explicate these experiences. What are some of the activities that lead to this stage? What are some of the activities that will follow this filling out of the form? How are these people implicated in a ruling practice that, on the surface, appears to be routine work that objectifies the child into a "folder" for monetary purposes? It also leads to an examination of the ways in which the "organizational features of professional work are, at the very least, likely to undermine good intentions" (Campbell and Gregor 2002: 108). Furthermore, in my analysis, I pay attention to understanding how the work of writing an Individual Education Plan (IEP), a Confidential Assessment Summary, Behavioral report, and similar documents becomes a specialized function and a documentary process that defines certain needs and ignores others. ISA texts produce numbers, categories, and description according to the set criteria of the profiles as indicated in Figure 12.1. The textual process takes up much of the time of professionals, who begin to perceive the student identified as high needs through the lens of the profiles and the various categorical distinctions set by the Ministry guidelines in the name of an equitable and fair accountability process.

As the data analysis proceeded, I was able to link concepts to arrive at a broad understanding as these emerging themes began to answer the questions I had posed. Interestingly, as I proceeded with my analysis, codes were changed and revised several times in the process. I began to develop a heightened sensitivity to the narratives of my informants. To summarize, institutional ethnographers first learn to understand and to describe the actual lived experience; second, they analyze how certain terms and discourses operate for the smooth functioning of an institutional setting (DeVault and McCoy 2002).

The Lived Reality of Text-Mediated Relations

The central argument of this chapter is that text-mediated social relations organize the work process to construct a decontextualized version of a student for ISA claims. Smith (1999) states that the social relations[5] of ruling are mediated by texts.

Earlier, I noted that the ISA claims process is essentially a bureaucratic process accomplished via the textual mode of documentation such as Confidential Assessment Summaries, IEPs, timetables, report cards, and medical certification. Texts are ubiquitous in that we take them for granted "as a basis for what we know in an ordinary way about the world" (Smith 1999: 33). The ISA process is one example of a text-mediated process organized through an intertextual dialogue in preparing claims for funding.

One supervising principal for Special Education programs at the local school board gave me a detailed description of the process to demonstrate the manner in which "members of the institution are trained to read and write in institutionally recognized ways...and linked through text and professional discourse" (Pence 1997: 91). Throughout this process, the Ministry profiles created the textual frame within which the work of preparing files and conducting audits took place:

> So, in the second "blitz" they changed the criteria; it was more inclusive of our kids, but again it involved a lot of reassessment. A lot of our DD (developmentally delayed) children, we took them in through medical diagnosis, but they wanted testing, adaptive testing, and things like that which we weren't doing with all our students. So, that involved a lot of redoing of testing. The LD (learning disability) had to have specific scores and that created a problem, too. And then of course we had to rewrite all the IEPs to meet the criteria and to cover all the things that were in the criteria.

Another special education consultant told me about the chain of textual organizational action from the moment the folder comes to her and as it proceeds to the next stages. The audit discourse is paramount in the organization of textual work, relations and experiences at each processing interchange:

> From me, the folder goes to the ISA guardian, the person in charge of the files at the board level. She enters it into a database. She then sends it to the board audit. Because I audit it, I make sure it is right in that the IEP and other documents match the requirements of the profiles. Then I give it to my coordinators, and they audit it. Then it goes to central audit—so in this way a file is audited at least three times before it gets to the Ministry level. They want to make sure it meets the requirements, because every file that fails—it brings our percentages down.

In these narrations we observe the way in which action is taken at each interchange, then connects to other steps in the claims exercise of preparing a folder with the appropriate "texts" that will be successful in securing funding for the respective boards. The work of different professionals and the social relations of ruling are organized by the dictates of the profiles in such a way that the practice is rendered routine to objectify the child/student into a category for claims. These forms of objectification are "organizational pathologies created by specialization and professionalization and compounded by rationalization and formalization" (Vislie and Langfeldt 1996: 66).

The language of the Ministry profiles coordinated the work of professionals in powerful ways. In an email I received on February 11, 2002 (reproduced here) from one of the coordinators, note the specific directions given on how to prepare a behavior report in which the intent of making a successful claim supersedes the objectification of a child as a textual reality. The email states:

> Under section (Assessment Summary) there needs to be a statement that the *student's behavior threatens the safety of self and others* (in these words). . . . In the sample report form given to you, the above statement is recommended since the behavior profile focuses on safety. In future reports please make sure the safety statement is made in section C even if safety is discussed in other parts of the report.

The original email gives more details about how and where the ISA language should be inserted. In this message, and several others, the discourse focuses on IEPs and reports, mainly an emphasis on texts; the student is not mentioned even once. The other part of the work process takes place at the Ministry audits of these files. The head auditor at the Ministry explained:

> The board will submit students [names] whose files they'd like to see audited. The forms are distributed to the designated auditors who contact the boards. They make arrangements for these files to be ready for audits. When they get there, they might have a brief meeting with the board people before they start. They might also meet with them again. In some boards, they have their people waiting in another room, in case clarifications are needed. In the end, they give feedback. There are specific "look-fors" for each profile, and these vary for each profile. But, all criteria for each profile must be met, or else the files would not pass the audit.

These narrations of the work process of submitting and auditing ISA claims demonstrate the intensity and complexity of this exercise, which made enormous demands on school boards in terms of human resources and in investment in precise and careful textual construction that followed the Ministry guidelines. School boards had to do this if they wanted to make claims that were going to pass the stringent audit process instituted by the Ministry to guarantee consistency and fairness across the province.

The process caused a great deal of stress and tension among and between people engaged in the ISA claims process. The sheer volume of paperwork was overwhelming. One supervising principal told me that she got very sick and was away for about six weeks due to stress. The careful reading of every piece of documentation and the different interpretations caused a lot of strain as people worked to fulfill the rigid claims requirements. One educational psychologist observed that:

> You had this enormous tension as people struggled because their work was tied to what the other person did. I know there were hurt feelings and anger. I know people dove for cover when they saw us coming because each time we had more paperwork for them or more tests for teachers to do. Some teachers refused to do them, and some dashed them off in anger so we couldn't use them anyway.

Another aspect of the organization of the social relations of ruling was that it took ownership away from the schools and teachers. School board officials were interested in identifying as many students as possible, and they wanted schools to comply with the necessary documentation. One educational psychologist who also served as one of the internal auditors experienced firsthand how some people got quite upset when things were sent back to them to be adjusted, edited, or changed:

> It was painful because people were doing a lot of work, and things were missing, because they didn't understand. We'd send the file back to the office, and they would send it back to the consultants, psychologists and others with a note for redoing parts of it. So, I don't think ISA people were loved for a while. And sometimes when you write things down, it comes across differently than if you could speak to the person.

Lessons Learned

The ISA policy process was a different way of funding special education in particular. Student-Focused Funding, the umbrella name for these new funding initiatives, turned out to be a misnomer. The focus was on everything but the student. We should remember, however, that the ISA policy does not appear in isolation but is part of the reconfiguration of traditional social institutions resulting from the increasing impact of the phenomenon of globalization that has changed the rules of the game. New rules based on cost-effectiveness and accountability have taken root in most social institutions. The discourse of business and management has become part of the hegemonic rightward turn within society in general and in education in particular.

Institutional ethnographic methodology allows us to deconstruct narratives to bring into view the activities of people that connect the local to larger spheres of influence. Research in education policy must make this connection because, if we focus entirely on global complexities, we exclude the lived experiences and perspectives of people in the local arena; conversely, if we focus entirely on the local context, we miss the larger arena of global influences. The text-mediated construction of a folder is achieved through organizational and institutionalized practices that match up an individual child against a standardized profile generated by the Ministry. Textually mediated work is achieved mainly through organizational practices of documentation and paperwork (to a large extent by computer-based technologies) that renders invisible the interpersonal work done in our everyday work practices (Diamond 1992; Rivers and Griffith 1995). In ISA work, organizational issues take precedence, with a greater emphasis on technical issues of diagnosis and assessments. In the exclusive focus on "disability" that leads to categorization according to prescribed criteria, scant attention is paid to the complexity of contextual features in the process. Institutional ethnography takes on that challenge to find space for greater sensitivity for the interpersonal work in the policy narrative.

The simple goal "to provide fair and equitable funding which recognizes that boards have differing proportions of high needs students and to ensure that funding matched the students' needs and the board's costs" (MET goals for ISA, 1999–2000) set in motion a set of processes and organizational bureaucracy that quickly spiraled out of control. Board and ministry officials might dispute this claim and argue that ISA funding procedures were needed to ensure that monies were distributed fairly. The recurring phrase in many interviews was "Of course we need consistency and we need to be accountable." Such perspectives are simple representations of a very complex reality. To facilitate better insights into fiscal matters, we need to seek answers that go beyond formulaic thinking. "It should include a broader understanding of how finance policies and mechanisms operate and affect educational processes and outputs" (Vislie and Langfeldt 1996: 60). The ISA process became a bureaucratic quagmire. In order to qualify, boards had to make successful claims that determined future funding.

Much was at stake in this funding exercise. The ISA funding formula did not account for many of the variables as the focus on consistency across the province took precedence over other considerations.

Funding policies should support and enhance the goals of an educational program. The ISA process, over the course of four comprehensive reviews, has failed to do that. In fact, the ISA process has led to demoralization and an erosion of trust. As one professional remarked:

> It's like they don't trust us any more. This is the first time that I am eagerly looking forward to retirement. This ISA work has sapped my energy and enthusiasm, and I hate feeling like that. I feel we have lost our integrity as professionals.

These remarks point to the practices put into place by the ISA process, which became self-regulating in that they sustained their power independent of people while at the same time appearing to be neutral as hegemony worked its way through "the disciplinary practices of the profession" (Pence 1997: 36) in the service of "good" organizational practices.

Texts are worked up by professionals in order to make a successful ISA claim. This case highlights the corruption of Special Education in the name of accountability and efficiency. A policy that started out with good intentions quickly spun out of control. The eligibility criteria of the Ministry profiles took on a completely different dimension. The ISA policy implementation took precedence over all other considerations and affected people in very real ways.

My analysis showed that the policy process, and its intersection with the everyday lived reality, was mediated mainly by texts, printed and electronic. It was the central frame that set up the ISA narrative. The biggest flaw in the plot of this narrative was that ISA was viewed solely as a funding exercise with little thought or planning for the contextual features and contingencies of the implementation process. Thus, by the end of the narrative, the plot was in shambles, the characters exhausted and demoralized, and the setting in disarray. The central theme of the ISA narrative of fair and equitable funding was lost in a shuffle of texts, documents, assessments, and percentiles, all in the name of procuring maximum funding for special-needs students. This lofty goal could have been attained, to some extent, if the policy had considered the involvement, the resistance, and the potential for subversion by people on the front line of this process. A little foresight and forethought could have prevented the competition between school boards for scarce funding.

Evidence of this money-grabbing exercise can be found in a recent review (July 28, 2004) conducted by the Ministry of Education (Ministry 2004). The review found that between 2001–2002 and 2003–2004, the number of claims for ISA funding doubled, from 27,000 to 54,000, although enrollment declined overall. Furthermore, the school boards' estimate of $63 million in June 2003 in funding for ISA students skyrocketed to $162 million in just four months. Last, the review concluded that school boards had placed approximately $80 million in reserves for their special-education needs.

In the lived reality of the funding exercise over the past few years, we perceive the manner in which the work in special education has become "bogged down in claims." Valuable time and resources are taken up in constructing a textual folder for funding in a complex web of social relations in which the work is seemingly "neutral" as people are linked across sites through an organized efficiency for ruling. The construction of an ISA folder relied upon the focus on pathology to meet the requirements of the profiles created by the Ministry. Through a proliferation of categories, labels, and numerical counts, in a discourse of accountability and audits, the ISA process became a game that had to be played well; it had winners and losers.

The ISA funding policy was conceived to bring equality and fairness in funding special-education needs in Ontario. The road from policy to practice turned out to be a rocky and controversial one. Policymakers had failed to take into account the contingencies of policy in local contexts. The ISA funding policy illustrates how "part of the significance of the discourse is the impossibility of reply . . . as the discourse replaces the articulation of interests with mechanisms such as technologies of measurement, testing, management" (Ball 1990: 58). This study of the ISA process shows that power over people operated in insidious ways as textual forms served to objectify and construct a child as "deviant" for funding purposes. The ISA process focused mainly on organizational work at the expense of interpersonal work. In deconstructing the process, we understand the different layers at work in text-mediated governance to enable us to move toward constructive and productive alternatives. We can begin to explore the possibilities of thinking otherwise.

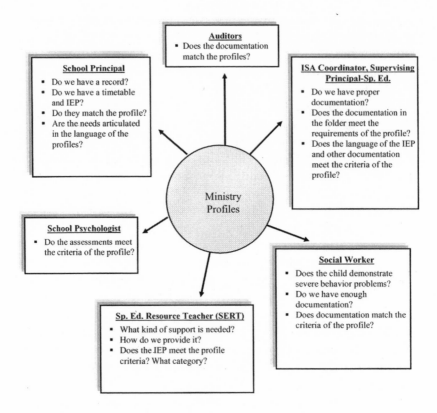

Figure 12.1 Collecting Textual Evidence (Profiles Coordinate ISA Claims).

NOTES

I wish to thank my mentor and friend, Dr. Alison Griffith, Professor, Faculty of Education, York University, for her continued support and encouragement.

1. Every claim is accompanied by a folder that holds all the relevant documentation pertaining to that claim. These folders are integral to the claims process.

2. The concept of work as used by Dorothy Smith is identified as what people do that requires some effort and time. "It is also the terminology in the discourse of the respondent's setting which is shared by others in the same setting and bears the social organization of their coordinated work" (Smith's list of concepts, given during her summer 2001 course at York University). Mehan's (1991) study claims: "The notion of work stresses the constructive aspect of institutional practice" (p. 89).

3. These "surfaces" both organize and conceal social relations (Smith 1999: 82).

4. Campbell and Gregor (2002) claim that "social relations may be a conceptualization, but the inquiry it supports is of material things. Something is actually connecting what happens here to what happens there" (p. 30).

5. In IE, as mentioned earlier, social relations are activities that are coordinated and that address the actual activities of people who may not be known to each other, yet whose activities are linked across time and distance, mainly through texts.

13

(Dis)continuity of Care
Explicating the Ruling Relations of Home Support

MARIE CAMPBELL

Editor's Introduction

This chapter is based on Marie Campbell's participatory research on home care for people with disabilities and its transformation as new managerial strategies are introduced into the Canadian health system. Her analysis here focuses on continuity of care, an explicit goal in service delivery. The puzzle she explores is how the new contracting and accounting arrangements displace continuity in favor of budgetary considerations, despite stated goals and good intentions. Campbell finds answers in a mode of supervision introduced to monitor the work of nonprofessional health aides and in a contracting system that shifts responsibility for continuity from the provincial funding entity to the agencies that hire and schedule workers.

New public management theorists suggest that decoupling funding and service delivery will allow the state to benefit from market efficiencies. But Campbell asks us to consider several different ways of knowing (and not knowing) built into these relations, suggesting that those with mandated responsibility for programs know financial impacts better than what happens in the service encounter. She also suggests that these accounting practices contribute to making health-support work one of the so-called bad jobs of the New Economy; it is not only low-paid work but increasingly work that does not provide the satisfaction of personal relationships with clients. Her analysis suggests that such jobs are not simply or inevitably "bad" ones; the work could be organized differently.

Like Daniel's study of her own work environment, Campbell's study illustrates how professionals and other front-line workers might join with clients to explore and map the social processes that govern their interactions.

* * *

Personal-support services have a particular and important place in the lives of people with disabilities who live in their own homes in the community. Too often, what these people need is not readily available to them. Approximately 2.4 million adult Canadians with disabilities—70 percent of adults with disabilities—require help with some type of daily activity, including light and heavy housekeeping; approximately 30 percent of them require some, or much more, help than they can get, according to the Canadian Council on Social Development (2005). Policy analysts agree that the implementation of approved policy framework and programs adequate to the needs of Canadians with disabilities have proceeded at a frustratingly slow pace (Prince 2004). The reasons for this are complex, and efforts to understand them include notions of social exclusion (Rice and Prince 2000), intentional and unconscious discrimination (Young 1990), and the politics of distribution (Brooks 2000). A more empirical analysis of the provision of Home Support, one that raises different questions and offers insights into the everyday and ordinary troubles that plague the provision of personal support, is the basis for this chapter.

The study of Home Support was designed at the instigation of a group of people with disabilities, and in collaboration with representatives of the Victoria, British Columbia, agencies responsible for offering personal support as a publicly administered service to people in their homes. People with disabilities who volunteered for interviews helped develop the focus for the research on Home Support and helped design a study to discover how recipients' experiences of Home Support were actually organized. The ethnography consisted of observations conducted at seventeen sites that preliminary mapping of the process of application, assessment, worker assignment, worker-client interaction, and so on had allowed the researchers to recognize as the important nodes of interaction between organizational/ agency actors and clients. Then, having observed instances of "what actually happens" in the identified sites, researchers conducted interviews and text analysis to learn about the "behind-the-scenes" organization from those who were responsible for the operation of the services.

This chapter analyzes one element of the study, beginning from and explicating observational data from one worker-client interaction. It illustrates how, in British Columbia, the provision of Home Support is exceedingly vulnerable to the ruling relations of "the new public management" of Canada's health-care system; the analysis suggests not only how an aggressive drive for more efficient management of health care undermines the provision of Home Support but how the connections between the organizational features and their effects on people disappear, leaving the official story as one of service improvement.

One instance of the ruling relations, as they appear in the everyday world of people's lives, provides the disjuncture chosen for explication here. We researchers learned, early on, that everyone involved in providing Home Support recognized the crucial importance of *continuity of care*.[1] Beginning with the ethnographic observations of a Home Support worker carrying out her work in the home of a man with a serious mobility restriction, questions arise about what happened, and especially, how the troubles observed might be characterized as expressing a lack of continuity. To problematize "continuity," the institutional ethnography that is conducted explores and illuminates a more or less hidden feature of this provision of Home Support: its translocal or interinstitutional organization. The analysis shows the particular textual character that is being introduced into the provision of these services through technologies of management and accountability. In the texts that describe, organize, and account for service provision, people, as subjects, disappear. Instead of being conducted as a relation between a worker and a client whose unique needs are thereby met, service provision is ultimately, but invisibly, subordinated to the ruling practices of health-care efficiencies operating in texts. It is this social organization, I suggest, that makes the personal support accessible to clients with disabilities particularly unsatisfactory.

Sketched from observations that researchers[2] made in the client's home, the following account serves as entry for the inquiry conducted as an institutional ethnography:

A Home Support worker, Teresa, arrives at the home of her client (Fred), with an assignment to do a spongebath, and Fred confirms that this is what he needs. Fred is still in bed when Teresa arrives and he needs her assistance to get ready for his day as a student at a near-by college. Teresa is a "casual" worker and she and Fred have never met before. He takes charge of the interaction between them. He calls for Teresa to "bring the Hoyer lift" and transfer him to the commode chair and thence to the bathroom. What happens next, according to ethnographic observers, is intensely challenging for Teresa and frustrating, as well as physically risky, for both her and Fred. Mistakes are made in managing the lift and miscommunication occurs. Fred instructs Teresa in how to use the lift; she appears to "not hear" his comments, or at least, not to accept them as instructions. So she gets into trouble with the lift. As the work unfolds, the sponge-bath that

Teresa envisions and the help that Fred needs are two different things. One observer, in the debriefing session following the observation, reported that when Teresa heard she would have to hoist Fred from bed to chair "this horrified look came over her face because, apparently, she had never used the lift. . . . She was really unprepared for all of that."

These observations provide a strong negative example of why "continuity" is an important consideration in the routine scheduling of Home Support workers; indeed, this story suggests why the regional health authority that bears the responsibility for provision of public-health services insists that the contractors who provide home support must offer continuity of care. As related in the excerpt, the Home Support worker who arrived to provide a specific service for a disabled man was a "casual" employee, someone who did not know this man and his particular needs. Along with the observers of that incident, we (readers) see a casual worker, assigned to give a "spongebath," finding herself in a situation that seems to be almost beyond her capacities. She doesn't seem to want to follow instructions from the client, and this creates more stress for herself and the client. Although the observers also knew that Teresa and Fred managed to get the sponge-bath done without either one of them suffering an injury, the whole visit went wrong, took far too much time, frightened both worker and client, and disrupted both their schedules.

Our informants made the point that for someone with a disability, continuity means having a regular worker. Consistency in assignment of workers would have guaranteed that Fred could trust that his care provider would understand his routine, know how to operate his equipment safely and efficiently, and respect his wishes, his schedule, and his plans. As we learned, having the same worker assigned consistently offers people with disabilities confidence that the services they receive will be adequate to support them in functioning as community members. Having consistent workers also means that clients or families of clients are not required, again and again, to "train" workers in how to meet their unique needs. Complaints that continuity is overlooked have always been taken seriously by the responsible agencies, even when it seems that there is little that can be done to improve that outcome of a tight scheduling process. Recently, however, the health authority that manages these services has been putting increased pressure on agencies to make sure that they schedule staff consistently into clients' homes.[3] When everybody wants continuity, what interferes? That is the puzzle that I explore. And that I propose to explain in terms of "ruling relations."

An Inquiry in Institutional Ethnography

As an institutional ethnographer, I draw on the methodological and analytic tools that other contributors in this volume have already explained, as I enter the socially organized world of health care and Home Support. Traditional methods of ethnographic data collection provide for observational data of the sort "written up" earlier in this chapter. My research task includes making analytic use of those data. Social phenomena, such as recorded about this Home Support setting, are understood to be "put together" in and of people's actions. But, as analyst, I choose for further exploration a particular aspect of the situation that is or would be relevant to those who live it, adopting the research stance that allows me to "take the standpoint" of those with whom and/or for whom the research is being conducted.[4] As an institutional ethnographer, I was puzzled about how this provision of service for the disabled client happened as it did—as less than optimally supportive. Other questions could be asked of the story (as was also the case of the kitchen-table stories that Griffith and André-Bechely explicated in chapter 2). Other standpoints are possible, and in research conceptualized differently, different interests would be addressed.[5] All researchers might be interested in similar organizational features, but as Daniel (chapter 12) argues, a ruling standpoint would focus on specific aspects of a client (or, in her study, of students). In my study, a managerial standpoint might focus on what the data would reveal about improving staff training, supervision, and scheduling, or how it informs quality assurance or some other institutional technology (Griffith and André-Bechely, chapter 2) among many other possible questions.

To explore the puzzle I had identified, I address the "institutional"—the social relations enacted in the setting that rule what can happen. To discover the ruling relations, I turn, as Daniel explained that she also did, regarding the activation of the ISA policy, to those who are the experts in doing what happens. People know how to conduct their everyday work, and when they talk about it, informed as their talk is by this kind of everyday expertise, their conversation necessarily carries traces of those social relations. Finding such traces in ethnographic data directs my inquiry into certain features of the Home Support worker's visit and her action and, thus, into its routine local and translocal organization. For instance, in the observational data reported here, the words "an assignment" reflect the presence of an organized and already learned work process, as well as an organized method of deploying workers that makes use of hourly assignments. Knowing that a Home Support worker is called a "casual" employee presupposes a particular mode of employment.[6] Hearing the different expectations expressed by the worker and the client about the spongebath suggests that, somehow, conflicting messages about the work prevail. All these features of the setting can be explored to discover how they exist, not just as experiential data but as social and socially organized practices.

In this volume, previous contributors have explained that institutional ethnography proposes that a complex organization of provision and accountability exists between the everyday world where people live and interact and the virtual worlds of educational, social services, and health-care policy management. And texts are central to this organization. Analysing the Home Support data, I could assume that certain policies frame what happens in the homes of people receiving Home Support; treating the activation of policy as the topic of inquiry problematizes the apparently objective nature of its funding, administration, and accountability. Institutional ethnography puts back into focus how such objectivity is organized and how the people who accomplish it are made to "disappear." As Smith says about institutional ethnography:

> Taking women's standpoint, we remember that we, the actual readers/writers/speakers/hearers, who disappear in the relations of intertextuality, are also those who participate, generate, provide the dynamic of the ruling relations. We are also those whose local activities are organized and shaped by and in these relations, just as [Marx's work shows] the interrelations of money and commodities relate people to one another and organize the local actualities of our/their lives. (Smith 1999: 80)

Smith's words provide an important reminder for the conceptualization of my inquiry. First, I am reminded of the "disappeared" participants in health-care work processes who are actually located at many different sites, bringing diverse expertise and interests to their work. Each participant in the process attends to his or her work through the relevancies of that position, its activities, the standpoint that employment responsibilities generate, and so on. Second, Smith connects intertextuality and ruling relations, using that association to explicate how capitalist society works at an intimate level in people's lives, as I will also do with respect to the provision of health care and Home Support. My analysis draws on Smith's account of ruling to attempt to show what happens in the research setting as the result of neither bad intentions nor flawed management; nor should it be accepted simply as the mysterious imposition of an external power. Just as Daniel's research (chapter 12) discovered that the actions of a cast of players carrying out different elements of educational policy accomplished everything that eventuated, I, too, need to learn how local actors begin to substitute outside interests for their own. As I explore the organization of (dis)continuity of care in Home Support, my ethnographic observations give me some sense of what actually happened in that one site at one time; now, both to understand that incident and to generalize further, I must explicate the relations that rule that and similar settings.

A comment made by a Home Support informant is redolent of the new ruling relations; she reported that "[the health authority's] financial people make us [Home Support administrators] feel as if we are robbing the system; they don't seem to recognize the need for any administrative costs" in the agencies' provision of Home Support. The next sections of the chapter explore the more or less invisible part played by the new approach to public management in organizing just such relations between personnel from Home Support agencies and those from the health authority that is at the root of this comment. Overlooked in the interactions where this comment arose, and in the regional health authority's insistence that Home Support agencies assume responsibility for ensuring continuity of care to clients, is how the new public management organizes a continual retreat from spending on *publicly* funded services.

Organizing for Provision of "Continuity" of Workers

The public provision of Home Support services in Victoria, BC, is organized through the regional health authority under the mandate of provincial legislation. Health authority staff assess applicants for eligibility[7] for several possible levels of funding and then contract the actual work of provision that the program offers to Home Support agencies who supply the workers. Both Home Support agencies and the regional health authority make claims for providing "continuity of care."[8] To fulfill their claims to excellence, a principled and systematically coordinated approach to the organization and management of provision of services has been put in place. In addition, agencies use a range of routine text-based practices to certify the abilities of Home Support employees, through the requirement for and monitoring of their basic qualifications. Hiring policies and practices and orientation and supervision procedures allow agencies to claim that all their employees have the required set of skills to do the job, including the capacity to read and understand agency standards and rules and the ability to follow these directives.[9] A working environment of careful overview by administrators and supervisors, using direct and. more often, indirect (or text-mediated) means, is thereby created.

Interviews with administrators reveal the scope of the textually mediated environment of Home Support. The health authority makes its contracting decisions on the basis of proposals in which agencies describe their standards of care and the systems through which they implement them. The provincial government's Case Management standards are the basis for the development and implementation of service provision by everyone—both professional and nonprofessional staff, interacting with service recipients and their families. Agencies' nonprofessional staff, the Home Support workers, provide the care that health authority professionals, the Case Managers, have determined from their assessments to be needed and that they outline. Because the provision of Home Support takes place between clients and agencies' *nonprofessional* service personnel, out of sight of agency supervisors, considerable effort is made to organize and coordinate carefully those interactions. It is in these person-to-person interactions that "continuity of care" and all other expectations and requirements are met, or not. This is the context in which administrative texts guide the actual work of personal support so as to standardize its provision.

The approach taken to managing (nonprofessional) Home Support workers is an extension and modification of how the work of health-care professionals is managed. Professionals have more leeway to use their judgment. A professional nurse's ministrations to patients leans heavily on the knowledge and skills that s/he brings to the setting from theoretical and practical education and on the attitudes, beliefs, and commitments that, inculcated through professional socialization, can be taken for granted by employers. Nursing registration not only carries a commitment to ethical guidelines that codify a registered nurse's otherwise internalized approach to patients but also maintains standards of professional behavior, backed by authorized and mandated disciplinary action. In contrast, Home Support workers are not professionally licensed and regulated but are trained for "task provision" in six-month educational programs that cover explicit areas of knowledge and responsibilities. The training establishes mastery of the level of skill needed to become Home Support workers and, along with that, establishes their proper and subordinate "role in the health-care team" (Camosun College, 2005).

A hierarchy of responsibility and knowledge is presupposed by the division of professional and nonprofessional labor that is codified in the official texts of the health authority and agencies. As suggested earlier, the regional health authority's professional staff (registered nurses and social workers) prepare the textual ground for provision of service by nonprofessional Home Support workers by determining a client's needed level of service, expressed in hours of service. Once service is approved, professional staff use their knowledge to translate abstract "hours of service" into care plans for individual clients with prescribed tasks to be provided by a Home Support worker. This mediation of people's needs and wishes to an organization's mode of action takes place in text, in preestablished official forms. The assessor "works up" into the form's categories, words, and/or numbers how an individual presents him or herself, as the beginning of the organizational process that constitutes the client as the object of a Home Support worker's attention. The assessor's write-up is one step of a text-mediated technology for providing care according to standards; another step determines a client's financial status, contributing to the health authority's involvement in and responsibility for government fiscal policy. The completed assessment text describes the client as an object of care in exactly the terms that constitute him or her (that is, the client) as organizationally actionable and textually accountable.

Knowing the work objectively, as a list of text-mediated activities or tasks, moves the process on to the next steps—assigning it to a worker to conduct it and eventually billing for it. Its standardization creates its usefulness for entering tasks into a Home Support agency's objective management processes of assignment and accountability. A Home Support worker is deployed to a client's home to fulfill an assignment as it has been officially constituted, defined as discrete tasks, listed in care plans, and absorbing a certain number of hours of approved and thus billable hours. Consider, for instance, how this precise description of Home Support tasks (that is, all tasks being textualized and timed) makes possible the precisely timed scheduling of workers. Besides facilitating scheduling, this kind of assignment also builds in a kind of text-mediated professional oversight, ensuring that individual workers are held to prescribed tasks and to a definite time frame. The worker is assigned and paid for doing the official task as it appears in a manual and in the time that is established by the length of the assignment. Thus, the worker is not just motivated but coordinated to complete the assignment expeditiously. Her next assignment follows with only the prescribed break between two assignments of a standard ten minutes of travel time. Agency rules that strengthen these scheduling arrangements (for example, to "avoid taking instruction from clients" and to "follow the care plan's listed tasks") encourage workers to stick to the assigned task, as formally inscribed, codified, and approved.

But this carefully orchestrated service provision is not as securely tied to timed tasks as it might seem. A problem often arises for workers who, as an intrinsic part of the fulfillment of any assignment, must handle the challenge of accomplishing it within the resources of the everyday world of the client. The textual version of the assignment must be materialized in action, in the local setting, in homes with many differences. Home Support workers take for granted, as do their supervisors, that they will bring the preapproved, precise textual descriptions and arrangements, together with the local actualities of an everyday situation that, far from being unitary, is diverse and complex. (We saw this to be the case in Fred's everyday situation where a spongebath was not just a spongebath.). Accomplishing this translation passes unnoticed as someone's work, when the work is already known officially and textually defined.

To institutional ethnographers, this taken-for-granted feature of Home Support work identifies a line of fault between the everyday world (where an assignment is actualized) and the assignment as it appears in accounts made for ruling purposes. A gap appears between the descriptions that differently located knowers would make about the task that otherwise appears to be "known in common." Such a conceptual line of fault appears for us, too, when we read the story about Teresa and Fred and try to put it together with the coordination of Home Support services that I have now sketched here. Not only is it jarring to read about it, but this sort of disjuncture must be suppressed or it would disrupt the work organization—the organization that guarantees that the assignment gets done well, in a timely fashion, efficiently, and accountably.

Those who do the work, those who are its recipients, and those who organize and account for it may all know it differently. Planners and managers know it through texts. For them the work is abstract. And the abstract quality of the assigned task plays a particularly important part in its successful management. Remember that the spongebath assignment remained abstract until it was materialized or actualized in the worker-client interaction. But there, in the everyday activity (or, sometimes, inactivity) in that home, the task took on a different character. There, a gap appeared between the assignment as expressed and known textually (as the client's assessment and identified level of care described him, as the care plan stated, as the task was defined, timed, and taught, and so on), and how it was enacted in the setting. Closing the gap between the official (textual) and the everyday (enacted) versions of "the assignment" is work done by Home Support workers and/or clients and families in their everyday process of activating the text/task as Home Support service. For the most part, the nature of this translation work remains institutionally unknown. If known about, that work and its associated knowledge and skill are largely treated as irrelevant and are unaccounted for.[10] The actuality and how it might differ from its description are not allowed to disturb the character of the work known abstractly.

As researcher or as readers of this analysis, you and I are now privy to the problems around service provision that the ethnographic observers caught, in this particular instance, on audiotape and in their observations. Teresa, the Home Support worker assigned to the client, appears to lack those additional and usually invisible skills for coordinating the everyday setting with the objective task assignment without undermining its performance. Is the explanation for the troubled visit that a *casual* worker had been assigned, one who couldn't make the vital but unaccounted for contribution to the actualization of the text/task? To attempt to follow up this query, to discover why such scheduling choices are made, even now when so much attention is given to scheduling for continuity, I must look beyond the boundaries of the original ethnographic setting to discover how this happens.[11]

Contracting of Home Support Hours:
Translocal Ruling Practices

Home Support, although organized and funded through the regional health-care authority, has a status different from that of the universal, publicly insured, system of acute health care mandated by the Canada Health Act. Provincial governments have wide discretion in the home-care programs they support. Canadian provinces and territories are allowed to use health-care funding (some of it from federal transfer payments) to subsidize "other" health-related programs such as home nursing care and personal support, but as a optional program; given that provinces already struggle to pay the major portion of funding for provision of health care anyway, Home Support has never been generously subsidized. In BC, Home Support falls within the Continuing Care Programs Regulation of the Continuing Care Act. This Act establishes eligibility criteria for subsidization of support services depending on the applicant's/client's capacity to pay.[12] The actual levels of funding made available for eligible recipients fluctuate according to decisions taken by regional health authorities that act for the provincial government, contracting with Home Support agencies for service provision.

In BC, Home Support agencies operate as businesses in a mixed (public/private) marketplace for their services. The agencies that currently have contractual relations with the health authority to provide Home Support services to subsidized clients stay in business almost exclusively through the funding these contracts bring in, a relationship that according to informants is increasingly untenable. Currently, the health authority pays a Home Support agency at the rate of $29.53 per hour of Home Support provision, and of that sum, the assigned (regularly employed) worker gets an average total hourly pay of $17.98. The difference between the workers' pay package and the total "hourly rate" paid by the health authority (currently, $11.55 from each hour of contracted work, or slightly less in the case of casually employed workers) is retained by the Home Support agency to cover administrative costs. Purchase of benefits for regular employees is the greatest fixed cost that agencies assume, and when a Home Support agency's contracts for funded hours fluctuate, those and other fixed costs keep mounting. Agencies that are reliant on funds from the regional health authority's allocation for its community programs are especially vulnerable to the health authority's exercise of its contracting discretion. They sign three-year agreements to supply Home Support services for the region, but they are always subject to competition from agencies that in the next tendering might offer to provide services better, cheaper, with fewer complaints from clients and their families.

It is in this pressured environment that the health authority's responsibility for achieving continuity of care to Home Support clients has been devolved to the Home Support agencies. And agency administrators feel it as personal pressure when they are called to answer for complaints made to the health authority. To attempt to accede to the health authority's demands for scheduling "continuity" and to handle any criticism that arises from failure to do so, the Home Support agencies have developed a system of accounting for their own scheduling of assignments that offers what the administrators call "continuity statistics." This gives them an overview of the scheduling practices from which they can look back and figure out the reasons that their schedulers departed from the best practices for continuous assignment of workers to clients.[13] A pincer-like effect occurs as the management of scheduling to accomplish continuity coincides with contradictory organizational practices aimed at efficiency or cost-cutting. Militating against the capacity to supply the same worker to a client consistently are new organizational conditions associated with changes in how contracts are being let to Home Support agencies. Also felt as "pressure," these conditions that conflict with continuity practices come more indirectly from the health authority than personally voiced demands to schedule workers consistently. Listed and discussed next are some of the organizational arrangements that have this indirect, and contradictory, effect.

Casual staffing/financial flexibility: Only when an agency can see its financial stability extending into the future can it commit to hiring *regular* employees; in conditions of organizational (i.e., financial) uncertainty, casual workers (for whom there are fewer guarantees made about weekly hours of paid work and, particularly, no financial commitment for purchase of benefits) offer some flexibility to the agency. Even though agencies have contracting agreements with the health authority that extend for three years, the funding environment is still uncertain. Historically, in Victoria, a retirement city, expenditures on home support have been high compared to those of other regions in the province, and they have been specifically targeted for reduction. The number and associated income of contracts for "funded hours" of Home Support may vary, month to month, by as much as by one thousand hours, according to one administrative informant. When the health authority cuts "contracted hours," an agency's income is reduced, but its administrative overhead does not shrink accordingly. Contract obligations, including guaranteed hours of work and "benefits" to a pool of regularly employed workers, stay the same. Not so with casuals. They can be called in as "hours" are ordered, and the difference between casuals' pay and the total income to agencies can be used to cover the agency's fixed costs. But that solution increases the potential for lack of continuity of assigned workers.

Shorter contracts/higher administrative overhead/more casuals: In the past few years, the pattern of contracts has changed to shorter assignments, and that, too, may increase agency costs. Now, assignments may be for half-hour and one-hour services, almost to the exclusion of two- or three-hour assignments. Several problems for agencies' finances arise from these shorter assignments. Travel time, and the fee paid to workers for excessive travel time using their own car, goes up. (Ordinarily, ten minutes is taken off each assignment to allow the worker to get to the next client; this ten-minute window doesn't change whether the assignment is for two hours or half an hour). However, a half-hour assignment, perhaps for medication supervision, often becomes the occasion for adding on to the visit other "little" tasks. "Just check this or that" may be how it is phrased (in contrast to the official timed task assignment). It may be that the client needs to be transferred from bed to chair or to the toilet, but the half-hour that is already reduced by one-third, for the ten-minute travel time, is often insufficient to fit in those added extras. A contract comes with a fixed compensation for the hours ordered. When workers cannot get the work done in the contracted time (minus ten minutes), they claim extra travel compensation, and this comes out of the agency "overhead." As explained earlier, financial instability encourages the employment of casuals; in this case, they help balance out rising overhead costs.

Bunched distribution of work times/staffing with casuals: The new short-assignment work tends to be "bunched" into early-morning and late-evening time slots. (This may happen because it is at these times that many acute-care patients return home from hospital and need their many medications reviewed and their administration supervised by Home Support workers.) When one client has as many as four half-hour assignments per day and, overall, the agencies' shorter assignments are concentrated in the morning and at bedtime, new problems arise in scheduling. Home Support administrators find that casual workers are easier to place than regular workers into the new shorter and more frequent assignments. For workers, bunched-up assignments means there is increased demand for worker availability between 7 A.M. and 12 noon and again between 7 and 10 P.M.; regular workers, who are hired for an eight-hour day, are unavailable for this configuration of assigned hours. For the agency's scheduling purposes, casual employees offer the necessary flexibility. They can be fitted into the new shorter time slots, avoiding, as well, the scheduling glitches that occur with regular staff for whom guarantees for a set number of paid hours must be met. Scheduling becomes a "nightmare," informants say, and may even be an increased cost, with more and specialized schedulers being hired; but, again, the flexibility of casual workers helps with difficult scheduling, even as it undermines "continuity."

Degraded jobs/scarce staff : Home Support is becoming "a bad job." Home Support workers are members of a low status, largely female, workforce doing a difficult job, in isolated working conditions. While it has never been an easy job, union contracts give it reasonable compensation and a measure of stability. Now the work is being intensified, and, beyond that, privatization of agencies threatens unionization. All the elements of contracting efficiency discussed earlier have negative effects. Also, "raising the bar" in assessing client eligibility has intensified the actual work. Here is what happens when applicants (or clients being routinely reviewed for continuing eligibility) are deemed ineligible. The clients who *are* approved for Home Support are sicker or more needy and are experienced by workers as "heavier"; they are the clients who remain on caseloads as those at the lower end of the assessed-need scale are restricted from subsidized services. Home Support goes increasingly to people assessed with higher needs. This means more heavy lifting and transferring, all of which are done in a home setting by one worker (not the two that a transfer protocol in a facility may require); this worker is usually a woman, and she is usually in a hurry. As the work is intensified, the workers are at risk of more injuries, as evidenced by increased Workers' Compensation claims. Besides the increasing effort demanded of workers, there is declining satisfaction in doing this work. Job satisfaction for Home Support workers has tended to reside primarily in the nature of the relations they establish with their clients (McMillan 2003). To know that they are needed and important to the people with whom they work offers an antidote to some of the work's negative features. As the work becomes more pressured and more tightly organized, the time it takes to develop warm and supportive relationships with clients is also diminished. Clients do not appreciate a rushing, anxious, worker or a worker who is a stranger to them. Lack of appreciation becomes the basis for complaints that both the agencies and the health authority must field and attempt to fix administratively; the other side of the story is that it undermines the one positive feature of the Home Support workers' jobs. Increasingly, it is difficult to keep workers in their jobs; they leave as soon as another opportunity presents itself. The new reality is that agencies have trouble finding enough workers to accommodate the contract hours.[14] Scheduling for continuity drops in priority when it is difficult to find anyone at all to take the assignment.

The negative effects as described here appear to be linked and a regular feature of how services are provided. I see these institutional practices as "translocal ruling relations" because they are carried into Home Support agencies as managerial arrangements; their impetus comes from elsewhere, and they become enacted in the local setting. There, they rule what actually happens, potentially eroding the nature of the care that everyone wants for Home Support clients. The next section identifies and describes some of the frameworks that rule the local settings, and rule, as well, the actual practices that participants in the settings enact. A contradiction emerges between the textual coordination of claims that are made about the goodness of the services and what I have been showing is the "impact" of translocal organization. I argue that when a ruling textual regime is in place, it is possible and even practicable for those mandated with responsibility to *not know* or *not care* about "impact" as experienced in the everyday world. It is the financial impact that is understood to be important.

The "New Public Management": The Ruling Relations of Home Support

It is not happenstance that conflicts over continuity of care emerge as Home Support agencies try but fail to supply workers consistently to clients. This section of the chapter suggests that the opposite is true—that such outcomes are actively but invisibly being organized. Reductions and downgrading of care represent targeted cost savings and efficiencies in the health-care system. I argue that these are outcomes of a ruling regime implemented not through debate and democratic decision making but through administrative reform put in place to stretch health-care dollars and target them more precisely. Often called "the new public management," the new regime valorizes the reduction of public provision of services, or at least *social* services, and encourages efficiencies through market-based competition (McLaughlin, Osborne, et al. 2002). Osborne and Plastrik (2000), new public management gurus, speak of the success of the Canadian government in driving "program spending, as a percentage of gross domestic product, back to its lowest level since 1950" (p. 5). This statistic suggests that Canada's traditional commitment to use social policy to meet citizens' needs is indeed being transformed.

Without understanding it, Canadians accept the philosophy of the new public management as they enact it through its technologies. If Canadians recognize what it accomplishes, it will likely be viewed positively, as "innovation" in public management (Rachlis 2004) associated with belt-tightening, or the government managing within its means, or as reducing the government debt and budget deficits. When it has been promoted this way, Canadians have accepted the need for huge reductions in social spending. Osborne and his associates (Osborne and Gaebler 1992; Osborne and Plastrik 2000) note that the new public management practices that they teach were being absorbed into Canadian governments beginning in the mid-1990s, when transfer payments for health care from federal to provincial governments were a key target for funding cuts. Provincial governments, left to make up a higher share of health funding, reacted to the cutbacks in a variety of ways, including, importantly, with strong efforts at restructuring health-care provision (Rankin and Campbell 2006). Among a range of responses, many hospital beds and some whole hospitals were closed, as were many operating theaters. Hospital staff were "dehired," the euphemism used for all the arrangements made to reduce staff and cut labor costs. Auxiliary services such as laundry, housekeeping, and food were contracted out. As a consequence of cuts in facilities and staff, wait lists grew, and it has now become commonplace for Canadians to view the public health-care system as "in crisis" and not sustainable.

In British Columbia, regionalization of health-care administration also occurred in the mid-1990s, creating the regional health authorities that are now responsible for managing the provision of all health care, including Home Support. Regionalization itself should be recognized as a part of the "new public management" movement. The uncoupling of government *accountability* from *provision* of health services is one of the features of regionalization that recommends it within the new public management philosophy (Osborne and Plastrik 2000). It works to regulate and "improve efficiency" in Home Support programming in Victoria. Uncoupling can occur not just between a government and a region; "the service or compliance organization [in this case the regional health authority] can also uncouple its role as a purchaser from its role as a provider" (Osborne and Plastrik 2000: 118). For instance, in BC, a regional health authority is accountable to the provincial government for provision of Home Support services but does not provide them itself. The uncoupling of the purchasing from the provision allows the purchaser (the health authority) to not have to know or care how provision of services is actually accomplished—that is, through what means. The advantages to be gained from uncoupling the purchaser-provider roles include, as Osborne and Gaebler state in *Reinventing Government* (1992), "freeing policy managers to shop around for the most effective and efficient service providers help[ing] them squeeze more bang out of every buck"; and "it allows them to use competition between service providers" (p. 35). It would seem that these precepts explain the health authority's decision unilaterally to "re-tender . . . the home support contracts to fewer agencies" over the past decade—from seventeen to nine in the first instance—and in the recent restructuring down "to approximately four or five" (Vancouver Island Health Authority 2004a: 23). And when this chapter was written, the number of Home Support agencies that the region was contracting with had shrunk to three. As I have begun to show, efficiency of this nature has costs that lie hidden inside what the texts show.

Performance Agreements between the regional health authority and the provincial government set the general framework for the relationship that is established between the health authority and Home Support agencies (Vancouver Island Health Authority 2004b: 1–11). In these agreements, targets are set for reductions and efficiencies in all aspects of service provision and administration, and these targeted levels are set to increase in each of the three years of the agreement. Budget commitments are tied to health authority plans for realizing the performance targets. At the top of the list is the provincial target for shifting the "mix of acute/institutional care to more home/community care" and reducing the costs and expenditures on health care. Among other effects, this particular target also creates, by default, a competition (among client categories) for available home-support services. As an arm of health care, Home Support becomes subordinated to the restructuring goals in acute health-care provision. For instance, in hospitals, ordering Home Support for a discharged patient helps reduce length of hospital stays (Rankin and Campbell 2006). Utilization of acute hospital beds—a high-priority goal of restructuring—can be improved when Home Support helps patients return home sooner. There, in the community, they become competitors for service along with other similarly "targeted" users for Home Support. For instance, new methods of service delivery innovated under supportive living programs deploy Home Support workers to help older people manage acute illnesses and infirmity in "assisted living residences"[15] or in their own homes, to prevent or defer hospital admissions. Again, these elderly clients "compete" for Home Support services in an environment where acute-care efficiency has top priority, according to provincial targets.

Contracting with fewer agencies has reduced the health authority's own administrative costs (another target of the performance agreements), freeing more of its global budget for actual provision of hours of Home Support services. While this may be a good economical decision for the health authority as purchaser, as argued earlier it is not without "impact" on agencies, workers, or clients. Over the past decade, health authority retendering decisions have engineered the demise or consolidation of many Home Support agencies. Certainly, competition among agencies has increased as they recognize that the retendering process means that they are in a struggle for survival. The consolidations have disorganized the provision of service, especially to people with disabilities, as increased reliance is placed on a casual workforce. Among the complaints made by these clients are the troubles caused them by loss of their regular workers when agencies go out of business, shift boundaries of service, or reorganize their workforces.[16]

There is a rolling impact to all of this. As shown here, Home Support agencies hire casuals when they must to solve the range of new problems faced; those problems, in turn, have arisen out of the purchasing strategies that health authorities adopt to help them manage their own budgets, targeted as they are to reduce expenditures (Vancouver Island Health Authority 2004a). The interests of the purchaser, the provider agency, the workers, and the clients/recipients of Home Support services are not the same; sometimes they conflict, as we have seen. Reductions in funding are not experienced in the same way by everybody they affect. For instance, the administrative uncoupling of purchasing from service provision "preserves maximum flexibility to respond to changing circumstances" (Osborne and Plastrik 2000: 36). Within the new public management regime, maximum flexibility is what health authorities need in order to manage their shifting and reduced budgets. That demand is passed down into the Home Support agency, not just by regional staff voicing concerns but as "changing circumstances." Already identified are some of the changing circumstances for which a casual labor force is a response. And that suggests how more flexibility for the health authority and the Home Support agency organizes different and troubled relationships between workers and clients.

Clients (such as Fred), with complex and specific needs, expect workers to know them and respond to their unique needs, understanding how to make themselves maximally useful in relation to client characteristics and resources. In Fred's case, familiarity with his equipment is an essential feature of an adequately supportive relationship. Long-standing relationships increase workers' knowledge of how to help clients, but it has already become apparent that organizing for "flexibility" outranks organizing for "continuity." How does this happen in a setting where everyone is alert to the desirability for greater continuity? The answer appears to lie in differences in *knowing* continuity. The health authority can insist that Home Support agencies provide continuity, while not having to know or care *how*. For instance, health authority officials don't need to know that Home

Support agencies need to spend money on administrative costs. One example of how "changing circumstances" might increase agency administrative costs is the need for additional schedulers to handle the flood of contracts for new, shorter assignments (especially to acute-care patients). The necessary degrees of separation that protect the health authority from knowing what actually happens when circumstances change are maintained through the arts and technologies of a regime of text-mediated ruling. Conducted in virtual reality, ruling is blind to experiences in the everyday world.

The activation of a text-defined Home Support task, on the other hand, happens in the everyday world, as we saw from the observations of Teresa and Fred. A spongebath given in bed might have made better use of Teresa's time, but that was not what Fred had in mind, and he expected that Teresa would accept his definition of the situation. Such expectations are key to service provision, but they stand in the way of easy and expeditious "responses to changing circumstances." Hired as a casual worker, Teresa, although trained (and thus possessing the "skills" she needed for the job), couldn't easily accommodate Fred's expectations for proper fulfillment of his needs. In many situations, a casual worker will offer a service that, while adequate, won't be tailored to the specific client. Clients will experience as a loss of trust in Home Support service what agencies call flexibility; they may complain about "new" workers and resist losing their known and reliable staff. They may begin to phone the agency frequently, to try to line up their hours of service with their known worker's employed days, and so on.[17] Eventually, when all their work of this sort fails, clients may learn to accept casuals and accept that they cannot expect "a new worker" to know and do exactly what they wish. This may help accomplish what in the Canadian context has often been called a necessary lowering of expectations of the health-care system.

Conclusions

Rendered into textual form, Home Support work becomes an objective entity for apparently precise management; its provision can be coordinated at arm's length—as is the case for any other division of productive/industrial labor. This form of the division of labor operates on the assumption that the work, the workers, and the clients, too, are the same in the everyday world of experience as they are in the objective, and *virtual*, form of textual representation; that is, a spongebath delivered can be treated as if it were the same as a spongebath conceptualized, and thus it can be assigned to any worker. Workers, too, are treated as identical: the fulfillment of eligibility requirements is expected to create a labor force whose members, having the same qualifications, are equally "skilled" for purposes of administration/deployment. Even more important, as the original story reveals, a client who needs a spongebath becomes an interchangeable object for the "provision of a service" and under the abstraction of a timed intervention is understood to be treated adequately as such. But we have seen how in this particular case, none of these assumptions actually holds.

Home Support cannot be adequately understood by reading it as a set of tasks that, once provided, is synonymous with its textual description. However, it is precisely the textualization of the work that makes it objectively manageable. Its ruling happens as the work is coordinated through practices that constitute assignments in text form and that account for their provision and its costs. It is this way of knowing the work officially that is relied on, under conditions of budget constraint, when strategies are put in place to stretch and reduce the funding. The practical responses of the administrators of the Home Support agencies that I have described here are solutions to the budgeting crunch that health-care authorities and the agencies themselves get caught up in. Their responses also become part of the problem that workers and clients absorb. We are able to see how the strategy of employing casual workers assists home support agencies to maintain their existence in a precarious environment. In the setting we observed, however, a casual worker added to the difficulties that a disabled client had to deal with. That troubling aspect of what actually happens will have gone missing from the official account of the service provision and from the reporting on how successfully the health authority managed its performance agreement. This inquiry explicates it and challenges claims made by the Health Authority about reducing expenditures on Home Support "without impact" on the clients.

This analysis makes it both apparent and relevant that personal support services to people with disabilities are organized within public health policy and Canada's new public management; now we can see how personal services are caught up in and undermined by a continuingly tightening health policy/implementation/accountability regime. Managerial strategizing around targets for performance measures and associated budget constraint results in changes in the amount and kind of support services made available and in the character and capacity of the Home Support labor force. It also matters to those whose claims on the system are for needed personal support that Home Support (funds) are being targeted toward the reduction of the costs (and expenditures) in public acute health care. In the increasing competition for resources, some people with disabilities will lose out entirely; others will lose the trustworthiness of services. These are effects of the ruling regime organizing the provision of Home Support. All the managerial and coordinating efforts described in this chapter belong to that analytic category; they address interests that are not those of clients with disabilities. Ruling enters into the everyday world of Home Support as organizational and accountability practices, where these institutional arrangements overrule participants' efforts to provide good consistent services to all clients. As a range of economies is put in place on the basis of the health authority's official knowledge of the work, the claim may be made that service provision is becoming more efficient—that providers can "do more with less" or "do the right things" consistently. The analysis offered here looks behind such slogans to the social organization of what actually happens and shows the personal costs that are being generated.

NOTES

1. Thanks to Janet Rankin for pointing out that "continuity of care" is institutional language whose meaning varies, depending upon the speaker's/writer's location within the institution. That nicely sums up what this chapter is attempting to show.

2. The data excerpt is assembled from the taped debriefing of a two-person observation that had been conducted in a client's home (as part of Project Inter-Seed), as reported in Campbell, Copeland, and Tate (1999).

3. According to one Home Support administrator interviewed, accreditation standards are putting increasing emphasis on "safety," and continuity of care plays a part in how safety of Home Support practice is demonstrated.

4. In this case, the standpoint of people with disabilities coincides with the principles of the "independent living" movement, also a priority for many of those involved in the original project.

5. Most evaluation research and organizational analysis, and as Smith (1990a, 1999) has argued, most sociology, is conducted from the taken-for-granted standpoint of those who rule institutional settings.

6. A large and growing literature on contingent work shows the diverse purposes "casualization" of a labor force serves and the contradictory ways it affects workers; see Fudge and Vosko (2003), Houseman (2001), and Park and Butler (2001), among others. Thanks to Roxana Ng for access to her and her associates' research on contingent work.

7. One category of eligibility is being in receipt of a disability pension.

8. The health authority upholds Case Management standards calling for continuity of care. A Home Support document, "Continuity of Care Indicators" (2004), offers guidelines used by Home Support agencies to schedule for continuity of provider.

9. At one local community college, the Home Support/Resident Care Attendant (HSRCA) program runs for twenty-four weeks. Admission requirements include English 12 or equivalent or an English placement test at the Grade 12 level, two letters of reference from an employer (regarding volunteer experience, work study, and so on, to be completed on college forms), an interview with program faculty, and the Food Safe level 1 certificate.

10. Home Support agency administrators told me that they refuse contracts that seem too short to accomplish the work that must be done. Yet, even though they recognize the difficulties that half-hour assignments may create for workers and clients, they are not entirely free to determine the length of the contracts or even to accept or reject contracts. Doing so will have consequences, as the chapter's analysis suggests.

11. For the details of how agencies schedule workers into hourly assignments, I rely on interviews conducted with informants who are administrators of Home Support agencies.

12. Light housekeeping work, one of the recognized (by the Canadian Council on Social Development [2005]) needs for people with disabilities, was struck from the services that could be offered within the subsidized Home Support program (BC reg. 217/2004). The revised regulations state that of daily personal care activities, only help with mobility, bathing, dressing, grooming, and eating (but not meal preparation) are "prescribed."

13. "Continuity of Care," a report internal to the Home Support agencies contracting with VIHA, set out the criteria that should guide schedulers.

14. Classes in the college courses that prepare Home Support workers have not been filling in the past few years, according to my informants.

15. The BC government has been innovating new methods of providing community-based care aimed at its efficiency, for example, through public-private partnerships in seniors' housing (where Home Support workers may be stationed to serve the residents). VIHA has instituted a new "service delivery model"—Cluster Care, that clusters Home Support workers in a particular area of the city that has a high level of demand for service in recipients' own homes.

16. Campbell, Copeland, and Tate 1999, pp. 70–71.

17. Campbell, Copeland, and Tate 1999, p. 60.

Conclusion

MARJORIE L. DEVAULT

In the months since I wrote the introduction to this book, I have traveled many times between my job in upstate New York and my home in Boston. All that back and forth is invisible in the text—and rightly so. But the travel, and also its invisibility, could serve as emblems for the twin foci of our book. Each contributor has considered people at work, attending to their activities and the material sites of their lives; each has also considered how those people's efforts are represented in the texts of economic restructuring and how those texts are hooked into the neoliberal ideologies that now dominate public discourse and policymaking. We mean to show that economic transformation takes place not in some abstract realm—labeled and discussed as "the economy" or "globalization"—but in people's embodied lives. In sites of policymaking and management, people are doing the work of restructuring. They devise strategies for maximizing profits, for building new markets, for tracking expenditures and monitoring quality, and so on, applying similar technologies across sectors as diverse as production, health care, and education. The changes that seem to "just happen" are the products of people at work.

Outside the sites of ruling and administration, people are at work sustaining themselves and the people with whom they share lives and fates. Many seek the "good jobs" (in the parlance of the New Economy) that provide a living wage and access to other benefits; when they cannot find or sustain such employment, they devise other strategies for making lives. Our analyses are meant to be rooted in those lives. As we examine people's activities, the changes associated with economic restructuring appear in concrete form in a world that is ruled, increasingly, through the abstractions of textual reality. Our analyses open windows on the ongoing transformations we are all now living through. We point to the ways these changes are lived and felt, in experiences that may look quite different (and carry very different consequences) but are nonetheless linked to and shaped by the same relations of economic restructuring.

Restructuring is implemented, we have argued, in large part textually, through processes of discursive coordination. In myriad local sites, people's activities are coordinated through their involvement with and activation of specific organizational texts. Such texts are hierarchically organized (Smith 2005): they include broad ideologies, specifications for particular institutional arenas, and specific texts of record-keeping and accountability which extend the reach of ideological power into front-line action. Frequently, these textualized modes of organizing action produce systematic practices of "not knowing" (chapter 13)—surely an ironic effect, in such an age of accountability.

My aim has been to offer the kind of "map" of ruling processes—however partial—that can make more visible the motors of change. In this concluding chapter, I pull together some overarching findings of the volume and draw out their implications for a critique of neoliberalism. Then I point to questions and possibilities that open up to continuing exploration and discuss, briefly, the ways in which some institutional ethnographers have been using this approach in collaboration with activists and other community organizations.

Restructuring Work and Workers

Our analyses contribute to a growing corpus of critical writing about neoliberalism and the ongoing economic restructuring based on its tenets. Neoliberal theory conceptualizes the market as central to social life, locating solutions to nearly every problem in market processes. Its logic relies on the fiction of an abstract and unattached individual, whose fortunes depend on participation in the market and on the unquestioned capacity to absorb any risks of that participation. Each individual (or each household) is expected to obtain—in a textually conceived market, imagined as an efficient distributive mechanism—whatever is needed to sustain life, primarily by working for pay. In the dominant discourses of the so-called New Economy, meeting that expectation has been defined as the central element in "personal responsibility," and personal responsibility has become the centerpiece of good citizenship. For both people and institutions, responsibility is increasingly constructed in relation to the needs of capital. And the social welfare systems built over the past half-century are increasingly deemed financially untenable. These ideas have been put in place and sustained by a network of influential scholars, commentators, and policymakers; they constitute a conceptual currency invented in an intentional project of transformation. These discourses in which they are embedded are reinforced by constant repetition, drawing viability by incorporating vocabularies of freedom, democracy, and empowerment. Working in "textual reality" (Smith 1990a), policymakers have been hard at work, weaving these ideas into a consensus view of the global economy.

This text-based view may seem compelling to some, but our studies show that much of what happens on the ground can slip from view if we remain in the documentary world of political and economic theory. Many scholars are now investigating the realities of the global economy and are helping to bring people's real lives back into the picture. Our intent has been to contribute to that project; our distinctive contribution is to examine the texts that too often engineer the disappearance of real lives in the world of policy. We have been able to visit only a few of the locations of work and life that are undergoing significant transformation; there are, of course, many others. Taken together, however, our studies highlight several kinds of change across sites, each change predicated on the extension and intensification of market logics.

First, more and more people are being drawn into a global capitalist labor force. We have discussed, for example, the welfare-to-work initiatives that, in the United States, have pushed more and more women with children into low-wage jobs. In job training for health-care work (chapter 7), young mothers are asked to do the "heavy lifting" of long-term care at wages that cannot reasonably sustain their own and their families' health. The immigrant workers who make North American flexible production possible—whether they are producing computer chips in Canada (chapter 1) or solving software problems (chapter 5)—are assigned pieces of a global production process, as needed, and then moved to other tasks. Some highly educated women now find positions of authority in university and corporate jobs (chapter 9); they must consider how (or whether) to become the kind of "star" worker who reaches the top of her field. We have also seen that people with disabilities are finding new opportunities to enter higher education and look toward employment (chapter 10); but they are still expected to shoulder themselves much of the work of inclusion, so that employment opportunities typically bring additional work for these employees.

In these different circumstances, one common element is that people are asked to sculpt themselves into a kind of worker envisioned not only in bureaucratic managerialism but also in the neoliberalism that now pervades organizational thinking. Joan Acker (1990) has shown how the bureaucratic workplaces associated with a Fordist production regime assumed an "unencumbered worker" whose needs outside of work would not interfere with dedication to the organization. For a time, women's household work made it possible for some men to operate relatively unproblematically in this mode; many other workers have struggled in their home lives and within organizations to construct themselves as "unencumbered." Employers have been free to practice "nonresponsibility" (Acker 2006), designing work as if people had no responsibilities outside the job.

The ideal worker in the New Economy is, increasingly, meant to be not only unencumbered but disembodied, as well (Acker 2004). People are now conceived as flexible components of work regimes, whether they are immigrants who are used in short spells of work and then expected to disappear, corporate employees now taught to embrace the "lifelong learning" that allows them to reinvent themselves in ways that serve employers' needs, or people in need, living with the stresses of poverty and their consequences, who are asked somehow to construct themselves as "typical" workers who need not be distracted by struggles to care for themselves or others. To the extent that workers can be mobilized into such projects of self-transformation, employers and the state can continue to shed responsibility for people's sustenance and collective support for daily lives.

Wider participation in paid work seems also to be leading toward a redefinition of citizenship and inclusion, with sharper lines drawn between those who work for pay and those who do not. This trend is highlighted in a shrinkage of public assistance that amounts to the abandonment of many who cannot meet the increasingly restrictive labor-force demands for unencumbered "normalcy"—those with disabilities that make paid jobs difficult to sustain, for example, but also many others who simply need collective arrangements that would better support lives that include both paid work and care for others. Advocacy movements for liberation and inclusion have brought significant expansions in citizenship rights, perhaps especially rights to work; it remains to be seen whether those gains will be rolled back through economic restructuring and whether rights of access to employment will transmute into ever harsher expectations that many cannot easily meet (chapter 4).

Even as more people enter paid labor, the necessary labors of care for others outside the workplace are taken for granted in organizational practices and are increasingly mobilized toward organizational goals, though not acknowledged in any positive way. We have discussed, for example, the intensification of mothers' unpaid contributions to public schooling (chapter 2) and the ways that family help with carework is appropriated and glossed in new public-assistance budgeting practices (chapter 11). The experiences of those in welfare-to-work programs (chapter 7), as well as those who leave or are cut off from assistance (chapter 8), are shaped by employment plans that make only the slightest nods toward burdens of care for children and partners who may have significant health problems. Immigrant workers like the Indian IT professionals who are "Bodyshopped" to U.S. firms are often treated as if they have no personal needs for stability and care—and no family connections (chapter 5). And the Mexican workers whose labor in agriculture and food processing literally feeds the residents of midwestern U.S. communities sustain themselves with only limited access to the public resources of those communities (chapter 6). Hard-won employer and public supports for the work of reproduction are diminished under a banner of fiscal inevitability, so that more and more essential carework is shifted from the public sector into households. Some people can buy needed services in the market, but many must struggle to do more and more with less and less.

These changes, taken together, seem deeply contradictory—surely at some point we all must confront the reality that workers live in bodies and must be sustained. Yet, the increasingly sophisticated discursive frames of neoliberalism conceal such problems and have also achieved a remarkably successful establishment of consensus vocabularies that carry the underlying ideologies of a new regime. "Ideological codes" (Smith 1999), like the cluster of meanings gathered around the language of "personal responsibility," give these discourses a pervasive and seductive power. Such codes are woven into political discourse, budgeting, policy implementation, media reports, and so on, in ways that give them purchase with different audiences; as people take up these vocabularies, they take up beliefs on which they rest, which come to be widely accepted. It may begin to seem only reasonable that "working families" take responsibility for themselves and that they do that most efficiently by seeking "market solutions" for sustaining both work and home life.

Finally, we have seen that accountability is a key element in a new regime and that budgetary practices related to accountability both conceal and justify the reorganization of work. Documentary measures of quality are increasingly consequential, whether in production (chapter 1), education (chapter 2), or human services (chapter 13), and textualized approaches to assessment and accountability continue to spread. In the public sector, business models are applied with increasing focus and consequence, and they are designed to carry frames of accountability that mystify the shrinkage of public provision. The rhetoric and ideology of what some call a "new managerialism" (Rankin and Campbell 2006) portray that shrinkage as empowering individuals while obscuring work transfers and budget cutting.

In this context, workers in the human services seem increasingly to be working across a line of fault (Smith 1987)—they act in face-to-face relations with their clients, and simultaneously in a virtual space of textualized accountability. We saw, for example, the fair-hearing procedure where Betty and an apparently well-intentioned case manager try to work out not only how to secure the care she needs—from actual people—but also how to formulate it in abstracted "hours" (chapter 11). The picture of Ontario teachers and administrators scrambling to textualize students' "special needs" (chapter 12) highlights even more sharply the sometimes bizarre experience of working in a documentary reality. Such practices in health and home care (chapter 13) are designed to control or sometimes cap spending on human services, but they are rarely presented straightforwardly to clients or to front-line workers as budget-cutting devices. The conceptualization and deployment of disability labels brings into view additional problems of abstracted knowing—as our report from Iceland suggests (chapter 4), young people may seek and obtain work (or not) for many reasons; yet those identified as having "disabilities" are channeled into programs that define them more as clients than as workers.

Objectified knowledge is critical in accomplishing the changes of economic restructuring. When we examine the so-called New Economy from the perspective of embodied workers, we can begin to see that neoliberal theory references and relies on documentary accounts of market processes, fictions stripped of the concrete history and social specificity of work and collective life. Too often, even sociological analyses of markets leave in place a conception of market processes as abstracted and disembodied exchange (Krippner 2001). By contrast, knowledge grounded in everyday life allows us to recognize and speak about matters that are unacknowledged and unspeakable in the textual world of restructuring.

Analyzing the Powers of Ruling

Institutional ethnography is designed for mapping "how it works," rather than for the theory building of more conventional sociological research. Still, institutional ethnographers share interests with scholars of other theoretical persuasions in attempting to make sense of how everyday life is put together. Like other postpositivist approaches, ours is one that brings language and discourse to the center of our view of social organization. Our emphasis on power diffused through multiple sites and exercised obliquely, through discourses of governance, resonates with analyses of what Michel Foucault (1980) has called "power/knowledge" and "governmentality." Institutional ethnographers, however, insist on grounding the organizing effects of discursive regimes in the activities of people who take up and use texts—those who create, revise, and reshape them and who sometimes also subvert and resist their effects. We envision active bodies, in their material diversity and their obdurate physicality. And, while we may draw upon the kinds of genealogical analyses that trace discursive histories (e.g., in Fraser and Gordon 1994; Naples 1997), institutional ethnographies perform a different analytical work; we are concerned with people's lives and how texts are used in those lives.

It is the distinctive capacity of institutional ethnography to underscore the sometimes startling power of text-based management, which organizes activity in ways that may not be obvious. The power to control and coordinate that is exercised through textual mediation and can be made visible in institutional ethnographies may otherwise escape notice precisely because it is so pervasive. Its effects are achieved through the many small moments of action that join people engaged in diverse yet coordinated courses of action. This view of organizational life—as well as its reach outside the organization—is attentive to the details of a text-based institutional regime, and it relies on the complete accounting of what's happening that analysts can make when they draw on the generous concept of work discussed in the first chapter. Such an accounting carefully maps how each moment of organizational action connects to others and how a concerted sequence of activities is designed to accomplish the goals of ruling (and I use the term literally— activities are designed consciously and artfully, in acts of administration). What it produces is not so much a theory as an ethnography of power.

Two significant features of contemporary ruling relations open topics for further investigation. First, the managerial strategies that are being de-

veloped to orchestrate economic restructuring often depend on the information-processing capacities of electronic data management, providing
opportunities to shape local activities and monitor their compliance with a
ruling discourse more closely and immediately than ever before. The strategies associated with these technologies aim at standardizing local activity
and reducing inefficiency and waste. Neoliberal discourses establish such
goals as reasonable and laudable; the thinking is that a properly designed decision system will generate the most efficient and effective action. But these
strategies depend on the design and implementation of measurement in
ways that tend to shift relations of power and authority. Local discretion is
displaced as key decisions increasingly reside at some remove from the local setting—with those doing the measuring (and devising the measures and
the information-processing systems that use them), rather than those who
are at work in particular places. New powers are vested in those who operate systems documenting the quality of electronics production, assessing the
effectiveness of teachers' work, or determining when hospital patients are
ready for discharge. The workers who make the chips, the classroom teachers who know the children, and the nurses who spend time with patients still
play essential roles in these work processes, but the scope for their judgment
and discretionary decision making is chipped away and transferred to more
distant workplaces where judgments arise from texts. As front-line workers
learn to operate these texts, they learn to think in the terms of ruling discourses (see, for example, Rankin and Campbell 2006, on how nursing leaders take up the discourses of health-care reform). Given such developments,
it is vitally important to consider the consequences of new knowledge-based
technologies, both for the workers who subordinate their grounded knowledge to objectified knowing and for the institutional "subjects" who are being authoritatively known only through such abstractions. It is important
to ask more questions about what can be measured and what cannot and
about what is lost in a process of measurement. Without such examination
of the new technologies, both the goals and the (often unanticipated) consequences of transformation and reform too easily remain outside the processes of democratic decision making and grassroots organizing.

A related development is a changing division of labor that the new institutional technologies elicit and support. These technology-based practices
produce new jobs, new job descriptions, and new entrepreneurial openings
related to the production, maintenance, and servicing of electronic data
and data processing. The erosion of professional discretion seen especially
in health and human services relates to the bundling in new ways of deci-

sion-making capacity within organizations. Strategies aimed at flexibility, for example, have produced not only the labor strategies that incorporate immigrant workers in production but also new positions for workers, such as schedulers, especially in organizations that manage services. Often, the work of schedulers is tied to electronic technologies, such as the bed management software being introduced into hospitals, or the software that manages work in call centers of various kinds (Rankin and Campbell 2006; Brunson forthcoming). In education, new commercial enterprises are offering print and Web-based products designed around a growing testing (and test-preparation) industry at all levels. The authors and producers of educational tests, software, and other materials or of risk-management technologies in social welfare work (Parada 2002) are often now the ones who define both problems and solutions in front-line work with clients; electronic technologies—as currently designed—may often seriously limit the scope of decision making in the face-to-face service encounter. Thus, these technologies are radically changing not only low-wage production and service jobs but also—perhaps less visibly—the character of work in the public sector. Professional knowing and work are increasingly fragmented, transposed, and reformulated into the skilled but more specific jobs—such as that of the scheduler—that are organized around managerial technologies. Professional knowledge, while still necessary, may increasingly serve the purposes of managing an efficient flow of clients through the organization, as when teachers' time is increasingly directed toward assessment and record keeping (chapter 2; Stock 2002), or the clinical expertise of the head nurse is deployed in chart review for problems that might interfere with timely discharges (Rankin and Campbell 2006).

As we explore such changes, our studies are not directed toward extending theory (which would pull our analyses into the textual realm we critique). Rather, we examine and explicate the forms of knowledge deployed in ruling institutions, in order to elaborate and strengthen those kinds of knowing that are rooted in embodied lives. This mode of analysis not only preserves the embodied experiences of real people but also brings into focus a larger picture, including forces that are at work outside their view. Our studies connect—as the segments of a quilt are pieced together—because of the common ontology of institutional ethnography (Smith 2005): we take as given that social coordination is always a matter of people's activities, and we always look for people at work in the making of social life.

The knowledge produced in this kind of study accumulates as we make connections across analytic settings. Once sensitized to the specific practices developing in different arenas, we are prepared to see clues to their operation elsewhere—to notice and then think beyond what's visible, tracing the local particulars into the generalizing motors of power. As I've worked with institutional ethnography, I've seen this effect in the ways I think about my own research data, about material in my students' dissertation studies, and—perhaps most strikingly—in my own daily life. Perusing memos I receive from the university administration, activating the newly computerized check-in procedure at my doctor's office, writing an on-line recommendation letter, and so on, I now notice with a small shock of recognition the new administrative technologies we've been studying—technologies designed so as not to call attention to themselves, that I'm aware of in only a partial way even as they are reorganizing my activities and interactions. These moments remind me that the changes we're living through are continuing all around us: they don't hold still for analysis. Studies of the sort we've presented here are rarely complete and settled. Smith speaks of them as "open at the edges," meaning that there are always more connections to be made. While the effect of such openness can be daunting, as the researcher is always looking toward a moving horizon, it can also be exhilarating, as we share work and find new insights in the connections among our various studies.

Research and People at Work Making Change

Institutional ethnography is being developed with the aim of providing tools that people might use not only to understand but also to change the forces governing their lives. Thus, the goal is to map coordinative processes with an eye to points of productive intervention. Change does not come automatically with the analysis, however; it requires partnership with actors involved in the institutional processes. Scholars and activists are often uneasy partners, given their different locations, interests, and insights, and such tensions are often heightened by the ways that scholarship is woven into and shaped by ruling practices. The institutional ethnography approach, with its emphasis on ruling knowledges, makes such connections visible—perhaps a first step toward productive collaboration. Some researchers have been working as well on the next steps required to deploy this method of inquiry in collective efforts to reshape institutional practices; I sketch one such effort here in order to point toward those possibilities.

The U.S. institutional ethnographer Ellen Pence, a long-time activist in the area of domestic violence, has developed an institutional community "auditing" procedure explicitly oriented toward change. The audit applies institutional ethnography to organizational processes and draws practitioners within those organizations together, with advocates and community members, in order to explore how routine practices may lead to unintended consequences (Pence and McMahon 2003). The team examines the work of case processing as a case moves from one stage to the next and how its organization affects the experience of the woman being "processed."

In Duluth, for example, an audit team investigated a rise in "double arrests" in which battered women involved in violent encounters were treated in the same way as their partners; they found that routine police procedures resulted in many arrests made properly, in the legal sense, but without adequate attention to contextual circumstances. As they examined the work of dispatchers, police officers and supervisors, prosecutors, and so on, they could identify solutions to these problems: they recommended changes in arrest policies and in oversight of all double arrests. In another project, a Native American women's group worked with Pence on a community audit of city police practices in cases involving Indigenous women (Mending the Sacred Hoop 2002), developing a methodology that combined Indigenous principles of collaborative deliberation and decision making with the audit method. They discovered, among other problems, a number of ways in which the fragmentation of case processing resulted in practitioners overlooking key elements of the stories women brought to the justice system.

The successes of Pence's auditing projects rely on a long and broad history of activism, rooted in the battered-women's movement and continuing over decades. Activities on multiple fronts have slowly created the openings that made space for activist interventions in the criminal-justice system, as well as producing new agencies and actors, linked in complex ways to state and social movement constituencies in the evolving field of domestic violence (Walker 1990). Clearly, then, change efforts aimed at policies and practices will require not only the kind of analysis that institutional ethnographies might produce but also strategies for commanding public attention and support from constituencies.

The audit methodology used by Pence and her community partners in the field of domestic violence is strongly tied to the case-processing organization of the criminal-justice system. It seems most easily transferable to other arenas where work is organized through the treatment of "cases," such as social work/social welfare, health care, and education (perhaps especially special education), and has been used by others in such arenas (Campbell, Copeland, and Tate 1998). It is less clear, perhaps, how it might apply in the areas of human resource or immigration policy (where a kind of batch processing rather than case management often seems to obtain). Still, it seems a promising model for approaching policy development and reform in ways that keep the experiences and interests of real people central. In a project focused on issues related to economic restructuring, Belinda Leach and Susan Turner are working with several rural Canadian women's groups on issues the groups identify as important (see http://www.rwmc.uoguelph.ca); as those projects develop, their reports will no doubt provide additional insight into how auditing and related strategies might be used in these areas.

The chapters in the last section of this book provide tentative models for research that might bring together workers in the human service fields and their clients—groups whose interests are not the same but are certainly linked. Frank Ridzi's analysis of fair hearing procedures (chapter 11), for example, brings to light the textual constraints of work in public assistance that must often present dizzying frustrations for workers, as well as their clients. Pence has found in her projects that workers in such institutional sites typically welcome the opportunity to explore with others how their activities are hooked into other sites and how that matters for other workers and the clients that all are attempting to serve. Yvette Daniel's work (chapter 12) suggests that practitioners can often use institutional ethnography to make sense of puzzles in their own work organizations—either in a formal research project like Daniel's or, less formally, as a way of thinking about organizational practice. Several institutional ethnographers incorporate this method of inquiry into undergraduate teaching (See, e.g., Naples 2002), and their discussions point toward the possibilities for even quite modest investigations carried out with limited resources. Finally, Marie Campbell's report on her participatory research project (chapter 13) suggests that clients on the research team can identify fruitful starting points—in this case, the unmet goal of providing continuity of care—for more extended investigations. She and her collaborators have written elsewhere (Campbell, Copeland, and Tate 1998) about the analytic benefits of working collaboratively, as well as the challenges of building and sustaining an effective research group.

What Pence's and Campbell's auditing projects do extremely well is to show how an evaluative investigation can proceed with a clear focus on the implications of organizational action for its clients. In Pence's (2001) study of judicial processing, "women's safety" is taken as the touchstone and remains so as investigators take up their investigation; in Campbell's study, the researchers continually return to questions of how clients with disabilities experience the provision of home support. In addition, Pence and McMahon (2003) point out that the audit methodology has the advantage of shifting critique from a blame model focused on individual front-line practitioners to the organization of the practices causing problems. Finally, the audit procedure provides a flexible model for exploring organizational process that can be used in various ways from positions both inside and outside institutions, by researchers, practitioners, and advocates.

More Work to Do

All people's lives unfold in local and particular contexts—even the increasingly mobile workers of the so-called New Economy travel from one particular place to another, and another. These are places of embodied experience, with all the uniqueness of individual lives. But those lives are profoundly shaped by the organizations that we encounter in the course of our lives, whether as workers, parents, clients, consumers, researchers, or policymakers. As we work in and with organizations (and their texts), we enter the ruling relations; we participate in them, activate them, sustain them, and sometimes challenge or try to subvert them. We cannot simply step outside these relations, and it is not easy to change or interrupt them.

The studies presented here are meant to open up a kind of road map, producing the kind of user's understanding that we gain from consulting a map, so that we can see more clearly the relations of power we confront and perhaps where to intervene or how things might be arranged differently. Our studies chart only a few sites in the landscape of economic restructuring; but we hope they will inspire further investigations—filling in maps that may be useful for those of us who wish to contest the harsh new realities of neoliberalism. In that spirit, I would note simply that there is much more to learn about the consequences for people of a rapidly changing regime, and a great deal more to do.

References

Acker, Joan. 1990. "Hierarchies, Jobs, Bodies: A Theory of Gendered Organizations." *Gender and Society* 4: 139–158.

_____. 1998. "The Future of 'Gender and Organizations': Connections and Boundaries." *Gender, Work, and Organization* 5: 195–206.

_____. 2003. "Gender, Capitalism, and Globalization." *Critical Sociology* 30:17–41.

_____. 2006. *Class Questions: Feminist Answers*. Lanham, Md.: Rowman and Littlefield.

Ackers, Peter, Chris Smith, and Paul Smith, eds. 1996. *The New Workplace and Trade Unionism*. London: Routledge

Acs, Gregory, and Pamela Loprest. 2001. *"Final Synthesis Report of the Findings from ASPE's "Leavers" Grants."* Washington, D.C.: Urban Institute.

Acuna, Rodolfo. 1981. *Occupied America: A History of Chicanos*. New York: Harper and Row.

Adams, Dale W., and J. D. Von Pishke. 1992. "Microenterprise Credit Programs: Déja Vu." *World Development* 20:1463–1470.

Aitken, S., M. Buultjens, C. Clark, J. Eyre, and L. Pease. 2000. *Teaching Children Who Are Deafblind*. London, England: David Fulton.

Albelda, Randy. 2001. "Welfare-to-Work, Farewell to Families? U.S. Welfare Reform and Work/Family Debates." *Feminist Economics* 7:119–135.

_____. 2002. "Fallacies of Welfare-to-Work Policies." In R. Albelda and A. Withorn, eds., *Lost Ground*, pp. 79–94. Cambridge, Mass.: South End Press.

Albert, V. N., and W. C. King. 1999. "The Impact of a Mandatory Employment Program on Welfare Terminations: Implications for Welfare Reform." *Journal of Social Service Research* 25(1/2): 125–148.

Alexander, M. Jacquie. 1997. "Erotic Autonomy as a Politics of Decolonization: An Anatomy of Feminist and State Practice in the Bahamas Tourist Economy." In M. Jacquie Alexander and Chandra Talpade Mohanty, eds., *Feminist Genealogies, Colonial Legacies, and Democratic Futures*. New York: Routledge.

Alexander, M. J., and C. Talpade Mohanty. 1997. "Introduction: Genealogies, Legacies, Movements." In M. Jacquie Alexander and Chandra Talpade Mohanty, eds., *Feminist Genealogies, Colonial Legacies, and Democratic Futures*. New York: Routledge.

André-Bechely, Lois. 2005. *Could It Be Otherwise? Parents and the Inequities of Public School Choice.* New York: Routledge.

Anzaldúa, Gloria. 1987. *Borderlands/La Frontera: The New Mestiza.* San Francisco: Spinsters/Aunt Lute.

Arndt, K. L. 2005. "'They Should Know They Have Usher Syndrome Around Here': College Students Who Are Deafblind." Ph.D. diss., Syracuse University, New York.

Arnone, Michael. 2003. "The Wannabes." *Chronicle of Higher Education,* January 3.

Aronowitz, Stanley. 2000. *The Knowledge Factory: Dismantling the Corporate University and Creating True Higher Learning.* Boston: Beacon Press.

Ayers, Kristen Ness, and Scott D. Syfert. 2002. "U.S. Visa Options and Strategies for the Information Technology Industry." *International Quarterly* 14(4):535–565.

Bailyn, Lotte. 1993. *Breaking the Mold: Women, Men, and Time in the New Corporate World.* New York: Free Press.

Bakker, Isabella, ed. 1994. *The Strategic Silence: Gender and Economic Policy.* London: Zed.

Balkin, Steven. 1993. "A Grameen Bank Replication: The Full Circle Fund of the Women's Self-Employment Project of Chicago." In Abu N. M. Wahid, ed., *The Grameen Bank: Poverty Relief in Bangladesh,* pp. 235–266. Boulder: Westview Press.

Ball, S. 1990. *Politics and Policy Making in Education.* London: Routledge.

Banerjee, Payal. 2006. "Indian Information Technology (IT) Workers in the U.S.: The H-1B Visa, Flexible Production, and the Racialization of Labor." *Critical Sociology* 32:425–445.

Bania, Neil, Claudia Coulton, Nina Lalich, Toby Martin, Matt Newburn, and Cara J. Pasqualone. 2001. *The End of Welfare as They Knew It: What Happens When Welfare Recipients Reach Their Time Limits?* Cleveland, Ohio: The Center on Urban Poverty and Social Change.

Barley, Stephen R., and Gideon Kunda. 2004. *Gurus, Hired Guns, and Warm Bodies: Itinerant Experts in a Knowledge Economy.* Princeton: Princeton University Press.

Barnes, C., and G. Mercer. 2005. "Disability, Work and Welfare: Challenging the Social Exclusion of Disabled People." *Work, Employment and Society* 19:527–545.

Barnes, C., M. Oliver, and L. Barton. 2002. *Disability Studies Today.* Cambridge: Polity Press.

Baron, Dennis. 2003. "Sharing Inside Information." *Chronicle of Higher Education,* December 19.

Bates, Timothy, and Lisa Servon. 1996. "Why Loans Won't Save the Poor." *Inc Magazine,* April, p. 27.

Baynton, Dannah. 2001. "America's $60 Billion Problem." *Training,* May, pp. 51–56.

Behn, R. D., and E. K. Keating. 2004. "Facing the Fiscal Crisis in State Governments: National Problem, National Responsibilities." Cambridge, Mass.: The Taubman Center for State and Local Government, John F. Kennedy School of Government, Harvard University.

Belfiore, Mary Ellen, Tracey Defoe, Sue Folinsbee, Judy Hunter, and Nancy Jackson. 2004. *Reading Work: Literacies in the New Work Order*. Mahwah, N.J.: Lawrence Erlbaum.

Benach, Joan, Fernando G. Benavides, Steven Platt, Ana Diez-Roux, and Carles Mutaner. 2000. "The Health-Damaging Potential of New Types of Flexible Employment: A Challenge for Public Health Researchers." *American Journal of Public Health* 90(8):1316–1317.

Benner, Chris. 2002. *Work in the New Economy: Flexible Labor Markets in Silicon Valley*. Malden, Mass.: Blackwell.

Beresford, Peter, and Chris Holden. 2000. "We Have Choices: Globalisation and Welfare User Movements." *Disability and Society* 15:973–989.

Besharov, D. J. 1995. "Using Work to Reform Welfare." *Public Welfare* (Summer):17–20.

Bhatt, Nitin, Gary Painter, and Shui-Yan Tang. 2002. "The Challenges of Outreach and Sustainability for U.S. Microcredit Programs." In James H. Carr and Zhong Yi Tong, eds., *Replicating Microfinance in the United States*, pp. 191–222. Washington, D.C.: Woodrow Wilson Center Press.

Biggart, N. M. 1989. *Charismatic Capitalism: Direct Selling Organizations in America*. Chicago: University of Chicago Press.

Bines, H. 1995. "Special Education Needs in the Market Place." *Journal of Education Policy* 10(2):157–171.

Blair-Loy, Mary. 2003. *Competing Devotions: Career and Family Among Women Financial Professionals*. Cambridge, Mass.: Harvard University Press.

Blau, Joel. 1999. *Illusions of Prosperity: America's Working Families in an Age of Economic Insecurity*. New York: Oxford University Press.

Bloom, Dan, Mary Farrell, Barbara Fink, and Diana Adams-Ciardullo. 2002. "Welfare Time Limits: State Policies, Implementation, and Effects on Families." New York: MDRC.

Bloom, Dan, James J. Kemple, Pamela Morris, Susan Scrivener, Nandita Verma, and Richard Hendra. 2000. *The Family Transition Program: Final Report on Florida's Initial Time-Limited Welfare Program*. New York: MDRC.

Bloom, Dan, Susan Scrivener, Charles Michalopoulos, Pamela Morris, Richard Hendra, Diana Adams-Ciardullo, and Johanna Walter. 2002. *Jobs First: Final Report on Connecticut's Welfare Reform Initiative*. New York: MDRC.

Bogdan, R. 1988. *Freak Show*. Chicago: University of Chicago Press.

Bonacich, Edna, and Richard P. Appelbaum. 2000. *Behind the Label: Inequality in the Los Angeles Apparel Industry*. Berkeley: University of California Press.

Borja, R. R. 2004. "Education Industry Eyes Opportunities in 'No Child' Law." *Education Week*, April 7.

Boswell, Terry, and David Jorjani. 1988. "Uneven Development and the Origins of Split Labor Market Discrimination: A Comparison of Black, Chinese, and Mexican Immigrant Minorities in the United States." In Joan Smith, Jane Collins, Terence K.

Hopkins, and Akbar Muhammed, eds., *Racism, Sexism, and the World System*, pp. 169–186. Westwood, Conn.: Greenwood Press.

Bowring, Finn. 2002. "Post-Fordism and the End of Work." *Futures* 34:159–172.

Brandon, Peter D., and Dennis P. Hogan. 2004. "Impediments to Mothers Leaving Welfare: The Role of Maternal and Child Disability." *Population Research and Policy Review* 23(4):419–436.

Brantlinger, E. 2003. *Dividing Classes: How the Middle Class Negotiates and Rationalizes School Advantage*. New York: Routledge.

Brantlinger, Ellen, Massoumeh Majd-Jabbari, and Samuel L. Guskin. 1996. "Self-Interest and Liberal Educational Discourse: How Ideology Works for Middle-Class Mothers." *American Educational Research Journal* 33(3):571–597.

Broadfoot, P. M. 1996. *Education, Assessment and Society*. Philadelphia: Open University Press.

Brock, Thomas, Claudia Coulton, Andrew London, Denies Polit, Lashawn Richburg-Hayes, Ellen Scott, and Nandita Verma. 2002. *Welfare Reform in Cleveland: Implementation, Effects, and Experiences of Poor Families and Neighborhoods*. New York: MDRC.

Brock, Thomas, Isaac Kwakye, Judy C. Polyné, Lashawn Richburg-Hayes, David Seith, Alex Stepick, and Carol Dutton Stepick. 2004. *Welfare Reform in Miami: Implementation, Effects, and Experiences of Poor Families and Neighborhoods*. New York: MDRC.

Brodie, Janine. 1994. "Shifting the Boundaries: Gender and the Politics of Restructuring." In Isabella Bakker, ed., *The Strategic Silence: Gender and Economic Policy*, pp. 46–60. London: Zed.

Brooks, M. G., and J. C. Buckner. 1996. "Work and Welfare: Job Histories, Barriers to Employment, and Predictors of Work among Low-Income Single Women." *American Journal of Orthopsychiatry* 66:526–537.

Brooks, S. 2000. *Canadian Democracy: An Introduction*. New York: Oxford University Press.

Brown, H. 2004. *Citizens Not Patients: Approaches to Meet the Needs of Disabled People*. Strasbourg: Council of Europe.

Brueggemann, B. J., ed. 2004. *Literacy and Deaf People: Cultural and Contextual Perspectives*. Washington, D.C.: Gallaudet University Press.

Brunson, Jeremy. Forthcoming. The Practice and Organization of Sign Language Interpreting in Video Relay Service: An Institutional Ethnography of Access. Ph.D. diss. in progress. Department of Sociology, Syracuse University, Syracuse, N.Y.

Bullard, Robert D., J. Eugene Grigsby, III, and Charles Lee, eds. 1994. *Residential Apartheid: The American Legacy*. Los Angeles: Regents of the University of California.

Bullard, Robert D., and Charles Lee, C. 1994. "Introduction: Racism and American Apartheid." In Robert D. Bullard, J. Eugene Grigsby, III, and Charles Lee, eds., *Residential Apartheid: The American Legacy*, pp. 1–16. Los Angeles: Regents of the University of California.

Bureau of Labor Statistics. 2006. *Tomorrow's Jobs.* (Occupational Outlook Handbook, Bulletin 2600). Washington, D.C.: U.S. Department of Labor.

Burkhauser, R.V., M.C. Daly, A. J. Houtenville, and N. Nargis. 2002. "Self-Reported Work-Limitation Data: What They Can and Cannot Tell Us." *Demography* 39:541–555.

Burrage, Michael, and Rolf Torstendahl. 1990. *Professions in Theory and History: Rethinking the Study of Professions.* Thousand Oaks, Calif.: Sage.

Burtless, G. T. 1997. "Welfare Recipients' Job Skills and Employment Prospects." *Future of Children* 7(1):39–51.

Butler, S. S., and S. Seguino. 1998. "Gender and Welfare Reform: Redefining the Issues." *Journal of Progressive Human Services* 9(2):51–82.

Camosun College. 2005. "Home Support/Resident Care Attendant." Available at http://www.camosun.bc.ca/learn/programs/hsrc.html.

Campbell, M. 2002. "Research for Activism and Institutional Ethnography: Understanding Social Organization from Inside It." Paper presented at the Sociology for Changing the World: Political Activist Ethnography Conference. Laurentian University, Sudbury, November 8–10.

Campbell, M., and A. Manicom, eds. 1995. *Knowledge, Experience, and Ruling Relations: Studies in the Social Organization of Knowledge.* Toronto: University of Toronto Press.

———. 1995. Introduction. *Knowledge, Experience, and Ruling Relations: Studies in the Social Organization of Knowledge,* pp. 3–17. Toronto: University of Toronto Press.

Campbell, Marie, and Frances Gregor. 2002. *Mapping Social Relations: A Primer in Doing Institutional Ethnography.* Aurora, Ontario: Garamond.

Campbell, Marie, Brenda Copeland, and Betty Tate. 1998. "Taking the Standpoint of People with Disabilities in Research: Experiences with Participation." *Canadian Journal of Rehabilitation* 12:95–104.

———. 1999. "Project Inter-Seed: Learning from the Health Care Experiences of People with Disabilities: Final Report." Victoria, British Columbia: University of Victoria.

Canadian Council on Social Development. 2005. "Disability Information Sheet #17: Supports and Services for Persons with Disabilities in Canada: Requirements and Gaps." Ottawa, Ontario. Available at http://www.ccsd.ca/drip/research/drip17/index.htm.

Cancian, Francesca M., and Stacey J. Oliker. 2000. *Caring and Gender.* Walnut Creek, Calif.: Altamira.

Cancian, Francesca, Demie Kurz, Andrew S. London, Rebecca Reviere, and Mary Tuominen, eds. 2002. *Child Care and Inequality: Re-Thinking Carework for Children and Youth.* New York: Routledge.

Cantú, Lionel. Forthcoming. *Border Crossings: Mexican Men and the Sexuality of Migration,* edited with an introduction by Nancy A. Naples and Salvador Vidal-Ortiz. New York: New York University Press.

Capella-McDonnall, M. E. 2005. "The Ticket to Work Program: Employment Networks' Views on Serving Beneficiaries Who Are Blind or Visually Impaired." *Journal of Visual Impairment and Blindness* 99(6):336–344.

Cappelli, P., and N. Rogovsky. 1994. "New Work Systems and Skill Requirements." *International Labour Review* 133(2):205–20.

Cappelli, P., L. Bassi, H. Katz, D. Knopke, P. Osterman, and M. Useem. 1997. *Change at Work*. New York: Oxford University Press.

Carnoy, Martin, Manuel Castells, and Chris Benner. 1997. "Labour Markets and Employment Practices in the Age of Flexibility: A Case Study of Silicon Valley." *International Labour Review* 136(1):27–48.

Castleton, Geraldine. 2000. "Workplace Literacy: Examining the Virtual and Virtuous Realities in (E)merging Discourses on Work." *Discours* 21(1):91–104.

Charlton, J. I. 1998. *Nothing About Us Without Us*. Berkeley: University of California Press.

Chavez, Leo. 1992. *Shattered Lives*. Orlando, Fla.: Harcourt, Brace, Jovanovich.

Christopher, Karen. 2004. "Welfare as We [Don't] Know It: A Review and Feminist Critique of Welfare Reform Research in the United States." *Feminist Economics* 10(2):143–171.

Clark, Peggy, and Amy Kays. 1995. *Enabling Entrepreneurship: Microenterprise Development in the U.S.* Washington, D.C.: Aspen Institute.

Clawson, Dan. 2003. *The Next Upsurge: Labor and the New Social Movements*. Ithaca, N.Y.: Cornell University Press.

Clinton, Angela. 1997. "Flexible Labor: Restructuring the American Workforce." *Monthly Labor Review* 120(8):3–17.

Cockburn, C. 1983. *Brothers: Male Dominance and Technological Change*. London: Pluto Press.

Cohen, A., J. C. Timmons, and S. L. Fesko. 2005. "The Workforce Investment Act: How Policy Conflict and Policy Ambiguity Affect Implementation." *Journal of Disability Policy Studies* 15(4):221–230.

Collins, Jane L. 2003. *Threads: Gender, Labor, and Power in the Global Apparel Industry*. Chicago: University of Chicago Press.

Collins, Patricia Hill. 1997. "How Much Difference Is Too Much?: Black Feminist Thought and the Politics of Postmodern Social Theory." *Current Perspectives in Social Theory* 17:3–37.

Connell, R. W. 1987. *Gender and Power*. Palo Alto: Stanford University Press.

Consumer Directed Choices, Inc. 2004. *Preliminary Proposal Establishing an Administrative Relationship between Consumer Directed Choices, Inc. and Living Resources, Inc.* Accessed September 1, 2004, at http://cdchoices.org/lresource.html.

Consumer Directed Personal Assistance Association of New York State. 2001. *Legislation*. Accessed September 1, 2004, at http://www.cdpaanys.org/sec_365f.htm.

Cooper, Marianne. 2002. "Being the 'Go-to Guy': Fatherhood, Masculinity, and the Organization of Work in Silicon Valley." In N. Gerstel, D. Clawson, and R. Zussman, eds., *Families at Work*, pp. 5–31. Nashville, Tenn.: Vanderbilt University Press.

Council of Europe. 2006. *Council of Europe Action Plan to Promote the Rights and Full Participation of People with Disabilities in Society: Improving the Quality of Life of People with Disabilities in Europe 2006–2015*. Strasbourg: Council of Europe.

Council of European Union. 2000a. "Council Decision 2000/750/EC of 27 November 2000 Establishing a Community Action Programme to Combat Discrimination (2001–2006)." *Official Journal of the European Communities*, L303, {02/12/2000}pp. 23–28.

———. 2000b. "Council Directive 2000/78/EC of 27 November 2000 Establishing a General Framework for Equal Treatment in Employment and Occupation." *Official Journal of the European Communities*, L303, 02/12/2000, p. 16.

Counts, Alex. 1996. *Give Us Credit: How Muhammad Yunus's Micro-lending Revolution is Empowering Women from Bangladesh to Chicago*. New York: Random House.

Coutin, Susan Bibler. 1993. *The Culture of Protest: Religious Activism and the U.S. Sanctuary Movement*. Boulder, Colo.: Westview Press.

———. 2000. *Legalizing Moves: Salvadoran Immigrants' Struggle for U.S. Residency*. Ann Arbor: University of Michigan Press.

Cowgill, Julie, and Nancy Jurik. 2005. "The Construction of Client Identities in a Post-Welfare Social Service Program: The Double Bind of Microenterprise Development." In Anne Schneider and Helen Ingram, eds., *Deserving and Entitled*. Albany: State University of New York Press.

Crow, Sarah, and Jacqueline Anderson. 2004. *Working Against the Clock: Implementing Five-Year Welfare Time Limits in California*. Berkeley: California Policy Research Project (CPRC) Policy Brief 16(4).

Daley-Harris, Sam, ed. 2002. *Pathways Out of Poverty: Innovations in Microfinance for the Poorest Families*. Bloomfield, Conn.: Kumarian Press.

Dalla Costa, Mariarosa, and Selma James. 1972. *The Power of Women and the Subversion of the Community*. Bristol, England: Falling Wall Press.

Darrah, Charles. 1997. "Complicating the Concept of Skill Requirements: Scenes from a Workplace." In Glenda Hull, ed., *Changing Work, Changing Workers*, pp. 249–272. Albany: State University of New York Press.

Darville, Richard. 1995. "Literacy, Experience, Power." In Marie Campbell and Ann Manicom, eds., *Knowledge, Experience, and Ruling Relations: Studies in the Social Organization of Knowledge*, pp. 249–261. Toronto: University of Toronto Press.

———. 1999. Knowledges of Adult Literacy: Surveying for Competitiveness. *International Journal of Educational Development* 19:273–285.

———. 1998. "Nowadays I Read Myself to Sleep: Media Narratives in the Adult Literacy Regime." Paper presented at the Pacific Sociological Association, San Francisco, April 16-19.

_____. 2002. "Policy, Accountability and Practice in Adult Literacy Work." Paper presented at the Canadian Association for Studies in Adult Education (CASAE) Ontario Institute for Studies in Education, Toronto, May 30–June 1. Available at http:www.oise.utoronto.ca/.CASAE/cnf2002/2002_Papers/darville2002w.pdf.

Davis, L. J., ed. 1997. *The Disability Studies Reader.* New York: Routledge.

Delbridge, Rick. 2000. *Life on the Line in Contemporary Manufacturing.* New York: Oxford University Press.

Desai, Manisha. 2002. "Transnational Solidarity: Women's Agency, Structural Adjustment, and Globalization." In Nancy A. Naples and Manisha Desai, eds., *Women's Activism and Globalization: Linking Local Struggles and Transnational Politics,* pp. 15–33. New York: Routledge.

DeVault, Marjorie L. 1991. *Feeding the Family: The Social Organization of Caring as Gendered Work.* Chicago: University of Chicago Press.

_____. 1999. *Liberating Method: Feminism and Social Research.* Philadelphia, Penn.: Temple University Press.

DeVault, M., and L. McCoy 2001. "Institutional Ethnography: Using Interviews to Investigate Ruling Relations." *Handbook of Interview Research: Context and Method,* pp. 751–775. Thousand Oaks, Calif.: Sage.

DeWolff, Alice. 2000. *Breaking the Myth of Flexible Work: Contingent Workers in Toronto.* Toronto: The Contingent Workers Project.

Diamond, T. 1992. *Making Gray Gold: Narratives of Nursing Home Care.* Chicago: The University of Chicago Press.

Dryburgh, Heather. 1999. "Work Hard, Play Hard: Women and Professionalization in Engineering—Adapting to the Culture." *Gender & Society* 13:664–682.

Dugger, Celia W. 2006. "Peace Prize to Pioneer of Loans for Those Too Poor to Borrow." *New York Times,*October 14, 2006, A1.

Duncan, G. J., J. Brooks-Gunn, and P. K. Klebanov. 1994. "Economic Deprivation and Early Childhood Development." *Child Development* 65:296–318.

Edin, Kathryn, and Laura Lein. 1997. *Making Ends Meet: How Single Mothers Survive Welfare and Low-Wage Work.* New York: Russell Sage Foundation.

Edin, K., K. M. Harris, and G. Sandefur. 1998. *Welfare to Work: Opportunities and Pitfalls.* Washington, D. C.: American Sociological Association.

Ehlers, Tracy, and Karen Main. 1998. "Women and the False Promise of Microenterprise." *Gender and Society* 12:424–440.

Ehrenreich, Barbara, and Arlie Russell Hochschild, eds. 2002. *Global Woman: Nannies, Maids, and Sex Workers in the New Economy.* New York: Metropolitan Books.

Ellis, Richard and B. Lindsay Lowell. 1999. "Foreign-Origin Persons in the U.S. Information Technology Workforce." IT Workforce Data Project: Report III. Available at http://www.cpst.org/ITWF_Reports.htm.

Ellwood, David T. 1988. *Poor Support: Poverty in the American Family.* New York: Basic Books.

Epstein, Cynthia Fuchs. 1981. *Women in Law.* New York: Basic Books.

Epstein, J. L. 2001. *School, Family, and Community Partnerships: Preparing Educators and Improving Schools.* Boulder, Colo.: Westview Press.

Espiritu, Yen Le. 1992. *Asian American Panethnicity: Bridging Institutions and Identities.* Philadelphia: Temple University Press.

Ethnic and Racial Studies. 1999. "Special Issue: Transnational Communities." *Ethnic and Racial Studies* 22(2).

European Commission. 1996. *Communication of the Commission on Equality of Opportunity for People with Impairment.* COM (96) 406 final.

_____. 2000a. *Benchmarking Employment Policies for People with Disabilities.* A study prepared by ECOTEC Research and Consulting for the Education and Culture Directorate-General. Retrieved January 15, 2007 at http://ec.europa.eu/employment_social/disability/bench_en.pdf.

_____. 2000b. *Towards a Barrier-Free Europe for People with Impairment.* Communication from the Commission to the Council, the European Parliament, the Economic and Social Committee, and the Committee of Regions, COM (2000) 284 final.

_____. 2001a. *The Employment Situation of People with Disabilities in the European Union.* A study prepared by EIM Business and Policy Research for the EU section on Employment and Social Affairs. Dublin: European Foundation for the Improvement of Living and Working Conditions. Available at http://ec.europa.eu/employment_social/news/2001/dec/2666complete_en.pdf.

_____. 2001b. *Attitudes of Europeans to Disability.* Eurobarometer 54.2. A report prepared by the European Opinion Research Group (EPRG) for the Education and Culture Directorate-General. Retrieved December 19, 2006, at http://ec.europa.eu/employment_social/disability/eu_bar_en.pdf.

_____. 2002. *Active Labour Market Programmes for People with Disabilities: Facts and Figures on Use and Impact.* A study prepared by EIM Business and Policy Research for the EU section on Employment and Social Affairs. Dublin: European Foundation for the Improvement of Living and Working Conditions.

_____. 2005. *Disability Mainstreaming in the European Employment Strategy.* European Commission, Employment, Social Affairs and Equal Opportunities. Available at http://ec.europa.eu/employment_social/disability/emco010705_en.pdf.

European Disability Forum. 2002. *The Madrid Declaration.* Available at http://www.madriddeclaration.org/en/dec/dec.htm.

European Foundation for the Improvement of Living and Working Conditions. 1999. *Employment Status and Health.* Dublin: Author.

Evans, Sara. 1979. *Personal Politics: The Roots of Women's Liberation in the Civil Rights Movement and the New Left.* New York: Vintage Books.

Evetts, Julia. 2003. "The Sociological Analysis of Professionalism: Occupation Change in the Modern World." *International Sociology* 18:395–415.

Fain, Paul. 2005. "Competitive Pressure Is Turning Research Universities into Look-Alike Universities." *Chronicle of Higher Education,* July 11.

Ferguson, J. 1994. *The Anti-Politics Machine: Development, Depolitization, and Bureaucratic Power in Lesotho*. Minneapolis: University of Minnesota.

Fernández-Kelly, María Patricia. 1983. *For We Are Sold, I and My People: Women and Industry in Mexico's Frontier*. Albany: State University of New York Press.

Filer, A., and A. Pollard. 2000. "Assessment and Parents' Strategic Action." In A. Filer, ed., *Assessment: Social Practice and Social Product*. New York: Routledge.

Fink, Deborah. 1992. *Agrarian Women: Wives and Mothers in Rural Nebraska 1880–1940*. Chapel Hill: University of North Carolina Press.

—————. 1998. *Cutting into the Meatpacking Line: Workers and Change in the Rural Midwest*. Chapel Hill: University of North Carolina Press.

Fish, Stanley. 2003. "All in the Game: Let Them Teach at Stanford." *Chronicle of Higher Education*, September 5.

Fitchen, Janet M. 1991. *Endangered Spaces, Enduring Places: Change, Identity, and Survival in Rural America*. Boulder, Colo.: Westview Press.

Flores, William V., and Rina Benmayor, eds. 1997. *Latino Cultural Citizenship: Claiming Identity, Space, and Rights*. Boston: Beacon Press.

Folbre, Nancy. 2001. *The Invisible Heart: Economics and Family Values*. New York: The New Press.

Foreman, D., A. C. Cohen, J. D. Kaplan, and R. Mitchell. 2001. *Spectrum Test Prep: Grade 2*. Grand Rapids, MI: McGraw Hill.

Foucault, Michel. 1972. *The Archaeology of Knowledge and the Discourse on Language*. New York: Harper and Row.

—————. 1980. *Power/Knowledge: Selected Interviews and Other Writings 1972–1977*. Ed. Colin Gordon. New York: Pantheon.

Frankenberg, Ruth. 1993. *White Women, Race Matters: The Social Construction of Whiteness*. Minneapolis: University of Minnesota Press.

Fraser, Nancy. 1989. *Unruly Practices: Power, Discourse, and Gender in Contemporary Social Theory*. Minneapolis: University of Minnesota Press.

Fraser, Nancy, and Linda Gordon. 1994. "A Genealogy of Dependency: Tracing a Keyword of the U.S. Welfare State." *Signs* 19:309–336.

Freeman, Harris, and George Gonos. 2005. "Regulating the Employment Sharks: Reconceptualizing the Legal Status of the Commercial Temp Agency." *WorkingUSA: The Journal of Labor and Society* 8:293–314.

Fudge, Judy, and Leah Vosko. 2003. "Gendered Paradoxes and the Rise of Contingent Work: Towards a Transformative Feminist Political Economy of the Labour Market." In W. Clement and L. Vosko, eds., *Changing Canada: Political Economy as Transformation*, pp. 183–213. Montreal and Kingston: McGill-Queen's.

Galabuzi, G. 2005. *Canada's Economic Apartheid: The Social Exclusion of Racialized Groups in the New Century*. Toronto: Canadian Scholars' Press.

Galinsky, Ellen. 2001. "Toward a New View of Work and Family Life." In R. Hertz and N. L. Marshall, eds., *Working Families: The Transformation of the American Home*, pp. 207–226. Berkeley: University of California Press.

Gennetian, Lisa A., and Pamela A. Morris. 2003. "The Effects of Time Limits and Make-Work-Pay Strategies on the Well-Being of Children: Experimental Evidence from Two Welfare Reform Programs." *Children and Youth Services Review* 25:17–54.

Gersick, Connie J. G., Jean M. Bartunek, and Jane E. Dutton. 2000. "Learning from Academia." *Academy of Management Journal* 43:1026–1044.

Geyer, R. R. 2000. *Exploring European Social Policy*. Cambridge: Polity Press.

Gilliom, J. 2001. *Overseers of the Poor: Surveillance, Resistance, and the Limits of Privacy*. Chicago: University of Chicago Press.

Giroux, Henry A. 2001. "Introduction: Critical Education or Training?: Beyond the Commidification of Higher Education." In H. A. Giroux and K. Myrsiades, eds., *Beyond the Corporate University: Culture and Pedagogy in the New Millennium*, pp. 1–12. Lanham, Md.: Rowman and Littlefield.

Goldberg, David Theo. 1993. *Racist Culture: Philosophy and the Politics of Meaning*. Oxford: Blackwell.

Gooden, Susan, and Fred Doolittle. 2001. *Exceptions to the Rule: The Implementation of 24-Month Time Limit Extensions in W-2*. New York: MDRC.

Gordon, Anne, Jacqueline Kauff, Carole Kuhns, and Renee Lauffler. 2002. *Experiences of Virginia Time Limit Families After Case Closure: 18-Month Follow-up with Cases Closed in 1998 and 1999*. Princeton, NJ: Mathematica Policy Research Institute.

Gottfried, Heidi. 1995. "Developing Neo-Fordism: A Comparative Perspective." *Critical Sociology* 21:39–70.

Graff, Harvey. 1987. *The Legacies of Literacy*. Bloomington: Indiana University Press.

Grahame, Kamini Maraj. 1998. "Asian Women, Job Training, and the Social Organization of Immigrant Labor Markets." *Qualitative Sociology* 21:75–90.

Grammenos, S. 2003. *Illness, Disability and Social Inclusion*. Dublin: European Foundation for the Improvement of Living and Working Conditions. Available at http://www.eurofound.europa.eu/pubdocs/2003/35/en/1/ef0335en.pdf

Green, Venus 2001. *Race on the Line: Gender, Labor, and Technology in the Bell System, 1880–1980*. Durham, N.C., and London: Duke University Press.

Grewal, Interpal, and Caren Kaplan, eds. 1994. *Scattered Hegemonies: Postmodernity and Transnational Feminist Practices*. Minneapolis: University of Minneapolis Press.

Griffith, Alison I. 1984. "Ideology, Education and Single Parent Families: The Normative Ordering of Families Through Schooling." Unpublished Ph.D. diss., University of Toronto.

———. 1992. "Educational Policy as Text and Action." *Educational Policy* 6(4): 415–428.

———. 1995. "Mothering, Schooling, and Children's Development." In M. Campbell and A. Manicom, eds., *Knowledge, Experience, and Ruling Relations: Studies in the Social Organization of Knowledge*, pp. 108–121. Toronto: University of Toronto Press.

_____. 2001. "Texts, Tyranny, and Transformation: Educational Restructuring in Ontario." In J. Portelli and P. Solomon, eds., *The Erosion of Democracy in Education.* Calgary, Alberta: Detselig.

Griffith, Alison I., and Dorothy E. Smith. 2005. *Mothering for Schooling.* New York: Routledge Falmer.

Gustavsson, A., J. Sandvin, R. Traustadóttir, and J. Tøssebro, eds. 2005. *Resistance, Reflection and Change: Nordic Disability Research.* Lund: Studentlitteratur.

Hagan, John, and Alberto Palloni. 1999. "Sociological Criminology and the Mythology of Hispanic Immigration and Crime." *Social Problems* 46(4):617–632.

Hagen, J. L., and L. V. Davis. 1995. "The Participant's Perspective in the Job Opportunities and Basic Skills Training Program." *Social Service Review* 69:656–678.

Hagen, J. L. and I. Lurie. August 1994. *Implementing JOBS: Progress and Promise. JOBS Implementation Study.* Albany, New York: The Nelson A. Rockefeller Institute of Government.

Handy, C. 1988. *Inside Organizations.* London: BBC Books.

Haney, Lynne. 1996. "Homeboys, Babies, Men in Suits: The State and the Reproduction of Male Dominance." *American Sociological Review* 61(3):759–779.

Haney, L., and M. March. 2003. "Married Fathers and Caring Daddies: Welfare Reform and the Discursive Politics of Paternity." *Social Problems* 50(4)(November):461–481.

Hantraris, L. 2000. *Social Policy in the European Union.* Basingstoke: Macmillan.

Harris, L. 1998. "Americans with Disabilities Still Face Sharp Gaps in Securing Jobs, Education, Transportation, and Many Areas of Daily Life." *SEE/HEAR* 3(4).

Harvey, David. 1989. *Condition of Postmodernity: An Enquiry into the Origins of Cultural Change.* Oxford: Basil Blackwell.

_____. 2005. *A Brief History of Neoliberalism.* New York: Oxford University Press.

Hautecoeur, Jean-Paul 1997. *Alpha97: Basic Education and Institutional Environments.* Toronto: Culture Concepts.

Hays, S. 2003. *Flat Broke with Children: Women in the Age of Welfare Reform.* New York: Oxford University Press.

Henderson, A. T., and N. Berla. 1995. Introduction to A. T. Henderson and N. Berla, *A New Generation of Evidence: The Family Is Critical to Student Achievement.* Washington, D.C.: Center for Law and Education.

Hertz, Rosanna. 1986. *More Equal Than Others: Women and Men in Dual-Career Marriages.* Berkeley: University of California Press.

Heymann, S. J., and A. Earle. 1999. "The Impact of Welfare Reform on Parents' Ability to Care for Their Children's Health." *American Journal of Public Health* 89(4): 502–505.

Hipple, Steven. 2001. "Contingent Work in the Late 1990s." *Monthly Labor Review* 124(3):3–27.

Hochschild, Arlie Russell. 1975. "Inside the Clockwork of Male Careers." In Florence Howe, ed., *Woman and the Power to Change,* pp. 47–80. New York: McGraw-Hill.

_____, with Anne Machung. 1989. *The Second Shift: Working Parents and the Revolution at Home*. New York: Viking.

Holland, Chris, Fiona Frank, and Tony Cooke. 1998. *Literacy and the New Work Order: An International Literature Review*. Leicester: National Institute of Adult Continuing Education.

Hondagneu-Sotelo, Pierrette. 2001. *Doméstica: Immigrant Workers Cleaning and Caring in the Shadows of Affluence*. Berkeley: University of California Press.

Hondagneu-Sotelo, Pierrette, and Michael Messner. 1994. "Gender Displays and Men's Power: 'The New Man' and the Mexican Immigrant Man." In Harry Brod and Michael Kaufman, eds., *Theorizing Masculinities*, pp. 200–218. Thousand Oaks, Calif.: Sage.

hooks, bell. 1990. *Yearning: Race, Gender, and Cultural Politics*. Boston: South End Press.

Houseman, Susan N. 2001. "Why Employers Use Flexible Staffing Arrangements: Evidence from an Establishment Survey." *Industrial and Labor Relations Review* 55(1):149–170.

Howells, Louise. 2000. "The Dimensions of Microenterprise: A Critical Look at Microenterprise as a Tool to Alleviate Poverty." *Journal of Affordable Housing and Community Development* 9:161–182.

Hull, Glenda, ed. 1997. *Changing Work, Changing Workers*. Albany: State University of New York.

Hull, Glenda, and Norton Grubb. 1999. "Literacy, Skills and Work." In Daniel Wagner, Richard Venezky, and Brian Street, eds., *Literacy: An International Handbook*, pp. 311–317. Boulder, Colo.:Westview Press.

Hvinden, B., and R. Halvorsen. 2003. "Which Way for European Disability Policy?" *Scandinavian Journal for Disability Research* 5:296–312.

Hyde, M. 2000. "From Welfare to Work? Social Policy for Disabled People of Working Age in the United Kingdom in the 1990s." *Disability and Society* 15:327–342.

Imai, Masaaki. 1997. *Gemba Kaizen*. New York: McGraw-Hill.

Jackson, Nancy S. 1987. "Skill Training in Transition: Implications for Women." In Jane Gaskell and Arlene McLaren, eds., *Women in Education: A Canadian Perspective*, pp. 351–369. Calgary, Alberta: Detselig.

_____. 1991. *Skills Formation and Gender Relations: The Politics of Who Knows What*. Geelong: Deakin University Open Campus Program.

_____. 1995. "'These Things Just Happen': Talk, Text, and Curriculum Reform." In M. Campbell and A. Manicom, eds., *Knowledge, Experience, and Ruling Relations: Studies in the Social Organization of Knowledge,* pp. 164–180. Toronto: University of Toronto Press.

_____. 2000/2001. Writing Up People at Work. *Literacy and Numeracy Studies* 10(1/2):5–22.

_____. 2005a. "Essential Skills: Essential Lessons Learner?" In Theresa Wallace, Nicole Murphy, Genevieve Lepine, and David Brown, eds., *Exploring New Directions in Essential Skills Research*. Ottawa: Public Policy Forum.

_____. 2005b. "Adult Literacy Policy: Mind the Gap." In Nina Bascia, Alister Cumming, Amanda Datnow, Kenneth Leithwood, and David Livingstone, eds., *International Handbook of Educational Policy,* pp.763–778. New York: Springer.

Jackson, Nancy, and Steve Jordan. 2000. "Learning for Work: Contested Terrain?" *Studies in the Education of Adults* 32:195–211.

Jacobs, Jerry A. 2004. "The Faculty Time Divide." *Sociological Forum* 19:3–27.

Jacobs, Jerry A., and Kathleen Gerson. 2004. *The Time Divide: Work, Family, and Social Policy in the 21st Century.* Cambridge, Mass.: Harvard University Press.

James, Paul, Walter Veit, and Steve Wright, eds. 1997. *Work of the Future: Global Perspectives.* St. Leonards, NSW: Allen and Unwin.

Jameson, Fredric, and Masao Miyoshi, eds. 1999. *The Cultures of Globalization.* Durham, N.C., and London: Duke University Press.

Joppke, Christian. 1998. "Immigration Challenges the Nation-State." In Christian Joppke, ed., *Challenge to the Nation-State: Immigration in Western Europe and the United States,* pp. 1–18. New York: Oxford University Press.

Jurik, Nancy. 2004. "Imagining Justice: Challenging the Privatization of Public Life." *Social Problems* 51:1–15.

_____. 2005. *Bootstrap Dreams: U.S. Microenterprise Development in an Era of Welfare Reform.* Ithaca, N.Y.: Cornell University Press.

Jurik, Nancy, Gray Cavender, and Julie Cowgill. 2006. "Searching for Social Capital in U.S. Microenterprise Development Programs." *Journal of Sociology and Social Welfare* 33:151–170.

Kaplan, Caren. 1996/2000. *Questions of Travel: Postmodern Discourses of Displacement.* Durham, N.C.: Duke University Press.

Kalleberg, Arne L. 2000. "Nonstandard Employment Relations: Part-Time, Temporary and Contract Work." *Annual Review of Sociology* 26:341–365.

Karides, Marina. 2002. "Linking Local Efforts with Global Struggle: Trinidad's National Union of Domestic Employees." In Nancy A. Naples and Manisha Desai, eds., *Women's Activism and Globalization: Linking Local Struggles and Transnational Politics,* pp. 156–171. New York: Routledge.

Katz, Michael. 1989. *The Undeserving Poor: From the War on Poverty to the War on Welfare.* New York: Pantheon Books.

Khan, M. 2000. *Does EFA Stand for "Except for Adults"?* Available online at http://www.iiz-dvv.de/englisch/Publikationen/Ewb_ausgaben/55_2001/eng_Khan.html.

Kidd, Paul T. 1994. *Agile Manufacturing: Forging New Frontiers.* Wolkingham, England, and Reading, Mass.: Addison-Wesley.

Kingfisher, Catherine, ed. 2002. *Western Welfare in Decline: Globalization and Women's Poverty.* Philadelphia: University of Pennsylvania Press.

Koeber, Charles. 2002. "Corporate Restructuring, Downsizing, and the Middle Class: The Process and Meaning of Worker Displacement in the 'New' Economy." *Qualitative Sociology* 25(2):217–246.

Krippner, Greta R. 2001. "The Elusive Market: Embeddedness and the Paradigm of Economic Sociology." *Theory and Society* 30:775–810.

Kunda, Gideon, Stephen R. Barley, and James Evans. 2002. "Why Do Contractors Contract? The Experience of Highly Skilled Technical Professionals in a Contingent Labor Market." *Industrial and Labor Relations Review* 55(2):234–261.

Kurz, D. 1998. "Women, Welfare, and Domestic Violence." *Social Justice* 25(1):105–122.

Lafer, Gordon. 2002. *The Job Training Charade*. Ithaca, N.Y.: Cornell University Press.

Lago-Avery, P. 2004. "13th Deaf-Blind International Conference." *The Deaf-Blind American* 43(3):26–31.

Lamphere, Louise, ed. 1992. *Structuring Diversity: Ethnographic Perspectives on the New Immigration*. Chicago: University of Chicago Press.

Lamphere, Louise, Alex Stepick, and Guillermo Grenier, eds. 1994. *Newcomers in the Workplace: Immigrants and the Restructuring of the U.S. Economy*. Philadelphia: Temple University Press.

Lareau, A. 1989. *Home Advantage*. Philadelphia: Falmer Press.

Lareau, A. 2003. *Unequal Childhoods: Class, Race, and Family Life*. Berkeley: University of California Press.

Lareau, A., and E. M. Horvat. 1999. "Moments of Social Inclusion and Exclusion: Race, Class, and Cultural Capital in Family-School Relationships." *Sociology of Education* 72(January):37–53.

Larson, Joanne, ed. 2001. *Literacy as Snake Oil: Beyond the Quick Fix*. New York: Peter Lang.

Lazarus-Black, Mindie. 1997. "The Rites of Domination: Practice, Process, and Structure in Lower Courts." *American Ethnologist* 24(3):628–651.

Legge, Karen. 1995. *Human Resource Management: Rhetoric and Realities*. London: Macmillan.

Leicht, Kevin T., and Mary L. Fennell. 2001. *Professional Work: A Sociological Approach*. Malden, Mass.: Blackwell.

Lengermann, Patricia Madoo, and Jill Niebrugge-Brantley. 1998. *The Women Founders: Sociology and Social Theory, 1830–1930*. Boston: McGraw-Hill.

Lens, V. 2002. "TANF: What Went Wrong and What to Do Next." *Social Work* 47(3):279–290.

Levin, Benjamin. 2001. *Reforming Education: From Origins to Outcomes*. New York: Routledge.

Levitan, Sar A., Frank Gallo, and Isaac Shapiro. 1987/1993. *Working but Poor: America's Contradiction*. Baltimore: John Hopkins University Press.

Lieberman, L. J., & J. MacVicar. 2003. "Play and Recreation of Youth Who Are Deafblind." *Journal of Visual Impairment and Blindness* 97(12):755–768.

Lightfoot, Sara Lawrence. 1978. *Worlds Apart: Relationships Between Families and Schools*. New York: Basic Books.

Linton, S. 1998. *Claiming Disability*. New York: New York University Press.

Lloyd, Marion. 2004. "In Mexico, Science Goes Begging." *Chronicle of Higher Education,* June 4.

London, Andrew S., Ellen K. Scott, and Vicki Hunter. 2002. "Health-Related Carework for Children in the Context of Welfare Reform." In Francesca Cancian, Demie Kurz, Andrew S. London, Rebecca Reviere, and Mary Tuominen, eds., *Child Care and Inequality: Re-Thinking Carework for Children and Youth,* pp. 99–112. New York: Routledge.

London, Andrew S., Ellen K. Scott, Kathryn Edin, and Vicki Hunter. 2004. "Welfare Reform, Work-Family Tradeoffs, and Child Well-Being." *Family Relations* 53(2):148–158.

Longmore, P. K. 2003. *Why I Burned My Book.* Philadelphia: Temple University Press.

Loprest, P. 1999. *Families Who Left Welfare: Who Are They and How Are They Doing?* Washington, D.C.: Urban Institute.

Lowe, Lisa. 1996. *Immigrant Acts: On Asian American Cultural Politics.* Durham, N.C.: Duke University Press.

Lowell, B. Lindsay. May 2000. "H-1B Temporary Workers: Estimating the Population." Working Paper no. 12. San Diego: University of California, Center for Comparative Immigration Studies.

————. 2001. "Skilled Temporary and Permanent Immigrants in the United States." *Population Research and Policy Review* 20:33–58.

Mangan, Katherine S. 2003. "The Great Divide." *Chronicle of Higher Education,* May 30.

Marchand, Marylyn. 1996. "Reconceptualizing Gender and Development in an Era of Globalization." *Millennium Journal in Culture and Society* 25(3):577–603.

Marchevsky, Alejandra, and Jeanne Theoharis. 2006. *Not Working: Latina Immigrants, Low-Wage Jobs, and the Failure of Welfare Reform.* New York: New York University Press.

Margolis, P. A., R. A. Greenber, and L. L. Keyes. 1992. "Lower Respiratory Illness in Infants and Low Socioeconomic Status." *American Journal of Public Health* 82:1119–1126.

Marshall, T. H. 1965. *Class Citizenship and Social Development: Essays by T. H. Marshall.* New York: Doubleday.

Massachusetts Department of Transitional Assistance. 2000. *After Time Limits: A Study of Households Leaving Welfare Between December 1998 and April 1999.* Boston, Mass.: Commonwealth of Massachusetts.

Massey, Doreen. 1994. *Space, Place, and Gender.* Minneapolis: University of Minnesota Press.

Massey, Douglas S. 1987. "Understanding Mexican Migration to the United States." *American Journal of Sociology* 92(6):1372–1403.

Maudient, M. 2003. *Access to Social Rights for People with Disabilities in Europe.* Strasbourg: Council of Europe.

McCoy, Liza. 1998. "Producing `What the Deans Know': Cost Accounting and the Restructuring of Postsecondary Education." *Human Studies* 21:395–418.

_____. 2006. "Keeping the Institution in View: Working with Interview Accounts of Everyday Experience." In Dorothy E. Smith, ed., *Institutional Ethnography as Practice*. Lanham, Md.: Rowman and Littlefield.

McInnes, J. M. 1999. *A Guide to Planning and Support for Individuals Who Are Deaf-blind*. Toronto: University of Toronto Press.

McInnes, J. M., and J. A. Treffry. 1982. *Deaf-Blind Infants and Children: A Developmental Guide*. Toronto: University of Toronto Press.

McLaughlin, K., S. P. Osborne, and E. Ferlie, eds. 2002. *New Public Management: Current Trends and Future Prospects*. London and New York: Routledge.

McMichael, Philip. 2000. *Development and Social Change: A Global Perspective,* 2nd ed. Thousand Oaks, Calif.: Pine Forge.

McMillan, R. 2003. "Unveiling the Invisible and Uncelebrated Aspects of Relational Practice: Enlightening Conversations with Experienced Community Health Workers." Masters thesis, Faculty of Human and Social Development, University of Victoria, Victoria, British Columbia.

Mehan, H. 1991. "The Schools' Work of Sorting Students." In D. Boden and D. Zimmerman, eds., *Talk and Social Structure: Studies in Ethnomethodology and Conversation Analysis*, pp. 71–90. Cambridge: Polity Press.

Mending the Sacred Hoop. 2002. "Community Based Analysis of the U.S. Legal System's Interventions in Domestic Abuse Cases Involving Indigenous Women." Minnesota Program Development, Final report to the National Institute of Justice. Available at http://praxisinternational.org/SA_frame.html.

Metzel, D. S., S. M. Foley, and J. Butterworth. 2005. "State-Level Interagency Agreements for Supported Employment of People with Disabilities." *Journal of Disability Policy Studies* 16(2):102–114.

Miano, John. 2005. "The Bottom of the Pay Scale: Wages for H-1B Computer Programmers." *Backgrounder.* Report by the Center for Immigration Studies, December. Available at http://www.cis.org/articles/2005/back1305.pdf. Accessed January 10, 2006.

Ministry of Education. 2004. "McGuinty Government Announces New Funds and New Accountability to Benefit Students with Special Needs." Ontario, Canada: Government of Ontario Newsroom. Available at http://ogov.newswire.ca/ontario/GPOE/2004/07/28/c6648.html?lmatch=&lang=_e.html.

Mink, Gwendolyn. 1998. *Welfare's End*. Ithaca, N.Y.: Cornell University Press.

Misra, Joya, Stephanie Moller, and Marina Karides. 2003. "Envisioning Dependency: Changing Media Depictions of Welfare in the 20th Century." *Social Problems* 50(4):482–504.

Mitchell, P. J., and C. Zampotella-Freese. 2003. "Using the Workforce Investment Act of 1998 to Benefit Youth with Blindness and Visual Impairment." *RE:view* 35(3):109–119.

Mitter, Swasti, and Sheila Rowbotham. 1994. *Dignity and Daily Bread: New Forms of Economic Organizing among Poor Women in the Third World and the First*. London and New York: Routledge.

Moghadam, Valentine M. 1999. "Gender and Globalization: Female Labor and Women's Mobilization." *Journal of World-Systems Research* 5(2):367–388.

Mohanty, Chandra Talpade. 1997. "Women Workers and Capitalist Scripts: Ideologies of Domination, Common Interest, and the Politics of Solidarity." In M. Jacquie Alexander and Chandra Talpade Mohanty, eds., *Feminist Genealogies, Colonial Legacies, and Democratic Futures*. New York: Routledge.

_____. 2003. *Feminism Without Borders: Decolonizing Theory, Practicing Solidarity*. Durham, N.C.: Duke University Press.

Momsen, Janet, and Janet Townsend. 1987. *Geography of Gender in the Third World*. Albany: State University of New York.

Montejano, David. 1987. *Anglos and Mexicans in the Making of Texas, 1836–1986*. Austin: University of Texas Press.

Moore, Wilbert E. 1970. *The Professions: Roles and Rules*. New York: Russell Sage Foundation.

Morduch, Jonathan. 1999. "The Microfinance Promise." *Journal of Economic Literature* 37:1569–1614.

_____. 2000. "The Microfinance Schism." *World Development* 28:617–629.

Morgen, Sandra, and Jeff Maskovsky. 2003. "The Anthropology of Welfare 'Reform': New Perspectives on U.S. Urban Poverty in the Post-Welfare Era." *Annual Review of Anthropology* 32:315–338.

Mykhalovskiy, Eric, and Liza McCoy. 2002. "Troubling Ruling Discourses of Health: Using Institutional Ethnography in Community-Based Research." *Critical Public Health* 12:17–37.

Naples, Nancy A. 1994. "Contradictions in Agrarian Ideology: Restructuring Gender, Race-Ethnicity, and Class in Rural Iowa." *Rural Sociology* 59(1):110–135.

_____. 1996. "A Feminist Revisiting of the 'Insider/Outsider' Debate: The 'Outsider Phenomenon' in Rural Iowa." *Qualitative Sociology* 19:83–106.

_____. 1997. "The 'New Consensus' on the Gendered 'Social Contract': The 1987–1988 U.S. Congressional Hearings on Welfare Reform." *Signs* 22:907–943.

_____. 2002. "Teaching Community Activism in the Introductory Women's Studies Classroom." In Nancy A. Naples and Karen Bojar, eds., *Teaching Feminist Activism: Strategies from the Field*. New York: Routledge.

_____. 2003. *Feminism and Method: Ethnography, Discourse Analysis, and Activist Research*. New York: Routledge.

Naples, Nancy A., and Manisha Desai, eds. 2002. *Women's Activism and Globalization: Linking Local Struggles and Transational Politics*. New York: Routledge.

National Association of State Budget Officers. 2003. *State Expenditure Report, 2002*. Washington, D.C.: National Association of State Budget Officers.

_____. 2001. *State Expenditure Report, 2000*. Washington, D.C.: National Association of State Budget Officers.

National Center for Education Statistics (NCES). 2003. "Highlights from the 2003 International Adult Literacy and Lifeskills Survey (ALL)—(Revised)." Washington,

D.C.: U.S. Department of Education. Available online at http://nces.ed.gov/pub-search/pubsinfo.asp?pubid=2005117.

Nelson, Margaret K. 2002. "The Challenge of Self-Sufficiency: Women on Welfare Re-defining Independence." *Journal of Contemporary Ethnography* 31(5):582–614.

New York State Department of Health. 2003. *Consumer Directed Personal Assistance Program (CDPAP)*. Retrieved August 30, 2004 from http://www.health.state.ny.us/nysdoh/medicaid/longterm/cdpap.htm.

New York State Department of Labor. 2000. *Welfare-to-Work Policy and Program Framework*. New York: Welfare-to-Work Division, New York State Department of Labor.

New York State Office of the Governor. 2004. *An Affordable Human Services Network*. Retrieved August 30, 2004, from http://www.state.ny.us/governor/dob/huserv.html#2a.

Newman, M. 1997. *Democracy, Sovereignty and the European Union*. London: Hurst.

Neysmith, Sheila, ed. 2000. *Restructuring Caring Labour: Discourse, State Practice, and Everyday Life*. Don Mills, Ontario: Oxford University Press.

Ng, Roxana. 1990. "Immigrant Women: The Construction of a Labour Market Cat-egory." *Canadian Journal of Women and the Law* 4:96–112.

Nightingale, D. S. 2001. *Program Structure and Service Delivery in Eleven Welfare-to-Work Grant Programs*. Department of Health and Human Services, Contract No. 100-98-0009, MPR reference No. 8550-121. Washington, D.C.: Urban Institute (sub-contractor from Mathematica Policy Research, Inc.).

Oboler, Suzanne. 1995. *Ethnic Labels, Latino Lives: Identity and the Politics of (Re)Presentation in the United States*. Minneapolis: University of Minnesota Press.

O'Brien, Ruth. 2001. *Crippled Justice: The History of Modern Disability Policy in the Workplace*. Chicago: University of Chicago Press.

O'Connor, Alice. 2001. *Poverty Knowledge: Social Science, Social Policy, and the Poor in Twentieth-Century U.S. History*. Princeton: Princeton University Press.

Office of Vocational and Educational Services for Individuals with Disabilities (VE-SID). 1999. Memorandum of agreement. Retrieved March 26, 2005 from http://www.vesid.nysed.gov/publications/mous/nov99.htm.

Ólafsson, S. 2005. *Disability and Welfare in Iceland in an International Comparison*. Report. Reykjavík: University of Iceland, Social Science Research Institute.

Oliker, S. J. 1995. "Work Commitment and Constraint Among Mothers on Workfare." *Journal of Contemporary Ethnography* 24(2):165–194.

Oliver, M. 1996. *Understanding Disability: From Theory to Practice*. London: Macmillan.

Olsen, T. 2003. "Orientation to Deafblind." Available at http://www.geocities.com/dblnj/dbreport.html.

Olson, K., and Pavetti, L. 1996. *Personal and Family Challenges to the Successful Tran-sition from Welfare to Work*. Washington, D.C.: Urban Institute. Department of Health and Human Services Contract No. 100-95-0021. Available online at http://www.urban.org/welfare/report1.htm.

Omi, Michael, and Howard Winant. 1986. *Racial Formation in the United States from the 1960s to the 1980s.* New York: Routledge.

Ong, Aihwa. 1991. "The Gender and Labor Politics of Postmodernity." *Annual Review of Anthropology* 20:279–309.

_____. 1999. *Flexible Citizenship: The Cultural Logics of Transnationality.* Durham, N.C.: Duke University Press.

Ong, Paul, and Evelyn Blumenberg. 1998. "Job Access, Commute and Travel Burden Among Welfare Recipients." *Urban Studies* 35(1):77–93.

Ong, Paul, Edna Bonacich, and Lucie Cheng, eds. 1994. *The New Asian Immigration in Los Angeles and Global Restructuring.* Philadelphia: Temple University Press.

O'Reilly, A. 2003. *The Right to Decent Work of Persons with Disabilities.* IFP/Skills working paper no. 14. Geneva: International Labour Organization.

Organization for Economic Cooperation and Development (OECD). 2002. "International Mobility of the Highly Skilled" (Policy Brief). *OECD Observer*, July. Retrieved October 15, 2004 from www.oecd.org/publications/Pol_brief.

_____. 2003a. *Employment Outlook.* Paris: Author.

_____. 2003b. *Transforming Disability into Ability: Policies to Promote Work and Income Security for Disabled People.* Paris: Author.

_____. 2003c. *Disability Programs in Need of Reform.* Paris: Author.

Organization for Economic Cooperation and Development (OECD) and Statistics Canada. 1995. *Literacy, Economy and Society.* Paris and Ottawa: Author.

Organization for Economic Cooperation and Development (OECD), Human Resources and Development Canada (HRDC), and Statistics Canada. 1997. *Literacy Skills for the Knowledge Society.* Paris and Ottawa: Author.

Organization for Economic Cooperation and Development (OECD), Human Resources and Development Canada (HRDC), and Statistics Canada. 2000. *Literacy in the Information Age: Final Report of the International Adult Literacy Survey.* Paris and Ottawa: Author.

Orloff, A. S. 2001. "Ending the Entitlements of Poor Single Mothers: Changing Social Policies, Women's Employment, and Caregiving in the Contemporary United States." In Nancy Hirschmann and Ulrike Liebert, eds., *Women and Welfare: Theory and Practice in the United States and Europe*, pp. 133–159. New Brunswick, N.J.: Rutgers University Press.

Osborne, D.. and T. Gaebler. 1992. *Reinventing Government.* New York: Basic Books.

Osborne, D., and P. Plastrik. 2000. *The Reinventor's Fieldbook: Tools for Transforming Your Government.* San Francisco: Jossey-Bass.

Ozga, J. 2000. *Policy Research in Educational Settings: Contested Terrain.* Philadelphia: Open University Press.

Parada, Henry. 2002. "The Restructuring of the Child Welfare System in Ontario: A Study in the Social Organization of Knowledge." Ph.D. diss., Ontario Institute for Studies in Education, University of Toronto.

Park, Lisa Sun-Hee. 1998. "Navigating the Anti-Immigrant Wave: The Korean Women's Hotline and the Politics of Community." In Nancy A. Naples, ed., *Community Activism and Feminist Politics: Organizing Across Race, Class, and Gender,* pp. 175–195. New York: Routledge.

Park, Y. S., and R. J. Butler. 2001. "The Safety Costs of Contingent Work: Evidence from Minnesota." *Journal of Labor Research* 22(4):831–849.

Parker, S., S. Greer, and B. Zuckerman. 1988. "Double Jeopardy: The Impact of Poverty on Early Childhood Development." *Pediatric Clinics of North America* 35:1227–1240.

Parrot, S. 1998. *Welfare Recipients Who Find Jobs: What Do We Know About Their Employment and Earnings?* Washington, D.C.: Center on Budget and Policy Priorities.

Pateman, Carole. 1988. *The Sexual Contract.* Stanford: Stanford University Press.

Pavalko, Ronald M. 1971. *Sociology of Occupations and Professions.* Itasca, Ill.: F. E. Peacock.

Pearlmutter, S., and E. E. Bartle. 2000. "Supporting the Move from Welfare to Work: What Women Say." *Affilia* 15(2):153–172.

Pearson, J., N. Thoennes, and E. A.Griswold. 1999. "Child Support and Domestic Violence: The Victims Speak Out." *Violence Against Women* 5(4):427–448.

Peck, Jamie. 2002. "Political Economies of Scale: Fast Policy, Interscalar Relations, and Neoliberal Workforce." *Economic Geography* 78(3):331–360.

Pence, E. 1997. "Safety for Battered Women in a Textually-Mediated Legal System." Unpublished Ph.D. diss., University of Toronto.

————. 2001. "Safety for Battered Women in a Textually Mediated Legal System." *Studies in Cultures, Organizations and Societies* 7:199–229.

Pence, Ellen, and Martha McMahon. 2003. "Working from Inside and Outside Institutions: How Safety Audits Can Help Courts' Decision Making Around Domestic Violence and Child Mistreatment." *Juvenile and Family Court Journal* 54(4):133–147.

Perea, Juan F., ed. 1996. *Immigrants Out! The New Nativism and the Anti-Immigrant Impulse in the United States.* New York: New York University Press.

Persuad, Randolph B., and Clarence Lusane. 2000. "The New Economy, Globalisation and the Impact on African Americans." *Race and Class* 42(1):21–34.

Petroff, J. 1999. "A National Transition Follow-up Study of Youth Identified as Deafblind: Parent Perspectives." Ph.D. diss., Temple University, Philadelphia.

Piore, Michael, and Charles Sabel. 1984. *The Second Industrial Divide: Possibilities for Prosperity.* New York: Basic Books.

Polit, Denise, Andrew S. London, and John M. Martinez. 2001. *The Health of Poor Urban Women: Findings from the Project on Devolution and Urban Change.* New York: MDRC.

Pollert, Anna, ed. 1991. *Farewell to Flexibility?* Oxford: Blackwell.

Polster, Claire, and Janice Newson. 1998. "Don't Count Your Blessings: The Social Accomplishments of Performance Indicators." In J. Currie and J. Newson, eds., *Universities and Globalization: Critical Perspectives,* pp. 173–191. Thousand Oaks, Calif: Sage.

Poovey, Mary. 2001. "The Twenty-First Century University and the Market: What Price Economic Viability?" *Differences: A Journal of Feminist Cultural Studies* 12:1–16.

Portes, Alejandro, and Jozsef Borocz. 1989. "Contemporary Immigration: Theoretical Perspectives on Its Determinants and Modes of Incorporation." *International Migration Review* 23(3):606–632.

Portes, Alejandro, and Rubén G. Rumbaut. 1996. *Immigrant America: A Portrait.* Berkeley: University of California Press.

Poster, Winifred, and Zakia Salime. 2002. "The Limits of Microcredit: Transnational Feminism and U.S. A.I.D. Activities in the United States and Morocco." In Nancy Naples and Manisha Desai, eds., *Women's Activism and Globalization*, pp. 189–219. New York: Routledge.

Priestley, M. 2003. *Whose Agenda for Disability Rights in Europe?* Plenary address presented at a conference of the Nordic Network on Disability Research, Jyväskulä, Finland, September 2003.

Prince, M. J. 2004. "Canadian Disability Policy: Still a Hit-and-Miss Affair." *Canadian Journal of Sociology* 29(1):59–82.

Prinsloo, Mastin, and M. Breier, eds. 1996. *The Social Uses of Literacy.* Capetown and Amsterdam: Sached Books and John Benjamin.

Quadagno, Jill. 1999. "Creating a Capital Investment Welfare State: The New American Exceptionalism." *American Sociological Review* 64:1–11.

Rachlis, Michael. 2004. *Prescription for Excellence: How Innovation Is Saving Canada's Health Care System.* Toronto: HarperCollins.

Rankin, Janet M., and Marie L. Campbell. 2006. *Managing to Nurse: Inside Canada's Health Care Reform.* Toronto: University of Toronto Press.

Raphael, J. 1999. "The Family Violence Option: An Early Assessment." *Violence Against Women* 5(4):449–466.

Rattansi, Ali. 2005. "The Uses of Racialization: The Time-Spaces of the Multicultural City." In Karim Murji and John Solomos, eds., *Racialization: Studies in Theory and Practice,* pp. 271–301. Oxford University Press.

Reid, Colleen. 2003. "'We're Not a Part of Society, We Don't Have a Say': Exclusion as a Determinant of Poor Women's Health." *Advances in Gender Research* 7:231–279.

Rice, J. J., and M. J. Prince. 2000. *Changing Politics of Canadian Social Policy.* Toronto: University of Toronto Press.

Rich, Adrienne. 1986. *Blood, Bread, and Poetry: Selected Prose, 1979–1985.* New York: Norton.

Ridzi, Frank. 2003. "Processing Private Lives in Public: An Institutional Ethnography of Front-line Welfare Intake Staff Post Welfare Reform." Ph.D. Diss., Syracuse University, Syracuse, N.Y.

_____. 2004. "Making TANF Work: Organizational Restructuring, Staff Buy-In, and Performance Monitoring in Local Implementation." *Journal of Sociology and Social Welfare* 31:27–48.

Ridzi, Frank, and Payal Banerjee. 2006. "The Spirit of Outsourcing: Corporate and State Regulation of Labor Under H-1B Visa and TANF Policies in the U.S." In Vicki Smith, ed., *Worker Participation: Practices and Possibilities*. Special Issue of *Research in the Sociology of Work*, 16:345–373.

Ridzi, Frank, and Andrew S. London. 2006. "'It's Great When People Don't Even Have Their Welfare Cases Opened': TANF Diversion as Process and Lesson." *Review of Policy Research* 23:725–743.

Riggio, M. 1992. "Population/Demographics: Reaction Paper." *Proceedings of the National Symposium on Children and Youth Who Are Deaf-Blind, USA*, pp. 20-27.

Rivas, L. M. 2002. "Invisible Laborers: Caring for the Independent Person." In B. Ehrenreich and A. Hochschild, eds., *Global Woman: Nannies, Maids, and Sex Workers in the New Economy*, pp. 70–84. New York: Holt.

Rivers, E., and A.Griffith. 1995. "Organizational Knowledge and Interpersonal Experience: Positioning Students in Inclusive Education." *Journal for a Just and Caring Education* 1(3):275–295.

Rizvi, F. 2004. "Theorising the Global Convergence of Restructuring Policies in Education." In S. Lindblad and T. Popkewitz, eds., *Educational Restructuring: International Perspectives on Traveling Policies*. Greenwich, Conn.: Information Age.

Roberts, Dorothy. 1997. *Killing the Black Body: Race, Reproduction, and the Meaning of Liberty*. New York: Vintage Books.

Robinson, William I. 1993. "The Global Economy and the Latino Populations in the United States: A World Systems Approach." *Critical Sociology* 19(2):29–59.

Rocheleau, Dianne, Barbara Thomas-Slayter, and Esther Wangari, eds. *Feminist Political Ecology: Global Issues and Local Experiences*. New York: Routledge.

Rodriguez, Cheryl Rene. 1995. *Women, Microenterprise, and the Politics of Self-Help*. New York: Garland .

Rogaly, Ben. 1996. "Micro-finance Evangelism, 'Destitute Women,' and the Hard Selling of a New Anti-poverty Formula." *Development in Practice* 6:100–112.

Roggero, P., R. Tarricone, M. Nicoli, and V. Mangiaterra. 2006. "What Do People Think About Disabled Youth and Employment in Developed and Developing Countries? Results from an E-discussion Hosted by the World Bank." *Disability and Society* 21:645–650.

Rosaldo, Renato. 1997. "Cultural Citizenship, Inequality, and Multiculturalism." In William V. Flores and Rina Benmayor, eds., *Latino Cultural Citizenship*, pp. 27–38. Boston: Beacon Press

Rose, Gillian. 1993. *Feminism and Geography: The Limits of Geographical Knowledge*. Minneapolis: University of Minnesota Press.

Roy, A. W. N., G. Dimigen, and M. Taylor. 1998. "The Relationship Between Social Networks and the Employment of Visually Impaired College Graduates." *Journal of Visual Impairment and Blindness* 92(7):423–432.

Rubery, Jill, and Damian Grimshaw. 2001. "ICTs and Employment: The Problem of Job Inequality." *International Labour Review* 140(2):165–192.

Rudrappa, Sharmila. 2004. *Ethnic Routes to Becoming American: Indian Immigrants and the Cultures of Citizenship*. New Brunswick, N.J.: Rutgers University Press.

Russell, Marta. 1998. *Beyond Ramps: Disability at the End of the Social Contract*. Monroe, Me.: Common Courage Press.

Sable, M. R., M. K. Libbus, D. Huneke, and K. Anger. 1999. "Domestic Violence Among AFDC Recipients: Implications for Welfare-to-Work Programs." *Affilia* 14(2):199–216.

Salzinger, Leslie. 2003. *Genders in Production: Making Workers in Mexico's Global Factories*. Berkeley: University of California Press.

Sapiro, Virginia. 1990. "The Gender Basis of American Social Policy." In Linda Gordon, ed., *Women, the State, and Welfare*, pp. 36-54. Madison: University of Wisconsin Press.

Sassen, Saskia. 1998. *Globalization and Its Discontents: Essays on the New Mobility of People and Money*. New York: New Press.

Sauerburger, D. 1995. *Independence Without Sight or Sound: Suggestions for Practitioners Working with Deaf-Blind Adults*. New York: American Foundation for the Blind.

Schram, S. F. 2000. *After Welfare: The Culture of Postindustrial Social Policy*. New York: New York University Press.

Schuck, Peter H. 1998. *Citizens, Strangers, and In-Betweens: Essays on Immigration and Citizenship*. Boulder, Colo.: Westview Press.

Schugurensky, D., B. Slade, and L. Yuo. 2005. "'Can Volunteer Work Help Me Get a Job in My Field?': On Learning, Immigration and Labour Markets." 2005 Work and Lifelong Learning Conference Proceedings, June 20–22, Toronto. Available online at http://lifelong.oise.utoronto.ca.

Schultz, Katherine 1997. "Discourses of Workplace Education: A Challenge to the New Orthodoxy." In G. Hull, ed., *Changing Work, Changing Workers: Critical Perspectives on Language, Literacy and Skills*, pp. 43–83. Albany: State University of New York Press.

Scott, E. D., A. S. London, and K. Edin. 2000. *Good Cause: Domestic Violence and the Mandates of Welfare Reform*. Paper presented at the Annual Meeting of the American Sociological Association, August, Washington, D.C.

Scott, Ellen K., Andrew S. London, and Allison Hurst. 2005. "Instability in Patchworks of Child Care When Moving from Welfare to Work." *Journal of Marriage and the Family* 67:370–386.

Scott, Ellen K., Andrew S. London, and Nancy A. Myers. 2002. "Dangerous Dependencies: The Intersection of Welfare Reform and Domestic Violence." *Gender and Society* 16(6):878–897.

Scott, Ellen K., Kathryn Edin, Andrew S. London, and Rebecca Joyce Kissane. 2004. "Unstable Work, Unstable Income: Implications for Family Well-Being in the Era of Time-Limited Welfare." *Journal of Poverty* 8(1): 61–88.

Scott, R. A. 1991. *The Making of Blind Men*. New Brunswick, N.J.: Transaction Publishers.

Servon, Lisa. 1999. *Bootstrap Capital: Microenterprises and the American Poor*. Washington, D.C.: Brookings Institution Press.

Shakespeare, T. 2006. *Disability Rights and Wrongs*. London: Routledge

Sharp, Rachel, and Anthony Green. 1975. *Education and Social Control: A Study in Progressive Primary Education*. London: Routledge and Kegan Paul.

Sherraden, Margaret S., Cynthia K. Sanders, and Michael Sherraden. 2004. *Kitchen Capitalism: Microenterprise in Low-Income Households*. Albany: State University of New York Press.

Shklar, Judith N. 1991. *American Citizenship: The Quest for Inclusion*. Cambridge, Mass.: Harvard University Press.

Shragge, Eric, ed. 1997. *Workfare: Ideology for a New Under-Class*. Toronto: Garamond Press.

Silvestrini, Blanca G. 1997. "'The World We Enter When Claiming Rights': Latinos and Their Quest for Culture." In William V. Flores and Rina Benmayor, eds., *Latino Cultural Citizenship: Claiming Identity, Space, and Rights,* pp. 39–53. Boston, MA: Beacon.

Simpson, Ida Harper. 1972. "Patterns of Socialization into Professions: The Case of Student Nurses." In R. M. Pavalko, ed., *Sociological Perspectives on Occupations*, pp. 169–177. Itasca, Ill.: F. E. Peacock.

Sivasubramaniam, Malini. 2005. "Teaching Adults, Reaching Children: Making the Case for Adult Education and Learning." Paper presented at the Canadian Association for the Study of Adult Education (CASAE), University of Western Ontario, London, Ontario, May 29–31. Available online at http://www.oise.utoronto.ca/CASAE/caf2005/2005online Proceedings/CAS2005Pro-Sivasubramaniam.pdf.

Slade, Bonnie. 2003a. "A Critical Feminist Analysis of the Marginalization of Immigrant Women Engineers: Subtle Semantics, Redundant Assessments and Conflicting Jurisdictions." M.A. thesis, OISE/University of Toronto.

————. 2003b. "The Uneven Terrain of 'Learning Organizations': The Deskilling of Immigrant Professionals." In *The Changing Face of Work and Learning: 2003 Conference Proceedings*, pp. 202–207. Edmonton: Work and Learning Network. Available online at http://www.wln.ualberta.ca/papers/pdf/36.pdf.

————. 2004. "Highly Skilled and Under-Theorized: Women Migrant Professionals." In R. Baaba Folson, ed., *Calculated Kindness: Global Economic Restructuring and Canadian Immigration and Settlement Policy*. New York: Routledge.

————. Forthcoming. "The Deprofessionalization of Immigrant Women Engineers in Canada: The Discursive Shift from Desirability to Skill." In D. Barnes, Z. Nazim, and R. Sin, eds., *Celebrating Resistance: WORKing from a Critical Race Perspective*.

Slade, Bonnie, and Kiran Mirchandani. 2005. "'You Just Have to Be Respectable to Talk To': Contingency, Learning and Definitions of 'Skill' in a Call Centre." Paper presented at the Canadian Association for the Study of Adult Education (CASAE), University of Western Ontario, London, Ontario, May 29–31. Available online at http:/www.utoronto.ca/CASAE/cnf2005/2005onlineProceedings/CAS2005Pro-Slade.pdf.

Slaughter, Sheila, and Larry L. Leslie. 1997. *Academic Capitalism: Politics, Policies, and the Entrepreneurial University.* Baltimore, Md.: Johns Hopkins University Press.

Smith, Dorothy E. 1987. *The Everyday World as Problematic: A Feminist Sociology.* Boston: Northeastern University Press.

_____. 1990a. *The Conceptual Practices of Power: A Feminist Sociology of Knowledge.* Boston: Northeastern University Press.

_____. 1990b. *Texts, Facts and Femininity: Exploring the Relations of Ruling.* New York: Routledge.

_____. 1993. "The Standard North American Family: SNAF as an Ideological Code." *Journal of Family Issues* 14:50–65.

_____. 1998. "The Underside of Schooling: Restructuring, Privatization, and Women's Unpaid Work." *Journal for a Just and Caring Education* 4(1):11–29.

_____. 1999. *Writing the Social: Critique, Theory, and Investigations.* Toronto: University of Toronto Press.

_____. 2000. "Schooling for Inequality." *Signs: Journal of Women in Culture and Society* 25(4):1147–1151.

_____. 2001. "Texts and the Ontology of Organizations and Institutions." *Studies in Cultures, Organizations, and Societies* 7(2):159–198.

_____. 2002a. "Institutional Ethnography." In T. May, ed., *Qualitative Research: An International Guide to Issues in Practice,* pp. 36–65. London: Sage.

_____. 2002b. Keynote Address. Delivered at the First Canadian Occupational Science Symposium: "Making Sense of What People Do." Dalhousie University, Halifax, Novia Scotia, May 24.

_____. 2005. *Institutional Ethnography: A Sociology for People.* Lanham, Md.: AltaMira.

_____, ed. 2006. *Institutional Ethnography as Practice.* Lanham, Md.: Rowman and Littlefield.

Smith, D. E., and A. I. Griffith. 1990. "Coordinating the Uncoordinated: Mothering, Schooling and the Family Wage." *Perspectives on Social Problems* 2:25–43.

Smith, George W. 1990. "Political Activist as Ethnographer." *Social Problems* 37:629–648.

Smith, Joan, Immanuel Wallerstein, and Hans-Dieter Evers, eds. 1984. *Households and the World Economy.* Beverly Hills, Calif.: Sage.

Smith, Vicki. 1997. "New Forms of Work Organization." *Annual Review of Sociology* 23:315–339.

_____. 2001. *Crossing the Great Divide: Worker Risk and Opportunity in the New Economy.* Ithaca, N.Y.: Cornell University Press.

Solomon, Brenda. 2001. "The Ins and Outs of Welfare-to-Work: Women as They Enter and Exit a Nursing Assistant Employment and Training Program in Upstate New York." *Sociology and Social Welfare* 28(3):157–186.

_____. 2003. "A 'Know It All' with a 'Pet Peeve' Meets 'Underdogs' Who 'Let Her Have It': Producing Low-Waged Women Workers in a Welfare-to-Work Training Program." *Journal of Contemporary Ethnography* 32(6):693–727.

Solomon, Catherine Richards. 2004. "'Sacrificing at the Altar of Tenure': Untenured Assistant Professors' Work/life Management." Ph.D. diss., Syracuse University, Syracuse, N.Y.

Somers, Margaret, and Fred Block. 2005. "From Poverty to Perversity: Ideas, Markets, and Institutions over Two Hundred Years of Welfare Debate." *American Sociological Review* 70:260–287.

Spivak, Gayatri Chakravorty. 1999. *A Critique of Postcolonial Reason: Toward a History of the Vanishing Present.* Cambridge, Mass.: Harvard University Press.

Stakes, R., and G. Hornby. 1997. *Change in Special Education: What Brings It About.* London: Cassell.

Standing, Guy. 1999. *Global Labour Flexibility: Seeking Distributive Justice.* New York: St. Martin's.

Stanley, Kathleen. 1994. "Industrial and Labor Market Transformation in the U.S. Meatpacking Industry." In Philip McMichael, ed., *The Global Restructuring of Agro-Food Systems,* pp. 129–144.

Starobin, P. 1998. "The Daddy State." *National Journal* (March 28):678–683.

Statistics Canada. 2003. "Learning a Living: First Results of the Adult Literacy and Life Skills Survey." Ottawa. Available online at http://www.statcan.ca/bsolc/english/bsolc?catno=89-603-X&CHROPG=1.

Steger, Manfried B. 2002. *Globalism: The New Market Ideology.* Lanham, Md.: Rowman and Littlefield.

Sticht, Thomas. 2001a. "Has the National Adult Literacy Survey (NALS) Defamed the Competence of America's Labor Force?" National Institute for Literacy (NIFL) Workplace discussion list, available at http://www.nifl.gov/nifl-workplace/2001/0254.html.

_____. 2001b. "The International Adult Literacy Survey: How Well Does It Represent the Literacy Abilities of Adults?" *Canadian Journal for the Study of Adult Education* 15(2):19–36.

Stock, Andree. 2002. "An Ethnography of Assessment in Elementary Schools." Ed.D. diss., University of Toronto.

Story, John. 1994. *New Wave Manufacturing Strategies.* London: Paul Chapman.

Stuber, Jennifer, and Karl Kronebusch. 2004. "Stigma and Other Determinants of Participation in TANF and Medicaid." *Journal of Policy Analysis and Management* 23(3)(Summer):509–530.

Swift, Karen. 1995. *Manufacturing "Bad Mothers": A Critical Perspective on Child Neglect*. Toronto: University of Toronto Press.

Tenner, Edward. 2004. "The Pitfalls of Academic Mentorship." *Chronicle of Higher Education*, August 13.

Theodore, Nik, and Jamie Peck. 2002. "The Temporary Staffing Industry: Growth Imperatives and Limits to Contingency." *Economic Geography* 78(4):463–493.

Thomas, Robert J. 1985. *Citizenship, Gender, and Work: Social Organization of Industrial Agriculture*. Berkeley: University of California Press.

Thomson, R. G. 1997. *Extraordinary Bodies*. New York: Columbia University Press.

Traweek, Sharon. 1988. *Beamtimes and Lifetimes: The World of High Energy Physicists*. Cambridge, Mass.: Harvard University Press.

Trotter, A., and K. K. Manzo. 2007. "Harcourt Sale Would Spawn Big 3 of Texts." *Education Week*. Available at http://lnk.edweek.org/edweek/index.html?url=/ew/articles/2007/08/01/44harcourt.h26.html.

Turner, S. 2001. "Texts and the Institutions of Municipal Government: The Power of Texts in the Public Process of Land Development." *Studies in Cultures, Organizations and Societies* 7:297–325.

United Nations. 1993. *Standard Rules on the Equalization of Opportunities for Persons with Disabilities*. Available at http://www.un.org/esa/socdev/enable/dissre00.htm.

United Nations Social Commission for Asia and the Pacific. 2002. *Guidebook on Integrating Unpaid Work into National Policies* (draft as of May 2002). Retrieved April 21, 2003 (http://www.unescap.org/stat/meet/wipuw/wipuw_guidebook.htm).

U.S. Department of Health and Human Services. 2000. *A Profile of Medicaid Chart Book 2000*. Washington, D.C.: U.S. Centers for Medicare and Medicaid Services, Health Care Financing Administration.

U.S. Department of Homeland Security. 2003. "Characteristics of Specialty Occupation Workers (H-1B): Fiscal Year 2002." Available at http://www.uscis.gov/files/article/FY2002Charact.pdf.

U.S. General Accounting Office (GAO). 2000. *H-1B Foreign Workers: Better Controls Needed to Help Employers and Protect Workers*. Washington, D.C.: Author.

_____. 2001, October. *Welfare Reform: More Coordinated Federal Effort Could Help States and Localities Move TANF Recipients With Impairments Toward Employment*. GAO-02-37. Washington, D.C.: Author.

_____. 2002. *Welfare Reform: With TANF Flexibility, States Vary in How They Implement Work Requirements and Time Limits*. GAO-02-770. Washington, D.C.: Author.

_____. 2003. *H-1B Foreign Workers: Better Tracking Needed to Help Determine H-1B Program's Effect on U.S. Workforce*. Washington, D.C.: Author.

Valocchi, S. 1994. "The Racial Basis of Capitalism and the State, and the Impact of the New Deal on African Americans." *Social Problems* 41(3): 347–362.

Vancouver Island Health Authority. 2004a. *Health Services Redesign Plan Summary.* April 22.

_____. 2004b. *Performance Agreement Between the Ministry of Health Services and the Vancouver Island Health Authority, April 1, 2004 to March 31, 2005.*

Vislie, L., and G. Langfeldt. 1996. "Finance, Policy Making and the Organization of Special Education." *Cambridge Journal of Education* 26(1):59–69.

Vollmer, Howard M. 1966. *Professionalization.* Englewood Cliffs, N.J.: Prentice Hall.

Walker, Britton A., and Amy Kays Blair. 2002. *The 2002 Directory of U.S. Microenterprise Programs.* Washington, D.C.: Aspen Institute.

Walker, Gillian A. 1990. *Family Violence and the Women's Movement: The Conceptual Politics of Struggle.* Toronto: University of Toronto Press.

Walsh, M. 2003. "Companies Jump on 'No Child Left Behind' Bandwagon." *Education Week* 22(August 6):8.

Watson, R. 1997. "Ethnomethodology and Textual Analysis." In D. Silverman, ed., *Qualitative Research: Theory, Method and Practice.* London: Sage.

Wehman, P., and G. Revell. 2005. "Lessons Learned from the Provisions and Funding of Employment Services for the MR/DD Population." *Journal of Disability Policy Studies* 16(2):84–101.

Wendell, Susan. 1996. *The Rejected Body: Feminist Philosophical Reflections on Disability.* New York: Routledge.

Wiens-Tuers, Barbara A. 1998. "The Relationship of Race and Outcomes of Non-Standard Labor." *Journal of Economic Issues* 32(2):575–585.

Wilson, Robin. 2005. "Deep Thought, Quantified." *Chronicle of Higher Education,* May 20.

Winant, Howard. 1994. *Racial Conditions: Politics, Theory, Comparisons.* Minneapolis: University of Minnesota Press.

Womack, James, Daniel Jones, and Daniel Roos. 1990. *The Machine That Changed the World.* New York: Rawson Macmillan.

Workability Europe (December 2006/January 2007). Public affairs e-bulletin. Retrieved February 18, 2007, from www.workability-europe.com.

World Bank. 1995. *Priorities and Strategies for Education: A World Bank Review.* Washington, D.C.: Author.

Worrall, A. 1990. *Offending Women: Female Lawbreakers and the Criminal Justice System.* London: Routledge.

Yoest, Charmaine. 2004. "Parental Leave in Academia: The Family, Gender, and Tenure Project." Unpublished paper, University of Virginia, February. Retrieved February 17, 2004, from http://www.faculty.virginia.edu/familyandtenure.

Yoken, C. 1979. *Living with Deaf-Blindness: Nine Profiles.* Washington, D.C.: Gallaudet College.

Young, I. M. 1990. *Justice and the Politics of Difference.* Princeton: Princeton University Press.

Zalewski, Jacqueline M. 2005. "'Rebadging': The In-House Outsourcing of Professional Workers." Paper presented at the Society for the Study of Social Problems Annual Conference, August 12–14, Philadelphia.

Zedlewski, Sheila R., and Jennifer Holland. 2003. "How Much Do Welfare Recipients Know About Time Limits?" No. 15 in the series *Snapshots of America's Families III.* Washington, D.C.: Urban Institute. Available at http://www.urban.org/urlprint. cfm?ID=8675.

Contributors

Lois André-Bechely is an associate professor in the Charter College of Education at California State University, Los Angeles. She teaches educational leadership and qualitative research methods. Her research on parents' experiences with educational policies and practices has been published in journals such as *Educational Administration Quarterly* and *Urban Studies*. Her book *Could It Be Otherwise: Parents and the Inequities of Public School Choice* was published by Routledge in 2005. Her upcoming publication, titled "Feminism and Education Politics: No Longer for Women Only," is a co-authored chapter with Catherine Marshall for the American Educational Research Association's *Handbook of Research on the Politics of Education*.

Katrina Arndt is an assistant professor of special education at St. John Fisher College in Rochester, New York. She taught in K-12 settings for eleven years and trained as a sign-language interpreter before entering higher education. Using a disability studies framework, she is interested in promoting inclusive experiences in schools, the workplace, and the community. Her research focuses on providing strategies for supporting inclusive practice. Her recent publications have appeared in *The Journal of Physical Education, Recreation, and Dance*; *Issues and Challenges in Conducting Qualitative Research Involving Deaf and Hard of Hearing Persons*; and *Building Pedagogical Curb Cuts*.

Payal Banerjee's research, based on fieldwork conducted in India and the United States, looks at the incorporation of Indian information technology, or IT, workers as immigrant labor in the United States. Her publications have focused on questions of gender and race/ethnicity, globalization, and U.S. immigration policies. They include "Indian Information Technology (IT) Workers in the U.S.: The H-1B Visa, Flexible Production, and the Racialization of Labor" (2006), in *Critical Sociology*, and other co-authored essays, such as "The Spirit of Outsourcing: Corporate and State Regulation of Labor Under H-1B Visa and TANF Policies in the U.S.," in *Worker Participation: Practices and Possibilities* (2006), a special issue of *Research in the Sociology of Work*, and "Ten Years After Beijing: A Conference on Collective Reflections About Gender Justice" (2006), in the *International Feminist Journal of Politics*. Her current research focuses on liberalization of trade in services and transnational mobility of labor, as well as on the historical and contemporary exchanges between India and China. Publications in the latter area include articles on Chinese minorities in India and on feminist interpretations of the current security discourse on India and China. Banerjee is a visiting adjunct professor in the Graduate Program in International Affairs, The New School. Currently, she is finishing her Ph.D. in the Department of Sociology at Syracuse University.

Marie L. Campbell is professor emerita at the University of Victoria, Canada, where she taught for twelve years in the interdisciplinary graduate program, Studies in Policy and Practice in Health and Social Services, in the Faculty of Human and Social Development. Her most recent book is *Managing to Nurse: Inside Canada's Health Care Reform*, co-authored with Janet Rankin and published by the University of Toronto Press in 2006.

Yvette Daniel is assistant professor at the Faculty of Education, University of Windsor, in Ontario, Canada. She teaches preservice and graduate-level courses. Her research interests are in the area of educational policy, theories of educational administration and leadership, and issues of urban education and teaching for social justice. She has recently completed a pilot study on the complexities of new teacher induction and another one on school discipline policies and practices in Ontario. She is currently involved in developing an urban education partnership with the local school community and another on the Wireless Writing Project in collaboration with the Ministry and the local school board. She has published several chapters in edited books and articles in journals such as the *Canadian Journal of Education* and *Canadian and International Education*.

Marjorie L. DeVault is professor of sociology and a member of the Women's Studies Program at Syracuse University. Her previous research has explored the "invisible work" in women's household and family lives and in the historically female field of dietetics and nutrition education. Trained in the sociological fieldwork tradition, and deeply influenced by the feminism of the 1970s, she has written broadly on qualitative and feminist methodologies. Since the 1980s, she has been learning about institutional ethnography from Dorothy Smith and others in the "IE network." She is currently chair of the IE Division in the Society for the Study of Social Problems, and she maintains an IE website at http://faculty.maxwell.syr.edu/mdevault. She is the author of *Feeding the Family: The Social Organization of Caring as Gendered Work* (1991) and *Liberating Method: Feminism and Social Research* (1999).

Alison Griffith is professor and director of graduate programs in the Faculty of Education at York University. She has published extensively in the area of families and schools. Most recently, she published "Constructing Single Parent Families for Schooling: Discovering an Institutional Discourse," in D. E. Smith, ed., *Institutional Ethnography as Practice*, and co-authored *Mothering for Schooling* with Dorothy E. Smith. She is past Division Chair (2005–2007) of the Institutional Ethnography Division of the Society for the Study of Social Problems. Her current research focuses on the audit processes that are transforming public education and parents' work.

Nancy Jackson is associate professor in Adult Education and Community Development at the Ontario Institute for Studies in Education, University of Toronto. Her primary research and teaching interests are in studies of working knowledge and critical perspectives on the international discourse of skill, including adult literacy. She is concerned with how the concept of skills works ideologically to mask and legitimize the production of systemic inequalities, often along lines of gender and race, in the labor market and workplace life. She has done research in sectors as diverse as office work, nursing, and auto manufacturing, as well as analyses of education and training policies in international comparative perspective. She is a co-author of *Reading Work: Literacies in the New Workplace*.

Nancy Jurik is professor and director of graduate programs in the School of Justice and Social Inquiry at Arizona State University. She teaches courses on "Women and Work" and "Economic Justice." Her publications focus on gender, occupations, work organizations, and economic development programs. She is the author of *Bootstrap Dreams: U.S. Microenterprise Development Programs in an Era of Welfare Reform* and *Doing Justice, Doing Gender: Women in Legal and Criminal Justice Occupations*. The first edition of *Doing Justice, Doing Gender* won the 1996 Gustavus Meyer Book Award for the Study of Human Rights in North America. Nancy is also a past president of the Society for the Study of Social Problems.

Andrew S. London received his Ph.D. in sociology and demography from the University of Pennsylvania in 1993. He is now professor of sociology in the Center for Policy Research in the Maxwell School of Citizenship and Public Affairs at Syracuse University. His research focuses on the health, well-being, and care of stigmatized and vulnerable populations. He has a long-term research agenda focused on health-care services and community-based care for persons living with HIV. For the past several years, he has been involved in two large-scale studies of the impact of welfare reform on poor women and their children, coordinated by MDRC: The Project on Devolution and Urban Change and the Next Generation Project. Drawing on longitudinal data from the Cleveland ethnographic component of Urban Change, which he co-directed with Ellen K. Scott, and data from the Urban Change survey, he has contributed to reports, book chapters, and journal articles on such topics as the health of poor, urban women; women's concerns about the effects on their children and teens of moving from welfare to work; the intersections of domestic violence and welfare reform; caring for children with chronic health problems in the context of welfare reform; and the post-PRWORA welfare, employment, poverty, and material hardship experiences of initially welfare-reliant women. Finally, and most recently, he has begun a series of investigations aimed at understanding how incarceration and/or military service early in the life course shape later-life trajectories, health, and mortality. He is a co-editor of *Child Care and Inequality: Rethinking Carework for Children and Youth*, and his recent publications have appeared in journals such as Demogra*phy, Research on Aging, Gender and Society,* and the *Journal of Marriage and the Family.*

Nancy Naples is professor of sociology and women's studies at the University of Connecticut, where she teaches courses on gender, politics, and the state; sexual citizenship; feminist theory; feminist methodology; and women's activism and globalization. Her research emphasizes the contradictory role of the state in reproducing and challenging inequality and the intersection between race, class, gender, sexuality, and region in community activism, citizenship, and social policy. She is author of *Feminism and Method: Ethnography, Discourse Analysis, and Feminist Research* and

Grassroots Warriors: Activist Mothering, Community Work, and the War on Poverty. She is also editor of *Community Activism and Feminist Politics: Organizing Across Race, Class, and Gender* and co-editor of *Women's Activism and Globalization: Linking Local Struggles with Transnational Politics* (with Manisha Desai) and *Teaching Feminist Activism* (with Karen Bojar). She served as president of Sociologists for Women in Society and is currently president of the Society for the Study of Social Problems.

Frank Ridzi is director of urban and regional studies and assistant professor of sociology at Le Moyne College. He has conducted research and written in the areas of social welfare policy, sociology of work, and student affairs. His recent work has appeared in such places as the *Journal of Sociology and Social Welfare, Research in the Sociology of Work, Review of Policy Research* and *The NASPA Journal of The National Association of Student Personnel Administrators*.

Ellen Scott is an associate professor of sociology at the University of Oregon and director of women's and gender studies. Her research focuses on the intersections of gender, race, and class inequality, most recently in the study of urban poor female-headed families. Recently, Scott has been involved with two large-scale studies of the impact of welfare reform on poor women and their children and has co-authored numerous journal articles, book chapters, and policy reports related to that research. Her current project grew from the project on welfare reform and examines cross-culturally the experiences of low-wage families juggling wage work and carework for children with disabilities. In this project, she is working collaboratively with a statewide community-based organization that serves families caring for children with disabilities to conduct in-depth, qualitative interviews in immigrant and nonimmigrant communities and to examine how factors such as social networks, experiences with social services, and employment conditions affect wage work and caretaking practices, and thereby also child well-being. Ellen Scott received her Ph.D. from the University of California, Davis, in 1997.

Bonnie Slade is a doctoral candidate in the Collaborative Women's Studies and Adult Education programs at the Ontario Institute for Studies in Education of the University of Toronto. Her areas of research are (1) gender, migration, and the labor market; (2) the study of engineering as a site of gendered and racialized power relations; (3) the social construction of skill; and (4) the use of institutional ethnography as a methodological and ontological tool to work for social change. Her Ph.D. dissertation focuses on the social organization of "Canadian work experience," beginning in the experiences of immigrants who undertake volunteer work to improve their access to the labor market.

Brenda Solomon is associate professor of social work at the University of Vermont. She is interested in the construction of work and family, the production of women workers, intersections of oppression, and the everyday practices of front-line workers in welfare, child welfare, and schools. She has published related articles in the *Journal of Sociology and Social Welfare*, the *Journal of Contemporary Ethnography*, the *Journal of Youth and Society*, and the *Journal of Poverty*.

Catherine Richards Solomon is a feminist sociologist who studies how individuals construct their work and family lives in relation to one another. She has examined this topic looking at variety of occupations, most recently exploring the work/life management of assistant professors. She also studies the intersection between work and family in later life. Catherine is an assistant professor of sociology and gerontology at Quinnipiac University.

Rannveig Traustadóttir is professor and director of the Center for Disability Studies in the Faculty of Social Sciences at the University of Iceland. Much of her work in disability studies has examined the intersection of disability and gender (and, to some extent, other dimensions of inequality, such as social class, race/ethnicity, age, and sexuality) and how these create multiple layers of discrimination and social exclusion in disabled people's lives. She has taken active part in the development of disability studies as a scholarly field in the Nordic countries and is currently the president of the Nordic Network on Disability Research.

Index

Access: of immigrants to community resources, 119; of people with disabilities to employment, 204; of professionals with disabilities to professional work settings, 217-218; and translation, for immigrants, 132

Accountability, 8, 294; auditing of education funding claims, in Ontario, 258; of home care agencies for continuity, 277-278; and information processing, 296; in new public management, 287; and "not knowing," 281, 290; performance measures, 283; in production work, 33; in public education, 40, 42-43, 249, 250; and public sector policies, 271; uncoupled from service provision, 282

Accounting: in home health care, 274-275; as representation, 1-2; of wage labor and carework, in U.S. social welfare, 240-241

Acker, J.: on idea of unencumbered worker, 2, 292; on nonresponsibility, 95, 292

AFDC (Aid to Families with Dependent Children, US social welfare program), 143, 163, 225

ALSS (Adult Life Skills Survey), 27

Americans with Disabilities Act (U.S. legislation), 204

Amsterdam, Treaty of, 85

Anglos. See White Americans

Anti-discrimination policies, of EU, 84, 85

"Bench," immigrant IT workers on, when between jobs, 107-109

Bill 160 (Ontario, Canada), 42, 54

Bodyshops, 102, 103

Borrowers' circles, 69, 71

Brueggemann, J., 219

Bullard, R., 119

Business logics: in education, 261; in home health support, 277; in social service delivery, 59, 71

Business training: in MDPs, 64-68; racial bias in, 66

Campbell, M., 142, 265n4

Canada Health Act, 276

Carework, 2; affected by changes in public sector, 45; community-based, in British Columbia, 288n15; and economic restructuring, 293; and participation in training, 67-68; management

of nonprofessionals in home health support, 273-275; subcontracting by welfare recipients, 232-233; and social policy, 11, 158; and textualized "provider," 240, 244; valuing, 244

Casualization of labor. See Contract workers; Temporary work

CDC (Consumer-Directed Care, Medicaid), 224. See also CDPAP

CDPAP (Consumer-Directed Personal Assistance Program, Medicaid, in New York State), 226-227, 234-239

Children: poverty and health, 146, 166-167; special needs and mothers' exemptions from time limits in U.S. welfare reform, 178n3; special-needs funding for, in Ontario, 249-250

Citizenship: broadening definition of, 114, 116-118; cultural, 117; and difference, 117 135; intersectional analysis of, 136; and race, 135-136; social regulation of, 118-120, 128, 133; as textual status, 112-113; and work, 85, 205, 242, 292

Clients: in MDPs, 64, 68-69; screening in MDPs, 70

Commission for the Blind and Visually Handicapped (CBVH, New York State agency), 216

Community: construction of belonging and outsiderness, 123; and demographic changes, in rural Iowa, 115, 120; fears of white residents, 127, 132; and interracial associations of youth, 133; and perceptions of cultural differences, 133; and politics of language, 130, 132; and regulation of citizenship, 112, 118-120; white residents' perceptions of racial tensions, 127; youth and language use, 133

Commuting: and "outsiderness" of immigrant workers in community, 124, 126

Competition, 44; naturalization of, 12

Conceptual currency: of neoliberalism, 291; "personal responsibility" in welfare reform, 158-159, 178, 224

Consolidation of educational publishing, 48

Contingent work. See Contract workers; Temporary work

Continuing Care Act (Canada), 277

Continuity of care, 266, 268-269, 287n1; standards for, 288n8; textualized, 268, 284-285

Continuous improvement, 30